THE CORPORATE DIMENSION

An exploration of developing areas
of company and commercial law.
Published in honour of Professor AJ Boyle.

THE CORPORATE DIMENSION

An exploration of developing areas
of company and commercial law.
Published in honour of Professor AJ Boyle.

Edited by Barry AK Rider.

JORDANS
1998

Published by
Jordan Publishing Limited
21 St Thomas Street
Bristol BS1 6JS

British Library Cataloguing-in-Publication Data
A catalogue record for this book is available from the British Library.

ISBN 0 85308 476 9

Typeset by Saxon Graphics Ltd, Derby
Printed in Great Britain by MPG Books Ltd, Bodmin, Cornwall

CONTENTS

FOREWORD

Since 1844, there have been 19 Companies Acts culminating in the Act of 1985 which consolidated and extended all that had gone before. The Act of 1985 contained 747 sections and 25 Schedules and has since been amended and extended by the Insolvency Act 1985, the Financial Services Act 1986, the Company Directors Disqualification Act 1986, the Companies Act 1989 and the Criminal Justice Act 1993. In addition, there has been European Union legislation incorporated, one hopes successfully, in the English legislation and the creation of the European Economic Interest Groupings, a creature half company and half partnership. For the past quarter of a century and more, Professor Boyle has illuminated and expounded company law and foreshadowed its future development.

Successive editions of *Gore-Browne on Companies* and *Boyle and Birds' Company Law* have been invaluable to the practitioner and the student in understanding the legislation and the hundreds of judicial authorities which govern the administration of companies. The contributions to this volume, published in honour of Professor Boyle, reflect the wide range of the subject to which the Professor has devoted his talents and his time. Those contributions also serve to remind the reader of the present state of the relationships between a company, its directors, its shareholders, its creditors and the public.

Company law is concerned with the regulation of management for the protection of creditors, investors, consumers and the public. That protection is sought by an insistence on transparency of operations, disclosure of interests, rigorous accountancy and open competition. Some of the contributions to this volume cast doubt on the effectiveness in practice of the protective measures imposed by the legislation. All the contributions are thought-provoking and erudite. They are all concerned with making company law a logical, effective and just method of disciplining modern business. They are therefore a fitting tribute to the work of Professor Boyle.

Lord Templeman

BIOGRAPHICAL NOTES

Barry AK Rider

Barry Rider is the Director of the Institute of Advanced Legal Studies and a Professor of Law at the University of London. He is also a Fellow of Jesus College, Cambridge and taught company law and financial services regulation at the University of Cambridge for 20 or so years, before becoming Director of the IALS. Barry Rider read law at Queen Mary College, London and then took an MA in Cambridge and PhDs from both the University of London and University of Cambridge. He has also been awarded an LLD by Dickinson Law School within Penn State University in the USA. He is a member of the English Bar. Professor Rider is general editor of *The Company Lawyer* and a contributor to *Gore-Browne on Companies*.

George P Gilligan

George Gilligan is based at the University of Melbourne, where he is involved in research for the Centre for Corporate Law and Securities Regulation and teaching in the Department of Criminology. He has a PhD and a Masters degree in criminology from the University of Cambridge and an MA in criminological studies from La Trobe University in Melbourne. He teaches and publishes across a range of criminological areas, and has specialist research interests in white collar crime, organised crime and the regulation of the financial services sector.

Chizu V Nakajima

Chizu V Nakajima is a Senior Lecturer at City University Business School, where she teaches financial services law and company law. She has a BA and MA in law from Keio University, Tokyo and a PhD in law from the University of London. She is general editor of the *Journal of Money Laundering Control* and editor of *The Company Lawyer*. She is also a Convenor of the annual Cambridge International Symposium on Economic Crime. Before returning to her academic work, she worked for Cazenove & Co and Lloyds Bank International in the City of London.

Eva Z Lomnicka

Eva Lomnicka is a Professor of Law at King's College, London. She is a graduate of Cambridge University (where she also took an LLM) and a member of the English Bar. Her main research interests are securities regulation and consumer credit regulation, being editor of the *Encyclopedia of Financial Services Law* (as well as of the relevant Part of *Palmer's Company Law*) and the *Encyclopedia of Consumer Credit Law*. She has written extensively on those areas and is on the Editorial Board of a number of legal journals, including the *Journal of Business Law* and *The Company Lawyer*.

Ned Swan

Ned Swan is a Partner in the Banking and International Finance Group of the international law firm Cameron McKenna. He has been a member of the Board of the Institute of Advanced Legal Studies since 1992 and is a Research Fellow at the Institute and a Visiting Professor of Financial Services Law at London Guildhall University. Mr Swan has a JD degree from New York University and is a member of the New York Bar. Ned Swan's main area of research is in derivatives markets and regulation, an area in which he has written and spoken widely and published three books. He is legal adviser to a number of markets and financial institutions in the UK, the US and Eastern Europe.

Helen Parry

Helen Parry is a Senior Lecturer in Law at London Guildhall University, teaching financial services law on the MSc Financial Services Regulation and the MSc Financial Markets and Derivatives. She is co-editor of *Futures Trading Law and Regulation* and *Swaps and Off Exchange Derivatives Trading: Law and Regulation*. Formerly a regulator in the derivatives industry, working for AFBD (Association of Futures Dealers and Brokers) and ICCH (International Commodities Clearing House) and securities and derivatives editor of the *FT Fraud Report*. She contributes regularly to journals in the field of financial services law and regulation, and financial crime.

John Birds

John Birds is Professor of Commercial Law and currently Head of the Department of Law at the University of Sheffield, where he has taught for nearly twenty years. Previously he was a lecturer at Queen Mary College, University of London. He obtained his LLB and LLM degrees from the University of London and is also a Fellow of the Royal Society of Arts. John Birds has written widely in the areas of company law and insurance law, and is, among other things, a contributor to *Gore-Browne on Companies*, co-editor of *Boyle & Birds' Company Law*, author of *Modern Insurance Law* and joint editor of *MacGillivray on Insurance Law*. He serves on the editorial board of *The Company Lawyer* (having been one of its founding assistant general editors) and of *Insolvency Law and Practice*.

Geoffrey Morse

Geoffrey Morse is Professor of Company Law and Head of the Department of Law at the University of Nottingham. A graduate of the University of Newcastle upon Tyne and a barrister of Lincoln's Inn, he has previously taught law at the Universities of Manchester, East Anglia and Liverpool. He has recently been appointed as an adjudicator of immigration appeals. Geoffrey Morse's main research interests are in the field of company law, partnership law and tax law. He is the principal editor of *Palmer's Company Law*, editor of *Charlesworth's Company Law*, author of *Morse on Partnership Law* and a contributor to *Davies Principles of Tax Law* and the *Journal of Business Law*.

Harry Rajak

Harry Rajak is a Professor of Law at the University of Sussex and Director of the Centre for Legal Studies at Sussex. He is also the Director of the Insolvency Research Unit at Sussex. He has been at the University of Sussex since 1 January 1995, prior to which he was Senior Lecturer in Law at the School of Law, King's College, London. He has also taught law at the University of Notre Dame (London campus) and at Georgetown University Law Center, Washington DC. From 1990 to 1995, Harry Rajak was a consultant to the non-contentious bankruptcy department of Lovell White Durrant and since 1992, he has been a joint editor of *Insolvency Law and Practice*. His main area of research is company law and corporate insolvency and he is a contributor to *Tolley's Insolvency*, as well as the author and editor of other texts in these areas.

Adrian Walters

Adrian Walters is a lecturer in law at Nottingham Trent University where he teaches company law, corporate insolvency law and securities regulation to both undergraduates and postgraduates. He has contributed several articles on company law and aspects of civil procedure to specialist journals including *The Company Lawyer*. He is also a qualified solicitor and an associate fellow of the Society of Advanced Legal Studies.

John P Lowry

John Lowry is a graduate of the University of London and was taught by Professor Boyle. He is currently Associate Director of the Centre for Consumer and Commercial Law Research at Brunel University. He was Associate Professor of Business Law at Fairleigh-Dickinson University in New Jersey between 1986 and 1991, and was elected an Honorary Fellow of the University in 1997. John Lowry has written widely in domestic and international law journals on aspects of company law, particularly minority shareholder rights and fiduciary obligations. He is a co-author of *Limitation of Actions* and *Consumer Law*. He is the company law editor (with Paul Davies) for the *Journal of Business Law*.

David Sugarman

David Sugarman is Professor of Law at Lancaster University. He studied at the Universities of Hull and Cambridge (where he was a William Senior Scholar in Comparative Law) and received his doctorate from Harvard Law School. His publications include: *Legality, Ideology and the State*; *Law, Economy and Society, 1750–1914: Essays on the History of English Law*; *Regulating Corporate Groups in Europe*; *Law and Social Change in England, 1780–1900*; *Professional Competition and Professional Power: Lawyers, Accountants and the Social Construction of Markets*; *A Brief History of the Law Society*; *Law in History: Histories of Law and Society*; and a special enlarged issue of *The Company Lawyer* on 'The Law Commission's Paper on Shareholder Remedies'. He is an Associate Research Fellow at the Institute of Advanced Legal Studies, London University and a Fellow of the Royal Historical Society. He serves on the editorial board of *The Company Lawyer*, *The International Journal of the Legal Profession*, *Law and Social Inquiry* (the Journal of the American Bar Foundation), *The Journal of Legal History*, *The Canadian Journal of Law and Society*, *Studies in Law, Politics and Society* and *Legal Ethics*. He has been a visiting professor at law schools in Canada, Japan, Spain and the United States.

Ben Pettet

Ben Pettet read law at University College London and graduated with LLB (Honours) in 1976. In 1977, he was called to the Bar at Gray's Inn where he was also awarded the Band Scholarship. He has practised as a barrister. He is currently a Senior Lecturer in Laws at University College London. He has also been a visiting adjunct Professor at Pace University, New York on their London programme and has taught part-time at St Edmund Hall, Oxford and Robinson College, Cambridge. His research interests span company law, corporate finance law, securities regulation and comparative law. Recent publications include the UK monograph for the *International Encyclopaedia of Laws: Corporations and Partnerships*, and an article published in *Current Legal Problems* examining economic approaches to the doctrine of limited liability. Other major publications include the *Second Cumulative Supplement* to Gower's *Principles of Modern Company Law* (4th edn) and the editing of a volume of essays *Company Law in Change*.

Joanna Gray

Joanna Gray is a Lecturer in Law at the University of Newcastle upon Tyne. She is a graduate of the University of Newcastle upon Tyne and Yale Law School. She is a former Fulbright Scholar and is a Solicitor of the Supreme Court of England & Wales. During 1998 she was Senior Research Fellow at the Institute of Advanced Legal Studies and is a member of the Law Society Standing Committee on Company Law. Her main research interest is in regulation of financial markets and financial services.

Brenda Hannigan

Brenda Hannigan is a Reader in Corporate Law at the University of Southampton. She took her MA degree at Trinity College, Dublin and an LLM at Harvard. Her principal research interests are in company and insolvency law, financial services and securities regulation. She is an editor of *Halsbury's Laws of England* and has written and contributed to a number of books on company law and securities regulation. She also served as a consultant to the Law Commission on its project on shareholder remedies.

Janet Dine

Janet Dine was called to the Bar in 1973. In 1978, she became a lecturer at King's College, an appointment she held until 1992 when she took up an appointment as Reader in Law at Essex University. From 1987–1989 she was on leave from King's having been appointed as the Law Society's Senior Research Fellow in company and commercial law at the Institute of Advanced Legal Studies, London University. From 1989–1992 she was Director of the Centre for European Law at King's College, London. In 1990, she acted as specialist legal adviser to the House of Lords Standing Committee on the European Communities when she assisted in drafting the report of that committee on the European Company Statute. In October 1992, she was appointed by HM Treasury to the post of Commissioner for Friendly Societies. In 1994, she was appointed Professor of Law at Essex University and was Head of the Department of Law until 1997. 1997–1998, Senior Visiting Fellow at the Institute of Advanced Legal Studies. Recent publications include *Company Law* (Macmillan, 1991, second edition 1994), *EC Company Law* (Jordans 1991, with 6-monthly updates) and *Criminal Law in the Company Context* (Dartmouth, 1995). A book on Eastern European company law will shortly be published by Wiley.

Mads Andenas

Mads Andenas is Director of the Centre of European Law, King's College, London. He was formerly legal adviser to the European Bank of Reconstruction and Development (EBRD) and Deputy Director General of the Royal Norwegian Ministry of Finance. He has a Cand Jur degree from the University of Oslo and a PhD degree from the University of Cambridge. He is an Advokat (Norway) and Barrister (England and Wales). His main areas of research are European Community law and comparative law and the law of financial markets and corporations. He is an editor of *The Company Lawyer* and the general editor of *European Business Law Review*.

INTRODUCTION

Barry AK Rider

The practice of publishing a collection of papers ranged broadly within a particular area of study, to mark the retirement of a leading scholar, is a relatively recent import into Britain from Continental Europe. It is, however, one of the most pleasant practices that we have adopted as a consequence of becoming closer to our neighbours across the Channel. Of course, the Festschrift is of German origin, although its reception into the academic societies of other European countries has been somewhat more pervasive than it has in ours. Indeed, traditionally, we have been rather reluctant to acknowledge, let alone fête, significant contributions to scholarship, particularly during the lifetime of the person concerned. This, no doubt, reflects our fear of bestowing an honour on someone who still has enough energy and opportunity to embarrass us. Therefore, we tend to be parsimonious in marking merit and cautious in the extreme in giving anyone, even our most deserving academicians, anything more than membership of a club! Consequently, it was a delight to be asked to put together a collection of papers, broadly within the remit of company law, to mark the contribution that Professor Anthony James Boyle has made to the study of law during his long and distinguished career as a teacher and author.

Tony Boyle has spent the last thirty-three years teaching law at the University of London, initially at King's College, in the Strand and then at Queen Mary College, now Queen Mary and Westfield College, to the east of Whitechapel. He took both his bachelors and masters degrees at London; therefore, by far the greater proportion of his career in law has been spent in the University of London. Tony started his teaching career, however, in Durham, where he taught for one year before taking up a lectureship at the University of Birmingham, where he taught for a further two years, before returning to London. Although the greater proportion of Tony's career has been spent in the capital, his scholarship has never been parochial. His decision to go to Harvard and submit a dissertation on the derivative action and minority shareholder protection in American and English law, which resulted in his being awarded an SJD in 1968, attests to his desire to learn from the experience of other jurisdictions. By the same token, Tony Boyle was one of the first English academic company lawyers to recognise the significance of Europe and, in particular, the European Community for corporate and commercial law.

The same lack of parochialism is indicated in Tony's appreciation of the very real contribution that practitioners can and should be encouraged to make in the development of the law, and also, for that matter, the assistance that academics can render to those involved in the practice or administration of the law. Consequently, Tony was keen, as soon as he took over the general editorship of

Gore-Browne on Companies, to strengthen the contribution made by practitioners, and not only those from conventional legal practice, but also those working in financial institutions. His involvement, often on an informal basis, in law reform projects has also underlined his concern to ensure that company law is not allowed to perch in an ivory tower. While Tony has himself rarely practised, although as a member of the Bar he was one of the first academic company lawyers to secure a foothold in chambers, he has always surrounded himself with those who are engaged in the cut and thrust of practice and, as a consequence, his own writing and thinking has always evinced a degree of authenticity and relevance that is not always immediately apparent in that of some of his colleagues. This is not to say, however, that Tony has at any time in his career been less than a scholar devoted to the highest ideals of academia. His appointment as a Reader in Law in 1971 and then election to a Chair of Law in 1974, were both early and well deserved.

I had the honour of arriving at Queen Mary College at the same time as Tony. He, as the newly appointed Reader, from King's College, and I as a bewildered second-year student transferring from the Polytechnic of North London. Even though Tony did not teach me for a further year, he was conspicuous as one of the more approachable and committed teachers and tutors. His lectures on company law tended to focus on the grey areas of law, and therefore did not and could not give to the audience the degree of certainty favoured by those who prefer to refrain from using their own grey matter. On the other hand, for those who were prepared to think and read, Tony's lectures proved to be stimulating and, in so many areas of the law, prophetic. Having said this, it was not until Tony started to supervise my own research, the following year, that I appreciated the very real depths of his knowledge and understanding, not only in English law, but other systems and, in particular, US law. The respect with which Tony was and is regarded overseas, was illustrated dramatically in the first correspondence that I had, in regard to my own work on insider dealing, with Professor Louis Loss, Tony's own former supervisor at Harvard. I had, rather naïvely, written to the great doyen of securities law asking whether he could give me a few references on the US law relating to insider abuse. Professor Loss responded, that I might as well ask a physicist to give me a few references on developments in the laws of physics over the last fifty years. Nonetheless, as I came to him recommended by Tony, I was invited over to Harvard to find the references myself!

As I and many others have found, Tony was and is a first rate research supervisor. His approach is rather the same as that when dealing with colleagues. He is not intrusive, but supportive and reassuring. A wealth of knowledge and experience is almost hidden behind his natural modesty which, on occasion, almost amounts to shyness. In my case, I had the privilege of working with Tony both as one of his students and as a junior colleague teaching on the contract law course, that Tony taught with Professor Roy Goode. Some years later, I had the pleasure of returning to Queen Mary College, again to work with Tony and also Roy, albeit as a visiting fellow at the Centre for Commercial Legal Studies. What I am saying, however, albeit in a rather roundabout manner, is that without Tony's advice and support I would never have finished my own PhD, let alone pursued a career in academia. I know many, some of whom sadly could not contribute to this work, who feel very much the same as I do.

Apart from teaching, developing and supporting the development of new courses in the University of London and for that matter elsewhere, including Cambridge; and in facilitating and supporting research, Tony has been a prolific legal writer and commentator. The editorial offices and appointments that he has and largely continues to hold on the editorial boards of legal journals are too numerous to mention. From my own standpoint, I am well aware of the support he gave to me, Elana Hew, another of his former students, and John Birds, now Professor of Commercial Law and Head of the Law Department at the University of Sheffield, but then one of his junior colleagues, in setting up and launching *The Company Lawyer* in 1979. It is, however, in regard to his General Editorship of *Gore-Browne on Companies*, published by Jordans, that Tony's greatest contribution to company law has been and continues to be made. He took over responsibility for the 42nd edition, which was published in 1972, and has carried this leading practitioners' work, through to its present 44th Edition. The 41st edition had been published in 1952 and was about as out of date as the First Edition of 1907. The 43rd Edition went into a loose-leaf format, given the pace of developments in the law, and the present edition, comfortably, fills two loose-leaf volumes. The last two editions have been and continue to be supplemented on a very regular basis. Indeed, as one of the contributors, it seems to me as though Tony must be continuously revising manuscript. If this was not a big enough commitment, in 1982, with John Birds, Tony brought out *Boyle and Birds' Company Law*, also published by Jordans. This is a student text, which while it draws heavily on *Gore-Browne* is in both a form and style which renders the material rather more accessible to those studying law, rather than seeking to ascertain a point of law in practice. This successful book is now in its third edition, Tony and John having been joined as authors by Charlotte Villiers, from the University of Sheffield, and Dr Eilis Ferran, from the University of Cambridge.

In a work such as this, which has been so generously and well supported by the publishers, it would be lacking in courtesy not to refer to the very special relationship that Tony has enjoyed for many years with Jordans. Tony has played a significant role, over a great many years, in assisting in the formulation of Jordans' publishing policy and has, I know from my own experience, played an important role in supporting titles and authors. Without the trust and confidence that Jordans have both obviously and rightly placed in Tony, a work of the proportions and significance of *Gore-Browne* could not have been saved and promoted to the quality it now has.

Tony has, over the years, contributed to a number of chapters to books and articles to legal journals. Some have reflected his other great academic interest, legal history. On the occasions that he has looked at an area of company or commercial law in its historical context, he has exhibited a depth of learning and scholarship which cannot but fail to impress the reader. On the other hand, as I have already pointed out, Tony is equally prepared to take on some of the most complex and controversial issues of the day. His many contributions to *The Company Lawyer* in particular, attest to this.

While Tony has never courted controversy, he has never gone out of his way to avoid it, if a principle or a friend is at risk. In defending what he considers to be right and proper, or in protecting something which he values, Tony on countless occasions has proved to be a powerful and often victorious protagonist. In fighting his corner, he has not confined himself simply to matters of academic company law. He has strong and committed views on education and on a wide range of social and moral issues. Although not great in physical stature, Tony is certainly not one for pushing around. This aspect of his character has manifested itself on many occasions, but here I wish to mention only two broad examples. First, Tony has always been prepared to be the first to jump in to the lion's den to defend someone who he considers has been given a raw deal. He is prepared to do this as much for a student as he is a colleague. Again, I can speak from experience, having worn both hats. Secondly, Tony is not shy in supporting new initiatives from the start — if he thinks they are worthwhile — and does not refrain from giving his personal support until he can see which way the wind is blowing. I have already mentioned his support of *The Company Lawyer*, but he was also one of the first to support the setting up of the British Institute of Securities Laws in 1976 and has readily agreed to serve as the first Chairman of the new Centre for Corporate Law and Practice at the Institute of Advanced Legal Studies, which was set up last autumn.

As I have already indicated, there were a number of others who would have liked to have had the opportunity to contribute to this book, but who, for a variety of reasons, were unable to do so. In selecting those papers that we have been able to include, I have attempted to draw together at least one or two discernible themes, while acknowledging that in a work of this nature, it is important that contributors are allowed latitude in selecting and exploring particular issues. We have been especially keen to focus on new and developing areas of the law. Therefore, we have not confined the scope of this book to what might be considered to be the traditional area of company law and practice. Hence, Dr George Gilligan addresses the development of financial regulation in Britain, and in particular, the institutional structures that have been put in place and are constantly being refined to protect investors. Dr Chizu Nakajima's essay focuses on the impact of anti money-laundering laws on financial intermediaries and, in particular, the interplay between such rules and what appears to be the developing law relating to proprietary remedies and civil accessory liability. Indeed, it is arguable that the new law relating to the prevention and control of money laundering, with its attendant compliance obligations, has had an even greater impact on the way in which business is conducted in the financial services sector than many aspects of the legislation which address directly the regulation and supervision of the financial markets. Professor Eva Lomnicka's essay is also in what might be described as the 'financial area', in so far as she discusses the law relating to open ended investment companies and, in so doing, raises several significant issues as to the corporate law implications of this investment vehicle.

Mr Edward Swan, in his paper on the historical development of derivative securities, plunges back in time rather further than even Tony's interest in legal history has taken him. In his discussion of the nature of such instruments and their regulation, Ned Swan harks back to both ancient Greece and Rome, and rather proves the adage that there is nothing new in the universe. Indeed, in many ways, the concerns that were then recognised are not too dissimilar from those we have today. Ms Helen Parry brings us firmly back to the present in her discussion of the control of company fraud, an issue that has long interested Tony, given his concern to see adequate protection for the rights and expectations of those adversely affected by companies and business. The theme of protecting investors from incompetent and dishonest management is also addressed, to some degree, by Professor John Birds, and by Professor Geoffrey Morse, Professor Harry Rajak, Mr Adrian Walters and Mr John Lowry. Professor David Sugarman addresses specifically the issue of minority shareholder protection and the derivative action, a matter always very close to Tony's heart. Mr Ben Pettet's essay, although focusing on the law relating to share buy-backs also addresses, at least in part, the control of abuses and protection of minority interests. Ms Joanna Gray raises similar issues, albeit across a much broader spectrum in her essay on corporate personality. Ms Brenda Hannigan's essay brings us back to an old but extremely important issue in the governance of companies, namely the legal basis and limits of directors' authority. Professor Janet Dine's thought- provoking contribution raises issues pertinent to the very structure of company regulation and control. Dr Mads Andenas addresses an issue that Tony has always considered to be of very considerable importance, namely the impact of European initiatives on English company law.

We are delighted that so many distinguished scholars have contributed to this work and regret that the confines, largely of space and time, have not permitted the inclusion of other papers. Nonetheless, those that have been included fairly reflect that dynamic quality of company law that Tony has done so much to chronicle and render lucid, not least through the pages of *Gore-Browne*. Needless to say, without the support and generosity of the contributors, our publishers Jordans and so many others, this book could not have been completed.

It should be plain to those who bother to wade through these, essentially, introductory comments, that I am presumptuous enough to consider myself a close friend of both Tony and Joan Boyle. I, like countless other former students, owe both of them a considerable debt. Although Tony has retired from his Chair, a little early — sadly on the grounds of ill health, I have no doubt that he will continue to make a very considerable contribution to company law scholarship. His agreement to chair the new Centre for Corporate Law and Practice at the IALS, and his willingness to support its activities, are firm testaments to the fact that Tony is still very much in the business of company law — and long may this be so!

Barry AK Rider
Jesus College
Cambridge
February 1998

Chapter 1

THE CITY OF LONDON AND THE DEVELOPMENT OF ENGLISH FINANCIAL SERVICES LAW

Dr George P Gilligan[1]

INTRODUCTION

When considering developments in UK company law over the last decade, perhaps the most dramatic changes have occurred in the area of financial services. This essay is being written on the forty-sixth day of the new Labour Government led by the Prime Minister, Tony Blair, and the proposals for reform have been coming thick and fast. Initiatives in health and education were widely expected, but the proposed rationalisation of the regulatory infrastructure of the UK's financial services sector surprised many commentators, regulators and the industry itself.[2] Indeed, one article describes '. . . the surreal chain of events that rocked the City supervisors'.[3] The timetable for reform suggested by the Chancellor of the Exchequer, the Right Hon Mr Gordon Brown MP and the Economic Secretary to the Treasury, the Right Hon Ms Helen Liddell MP is approximately eighteen months and allows for lengthy consultation with the industry. The financial services sector has always been an active participant in its own supervision since financial service regulation began evolving in the Middle Ages. Perhaps the most important point to make about the evolution of UK financial services regulation is that, in fact, it is effectively the history of the City of London;[4] and, consequently, the City is the central focus of analysis. In this essay, Ingham's working definition of the City is adopted:

> '. . . the institutional structures of short term money markets (or exchanges) in commodities, securities, money and services . . . the essential character of the City is that of a commercial entrepot in all commodities, including money, at both the domestic and international level.'[5]

The regulatory history below highlights how the City is different from other

---

1 University of Melbourne.
2 The editorials of 21 May were a mixture of shock, caution and admiration regarding the proposals to make the SIB a *super-regulator*. For example: Comment, 'All change for the super-SIB' (1997) *Financial Times*, 21 May, p 23; and Commentary, 'Regulators back in the melting pot' (1997) *The Times*, 21 May, p 31.
3 Farrelly, P, 'Regulators in Wonderland', (1997) *The Observer*, 25 September, Business p 7.
4 Hereafter referred to as the City, the generally accepted term for the financial and associated markets of the City of London.
5 Ingham, G, *Capitalism Divided? The City and Industry in British Social Development* (London: Macmillan, 1984), p 60.

leading financial centres. The early history of the City is examined and, in particular, its influential relationship with the Crown and the State, both of which became dependent upon the City for financial support. The dependent nature of these relationships established the traditions of the City's regulatory autonomy and the domination by essentially private models of self-regulation of Britain's financial sector.

The analysis stresses historically contingent factors, not least the international traditions of the City as the world's commercial and not merely financial clearing house, and the regular convergence of the often separate policy goals of the City, the Treasury and the Bank of England. It has been the reflexive interaction of all these factors and their sometimes unintended consequences which have provided the City with the political and commercial power to resist external intervention and formal patterns of censure. It is acknowledged that the City's relative autonomy has also been due to the fact that, for centuries, it was able to provide a generally secure and profitable trading environment. A unique feature of the City is that, even though it has been the world's most important financial centre, for a long time it remained a village both in terms of its social confines and its social mores.[1] This analysis emphasises the reflexive interdependence that the City's institutional structures have had with its human inhabitants as they have developed their regulatory environment over generations.

THE ESTABLISHMENT OF THE CITY'S FINANCIAL MARKETS

This section examines how the City's financial and associated markets have been shaped by: (i) the international character of the City; (ii) the economic and political influence that the City has exerted over the Crown and central government; and (iii) the interaction of broader legal developments with the traditional weakness of the central State in England.

The various financial and associated markets of the City have merged with cultural, economic and political influences specific to the City to form institutional social structures. These structures have combined with the human agency activities of numerous City interest groupings over several centuries to equip the City with a significant degree of political influence. This political influence has, in turn, provided the City with enough regulatory autonomy to mould its own regulatory culture and structures. A crucial factor in this regulatory autonomy is the international nature of the City, which has had a significant effect upon Britain's social and economic history:

> 'The City is unique: no other international commercial, banking and financial centre has ever enjoyed such a lengthy and continuous period of operation — over 250 years. And in this crucially important respect, Britain is also unique: no other industrialised society has ever acted as host to a centre which has undertaken such

---

1 For a detailed analysis of the enduring regulatory influence of the City as a village refer to: Gilligan, GP, 'The Michael Lawrence Sacking – A Confirmation of the Regulatory Traditions of the Stock Exchange and the City of London?' (1997) 4 *Journal of Financial Crime*, 3, pp 207–214.

a large share of the world capitalist system's commercial, banking and financial activities. Britain was not only the "workshop of the world", but also its "clearing house" and whilst the former status has been lost, the latter — despite some recent competition from other centres — has not. The consequences of this enduring economic activity for the development of the dominant classes, the state system and the economy of Britain can scarcely be over estimated.'[1]

This unique character and the importance of the City to the organisation of British society and its economy is the focus of this essay. This section charts how the City came to occupy this strategic position and the central importance of its 'international clearing house' role.

The regulation of securities in Britain derives from theories of markets, with the concept of barter markets being the earliest authority; and in England from AD 1000 a sophisticated form of market regulation emerged gradually. Its central purpose was to introduce more certainty into economic exchange by impacting upon the processes of supply and demand. The ancient common law offences of engrossing (buying in quantity corn, etc, to sell again at a high price), forestalling (raising the price of certain goods by holding up supplies, etc), and regrating (buying corn or other grains in any market so as to raise the price, and then selling it again in the same place) were all rendered statutory offences in the fourteenth century.[2] These statutes could be viewed as the legislative origins of UK financial services regulation. As is true of many contemporary regulatory initiatives,[3] these statutes were a legislative response to the social and political pressures exerted by the moral economy of English society at that time. These pressures often stimulated crowd protest and, for several hundred years, mass protest was a common response to grain shortages.[4]

London's importance as a national and international trading centre really began in the twelfth century. In England, from 400 to 1200, there was a change from tribalism, to feudalism, to nationalism. State justice replaced feudal justice and common law emerged as the law of the Crown available to all men.[5] The principles of common law grew from the forms of justice administered by the King's courts.[6] The common law helped shape contemporary social structures and it promoted the belief that commercial transactions were essentially private in nature. This idea was rooted in the practice of the late Middle Ages when the

---

1 Ingham (1984), *ibid, supra*, p 40.

2 *Statutes of the Realm* (1363), 37 Edw III c 8.

3 For example, increased regulatory oversight of pension funds and the pensions industry generally, following strident public criticism of the scandals involving the late Robert Maxwell, and also the widespread mis-selling of personal pensions.

4 There is a substantial literature upon the importance of the moral economy of pre-industrial England and its effects on legislation and law enforcement. Prominent examples include: Brewer, J and Styles, J (eds), *An Ungovernable People: The English and their Law in the Seventeenth and Eighteenth Centuries* (New Brunswick, 1980); Gatrell, VAC, Lenman, B and Parker, G, *Crime and the Law: The Social History of Crime in Western Europe since 1500* (London, 1980); Rude, G, *The Crowd in History — A Study of Popular Disturbances in France and England 1730–1848* (New York: Wiley, 1964); Thompson, EP, 'The Moral Economy of the English Crowd in the Eighteenth Century' (1971), *Past and Present*, 50, pp 76–136.

5 Jeffery, CR, 'The Development of Crime in Early English Society', in Chambliss, WJ (ed), *Crime and the Legal Process* (New York: McGraw Hill, 1969), pp 25, 31.

6 Baker, JH, *An Introduction to English Legal History* (London: Butterworths, 1990), p 63.

Crown deferred to the professional expertise of the merchant guilds and permitted them to develop rules governing trade. During the fourteenth century,
the main commercial towns were granted Courts of Staple in which merchants
judged their own customs and this 'law merchant' was absorbed into the common law.[1] This process was accelerated by the eighteeenth century judiciary led
by Lord Mansfield, who empanelled special jurors from the City of London to
determine crucial cases on the import of financial, insurance and trading customs.[2] This regular use of City professionals in key commercial cases is an early
indication of the strategic political position of City interests, and reflects their
ability to influence important regulatory developments in commerce.

Contemporary changes in legal controls, such as these special courts, were often
unplanned, contingent responses to the conflicts of the emerging market economy.[3] Unlike many countries in Continental Europe, there was no justice ministry in Britain, and consequently no tradition of a ministry to oversee law
reform and the general law. This lack of a justice ministry is symptomatic of the
weak position of the State in England in comparison to the rest of Europe.
Traditionally, in Continental Europe, the concept of the State has been more
important, and there is a greater sense of people 'belonging' to the State.[4] This
'belonging' carries with it expectations about subsequent responsibilities that
the State owes to its people and is expected to fulfil. Centralised police forces,
stronger central bureaucracies and less concern for ideologies of individualism
are manifestations of this 'strong State: weak State' comparison.

Even as late as the nineteenth century, in England, many economic and political functions, as well as the administration of the civil and criminal law itself,
continued to operate in many ways at a local rather than a centralised level. This
strong local emphasis and lack of central State interference heavily influenced
the development of English markets and industries. All English markets and
not just London's financial markets have firm, long-held traditions of self-regulation. They are grounded legally in the law merchant and common law, and
have at their heart the belief that commerce is a domain of private transactions.
The private regulatory structures of the City's markets, therefore, reflect
national characteristics and are explained partially by the relative weakness of
the central State.

However, the key relationship that has established, nurtured and maintained
the City's pre-eminence in the British economy has been its connection with
the Crown and central government.[5] There is a long history of mutual self-
interest between the City of London and the monarchy, which has been crucial
in developing the relative autonomy of the City of London. There is the obvious

---

1 Cornish, WR and de Clark, G, *Law and Society in England 1750–1950* (London: Sweet &
   Maxwell, 1989, pp 197–198.
2 *Ibid*, pp 36–37.
3 Sugarman, D and Rubin, GR, 'Towards a New History of Law and Material Society in England,
   1750–1914', in Rubin, GR and Sugarman, D (eds), *Law, Economy and Society, 1750–1914: Essays
   on the History of English Law* (Abingdon, Oxon: Professional Books Limited, 1984), p 67.
4 Dyson, KHF, *The State Tradition in Western Europe* (Oxford: Martin Robertson, 1980)
5 The international character of the City is developed in more detail below, with a particular
   emphasis upon how the City has utilised its political influence to control its own regulation and
   secure a significant degree of relative autonomy from the central State.

importance to the Crown of a supportive and peaceful major economic centre to assist royal stability through the country as a whole. The City of London and the City of Westminster were separate entities, with the majority of the Royal Court resident in Westminster, but the cooperation and support of the City of London were vital to the Crown's interests. The monarchy's need for this support was acute during the Middle Ages when the baronial class was extremely powerful. Consequently, the City's relationship with the Crown was particularly close on matters of public order, trade and taxes, (for example, the City Levies, The Fifteenth and Tenth, and The Subsidy which provided the Crown with revenue and military recruits). The tradition of London as a generally peaceful city was principally dependent on this cooperative relationship and, by the reign of Henry VIII, London was largely self-governing.[1] A self-governing London suited the Crown as it avoided the expense of a large civil bureaucracy. Nevertheless, the Crown still sought frequently to influence distribution of patronage within the City to ensure a steady supply of tax revenue. From the Elizabethan period, this reliance of the Crown on the City for revenues meant that, in practical terms, the dependence of the Crown on the City was usually greater than any reliance of the City upon the Crown.[2]

This royal dependence on the City of London allowed the City latitude freely to pursue trade matters. It was during the fifteenth century that England's international trade role developed in a substantial way, and Italian merchants and financiers were integral in this process.[3] This development of international trade was boosted during the late fifteenth century when Edward IV traded as a merchant himself and carried on many private ventures. He fostered the development of trade and trade-oriented treaties, and his most important legislation was commercial.[4]

However, not all monarchs have had such warm relationships with the City as Edward IV. For example, Charles II had a prolonged struggle with the City of London to alter its property rights.[5] Nevertheless, as the seventeenth century progressed, the commercial interests of the City, with its increasingly powerful and profitable joint-stock trading companies, dovetailed with those of the Crown, because:

> 'The growing power of the central government was raising the costs of administration, wars were becoming larger and more expensive, and the rise of prices in the late sixteenth and early seventeenth centuries caused an ever-growing discrepancy between the traditional source of revenue and the expenses of the state.'[6]

As costs of government rose dramatically during the sixteenth and seventeenth centuries, the Crown's borrowing requirement soared and it was the City which funded that borrowing. Direct taxation was unpopular and the lack of a strong central bureaucracy depleted the Crown's tax-gathering potential. As a result,

---

1 Allen, JW, *A History of Political Thought in the Sixteenth Century* (London, 1928), p xv.
2 Foster, FF, *The Politics of Stability: A Portrait of the Rules of Elizabethan England* (London, 1977), p 6.
3 Hall, J, 'Theft, Law and Society: The Carrier's Case', in Chambliss, WJ (ed), *Crime and the Legal Process* (New York: McGraw Hill, 1969), pp 46–47.
4 *Ibid*, p 48.
5 Sugarman, D and Rubin, GR (1984), *ibid, supra*, p 32.
6 Morgan, EV and Thomas, WA, *The Stock Exchange — Its History and Functions* (London: Elek Books, 1962), p 17.

collection of tax revenue was extremely difficult, and the Crown became heavily dependent upon loans from City merchants and financiers to cover expenditure.

The Crown's credit requirements were a significant factor in the establishment of the City's two most important financial institutions:

> '. . . Both the Bank of England and the Stock Exchange were the products of England's "second revolution" in the late seventeenth century which ended Charles II's attempts to restore arbitrary royal powers in financial matters . . . Over 1,000 subscribers, including London's leading merchants, were incorporated as the Governor and the Bank of England in 1694. The Charter was granted in return for an initial loan of £1.2 million, and in 1708 the Bank was extended by Act of Parliament the privileged status of the country's only joint-stock bank. This early monopoly which lasted for over a century, meant that other banks could only be partnerships, which were limited in number to six persons. This legislation was the direct result of the City's power and effectively retarded the development of provincial branch banking on any scale.'[1]

The essentially private character of the Bank of England and the Stock Exchange moulded the self-regulatory system of the UK financial services sector.[2] Their privileged market positions and the UK's system of financial self-regulation flow from the post-medieval financial dependence of the Crown upon the City of London. They provide a neat illustration of how prevailing power relations and economic conditions will inevitably shape regulatory structures. These powerful influences can also be seen at work in the emergence in the Middle Ages of the guild system (which controlled the professions through restrictive trade practices), and the granting by the Crown of trade monopolies through royal charters or franchises. The Crown and Aldermen of the City of London formed a natural alliance as these monopolies concentrated economic wealth. The Crown gained increased taxation revenue and established traders made enormous profits as they ordered and controlled markets. It was not until the seventeenth century that the Crown dropped its support of national monopolies, and the middle of the nineteenth century before foreign trade monopolies were proscribed.

By 1700, international trade had become so important to London and England that London was the largest city in the world, with a population of 600,000, and one quarter of those people worked in the City and its ports. During the nineteenth century, London overtook Amsterdam as the world's main financial centre. The international money market centred around London's merchant banks, discount houses and the Bank of England; and the Bank became the guardian of the international money system with the gold standard as the fulcrum of that system.[1] By the end of the nineteenth century, the importance of

---

1 Ingham (1984), *ibid, supra*, p 47.

2 Only in recent times has the Stock Exchange become more open and more publicly accountable. The Bank of England was nationalised by the *Bank of England Act 1946*, but the process of choosing the Governor remained unchanged and nationalisation had virtually no effect on the Bank's methods of operation. See generally: Eatwell, R, *The 1945–1951 Labour Governments* (London: Batsford Academic, 1979), pp 54–55; and Lloyd, TO, *Empire to Welfare State* (Oxford: Oxford University Press, 1970), pp 284–285.

London's financial markets to the British economy was manifested in the fact that:

> '. . . one fifth of the nation's wealth was invested in company shares . . . more than double the amount of French and German company investment combined, and it did not even include money invested in colonial or foreign companies. It has been estimated that British overseas investment grew from around £100 million in 1829 to £230 million in 1854 to a staggering £4 billion by 1914.'[2]

These totals reflect the astonishing wealth of Victorian Britain. By 1800, Britain's manufacturing output was almost 40 per cent of the world's total. This was augmented by the City's earnings, which in 1820 accounted for 30 per cent of exported products, rising to 50 per cent by the 1880s. The City through its 'commercial broker' role became the 'natural' commercial and financial centre of the world system.[3]

During the nineteenth century, Britain was the dominant world power and, unlike France and Germany, did not require protectionism. She embraced *laissez-faire* principles and imposed her commercial hegemony upon the rest of the world. The economic medium that acted as the conduit for that hegemony was the collective institutional structure of the City. This paramount political significance gave City professional groups and markets enormous influence with the Crown and central government. Britain is no longer the dominant world power, but the international character of the City has allowed it to retain its status as the world's most important financial centre. In turn, this has ensured its central importance to the British economy, sustained its political influence and secured its relative autonomy.

THE REGULATORY HISTORY OF THE CITY

This section explains specific regulatory patterns in the UK financial services sector by examining regulatory milestones in the evolution of the City. In particular, it analyses how, during the last 300 years, any significant regulatory developments in the City have been directed largely by its own constituent interest groups. These groups have achieved their regulatory autonomy through their reflexive interaction with external economic and political structures. The analysis shows the way in which the City has utilised these relationships to defeat or deflect consistently external attempts at regulatory intervention, and to consolidate its own regulatory authority and systems of self-regulation.

Initially, there are some general points that can be made about the way in which UK financial services law has developed. First, the historical development of the law governing business is full of paradox, and all traders and entrepreneurs have, historically, thrived when legal systems are complex and confusing.[4] This

---

1 McRae, H and Cairncross, F, *Capital City, London as a Financial Centre* (London: Methuen, 1985), pp 2, 6, 7.
2 Robb, G, *White-Collar Crime in Modern England, Financial Fraud and Business Morality, 1845–1929* (Cambridge: Cambridge University Press, 1992), p 28.
3 Ingham (1984), *ibid, supra*, pp 96–98.
4 Sugarman and Rubin (1984), *ibid, supra*, p 5.

is particularly the case for UK securities regulation, which resembles the British Constitution and operates under an umbrella concept, with a host of interacting rules, laws and practices.[1] Secondly, securities regulation is not a static phenomenon but is the product of compromises between different social and commercial forces which set out the legitimate parameters for commercial activity. The business community is generally antipathetic to regulation, and company and financial law reform has been largely reactive to the agency of affected practitioners.[2]

The earliest statutory instances of City regulation relate to brokers and the most significant Acts were: 13 Edward I stat. 5 (1284); I James I c 21 (1604); 8 & 9 William III c 32 (1697); 6 Anne c 16 (1707); 10 Anne c 19 (1711); 6 George I c 18 (1720); 3 George II c 31 (1730); 7 George c 8 (1734).[3] The 1284 statute authorised the Court of Aldermen to license brokers (or *broggers* as they were then called) in the City of London and also to prosecute unlicensed brokers.[4] This statute firmly established the traditions of self-regulation and restrictive trade practices in the City of London as reward for its financial and political support of the Crown.

Statutory obligations upon the financial services sector only became entrenched in 1986 with the Financial Services Act (FSA), and from 1284 until that time traditions of internal self-regulation by the City were dominant. Before completing a chronology of significant regulatory milestones affecting the City, it is worth drawing comparisons between the Act To Restrain The Numbers and Practice Of Brokers And Stock Jobbers (1697) and the FSA, because they are probably the most interesting statutes regarding the development of financial services in Britain. They also illustrate the continuing influence of the City upon how patterns of securities regulation emerge in the UK. The content of the FSA is quite well known, but the 1697 statute is known by few. However, the key features of the 1697 Act were:

- brokers and jobbers had to be licensed;
- the numbers of brokers should be restricted to 100, they must swear oaths and pay a bond;
- maximum limits were placed upon commissions;
- all brokers should keep a broker's book naming all parties and recording details of all contracts, agreements and bargains within three days of being instigated.[5]

The statute provided a fairly comprehensive set of guidelines and sanctions regarding brokers, and contains some features that are central concepts of the FSA. There are also differences between the two statutes, the most important being that the 1697 Act confirmed restrictive practices associated with numbers of brokers, whereas the 1986 statute encourages more open access to the securities markets.

---

1 Rider, BAK, Abrams, C and Ferran, E, *Guide to the Financial Services Act 1986*, 2nd edn (Bicester, Oxon: CCH, 1989), p 7.
2 Robb (1992), *ibid, supra*, p 147.
3 Baily, F, *The Rights of the Stock-Broker defended against the Attacks of the City of London* (London, 1806), p v.
4 Loss, L, *Fundamentals of Securities Regulation* (Boston: Little Brown and Company, 1983), p 1.
5 Baily (1806), *ibid, supra*, pp 10–11.

It is important to remember that the late seventeenth century was a period of profound change which was marked by increased levels of concern about England's financial markets centred in the City of London. These concerns became more pronounced during the boom of 1693–1695 and the crisis that followed. A parliamentary inquiry was appointed in November 1696 '. . . to look after the Trade of England . . .' as a response to widespread public disquiet about the rapacious nature of England's early capital markets. The Royal Commissioners were alarmed by the promotion of frauds and manipulation of the market, they complained that:

> 'The pernicious Art of Stock-jobbing hath, of late, . . . wholly perverted the End and Design of Companies and Corporations, erected for the introducing, or carry-ing on of Manafactures, . . . by selling their shares for much more than they are really worth . . . Thus, . . . the Management of that Trade and Stock comes to fall into unskilful Hands, whereby the Manafactures . . . dwindle away to nothing.'[1]

It was the damning report of the Royal Commissioners which prompted Parliament to pass the 1697 Act. However, as is discussed below, the restrictive trade practices of stock-jobbers remained in force and their self-regulatory monopoly of the City's securities markets was not seriously threatened. They retained this control despite continuing public anger about market manipula-tion, and widespread accusations that brokers were manipulating rumours about foreign wars and share prices in order to increase their volumes of trade.[2]

Nevertheless, despite its limited effects in practice, the 1697 Act was a crucial legislative initiative because it was the first attempt by any government to impose certain standards of probity and competence upon those dealing in the embryonic securities market. All broking business not with a licensed broker was considered unlawful and available penalties included: imprisonment, £500 fines, disqualification as a broker and the pillory. The legislation was both punitive and preventive, emphasising the twin concepts of anti-fraud and due diligence, and merging administrative and criminal justice processes. The statute also recognised, for the first time, the value of public esteem and censure as a sanction in the financial sector, and interestingly, this sanction is now contained in s 60 of the FSA.[3] The 1697 Act was markedly forward-looking in many of its objectives but was repealed in 6 Anne c 16 (1707). This was in spite of a Committee of the House of Commons ruling that the Act was ' . . . fit to be continued'.[4] The reasons for the Act lapsing are not absolutely clear, but what is interesting, for the purposes of this essay, is to consider why it was not renewed, and also what factors prompted such a notable statutory intervention upon the City.

The Royal Commission on the Trade of England (1696), in its report submitted to Parliament, had been highly critical of widespread fraud and market manip-ulation and '. . . the pernicious trade of stock-jobbing'.[5] This report and its fear

---

1 *House of Commons Journals* (1696), 25 November.
2 Mortimer, T, *Every Man His Own Broker* (London, 1791) pp 40, 53–64.
3 Under s 60, the Securities Investment Board (SIB) may publicise the fact that a person or firm has breached the requirements of the FSA. It has the potential to be a powerful sanction in an industry where reputation is crucial, but it is one that the SIB has been reluctant to apply.
4 Morgan and Thomas (1962), *ibid, supra*, p 26.
5 *House of Commons Journals* (1696), *ibid, supra*.

of market manipulation was the precursor of the 1697 Act which passed through Parliament quickly, receiving the royal assent less than a week after being introduced by Sir Joseph Tiley.[1] However, it was not government altruism towards the investor, but concern about its own finances that ensured the Bill's success and speedy passage. The State was in dire financial distress because speculative investment was haemorrhaging the flow of available capital and loans away from the government, and Exchequer tallies were at 30 per cent discount.[2] The stringent conditions of the Act upon brokers were the means by which the government expected to re-establish its own supplies of capital, rather than a concerted effort at raising levels of investor protection through improved broker competence and probity. The City subsequently responded to the government's need for loans and the Act was not strictly enforced, although City opposition to it remained strong.

The 1697 Act was made for three years, continued for seven years longer and then, on 17 January 1707, petitions were made for it to continue. On 3 February 1707, a counter-petitition submitted that it be discontinued, but on 6 February the House of Commons Committee on Expiring Laws judged it fit to be continued. They recommended that its report and all petitions be considered by Parliament on 14 February 1707. However, on 24 January 1707, the Levant Company had presented a petition to repeal the Act for the Well Garbling of Spices James I c 19. The Chief Garbler (collector of levies on trading in spices) at that time, William Stewart, petitioned against loss of income if the Act was repealed.[3] The House decided to repeal the Spices Act in 6 Anne c 16 (1707), but at the same time, in order to cover losses in revenue, the Act imposed an annual levy of 40 shillings upon brokers of the City.[4] Previously, this figure of 40 shillings had been a maximum not a minimum levy, and so brokers petitioned that they should not have to bear both the new levy and the costs of the 1697 Act. As a consequence of their lobbying pressure, the 1697 Act was allowed to lapse, an early indicator of the lobbying power of the City.

The City's lobbying power combined human agency and structural pressures, a combination which proved to be extremely effective in the continuing public debates concerning the legitimacy of the regulation of stock-jobbers and brokers in eighteenth century England. Many of the surviving records of these debates are anonymous pamphlets presented to the House of Commons. The practice of delivering pamphlets to the Commons was a key strategy for the various interest groups in the discourse upon financial regulation. These groups made constant appeals to the virtues of both equity and efficacy, by either emphasising the allegedly unfair practices of stock-jobbers and the harm they caused to England's trade, or refuting these allegations and lobbying strongly for broking interests. One such pamphlet, which supported the 1697 Act, was produced by a coalition of merchants, who lobbied parliamentarians to strengthen the regulation of stock-jobbers, and argued vehemently that:

---

1 *House of Commons Journals* (1697), vol XI, p 595.
2 Baily (1806), *ibid, supra*, p 20.
3 *Ibid*, pp 20–24.
4 Anon, *Bond signed by all those intending to be Brokers* (London, 1707).

'. . . Stock Jobbing hath been found so Pernicious to Trade in general, and Ruinous to many Families in particular, It's therefore very necessary that a more effectual Law, than the late Brokers Act should be made against that pernicious Practice.'[1]

Twenty years later the public image of stock-jobbers was still quite low, as shown by an appeal to the 'noble instincts' of Parliament to legislate against those dealing in Share Contracts:

'The Buyers for Ready Money are allowed to be the Gentry and Merchants, as well as the Buyers for Trust, and the cunning Jewellers are the same in both Cases, viz, the late Directors, their Agents, Confederates, Brokers and Stock Jobbers, who by a dismal reverse in Affairs have, by Collusion and Fraud, raised Fortunes to themselves, too large for any Subjects . . .

But as all honest Men will consider, that there are a great many of these Bargains, which stand in the Names of these hidden and secret Villains.'[2]

This pamphlet highlights the widespread existence of share frauds and also the popular mistrust of financial professionals which had been prevalent for several hundred years. This entrenched distrust is shown by the fact that although banking is now a high-status occupation, in the Middle Ages financiers were considered to be '. . . usurers and were universally deprecated and formally anathematised.'[3] Similarly, stock-broking is now a very highly paid and high-status occupation, but it was under attack even up to the end of the eighteenth century. Critics vilified 'the diabolical art of stock-jobbing', alleging that stock-jobbers abused public credit in general and exploited the fortunes of women in particular.[4]

Whatever the relative merits of stock-broking as a profession, one can only muse on how different the history of the City and the industrial development of Britain might have been if the 1697 Act had remained in existence and its provisions enforced. The 1697 Act was a watershed in the regulatory history of the City and cemented its regulatory authority. It assured the restricted numbers of City brokers and actually extended their ambit by allowing them to deal in Exchequer and Bank of England bills and tallies. The chief motivation for City resistance was that the Act represented external intervention into its systems of self-regulation. The struggles surrounding the 1697 Act illustrate the forces of duality of structure at work. Interdependent agencies and structures in the City and in Parliament attempted reflexively to maintain or repeal the Act, with unintended consequences also playing their part. The City could see how far-reaching the consequences of the 1697 Act were to its independence and methods of operation, even though those consequences were not the primary concern of a government determined to assert its funding priorities. There

---

1 Anon, *Reasons on behalf of many eminent merchants for continuing the late Brokers Act under further regulations, humbly submitted to the consideration of the Honourable the Commons of Great Britain in Parliament assembled* (London, 1700).

2 Anon, *Some Considerations with respect to the Bill for preventing the infamous Practice of Stock-Jobbing; being Remarks upon the Supplement to the Reasons for making void and annulling those Fraudulent and Usurious Contracts, into which etc. and upon the Reply to a modest Paper, etc. both delivered at the Door of the House of Commons on Friday last* (London, 1721).

3 Bridbury, AR, 'Markets and Freedom in the Middle Ages', in Anderson, BL and Latham, AJH (eds), *The Market in History* (London: Croom Helm, 1986), p 83.

4 Mortimer, T (1791), *ibid, supra*, pp vi, xi, 25.

were subsequent failed attempts in Parliament in 1711,[1] 1719 and 1721[2] to revive the 1697 Act or produce an equivalent, but intensive lobbying by the City ensured that they did not receive a third reading.[3]

It is worth drawing some comparisons between the saga of the 1697 Act and the struggles that produced the FSA, because they demonstrate the recurring features of the City's regulatory autonomy. The major impetus for the FSA came in 1979, with the removal of exchange controls and the reference by the Director-General of Fair Trading of the Stock Exchange Rule Book to the Restrictive Practices Court. In July 1981, the Conservative Government of Margaret Thatcher asked Professor Jim Gower to conduct an inquiry into the need for statutory control of the financial services sector and advise on new legislation. Gower realised what the City expected from him, but was also very aware of the inadequacies of City self-regulation:

> 'The City would welcome continued self-regulation, for which it believed it had a genius. But self-regulation to most of the City then meant leaving everybody to regulate himself in his own interests subject only to a possible unpublicised reproof from his professional or trade association if he transgressed too blatantly . . . Nor would the City establishment welcome the establishment of anything like the . . . SEC, of which it had an almost paranoid fear and dislike.'[4]

When Gower published his provisional views in a discussion document in January 1982, he stated that he wanted to establish a US-style securities commission, but acknowledged that political constraints (ie City opposition and its enormous political influence) made that impossible. Instead, he recommended a new Securities Act which would establish wide-ranging self-regulatory authorities which would be funded by the industry.[5] City reaction was hostile:

> '. . . the main City bodies were livid. They denounced me for having, in their view, exceeded my brief by suggesting regulation of the elite merchant banks and Stock Exchange firms when all that was needed was effective regulation of the fringe operators. And they argued that self-regulation (in their sense) was the panacea and that it only works when it is left free of any form of governmental surveillance.'[6]

Here we see the tactics of 1697–1707 re-emerging as City interests lobbied fiercely to stave off the prospect of strong external supervision. The City's traditional alliances and kinship with the Bank of England and the Treasury were activated in efforts to militate against Gower's final report harming City independence. In an important initiative in May 1984, the Governor of the Bank of England formed an advisory group of City dignatories under the Chairmanship of Mr (now Sir) Martin Jacomb to advise on the structure of self-regulation. At the same time, the Parliamentary Under-Secretary of State asked Mr Marshall Field to set up another group to advise on life assurance and unit

---

1 Anon, *Reasons for putting the Bill for the better Preserving of Publick Credit, by reviving and continuing the Act made in the Eighth and Ninth Years of the Reign of the late King William III. Entitled An Act to Restrain the Number and Ill Practices of Brokers and Stock Jobbers* (London, 1711).
2 Anon (1721), *ibid, supra*, pp 1–2.
3 Baily (1806), *ibid, supra*, pp 26–27.
4 Gower, LCB, 'Big Bang and City Regulation' (1988), *Modern Law Review*, Vol 51, No 1, p 8.
5 Gower, LCB, *Review of Investor Protection: A Discussion Document*, Cmnd 7937 (London: HMSO, 1981).
6 Gower (1988), *ibid, supra*, p 9.

trusts. Gower is scathing about these outflanking manoeuvres by the City and Whitehall:

> 'Precisely what the Governor's group reported I cannot tell you since its report was never published; indeed, officially it never made a written report (GAG, the acronym by which the Governor's Advisory Group was known, was singularly apt).

> There were then intensive discussions and arguments between the Bank of England and the Department of Trade and Industry which led to what was known by those involved as the Treaty of London. This is another document which officially does not exist but the general lines of the concordat reached were outlined in ... a White Paper published in January 1985,[1] and now implemented in the *Financial Services Act* 1986.'[2]

The irony of the White Paper is that, rather than being a new framework for investor protection as its title states, it is more a new framework for the protection of the relative autonomy of the City. Gower himself describes the White Paper as being so ingenious as to be :

> '... almost a confidence trick. The White Paper described its proposals as "self-regulation within a statutory framework" but in fact a more accurate description of what has emerged is "statutory regulation monitored by self-regulatory organisations recognised by, and under the surveillance of a self-standing Commission".'[3]

The self-standing commission is, of course, the SIB, which is a private company limited by guarantee which exercises delegated statutory powers. It is a remarkable constitutional hybrid and it would be hard to imagine its emergence in any major financial centre other than a zealously insular and politically powerful City of London. The City had, effectively, outflanked Gower and his final report which was published in January 1984.[4] The intense lobbying by the City produced the FSA, a statutory model in its own self-regulatory image. The then Secretary of State for Trade and Industry, Mr Norman Tebbit MP (now Lord Tebbitt), confirmed, when tabling the White Paper in the House of Commons, that the financial services industry would be regulated by its practitioners.[5] The circumventing of Gower's preferred regulatory model can be regarded as an opportunity missed and represents another successful lobbying campaign by the City to protect its regulatory autonomy. Gower's proposed reforms and Securities Act had been emasculated in much the same manner as the 1697 Act had been and, in the intervening two centuries, the City has also scored other important regulatory victories.

As discussed above, there is evidence stretching back to 1697 of the reflexive lobbying power of City interests and their ability to maintain restrictive trade practices.[6] Another pamphlet, in 1700, argues that the national interest is entwined with limiting the numbers of brokers.[7] It is ironic that a 1756

---

1 Department of Trade and Industry, *Financial Services in the United Kingdom: A new framework for investor protection*, Cmnd 9432 (London: HMSO, 1985).
2 Gower (1988), *ibid, supra*, p 11.
3 *Ibid*, p 11.
4 Gower, LCB, *Review of Investor Protection*, Cmnd 9125 (London: HMSO, 1984).
5 *Hansard* (1985), 29 January, pp 157–158.
6 Anon, *Some observations on the Bill now depending Intitled, An Act to prevent the Infamous Practice of Stock-Jobbing* (1697), p 3.
7 Anon (1700), *ibid, supra*, p 1.

pamphlet employs free trade ideology to justify restrictive broking practices, conflating those practices with the sanctity of the individual right to trade and linking them with loyalty to the nation.[1] In the nineteenth century, City lobbying efforts were channelled through the parliamentary-based Political Reform Club. It was composed almost exclusively of City merchants and aristocrats, and was the most powerful and effective political lobby group in Victorian England.[2]

However, the City's regulatory autonomy has not been solely reliant on lobbying power. During the eighteenth and nineteenth centuries, its autonomy was boosted by a widely held belief that if the City were left free of external interference then national prosperity would continue. This was thought to be a self-evident justification of *laissez-faire*.[3] In fact, as intervention by the central State into other areas of the economy increased during the nineteenth century, the hostility that administrators met from City interests obliged them to adopt practices based upon conciliatory tactics.[4]

In addition to skilful lobbying and ideological justifications, the City's regulatory autonomy has been strengthened continually over the years by the social, cultural and business connections that City professionals share with senior civil servants and influential politicians. These diffused networks of patronage within the British élite have been extremely influential, particularly in the Victorian era when:

> '... politicians were so inextricably bound up in business activity that they were incapable of initiating serious reform. Large numbers of both Houses were directors of public companies, as were members of the civil service. There were no rules governing politicians' associations with trade and industry, and so lax were standards of conflicting interests that during the 1870s the Chief Railway Inspecting Officer at the Board of Trade was himself the director of a railway company.'[5]

The issue of politicians' links with business, and the conflicts of interests they raise has remained a continuing regulatory dilemma.[6] Political and social connections have helped the City's social praxis to become the normative order of the UK financial services sector and militated against public models of regulation. The reflexive interaction of City structures, their social and political connections, and the lobbying efforts of City professionals have protected the City's regulatory autonomy. This allowed it to benefit from the spectacular profits of the colonial era and insulated it from the subsequent decline suffered by other sectors of the UK economy.[7] The key political connections in these networks of patronage have been the City's links with the Treasury, which has

---

1 Anon, *Reasons against passing into an Act at this time any further Bill relating to Stockjobbing* (London, 1756), p 1
2 Ingham (1984), *ibid, supra*, pp 126–127.
3 Ingham (1984), *ibid, supra*, p 131.
4 Cornish and de Clark (1989), *ibid, supra*, pp 54–60.
5 Robb (1992), *ibid, supra*, p 173.
6 This has been demonstrated graphically in recent times by the 'cash for questions' parliamentary scandal, and the efforts of Lord Nolan and others to find ways of improving ethical standards in public life.
7 Ingham (1984), *ibid, supra*, p 152.

enormous power located in its dual role as the ministry of finance and head of the government bureaucracy.[1]

Returning to the regulatory chronology, the next significant legislation after the 1697 Act was the Bubble Act 6 Geo II c 18, passed on 9 June 1720, in order to dampen the speculative fever of the South Sea Bubble.[2] The South Sea Company had been established in 1711 by converting £900,000,000 of unfunded national debt (a legacy of the War of Spanish Succession) into shares of the new South Sea joint-stock company and layers of subsequent dubious promotions created the infamous bubble which involved as subscribers, or borrowers, or both:

> '. . . not only the traders and financiers of the City, but the King and the Prince of Wales with their Courts, the majority of members of both Houses of Parliament, army officers and senior civil servants, and a great mass of country gentry, large and small. In fact most of the people who wielded political power and influence were involved.'[3]

The draconian penalties of the Bubble Act were aimed at those operating non-chartered companies and included life imprisonment or forfeiture of all property. The sanctions were a symbolic deterrent and although the Act remained on the statute books until 1825, there was only one prosecution under its provisions.[4]

The next legislative attempt to regulate the City was An Act to Prevent the Infamous Practice of Stock-Jobbing, passed on 16 April 1734 and more commonly known as 'Barnard's Act'.[5] The Act outlawed the common practices of short-selling and forward transactions, and initiated mandatory recording of all transactions in the name of the principal. There were criminal penalties for failure to comply, but the Act was not strictly enforced and so the City again evaded external accountability measures.[6] There were further Private Members' Bills to regulate stock-jobbing in 1737, 1746, 1756 and 1765, but all were defeated by City lobbying efforts.[7] These efforts stressed the harm the proposed Bills would do to the national interest by restricting City trade,[8] and one pamphlet argued that mandatory recording of brokers and their transactions would assist:

---

1 The City/Treasury relationship has been changing in recent years as the Treasury has assumed greater regulatory oversight.

2 See generally: Carswell, J, *The South Sea Bubble* (London: Crescent Press, 1960); and Cowles, V, *The Great Swindle* (London: Collins, 1960).

3 Morgan and Thomas, (1962), *ibid, supra*, p 39.

4 *R v Caywood* 1 [1723] Stra 472 and 2 Ld Ray 1362.

5 Sir John Barnard was an Independent Whig parliamentarian, who championed the interests of the smaller merchants, tradesmen and craftsmen on trade and finance issues. This brought him into conflict frequently with the large trading and finance companies and the government of Sir Robert Walpole. See: Sedgwick, R, *The House of Commons 1715–1754*, Vol 1 (London, 1970), pp 435–437.

6 Rider et al, (1989), *ibid, supra*, pp 2–4.

7 Baily, (1806), *ibid, supra*, pp 30–32.

8 Anon, *Reasons humbly offered to the Members of the Honourable House of Commons, against a Bill now depending, to render more effectual, an Act made in the Seventh Year of His Majesty's Reign, intitled, 'An Act to prevent the infamous practice of Stock-Jobbing'* (London, 1737), pp 1–2.

'. . . those confederated Monopolisers, (detestable and pernicious to the last degree to the Publick and the Proprietors) who . . . will have all the Game to themselves, and play into one another's Hands . . . and their great Connections with the Monied Interest, have domineered over the Stocks.'[1]

Once again, we have the irony of City interests warning of the dangers of monopolisers, when they themselves were speaking from a restrictive entry position to the 'Game' of stock-broking. The same pamphlet warns that increased external regulation would initiate many litigation claims and provide an '. . . inexhaustable source of income for lawyers.'[2] These successful lobbying efforts prompted Stock Exchange members to describe Barnard's Act as inoperative and it was widely flouted.[3] Broader economic forces also assisted City autonomy, because 1750–1825 was the period of the 'Great Transformation' when Britain became the world's major industrial power, and the market society, with its *laissez-faire* philosophy, was dominant.

The mid-nineteenth century saw the next major legislative developments in the financial services sector, through the Joint Stock Companies Act 1844 which established sufficient and timely disclosure as the cornerstone of English company law, and the Limited Liability Act 1855. Corporations and limited liability were not new ideas; pre-Christian Rome had developed concepts of corporation and limited liability, but the Romans had not tried to link the two.[4] The traditional purpose of corporations in the Middle Ages was one of association, and corporate personality could then only be granted by Royal Charter or an Act of Parliament, but the pressures of the Industrial Revolution saw it emerge from the model of joint-stock companies as an investment vehicle which could reduce risk. However, the speculative disaster of the South Sea Bubble had made governments wary of granting many charters of incorporation, and limited liability was considered by Adam Smith[5] and others as contrary to free market principles, because it evaded full personal responsibility for personal business decisions. Despite these fears, by 1844 the three main pressures for incorporation were: (i) the need for large amounts of capital for major projects such as railways; (ii) the popularity of financial gambling on stocks and shares through the London Stock Exchange; and (iii) the desire to risk capital without exposing entire personal fortunes.[6]

For obvious commercial reasons, the City was lobbying hard for universal limited liability as well as incorporation. There was opposition in some quarters to limited liability because it was seen as being solely for the benefit of owners of capital and financial traders, and not in the interests of customers, employees and suppliers. In 1808, Lord Ellenborough labelled moves towards limited liability as '. . . a mischievous delusion to ensnare the unwary public'.[7] However,

1 Anon (1756), *ibid, supra*, p 1.

2 *Ibid*, pp 2–3.

3 Ferguson, RB, 'Commercial Expectations and the Guarantee of the Law: Sales Transactions in Mid-Nineteenth Century England', in Rubin and Sugarman (eds), *ibid, supra*, p 195.

4 Perrott, DL, 'Changes in Attitude to Limited Liability — The European Experience', in Orhnial, T (ed), *Limited Liability and the Corporation* (London: Croom Helm, 1982), pp 85–86.

5 Smith, A, *The Wealth of Nations* (London: T Nelson & Sons, 1884).

6 Cornish and de Clark (1989), *ibid, supra*, p 247.

7 *R v Dodd* [1808] 9 East 516.

City interests argued that the depression of 1846–47 was evidence that limited liability should become readily available and not remain a privilege. A Bill was eventually introduced into Parliament in 1855 and immediately denounced as 'The Rogues Charter' by *The Law Times*.[1] Nevertheless, the Bill became the Limited Liability Act 1855 and was confirmed and developed in the Joint Stock Companies Act 1856 and the Companies Act 1862. So the City had won a long lobbying battle on limited liability and, as a result, there were massive increases in the flotation of limited liability companies. However, criticism still endured and, in 1859, Professor JR McCulloch, first Professor of Political Economy at the University of London, wrote about the Limited Liability Act 1855 in these terms:

> 'Were Parliament to set about devising means for the encouragement of speculation, over-trading and swindling, what better could it do?'[2]

The City was, of course, not likely to complain about high levels of speculation and over-trading because these increase commission revenues. In fact, insider dealing and market manipulation were accepted as common practice on its markets. The 1860s saw a huge amount of speculative activity culminating in the disastrous collapse of Overend Gurney, the City's largest discount house, but even then the Stock Exchange:

> '. . . showed itself nakedly hostile to any attempt from outside to impose requirements for disclosure in new promotions.'[3]

Concerns about inadequate disclosure requirements, problems associated with limited liability and complaints about City market practices were repeated by many witnesses before Parliamentary Committees in 1867, 1875, 1877 and 1878, and in 1886 before the Royal Commission on the Depression in Trade. Public distaste for financial professionals has been a continuing feature of English social history, but it was especially pronounced in the Victorian era:

> 'The Victorians had few illusions regarding the world of finance. The stereotypical image of the virtuous and respectable Victorian businessman is almost wholly the creation of twentieth-century sentimentalists and conservative ideologues. The Victorians themselves were plagued by white-collar crime as no other people before or since.'[4]

Scandals are still a feature of UK financial services in the 1990s, but ethical standards have risen steadily since the Victorian era, largely because there has been an inexorable rise in professionalisation within the industry.[5] Even fraudsters such as Peter Clowes would find it hard to compete with Victorian white collar offenders such as Ernest Hooley, who bought companies on borrowed money and then resold them to the public with as much capital tacked on as possible. Inevitably, most of these companies swiftly became bankrupt and an article in the *National Review* reflects contemporary sentiment:

---

1 Diamond, AL, 'Corporate Personality and Limited Liability', in Orhnial (ed), (1982), *ibid*, *supra*, p 33.
2 *Ibid*, p 43.
3 Cornish and de Clark (1989), *ibid*, *supra*, pp 258–259.
4 Robb (1992), *ibid*, *supra*, p 3.
5 Clarke, M, *Business Crime: Its Nature and Control* (Cambridge: Polity Press, 1990), p 232.

'Technically there may have been no legal flaw in these gigantic shuffles, but anything more mischievous and contrary to the spirit of sound finance it would be hard to conceive . . . If the moral sense of the nation were to permit such finance to be carried on, we should soon degenerate into a gang of blacklegs. There would be less honour or less honesty in the City than there is on the racecourse.'[1]

Unfortunately, some of the business practices employed by Hooley were still commonplace in the 1980s, when ludicrously high negative gearing and asset stripping strategies were widely engaged in by aggressive entrepreneurs, both individual and collective. These strategies were often used to fund massive acquisitions, many of which proved ruinous following the October 1987 stock market crash. Despite the well-publicised intolerance of Victorians for white collar crime activities, ambiguous legislation and ambivalent industry attitudes assisted scoundrels like Hooley, just as they have facilitated the operations of his modern counterparts such as Robert Maxwell, Peter Clowes and Roger Levitt.

The Victorian and Edwardian communities (like their modern successors) demonstrated systematic bias in how they prosecuted known instances of white collar crime. Few senior industry figures were charged,[2] but there were thousands of prosecutions for clerical embezzlement. Those white collar criminals who were prosecuted often received relatively lenient sentences in comparison to low-status offenders, and it is interesting to note that a justification often mooted for this differential sentencing was that:

'. . . the shame and social disgrace attendant on criminal conviction were punishment enough for middle-class persons. Exclusion from polite society was viewed as a more serious penalty than imprisonment . . . For white collar criminals prison was seen as ancillary to their personal sense of shame and loss of social status.'[3]

These examples illustrate how the social and cultural attitudes of an era are crucial in the differential implementation of the legal process against the white collar criminal. This is evident throughout much of the Victorian era, when, despite overwhelming evidence of widespread fraud being presented to them, legislators did not impose stricter regulation because they feared alienating the financial community.[4] An exception was Leemans Act 1867, which sought to stop the widespread practice of not recording transactions individually (but instead recording them as house transactions), and also aimed to reduce speculative dealing in banking securities. However, the traditional disregard of the City, even for existing statutory controls, is clear in the evidence given to a parliamentary committee in 1875 by Mr Samuel Herman de Zoete, the then chairman of the London Stock Exchange:

---

1 Robb (1992), *ibid, supra*, p 106.
2 Robb cites the examples of the government prosecuting the directors of the Royal British Bank for fraud in 1858, when many newspapers, including *The Times*, alleged that they were only prosecuted because they were not prominent City people, while other equally guilty City people were shielded by their City influence and connections. In a case with similarities to the 1993 Levitt case, there was public outcry in 1878 when the directors of the City of Glasgow Bank received sentences of only five to eighteen months imprisonment, even though their fraud had involved millions of pounds. *Ibid*, pp 163,164.
3 *Ibid*, p 165.
4 Robb (1992), *ibid, supra*, p 150.

'Sirs, we disregarded for years Sir John Barnard's Act and we are now disregarding in the same measure Mr Leeman's Act.'[1]

This dismissive attitude of the Stock Exchange towards restrictive legislation had, in 1860, prompted it to establish a sub-committee to press for the repeal of Barnard's Act.[2] These efforts were successful and the Act was repealed.[3] Leeman's Act, like Barnard's Act, was ignored by the government and practitioners for many years, before being quietly repealed in 1966 under the procedure for removing 'obsolete, spent, unnecessary or superseded enactments'.[4]

Following a series of scandalous promotional frauds during the 1870s, Lord Penzance was appointed, in March 1877, to inquire into the administration and operation of the London Stock Exchange. His major recommendations were:

(i)   that enforcement against fraud relating to financial markets should be vested in some public functionary;
(ii) that all transactions on the Stock Exchange should be individually recorded; and
(iii) that the Stock Exchange should be constituted in statute and be regulated by that statute.[5]

Lord Penzance argued that only increased public accountability on an external level could justify the restrictive practices operated by the Stock Exchange regarding membership and fixed minimum commissions. Unsurprisingly, the lobbying power of the City ensured that Penzance's recommendations were not put into practice by the government and it took over a century for some of them to seep into the regulatory structure of Britain's financial markets. Penzance was a predictor of several of the central reforms of the FSA, and ss 1–3 of the Criminal Justice Act 1987 created a statutory authority in the SFO which has responsibility to act against major frauds. Subsequent inquiries on the financial services sector, such as the Bodkin Committee of 1936 and the Wilson Committee of 1980 have met a similar fate.[6] The regulatory authority of the City has enabled it to marshal sufficient political influence to deflect or defeat negative assessments of its self-regulatory systems by such inquiries.

There have been other statutes affecting the City prior to the FSA and the Big Bang era, including a whole series of Companies Acts, but none have hampered its intrinsic independence. Any provisions of these that have hinted at threatening City autonomy, such as the Company Bills of 1877 and 1888, were quietly and efficiently buried in the committee stages of the parliamentary process.[7] Most financial services legislation this century has concentrated on improving

---

1 *House of Commons Journals* (1875).
2 Roy, H, *The Stock Exchange: Strictures on the Repeal of Sir John Barnard's Act* (London, 1860), p 30.
3 Sir John Barnard's Act Repeal Act [1860] 23 Vict c 28.
4 Ferguson (1984), *ibid, supra*, p 197.
5 Penzance, *London Stock Exchange Commission, Report of the Commissioners*, Cmnd 2157 (London, 1878).
6 Bodkin Committee, *Share Pushing — Report of the Departmental Committee appointed by the Board of Trade 1936–1937*, Cmnd 5339 (London, 1937); and Committee to review the functioning of financial institutions, *Report*, Cmnd 7937 (London: HMSO, 1980).
7 Robb (1992), *ibid, supra*, p 154.

operating standards within the industry and ensuring public access to financial information, so that investors can, allegedly, make fair and informed decisions, under *caveat emptor* principles. The reality is that the structural imbalances of the industry remain, an example of which can be seen in the unfair spread of losses at Lloyd's between insider and outsider 'Names'.[1] No legislation has struck at these inherent imbalances, but the Prevention of Fraud (Investments) Act 1939 and the Prevention of Fraud (Investments) Act 1958 were notable for the improvements they brought in licensing standards. These two statutes represent the last significant statutory developments in UK financial services regulation prior to the FSA and bring this regulatory history of the City to a close.[2]

CONCLUSION

There have been improvements in the standards of UK financial services regulation in recent years, but these have been largely dependent upon the City's cooperation. There are three factors which chiefly explain why the City has been able to develop its high levels of regulatory independence over the years: (i) the growing dependence of first the Crown and then the State on the City and the access to capital it provided; (ii) the City's efficiency as a world finance centre and the economic advantage this has brought to Britain; and (iii) the close social, political and cultural ties between those in the City and their peers in the Treasury and the Bank of England. This regulatory history of the City has sought to show how these factors have combined to ensure that issues such as investor protection are subordinate to the City's determination to retain high levels of relative autonomy over the regulation of its markets. This pattern of resistance to external intervention has been repeated throughout the history of the City. Its various constituent interest groups have utilised their shared social and political connections, their lobbying power and the industry's strategic importance in order to maintain the City's regulatory authority and preserve its self-regulatory traditions. These traditional networks and regulatory arrangements have stood the test of time, but they are coming under increasing pressure as late-modern capitalism creates new trading environments. It will be interesting to observe how the Labour Government's blueprint for reform takes shape over the next couple of years and, in particular, whether this process of change substantially alters the degree of regulatory influence held by the City over its regulatory infrastructure.

---

1 Springett, P, 'Lloyd's battleground switches to the courts' (1994) *The Guardian*, 15 February, p 17.
2 The effects of the Big Bang and subsequent regulatory developments have been so substantial that they merit a separate critique and could not be covered within the constraints of this essay. However, the earlier discussion of the struggles surrounding the regulatory passage of the FSA are an indicator of not only how different forces are participating in moulding the regulatory shape of the UK financial services sector since the early 1980s, but also how traditional City power groupings are adapting to changing trading and political conditions in an effort to maintain their levels of influence.

Chapter 2

MONEY LAUNDERING AND CONSTRUCTIVE LIABILITY

Chizu V Nakajima[1]

INTRODUCTION

The world-wide effort to combat serious criminal enterprises through depriving criminal organisations of the profits that they make through their subversive and illicit activities, has led to the creation of wide ranging laws and regulatory systems designed to outlaw and inhibit the laundering of the proceeds of criminal acts. Given the increasing recognition of the significance of the financial services industry in laundering the proceeds of serious crime,[2] and the dangers this presents to financial institutions, it is the declared policy of many regulatory authorities to 'ring fence' probity in the financial services industry by imposing onerous obligations on those who handle other people's money or who facilitate transactions, to take steps in the exercise of due diligence to ensure that their contribution is both lawful and proper. The rules, thus promulgated, place significant burdens of compliance on those operating in the financial and banking industries to, *inter alia*, ascertain a great deal of information about their clients and their transactions. Failure to comply with such obligations may well have serious implications for those who operate in the financial services industry, and the advent of such regulation has, therefore, had a major impact on the way in which they conduct their business.[3]

In addition to the direct threats posed by organised crime to the stability and integrity of financial institutions, there is the danger that intermediaries may innocently, or otherwise, be exposed to legal or disciplinary liability as a result of handling other people's money. Of course, even under the most Draconian provisions criminal liability is unlikely, unless the intermediary is aware of the

---

1 Senior Lecturer in Financial Regulation, City University Business School.
2 See, for example, House of Commons Select Committee on Home Affairs, *Organised Crime, Minutes and Evidence and Memoranda*, HC (1994–95) 18-II, HMSO, London.
3 See, generally, Rider, BAK, 'The Practical and Legal Aspects of Interdicting the Flow of Dirty Money' (1996) 3 *Journal of Financial Crime* 234; and Clark, NJS, 'The Impact of Recent Money Laundering Legislation on Financial Intermediaries' (1995) 3 *Journal of Financial Crime* 131. Note also that, at a meeting of experts in Italy, on the development of a Single Market for financial services in the European Union, senior officials from the European Commission admitted that the impact of the European Directive on Money Laundering (91/308/EEC), taken together with the Directive Coordinating Regulations on Insider Dealing (89/592/EEC), has had a greater impact on the way in which business is actually carried out within the Member States than any other measure promulgated by the Community in the context of financial regulation. On the conference organised by the University of Genoa, 8–10 November 1996, see the proceedings to be published in Ferrarini, G (ed), *Implementing the Investment Services Directive* (London: Kluwer, 1988).

criminal origins of the funds in question, but developments in the law of imputation and attribution of knowledge render it far more likely that the requisite
degree of scienter will be found. As was demonstrated dramatically in *Re Supply
of Ready Mixed Concrete (No 2)*,[1] even the existence of a sound compliance procedure, and the fact that the relevant transactions were undertaken without any
semblance of authority by an employee who nonetheless was able to do what
was done in the context of his employment, will not necessarily allow the corporate employer to deny personal responsibility.[2] The implications of this decision, supported by other cases, for financial intermediaries are profound.[3]
Furthermore, there have been very important developments in the civil law in
regard to receipt of the proceeds of crime and furnishing assistance in the laundering of the proceeds of a breach of fiduciary duty. The majority of litigated
and contested cases before the Chancery Division of the High Court concern
actions by liquidators and others against those who, while not directly involved
in the commission of specific crimes and wrongdoing, have nevertheless
become inveigled in handling the proceeds.[4] Furthermore, it seems to be the
intention of many regulatory authorities around the world to convert those who
act as professional intermediaries into a first line defence against fraudsters –
the 'reluctant policemen' of the system.[5]

In the context of our discussion, the most significant area of money laundering
control is that relating to the inquiries that must be made in relation to the identity of clients and the nature of their transactions. While the so-called 'know
your client' rule has existed for some considerable time, often as an element
within establishing suitability of investment advice, the extent to which intermediaries now have to ensure that they are in possession of information pertaining
to the identity, standing and character of clients and their transactions, is much
greater. The implications that this additional knowledge may have for the standard of care expected in the provision of advice and services have yet to be

---

1 [1995] 1 AC 456.
2 See Nakajima, C, 'The Cost of Laundry' (1995) 3 *Journal of Financial Crime* 172.
3 But this area of the law has thrown up decisions which are, seemingly, contradictory. See, for
   example, the recent case of *Russell v DPP*, reported in (1997) *The Times*, 28 January, in which the
   Queen's Bench Divisional Court held that it was not necessary for the defendant to show that he
   personally had exercised all due diligence to avoid the commission of the offence, in order to
   establish the defence of due diligence to a charge of selling alcohol to a person under age.
   Whereas, in *Shanks and McEwan (Teesside) Ltd v The Environment Agency*, reported in (1997) *The
   Times*, 28 January, the Court of Appeal held that the site manager's knowledge was sufficient to
   render his company guilty of an offence under the Environmental Protection Act 1990, as he
   was 'part of the directing mind and will of the company'.
4 See Rider, BAK, 'Civilising the Law – The Use of Civil and Administrative Proceedings to
   Enforce Financial Services Law' (1995) 3 *Journal of Financial Crime* 11. Indeed, Sir Peter Millett,
   in his much quoted extra-judicial writing stated: 'In England, and, no doubt, other financial
   centres, the courts are increasingly concerned with attempts by the victims of fraud to trace
   their money and recover it, not from the fraudsters or their confederates, who have usually
   disappeared, but from those through whose hands it has passed.' See Millett, PJ, 'Tracing the
   Proceeds of Fraud' (1991) 107 *LQR* 71 at p 71.
5 See Nakajima, C, 'The Cost of Laundry' (1995) 3 *Journal of Financial Crime* 172; and Froomkin,
   S, *The Reluctant Policemen* (Singapore Academy of Law Press, 1991). See also the SIB's now
   de-designated Core Conduct of Business Rule 28 placing primary responsibility of policing
   insider abuse on financial intermediaries, and the Treasury's Money Laundering Regulations
   1993 (SI 1993/1933) in regard to money laundering.

resolved in any jurisdiction. Indeed, seemingly very little thought has been given to the inter-relationship of these obligations. Added to this, is the problem[1] that, as the law of restitution develops, albeit haltingly in England,[2] the basis of liability in many respects is knowledge, actual or imputed. Thus, the obligation to know far more about clients and their activities must impose on financial institutions much more onerous obligations in regard to what might be considered these collateral areas of liability. The potential for conflict is, therefore, so much greater.

There are five specific money laundering offences which relate to three areas of criminal activity, namely drug trafficking, terrorism and serious criminal conduct.[3] It was not until 1993 that comprehensive legislation was introduced to criminalise the laundering of the proceeds of all types of serious crime.[4] The Treasury advises financial institutions to integrate into their own internal compliance programme mechanisms for policing these now numerous provisions, and the burden that this relatively new form of enforcement places on intermediaries should not be underestimated. Despite the responsible attitude of UK financial institutions, the requirement to report knowledge or a suspicion under the criminal law has created a duty that may conflict directly with a number of duties under the civil law. This essay focuses on the somewhat unclear relationship between financial intermediaries' duty to report knowledge or a suspicion under the criminal law, and the degree of knowledge sufficient to render them liable for knowing assistance in breach of trust.[5]

SUSPICION THAT MONEY IS BEING LAUNDERED

Under the UK law relating to money laundering, it is an offence, if a person comes to know or suspect, that money is being laundered, and that such money represents the proceeds of drug trafficking[6] or funds related to terrorism,[7] 'in

1 See *supra* n 4 on p 22.
2 See Lord Goff's reference to the 'tension between aims and perceptions' of restitution lawyers and equity lawyers in *Westdeutsche Landesbank Girozentrale v Islington London Borough Council* [1996] AC 669 at 685. But note the distinction between different types of trustee – beneficiary relationship, and different remedies available, as pointed out by Lord Browne-Wilkinson in *Target Holdings Ltd v Redferns (a firm)* [1996] 1 AC 421.
3 See, generally, Bosworth-Davies, R and Saltmarsh, G, *Money Laundering: A Practical Guide to the New Legislation* (London: Chapman and Hall, 1994).
4 The Criminal Justice Act 1993. See, generally, Rider, BAK, 'The Practical and Legal Aspects of Interdicting the Flow of Dirty Money' (1996) 3 *Journal of Financial Crime* 234 and Clark, NJS, 'The Impact of Recent Money Laundering Legislation on Financial Intermediaries' (1995) 3 *Journal of Financial Crime* 131.
5 Due to the confines of space, this essay does not cover liability for knowing receipt. Furthermore, liability of financial intermediaries for handling other people's money is less likely to fall under the 'knowing receipt' head, as the recipient 'must have received the property for his own use and benefit. This is why neither the paying nor the collecting bank can normally be brought within it'. See Millett J in *Agip (Africa) Ltd v Jackson* [1990] 1 Ch 265 at 292.
6 Section 52 of the Drug Trafficking Act 1994.
7 Section 18A of the Prevention of Terrorism (Temporary Provision) Act 1989, as inserted by s 51 of the Criminal Justice Act 1993; and s 54A of the Northern Ireland (Emergency Provisions) Act 1991, as inserted by s 48 of the Criminal Justice Act 1993.

the course of his trade, profession, business or employment',[1] unless he discloses his knowledge or suspicion. Anyone who enters into an arrangement with another to facilitate that other's retention of proceeds from drug trafficking, criminal conduct, or of terrorist funds, is guilty of an offence unless he discloses his knowledge or suspicion to the relevant authorities. Financial intermediaries, such as banks and lawyers, are under an additional obligation to report knowledge or suspicion of anyone laundering proceeds of drug related crime or terrorist funds.[2] Failure to report knowledge or suspicion is a criminal offence, punishable by up to five years' imprisonment. The report can, instead, be made to the 'reporting' or 'compliance' officer authorised by the company, and this will count as reporting under the relevant sections.

Regulation 5(3) of the Money Laundering Regulations 1993[3] states that:

> 'In determining whether a person has complied with any of the requirements [for identification and record keeping procedures set by the Regulations], a court may take account of (a) any relevant supervisory guidance which applies to that person; [or] (b) . . . any other relevant guidance issued by a body that regulates, or is representative of, any trade, profession, business or employment carried on by the person.'

Identifying the parties

Identification of prospective parties, or at least those who appear to be the parties, is a key issue in combating money laundering, as the objective of laundering is to conceal the ownership as well as, of course, the source of the money. Regulation 7 requires an intermediary to obtain satisfactory evidence of the identity of the applicant for business. If the intermediary cannot do so it should not proceed further with the business. Regulation 9 requires that when 'an applicant for business is or appears to be acting otherwise than as principal, . . . reasonable measures [are] to be taken for the purpose of establishing the identity of any person on whose behalf the applicant for business is acting.' This is an important requirement, as it is often the case that an intermediary, such as a bank or a lawyer, will be acting as an agent for a possible money launderer.

The 'know your customer' rule, which now permeates banking and financial regulation, has a strange origin. Ancient 'laws and customs' of the City of London required executing brokers to disclose to the other party in the ordinary course of business, the identity, or alternatively vouch for the financial soundness of their client, if there remained a contingent liability in the transaction. Laws also require the disclosure of 'foreign parties' or those who were not,

---

1 Section 52(1)(b) of the Drug Trafficking Act 1994; s 18A(1)(b) of the Prevention of Terrorism (Temporary Provisions) Act 1989; and s 54A(1)(b) of the Northern Ireland (Emergency Provisions) Act 1991.

2 The report must be made to the National Criminal Intelligence Service (NCIS). The UK government decided against the introduction of a reporting system similar to that of the US, where it is a requirement of the Federal Law for financial institutions, and in certain circumstances individuals, to report all cash and certain other financial transactions in excess of a set amount by filing a Currency Transaction Report (CTR). See, generally, Rider, BAK, 'The Practical and Legal Aspects of Interdicting the Flow of Dirty Money' (1996) 3 *Journal of Financial Crime* 234.

3 SI 1993/1933

generally, amenable to ordinary jurisdiction.[1] In more modern times, 'know your customer' rules have developed from notions that professional intermediaries, such as brokers, should, as far as is reasonable, ensure that the advice that they give or management of discretionary funds, is 'suitable' to the circumstances of the client.[2] They must know, therefore, who the client is.[3] Regulators seized upon these principles, especially in the US, as a means of requiring intermediaries to disclose the identity of their customers in cases of insider dealing and market abuse – a broker executing a suspicious transaction could not assert he did not know who his client was, as this might well be a breach of his obligation to ensure that his advice and management is suitable to the circumstances of this client.

It may be argued that merely establishing the identity of a client would not of itself give sufficient knowledge to render an intermediary liable as a constructive trustee, in regard to the particular objectionable transaction. Nonetheless, the compliance procedures set up by many intermediaries are such that they often require, perhaps in purely practical and commercial terms unwisely, far more detailed information about their clients than the Regulations actually require. The Guidance Notes issued by the Joint Money Laundering Steering Group in October 1993 stipulate that it is necessary not only to verify the identity of the intermediary, but also to 'look through him to his underlying clients'[4] when dealing with stockbrokers, fund managers, solicitors, accountants and other intermediaries.[5] It is not sufficient to rely on the reputation of the introducer of a prospective client, such as the firm's director introducing a person that he has known for many years, or a fellow professional. The Guidance Notes state: 'An introduction from a respected customer personally known to the manager, or from a trusted member of staff, may assist the verification procedure, but does not normally replace the need for address verification set out in [the previous subparagraph]. Details of the introduction should be recorded on the customer's file.'[6] This approach is in line with the view that the courts have taken. In the case of *Agip (Africa) Ltd v Jackson*, in the Court of Appeal, it was found that 'The respectability of the person[7] making the introduction did not relieve Mr Jackson from the obligation to make proper enquiries as to suspicious circumstances coming to his notice then or subsequently.'[8]

---

1 See, generally, Rider, BAK, Abrams, C and Ferran, E, *The Guide to the Financial Services Act 1986* (1989), Bicester, CCH, ch 1.

2 See, for example, the SIB's principle 4 in respect of 'Information about Customers' and Core Rule 16 on 'suitability', and SFA Conduct of Business Rule 5–31 on 'suitability'.

3 See rule 405 of the New York Stock Exchange. This itself, of course, is based on the 'shingle theory' that those who offer professional service should meet the required (or expected) standards of that profession.

4 For example, para 75 of *Money Laundering Guidance Notes for Mainstream Banking, Lending and Deposit Taking Activities*.

5 A similar provision is s 178 of the Financial Services Act 1986 – where an inspector, in respect of insider dealing, requires the identity of principal it is not 'reasonable' for an intermediary to say that he does not know – nor is it a defence to a referral to the High Court as a contempt, that foreign laws preclude disclosure if such laws contain provisions 'permitting disclosure or waiver of confidentiality' – irrespective of whether permission has, in fact, been obtained.

6 Para 54 (iv) of *Money Laundering Guidance Notes for Mainstream Banking, Lending and Deposit Taking Activities*.

7 A French lawyer with whom Mr Jackson had had previous dealings.

8 [1991] Ch 547 at 568.

A BANK OR INTERMEDIARY AS A CONSTRUCTIVE TRUSTEE

As we will see, 'knowledge' can act as a two-edged sword for those in the financial services industry. While a financial intermediary is under an obligation to know its customer, this knowledge might well expose the intermediary to the possibility of becoming a constructive trustee.[1] The most significant risk that an intermediary or professional adviser, such as a solicitor, may face after reporting a suspicion to the authorities, is a civil action seeking the declaration of a constructive trust, brought by the lawful owner of the money. By virtue of his reporting his suspicion that the money in question is the proceeds of serious crime, he proves his knowledge. The courts have, increasingly, become prepared to impose a constructive trust, or to find liability to account for monies as if a constructive trust had been imposed, in cases involving breach of fiduciary duty. Indeed, the use of the civil law as a means of depriving fraudsters of their ill-gotten gains has been advocated not just by academics, but by the SIB.[2] Financial intermediaries, and in particular professional advisers, represent relatively easy targets in such proceedings. They remain within jurisdiction, unlike the criminals and, as they are often subject to a regulatory structure, maintain records, and are amenable to regulatory and disciplinary procedures. Furthermore, as has been pointed out, it has become the policy of many regulators to place responsibilities on such persons to almost vouch for the integrity of their clients and their customers. In other words, if you hold yourself out as being prepared to offer professional services, you must ensure that you comply with the relevant standards of that profession.[3] While there are no cases in England which go anywhere near as far as what is thought to be the position in the US in this regard, the recent decisions of the English courts do indicate a willingness to develop the law. Perhaps the best example of this is the decision of the Court of Appeal[4] and, in particular, Millett J at first instance, in *Agip (Africa) Ltd v Jackson*.[5]

---

1 See, for example, the SIB's principle 4 in respect of 'Information about Customers' and Core Rule 16 on suitability, and SFA Conduct of Business Rule 5–31 on 'suitability'. Furthermore, a financial intermediary is less likely 'to seek to rebut an inference of knowledge by pleading that it was too foolish to perceive the reasonably perceptible', see Gardner, S, 'Knowing Assistance and Knowing Receipt: Taking Stock' (1996) 112 *LQR* 56 at 60. It is equally unlikely that it would wish to draw its clients' attention to the fact that it is not doing its best in seeking and utilising information by contractually delimiting its responsibility as their agent, see Rider, BAK, *Insider Trading* (Bristol: Jordans, 1983), at pp 278–279.

2 See, generally, Rider, BAK, 'Civilising the Law – The Use of Civil and Administrative Proceedings to Enforce Financial Services Law' (1995) 3 *Journal of Financial Crime* 11; Comment, 'Day of the Civil Sanction? (1996) 17 *Company Lawyer* 257; Large, A, *Financial Services Regulation: Making the Two Tier System Work* (London: SIB, May 1993), and more recently, Hilton, A, 'Civil Law to Deal with City "Crimes"' (1997) *Evening Standard*, 4 June, quoting Sir Andrew Large, Chairman of the SIB. Of course, the development of civil remedies to combat fraud is not confined to the area of equitable remedies. If a financial intermediary itself is implicated in a fraud, civil law of damages may be utilised to compensate the victims, as was clearly demonstrated by the recent House of Lords case of *Smith New Court Securities Ltd v Scrimgeour Vickers (Asset Management) Ltd* [1996] 4 All ER 769.

3 Note the so-called 'Shingle Theory' and see, for example, rule 405 of the New York Stock Exchange, and see *supra* n 3 on p 25.

4 [1991] Ch 547.

5 [1990] 1 Ch 265.

In this case, a chartered accountant based in the Isle of Man was held personally liable, as if he was a constructive trustee, for the losses to the plaintiff corporation, by the fraud of one of its employees. The chartered accountant had set up five shell companies and opened bank accounts for them, on the instructions of a French lawyer, who was one of the conspirators. While what was done, in this case, was no different to what the chartered accountant had done in a number of others, the courts thought that he had deliberately turned a blind eye to his role in assisting in what was, in effect, the laundering of the proceeds of fraud. The allegation of dishonesty against him was not rebutted, in large measure because of his failure to give evidence himself, as to why he did not make the inquiries, which the courts thought he should have made in the circumstances. It is important to appreciate that the implication of lack of probity, upon which liability was in fact based, did not arise simply because he turned a blind eye — it was an inference that was drawn fairly from his conduct as a whole. His failure to question what was going on, in the light of his refusal to give evidence at trial, certainly raised the implication of dishonesty. Nonetheless, while there is little doubt that the chartered accountant was not a paragon of virtue, as criminal proceedings in France later showed, it is true that the English courts were prepared to find the requisite lack of probity on what many might have thought to be somewhat circumstantial and nebulous evidence. It appears from the case that, in order for a third party to be held liable, as if he was a constructive trustee, it has to be proven that the third party knew the relevant facts or deliberately turned a blind eye and acted with a lack of probity.[1] It therefore seems unlikely that the courts will find a bank or other professional intermediary liable personally for participating negligently in money laundering. It must be proved that the accessory or facilitator actually knew or deliberately chose to ignore the facts indicating to him that the money in question was being transferred or dealt with in breach of a fiduciary obligation to another. The determination as to whether, knowing these facts, the facilitator behaved honestly or dishonestly is, however, an objective one. The question is, as we shall see, whether an honest person, knowing what he knew, would have acted as he had.[2] This is, of course, an important difference between the civil and criminal law. In a criminal prosecution, the issue of *mens rea* is a subjective one.[3]

The relationship between the obligation to report and the degree of knowledge

As we have seen, perhaps the most worrying aspect of money laundering legislation, for financial and other professional intermediaries, is that the

---

1 This was underlined in the more recent Privy Council case of *Royal Brunei Airlines Sdn Bhd v Tan* [1995] 2 AC 378. For a discussion of this case, see *infra* n 5 on p 38 *et seq* and accompanying text.
2 *Ibid* at 391.
3 But note the introduction of what is arguably an objective element, of 'having reasonable grounds to suspect', to the *mens rea* for the offences of concealment or transfer of proceeds, under s 93C of the Criminal Justice Act 1988, as inserted by s 31 of the Criminal Justice Act 1993, in respect of criminal conduct and s 49(2) of the Drug Trafficking Act 1994, in respect of drug trafficking. See also s 17 of the Prevention of Terrorism (Temporary Provisions) Act 1989, as amended by s 50 of the Criminal Justice Act 1993, in regard to investigation of terrorist activities, where there is reference to 'having reasonable cause to suspect'.

relationship between the obligation imposed by the legislation to report suspicions to the authorities and the degree of knowledge in the civil law is rather unclear. It may be possible to argue that the intermediary's act of reporting suspicions to the authorities or, indeed, its compliance officer, could amount to sufficient a proof of knowledge for the bank to be held liable, as a constructive trustee, for knowing assistance in the civil law. An intermediary may protect itself from a subsequent charge of money laundering by reporting its suspicions to the authorities, and by receiving its consent to continue the transaction concerned,[1] but it is not so clear as to whether this would protect it from civil actions. Indeed, the relevant statutory provisions simply state: 'the disclosure shall not be treated as a breach of any restriction upon the disclosure of information imposed by statute or otherwise',[2] thus, seemingly, only affording financial and other professional intermediaries immunity from liability arising from breach of confidence. In other words, in regard to claims made against such intermediaries, for example, for breach of trust, there is no statutory protection. It has been argued that this falls short of implementing the EC Money Laundering Directive, which, it has been asserted, provides complete immunity from 'liability of any kind', if disclosure is made in good faith.[3] It is, however, submitted that even this provision is, on a closer analysis, found to be limited in scope. It provides, 'The disclosure in good faith to the authorities . . . shall not constitute a breach of *any restriction or disclosure of information* imposed by contract or by any legislative, regulatory or administrative provision, and shall not involve the credit or financial institution, its directors or employees in liability of any kind'.[4] While the latter part of this provision may be construed as to provide complete immunity from 'liability of any kind', as it has been contended, when read in its entirety, it is submitted that the provision only addresses liability arising directly from obligations in respect of disclosure. In other words, the provision protects intermediaries from liability arising from a duty of confidentiality, be it statutory, contractual or otherwise, but not from liability arising *as a result* of disclosure, such as breach of contract or, for that matter, liability as a constructive trustee, founded on knowledge or a suspicion that is obtained as a result of complying with statutory obligations.[5] It is, therefore, arguable that

---

1 See ss 93A(b) and 93B(b) of the Criminal Justice Act 1988, as inserted by ss 29 and 30 of the
   Criminal Justice Act 1993 ; ss 50 (3)(b) and 51(5)(b) of the Drug Trafficking Act 1994; and
   s 53(5A)(b) of the Northern Ireland (Emergency Provisions) Act 1991, as inserted by s 47 of the
   Criminal Justice Act 1993.
2 Sections 50(3)(a) and 51(5)(a) of the Drug Trafficking Act 1994; ss 93A(3)(a) and 93B(5)(a) of
   the Criminal Justice Act 1988, as inserted by ss 29 and 30 of the Criminal Justice Act 1993; and
   ss 53(3A) and 53(5A)(a) of the Northern Ireland (Emergency Provisions) Act 1991, as inserted
   by s 47 of the Criminal Justice Act 1993. See also provisions in regard to failure to disclose
   knowledge or suspicion: relating to drug money laundering, s 52(4)(b) of the Drug Trafficking
   Act 1994; and relating to laundering of terrorist-related activities, s 54A(4)(b) of the Northern
   Ireland (Emergency Provisions) Act 1991, as inserted by s 48 of the Criminal Justice Act 1993
   and s 18A(4)(b) of the Prevention of Terrorism (Temporary Provisions) Act 1989, as inserted by
   s 51 of the Criminal Justice Act 1993.
3 See, for example, Clark, NJS, 'The Impact of Recent Money Laundering Legislation on
   Financial Intermediaries' (1995) 3 *Journal of Financial Crime* 131 at p145.
4 Article 9 (emphasis added) of the Council Directive on Prevention of the Use of the Financial
   System for the Purpose of Money Laundering (91/308/EEC).
5 See, for example, *Finer v Miro* [1991] WLR 35, discussed at *infra* n 6 on p 41 *et seq* and
   accompanying text.

specific protection by legislation should be given to those that report suspicions to the relevant authorities, from claims of breach of trust in regard to any subsequent dealings that take place involving those funds. Of course, if the intermediary, after reporting his suspicions, refrains from taking any action whatsoever in regard to the funds, it may well be that he will not be at risk. It should be noted, that once an intermediary has made a report, he is not obliged to deal with the funds in accordance with the instructions of the authorities, unless they obtain a court order. The legislation simply protects the intermediary from the risk of prosecution for money laundering,[1] if he acts in accordance with the instructions of the authorities, and, therefore, does not place an affirmative obligation on him to do so. However, even in cases where he does absolutely nothing in regard to the funds, it is at least arguable that he is in breach of his duty to the ultimate beneficiary for not disclosing the status of the funds. There is also a possibility, albeit perhaps remote, that the client, that is the person about whom the report has been made, might pursue the intermediary for failing to execute his instructions. As we have seen, the legislation does not deal with this. Of course, it would be ridiculous for a person guilty of money laundering or desiring to launder money within the scope of the Acts to sue, and, in such cases, it is probable that the doctrine of illegality would intervene. Where, however, it turns out that the suspicious transaction is not objectionable, then it may well be that the client has a good cause of action for any loss suffered, whether this be on his contract, for breach of fiduciary duty or in tort.

A proprietary claim sufficient for the imposition of a constructive trust

It is not without interest, however, that one of the reasons that the Treasury's own lawyers have been so reluctant to acknowledge the possibility of conflicts in this area of the law, is that they cannot accept that a person engaged in promoting a money laundering transaction could maintain a viable action based on breach of fiduciary duty, because he is not likely to have sufficient title. This is misconceived for a variety of reasons, not least that unless others come forward, they are likely to have sufficient possessory title to sue, and it does not follow, that in all cases, they would be ruled out of court on public policy grounds. Even a thief, in possession of property, has certain rights against third parties, and it must be remembered that, generally speaking, even a fraudster will have good title until the relevant transaction is rescinded. Furthermore, the view that, in most cases of crime, there would not be a sufficient fiduciary nexus to found a constructive trust, a view also maintained by the Treasury's lawyers, is also misconceived. While this may well be the case in regard to drug related crimes, where the proceeds are unlikely to belong to anyone other than the drug dealer, this is certainly not likely to be the case in most property based crimes. It is a matter of regret that so much of the thinking in this area of the law has been based on combating the illicit market in drugs, which,

---

1 For relevant statutory provisions, see *supra* n 2 on p 28.

although of critical importance, throws up issues so different from those in other areas.[1]

The possible dilemma for financial intermediaries, or at least the uncertainty, has been somewhat intensified by the recent opinion of the Board of the Privy Council in the case of *Attorney-General for Hong Kong v Reid*.[2] The Privy Council, in an appeal from New Zealand, extended the reach of the law relating to constructive trusts by allowing the tracing remedy in the case of a bribe. While a bribe, in the hands of the agent who has taken it, is recoverable by an action for account, this is a personal obligation and it was generally thought, on the basis of *Lister & Co v Stubbs*,[3] that such an obligation could not justify the implication of a constructive trust. In other words, for the declaration of such a trust or the imposition of personal remedies on an individual as if he were a constructive trustee, there had to be some kind of misdealing in property, or at least a claim involving property. The mere duty to account for a bribe or other secret profit, did not give rise to a sufficient proprietary nexus to bring into play the law of constructive trusts. Exactly what this meant was, and perhaps still remains, uncertain.[4] To require a proprietary relationship, in many cases, merely transfers the problem to determining what, in contemplation of the law, may be considered property capable of being the subject matter of a trust.[5] The Privy Council, following the lead of the Singapore courts,[6] disapproved of the much criticised but long established case of *Lister & Co v Stubbs*.[7] In this case, the plaintiff sought an order to restrain the defendant from dealing in certain investments that he had made with money that the defendant had received as bribes from third parties. The plaintiff argued that the bribes were held on constructive trust for the plaintiff, from the time they were received by the defendant. The significant issue in the case, being whether the plaintiff was entitled, as a right of property, to call the defendant to account for not only the sum of the bribes received, but also profits and interest derived from the monies' investment. The Court of Appeal did not allow the plaintiff to establish a tracing claim into the investment funds, as it regarded the relationship between the plaintiff and defendant as merely that of a debtor and a creditor, and not that of a trustee and a beneficiary. Thus, the defendant was ordered to pay to the

---

1 Such an emphasis may be inevitable given the fact that the fight against the drugs trade is the priority of the US government, which has been pioneering various measures to this end. See Grime, VP, '$16bn US Anti-Drug Budget' (March 1997) 7 *INTERSEC* 100, reporting that the Clinton Administration has allocated $16 billion to counter-narcotics programmes in its 1998 federal budget. For a discussion of the US extraterritorial initiatives, see Munroe, K, 'The Extraterritorial Reach of the United States Anti-Money Laundering Laws' and Parker, W III, 'Nowhere to run; Nowhere to hide – The Long Arm of the US Law Enforcement' in Rider, BAK and Ashe, TM (eds), *Money Laundering Control* (Dublin: Round Hall Sweet & Maxwell, 1996).

2 [1994] 1 AC 324.

3 (1890) 45 Ch D 1.

4 See Professor Boyle's analysis in '*Attorney-General v Reid*: the Company Law Implications' (1995) 16 *The Company Lawyer* 131. See also Nolan, RC, 'The Wages of Sin: Iniquity in Equity following *A-G for Hong Kong v Reid*' (1994) 15 *The Company Lawyer* 3; Comment (1994) 15 *The Company Lawyer* 34.

5 See, for example, the treatment of information as trust property in *Boardman v Phipps* [1967] 2 AC 46.

6 *Sumitomo Bank Ltd v Kartika Ratna Thahir* [1993] 1 SLR 735.

7 (1890) 45 Ch D 1.

plaintiff only the sums received as bribes and not the profits that he had obtained by their use. The plaintiff had no proprietary right over the bribes of the defendant. The money paid as bribes never came into the possession of the plaintiff, unlike the case of misapplication of property held on trust. This decision had been criticised for various reasons, not least its seeming unfairness.[1] Why should a person who has betrayed his principal by taking a bribe be allowed to retain the benefit that may accrue by investing his ill-gotten gains? Indeed, before *Lister v Stubbs*, it was thought that the plaintiff could recover twice over. He could seek the amount received as a bribe from the fiduciary who had betrayed his 'trust' on the basis of a personal duty to account for essentially a 'secret profit', and also from the third party; the briber, through a proprietary claim.[2] In *Mahesan v Malaysia Government Officers Co-operative Housing Society*,[3] the Board of the Privy Council held subsequently that the plaintiff had to decide between the two claims, personal or proprietary, as they were alternative, not cumulative.

While the decision in *Lister & Co v Stubbs*, technically, remains the law in England, given the strength of the opinion of the Privy Council in the *Reid* case, it would be a bold person who still regarded it as good law in regard to bribes.[4] The Privy Council placed great reliance on the excellent judgment of Lai J in the Court of Appeal of Singapore,[5] who reviewed the older cases carefully and diverted from the strict English rule, not only on the basis of principle but also authority. Academics and commentators have long disapproved of the iniquity of the rule and Australian courts, while hesitant to depart from it, have, on a number of occasions, expressed their disapproval.[6] Perhaps, however, the most influential factor in swaying the Board of the Privy Council was a learned article written by Sir Peter Millett,[7] which was cited with approval by Lord Templeman.[8] As a result, both as a matter of law and fairness, the Privy Council could see no reason to allow a person such as Mr Warwick Reid, who had grossly betrayed the trust of society, to keep the profits of his ill-gotten gains. Lord Templeman, in particular, thought that the law should ensure that such persons could not whisk their ill-gotten gains away to some haven.[9] The

---

1 See, for example, Goff, R and Jones, G, *The Law of Restitution* 4th edn (London: Sweet & Maxwell, 1993), p 666; Pettit, PH, *Equity and the Law of Trusts* 6th edn (London: Butterworths, 1989), p 152; Hayton, DJ, *The Law of Trusts* 2nd edn (London: Sweet & Maxwell, 1993), p 140; Oakley, AJ, *Constructive Trusts* 2nd edn (London: Sweet & Maxwell, 1987), p 56; Millett, PJ, 'Bribes and Secret Commission' [1993] *Restitution Law Review* 7.

2 See *Salford Corporation v Lever* [1891] 1 QB 168, and Oakley, AJ, *Constructive Trusts* 2nd edn (London: Sweet & Maxwell, 1987), p 56.

3 [1978] 2 All ER 405.

4 See, for example, in *Attorney-General v Blake* [1996] 3 All ER 903, at 912. Sir Richard Scott V-C, *obiter*, as this point was not raised in the case, while acknowledging the fact that Courts of Chancery were bound by authority in the Court of Appeal decision of *Lister & Co v Stubbs*, nevertheless gave his support for *Reid* by stating, 'I am . . . persuaded by the reasoning of Lord Templeman in his judgment in *Reid*'s case that *Lister & Co v Stubbs* ought no longer to be regarded as good law.'

5 *Sumitomo Bank Ltd v Kartika Ratna Thahir* [1993] 1 SLR 735.

6 See *supra* n 1 on this page, and *Consul Development v DPC Estates* (1975) 132 CLR 373 and *Daly v The Sydney Stock Exchange* (1986) 160 CLR 371.

7 Millett, PJ, 'Bribes and Secret Commission' [1993] *Restitution Law Review* 7.

8 [1994] 1 AC 324 at 337.

9 See Lord Templeman's reference to 'the proceeds whisked away to some Shangri La', *ibid* at 339.

decision to impose a constructive trust over Mr Reid's property in New Zealand was based on the notion that equity looks as done that which should be done.[1] The old maxim was invoked to translate Reid's personal obligation to account for the bribe into, essentially, a proprietary claim which could found the imposition of a constructive trust. In contemplation of equity, the monies which could be called to account were transferred into the hands of the claimants, and therefore in the mind of equity, the claim in the present case was a tracing of these sums into the property, in which they had been invested. While none could find fault with the actual decision in this case, the implications of allowing the law of constructive trust such a wide reach are unclear. For example, Lord Templeman spoke not just in terms of bribes, but also secret profits.[2] It had been thought that the taking of a secret profit by a fiduciary involved only a personal obligation to account for this sum to his principal. A literal reading of Lord Templeman's judgment would extend the tracing remedy to such claims. This could have profound implications for directors' duties and, for instance, the circumstances in which a minority shareholders' action could be brought.[3] Moreover, in analysing the authorities, his Lordship stated: '[t]he rule must be that property which a trustee obtains by use of knowledge acquired as trustee becomes trust property'.[4] On the basis of this, it may be arguable that the proceeds obtained by use of knowledge, such as insider dealing, could be traced and be subject to the imposition of a constructive trust, enabling the development of this area of law akin to that demonstrated in the Hong Kong High Court decision of *Nanus Asia Inc v Standard Chartered Bank*.[5] It is reasonably clear, however, that their Lordships did not have these wider issues in mind in the *Reid* case, and as has been pointed out by Professor Boyle,[6] it is likely that the net has not been thrown anywhere near as widely as some might argue.

What is clear from the authorities is that not all breaches of fiduciary duty will give rise to the imposition of constructive trust. In *Nelson v Rye*,[7] Laddie J cited, with approval, Sir Peter Millett's view, expressed extra-judicially.[8] In this paper, which, as we have seen, was also cited with approval by Lord Templeman in *Reid*, Sir Peter argues that the imposition of constructive trust is appropriate when an agent receives property himself in circumstances where it should have gone to his principal. In the company law cases, this principle has long been recognised. In *Warman International Ltd v Dwyer*,[9] the Australian High Court distinguished cases in which a fiduciary benefits by use of his principal's property or an opportunity coming to him by virtue of acting for his principal, where a constructive trust might be appropriate, from other

1 *Ibid* at 331.
2 *Ibid* at 337–338, referring to Sir Peter Millett's extra-judicial writing, 'Bribes and Secret Commission' [1993] *Restitution Law Review* 7, and *Boardman v Phipps* [1967] 2 AC 46.
3 See Comment, (1994) 15 *The Company Lawyer* 34.
4 [1994] 1 AC 324, at 332.
5 [1990] 1 HKLR 362.
6 See Boyle, AJ, '*Attorney-General v Reid*: the Company Law Implications' (1995) 16 *The Company Lawyer* 131.
7 [1996] 2 All ER 186.
8 Millett, PJ, 'Bribes and Secret Commission' (1993) *Restitution Law Review* 7.
9 (1995) 69 ALJR 362.

cases, in which the fiduciary is merely guilty of a breach of his duty of loyalty. In the latter cases, while there may be an obligation to account for all or part of his 'secret profit', the more exacting relationship of a trustee may not be appropriate.

KNOWING ASSISTANCE

The nature of liability imposed on those who knowingly assist in the laundering of funds under these principles is personal. In many cases, no property upon which a constructive trust can be attached is received by the defendant, as he is merely a facilitator.[1] It is established English law, as we have seen, that in order for a constructive trust to be imposed there has to be identifiable property upon which it can be imposed.[2] But, as has already been discussed, what is and is not property for this purpose is a moot point. In the context of the cases on directors' duties, it would seem that more turns on the remedy sought by counsel than any underlying principles of jurisprudence.[3] The law of property outside its traditional parameters being notoriously undefined, if information may be considered property, then information allowing a person to benefit would itself be capable of constituting trust property. The Privy Council, in the *Reid* case, was of the view that certain types of information could be the basis of a trust relationship and explained the majority's decision in the House of Lords in *Boardman v Phipps*[4] on this basis.[5] The same is true in regard to opportunities which are being developed in the interests of the principal; such as in the case of *Industrial Development Consultants Ltd v Cooley*.[6] It is a device of constructive trusteeship whereby a person who knowingly assists may be treated as if he was acting as a constructive trustee, 'as a formula for equitable relief by way of personal liability to account',[7] thus, providing 'a useful remedy where no remedy is available in contract or in tort'.[8] To this extent, the constructive trust may be seen to function as a remedial or restitutionary device, rather than an institution for the ownership of property. On the other hand, as Lord Browne-Wilkinson, in the recent House of Lords case of *Westdeutsche Landesbank Girozentrale v Islington London Borough Council*[9] emphasised, English law, for most part, has only recognised an institutional constructive trust, under which

---

1 For example, *Eaves v Hickson* (1861) 30 Beav 136. See also *supra* n 5 on p 23.

2 See, for example, Kekewich J in *Re Barney* [1892] 2 Ch 265, at 273.

3 See Sealy, LS, *Cases and Materials in Company Law* 1st edn, (Cambridge: Cambridge University Press, 1971), p 391, as was noted in Rider, BAK, 'Amiable Lunatics and the Rule in *Foss v Harbottle*' [1978] CLJ 270 at 273, n 22.

4 [1967] 2 AC 46. While much of the analysis of this case has focused on the treatment of information as trust property, it is worth noting that, in this case, the defendant was a solicitor, who, similarly to the defendant in the *Reid* case, arguably was in the position in society where a somewhat higher standard of probity may have been expected of him.

5 [1994] AC 324 at 337–338.

6 [1972] 1 WLR 443.

7 Hayton, DJ, *Hayton and Marshall Cases and Commentary on the Law of Trusts* 8th edn, (London: Stevens, 1986) at p 444.

8 Hayton, DJ, 'Personal Accountability of Strangers as Constructive Trustees' (1985) 27 *Malaya Law Review* 313 at 314.

9 [1996] AC 669. See also, in regard to the law of restitution, the Privy Council decision of *Murray Stanley Goss v Laurence George Chilcott* [1996] AC 788.

the trust arises by operation of law. Therefore, the court's function is merely to declare its existence, and not to give effect at its discretion. His Lordship distinguished this carefully from 'the concept of a *remedial* constructive trust', as developed in the US, where it is at the discretion of the court to impose such a trust as a judicial remedy.[1] While the law of restitution under English law is clearly in need of clarification, as their Lordships themselves admitted,[2] those who turned to the *Westdeutsche* case for such clarity had to be disappointed. Lord Goff was not prepared to give 'broad statements of principle which may definitively establish the future shape of this part of the law',[3] as he was of the view that 'it is not the function of your Lordships' House to rewrite the agenda for the law of restitution, nor even to identify the role of equitable proprietary claims in that part of the law. The judicial process is neither designed for, nor properly directed towards, such objectives'.[4] Lord Browne-Wilkinson expressed his favour for the remedial constructive trust as a suitable basis for developing proprietary restitutionary remedies, as it can be 'tailored to the circumstances of the particular case', so that 'innocent third parties would not be prejudiced and restitutionary defences, such as change of position, are capable of being given effect.'[5] Unfortunately, his Lordship stated that whether English law should adopt the remedial constructive trust, as in the US or Canada, had to be decided 'in some future case', as the present case was not directly concerned with this issue.[6]

The liability imposed on a person who has assisted in bringing about a disposition of trust in breach of trust was set out by Lord Selborne LC in *Barnes v Addy*.[7] In this case, the Lord Chancellor was considering the position of agents of a trust, such as solicitors and bankers, who as a result of following the instructions – which were given to them in breach of trust by the trustees – have assisted in the breach of trust. They are not recipients of trust property, nor are they acting beyond the scope of their fiduciary duties or authority. Such persons would be held liable to account to the beneficiaries. They have not induced the trustees to make the disposition in question.[8] Lord Selborne held that only those strangers to the trust who 'assist with knowledge in a dishonest and fraudulent design on the part of the trustees'[9] would be liable personally to account to the beneficiaries. It was the requirement that the facilitator acted 'with knowledge' that attracted most controversy, and the debate focussed upon the extent of knowledge required. In *Williams v*

---

1 [1996] AC 669 at 714–715. For an analysis of the relevant cases, see G McCormack, 'The Remedial Constructive Trust and Commercial Transactions' (1996) 17 *The Company Lawyer* 3; 'Fiduciaries in a Changing Commercial Climate' (1997) 18 *The Company Lawyer* 38; and *Proprietary Claims and Insolvency* (London: Sweet & Maxwell, 1997) London.

2 See [1996] AC 669, Lord Goff, at 685; Lord Browne-Wilkinson, at 716; and Lord Woolf, at 723.

3 *Ibid* at 686.

4 *Ibid* at 685.

5 *Ibid* at 716.

6 *Ibid*.

7 (1874) 9 Ch App 244.

8 *Eaves v Hickson* (1861) 30 Beav 136.

9 (1874) 9 Ch App 244 at 252.

Williams,[1] Kay J held that a solicitor was not liable though he was negligent. He mentioned that the outcome would have been different had the solicitor 'wilfully closed his eyes'.[2]

Elements of liability

Peter Gibson J, in the case of *Baden Delvaux and Lecuit v Société Générale pour Développement du Commerce et de l'Industrie en France SA*,[3] set out the following four elements which must exist in order for liability to be imposed under the 'knowing assistance' head. First, there must exist a trust.[4] There is no need for the trust to be express, and it seems that the interpretation of trust is wide enough to extend to many types of fiduciary relationship, including that of a bank and its customer.[5] The courts may be prepared to widen the scope of fiduciary relationship, to such an extent that it may become difficult, for example, for banks to recognise, in the ordinary course of their business, that such a relationship has arisen.[6] This is all the more possible after the decision in *Attorney-General for Hong Kong v Reid*,[7] as we have seen. However, the second element that Gibson J set out requires the existence of a dishonest and fraudulent design on the part of the trustee of the trust, or fiduciary, applying the earlier interpretation of trust, as stated by Lord Selborne LC in *Barnes v Addy*.[8] In *Belmont Finance Corporation Ltd v Williams Furniture Ltd*,[9] it was held that there was no distinction between 'dishonest' and 'fraudulent'. Further refinement of the interpretation of the term 'dishonest and fraudulent design' was made in the subsequent decisions.[10] While this second requirement was once thought to be an 'essential prerequisite' of liability for knowing assistance,[11] this view is now doubted after the recent case of *Royal Brunei Airlines Sdn Bhd v Tan*.[12] In this case, the Board of the Privy Council stated clearly that a third party who assisted a trustee to commit a breach of trust, or procured him to do so, was liable to the beneficiaries for the resulting loss provided that the third party had acted dishonestly and not merely negligently. However, it was not

---

1 (1881) 17 Ch D 437.
2 *Ibid* at 455.
3 [1993] 1 WLR 509. First reported [1983] BCLC 325.
4 See *In re Diplock* [1948] Ch 465. See also *Agip (Africa) v Jackson* [1990] 1 Ch 265, at 290, Millett J stating: 'The only restriction on the ability of equity to follow assets is the requirement that there must be some fiduciary relationship which permits the assistance of equity to be invoked. The requirement has been widely condemned and depends on authority rather than principle, but the law was settled by *In re Diplock* . . .'
5 See *Lipkin Gorman v Karpnale Ltd* [1992] 4 All ER 409, affirming in part [1987] Ch 264.
6 Clayton, NA, 'Banks which Knowingly Assist' (1989) 2 *Journal of International Business Law* 71.
7 [1994] 1 AC 324.
8 See *supra* n 9 on p 34.
9 [1979] Ch 250 at 267.
10 See Peter Gibson J in *Baden Delvaux and Lecuit v Société Générale pour Développement du Commerce et de l'Industrie en France SA* [1993] 1 WLR 509, at 574–575; Ungoed-Thomas, J in *Selangor United Rubber Estates Ltd v Cradock (No 3)* [1968] 1 WLR 1555, at 1582 and 1590.
11 See, for example, *Belmont Finance Corporation Ltd v Williams Furniture Ltd* [1979] Ch 250, 267, and Oakley, A, *Parker and Mellows The Modern Law of Trusts* 6th edn (London: Sweet & Maxwell, 1994), p 256.
12 [1995] 2 AC 378. See also Harpum, C, 'Accessory Liability for Procuring or Assisting a Breach of Trust' (1995) 111 *LQR* 545 at 547, stating that this case has 'despatched Lord Selborne's dictum'.

necessary for the conduct of the trustee to have been dishonest or fraudulent.[1] Thus, what is important is the dishonesty of the person who is sought to be made liable – and not necessarily that of the person who committed the initial breach of trust.

The third element is the existence of assistance by the person sought to be made liable as a constructive trustee in the dishonest and fraudulent design. In the *Baden* case, Gibson J stated that this was simply a question of fact. He thought that a bank would have given assistance if, on the orders of directors who were misapplying their company's funds in breach of trust, it had transferred funds to another. In *International Sales and Agencies Ltd v Marcus*,[2] Lawson J thought that when 'funds disposed of in breach of constructive trust reach other quarters', assistance had been given. A similar view was given in *Nanus Asia v Standard Chartered Bank*.[3]

The fourth element that needs to be shown, is that the person whom it is sought to make liable was aware that there had in fact been a breach of trust, or that his actions would materially assist in such. It is the scope and extent of knowledge that must be found, before liability can be imposed, that has attracted so much debate. In the *Baden* case, Gibson J thought that there were five categories of knowledge:

> '(i) actual knowledge; (ii) wilfully shutting one's eyes to the obvious; (iii) wilfully and recklessly failing to make such inquiries as an honest and reasonable man would make; (iv) knowledge of circumstances which would indicate the facts to an honest and reasonable man; (v) knowledge of circumstances which would put an honest and reasonable man on inquiry.'[4]

Where much of the confusion has occurred is in the relationship of scienter to the critical requirement of dishonesty or lack of probity. While there can, obviously, be knowledge without dishonesty, there can hardly be dishonesty without knowledge. The two issues are inextricably linked.[5] Hence the confusion. The level of inequity that has to be shown will govern the degree of knowledge that must be established. If liability can be based on mere negligence on the part of the facilitator, then it may be necessary to show only a very basic level of knowledge, or, indeed, no subjective knowledge at all. It may be sufficient to show that an ordinary reasonable person in the position of the facilitator would or should have known the facts; and the standard of culpability is then fixed on this. Of course, in cases of negligence simpliciter, it is not usual to refer to culpability, but there are instances where the standard of responsibility is still, essentially, an objective one founded in negligence, but which smacks of gross negligence. However, the determination is still an objective one. Often, the

---

1 [1995] 2 AC 378, at 392. See also *infra* n 3 on p 37 and accompanying text.
2 [1982] 3 All ER 551.
3 [1990] 1 HKLR 392.
4 [1993] 1 WLR 509 at 575–576.
5 As was clearly demonstrated in *Royal Brunei Airlines Sdn Bhd v Tan* [1995] 2 AC 378, where Lord Nicholls, having deemed 'knowingly inapt' as a criterion for accessory liability, still had to refer to knowledge in regard to a misapplication of trust assets, see *infra* nn 7 on p 38 and n 3 on p 39 and accompanying text. See also *infra* n 3 on p 37 and accompanying text and *Brinks Ltd v Abu-Saleh(No 3)* (1995) *The Times,* 23 October.

notion of gross negligence or, as Templeman J described in *Daniels v Daniels*,[1] culpable negligence, is simply allowing the court to draw an inference from the facts as proved, which would be justified in terms of objectivity, which might not go as far as to confirm subjective lack of probity. Thus, in *Daniels*, although there was no direct evidence that the directors had acted with the degree of dishonesty that would be required for a minority shareholders' action predicated on the so-called 'fraud on the minority' exception to the rule in *Foss v Harbottle*,[2] Templeman J thought that proof that the directors had, in effect, sold a piece of corporate property to themselves at a price which three years later led to them taking a profit over twenty times greater, gave a fair basis for finding culpable negligence. Where, however, the standard of dealing required for liability involves culpability in the conventional sense of a subjective state of mind involving lack of probity, the degree of knowledge of the pertinent facts will be much greater. Insofar as, today, we recognise that the only justifiable basis for imposing personal liability on a person, as if he was a constructive trustee, is his dishonest involvement in a breach of trust,[3] then it will be necessary to prove a degree of scienter which allows that person to form a dishonest intent. Consequently, knowledge must be actual and sufficiently comprehensive. It must be remembered, however, that, in practice, proof of knowledge, of whatever level and specificity, will almost certainly depend upon circumstantial and inferential evidence. Direct evidence of knowledge, at least in litigated cases, is rare, particularly when there are allegations of dishonesty. Finally, in this regard, it must be remembered that while dishonesty is obviously a subjective notion, the test of what may be considered to be dishonest in the case of knowing assistance, will be determined objectively.[4] This as we have seen is where the civil law departs from the criminal law.

Knowledge and state of mind

The inter-relationship of knowledge and the state of mind of the accessory was re-emphasised in *Consul Development Property Ltd v DPC Estate Property Ltd*.[5] Stephen J thought that the conscience of the defendant had to be taken into consideration, and, thus, found that only the first two categories of knowledge, that is to say the actual knowledge and 'Nelsonian knowledge',[6] would be sufficient to impose liability under the knowing assistance head. On the other hand, in *Lipkin Gorman*, the court thought that it would be sufficient to establish that

---

1 [1978] Ch 406.
2 (1843) 2 Hare 461. For an analysis of the case, see Rider, BAK, 'Amiable Lunatics and the Rule in *Foss v Harbottle*' [1978] CLJ 270.
3 In other words, the question the courts should be asking is 'was the defendant at all dishonest as opposed to merely negligent?'. As Millett J stated in *Agip (Africa) Ltd v Jackson* [1990] Ch 265 at 293: 'There is no sense in requiring dishonesty on the part of the principal while accepting negligence as sufficient for his assistant. Dishonest furtherance of the dishonest scheme of another is an understandable basis for liability; negligent but honest failure to appreciate that someone else's scheme is dishonest is not.' As Alliot J stated in *Lipkin Gorman v Karpnale Ltd* [1987] 1 WLR 987: 'want of probity is a key aspect in the approach the court should take'.
4 As was stated by Lord Nicholls in *Royal Brunei Airlines Sdn Bhd v Tan* [1995] 2 AC 378.
5 (1975) 132 CLR 373.
6 At the Battle of Copenhagen, Admiral Lord Nelson, when signalled to withdraw, reportedly put his telescope up to his blind eye and claimed he could see no signal.

the accessory had knowledge, within the first three categories, to substantiate a showing of want of probity.[1] Other judges have tended to sit on the fence between the second and third category, allowing the 'smell of fraud' to influence how far they are prepared to climb over the fence. Indeed, in this area of the law, the actual decisions have far more to do with the underlying issues of fact than principles of law.[2] Judges are prepared to 'bend' legal rules where they smell fraud, as was so clearly indicated at first instance in the case of *Prudential Assurance Co Ltd v Newman Industries Ltd (No 2)*.[3] As we shall see, the courts today, largely at the behest of Sir Peter Millett's judicial and extra-judicial pronouncements,[4] have veered away from a rigid categorisation of levels of scienter, and require only such knowledge as may justify the determination of dishonesty.

In the more recent case of *Royal Brunei Airlines Sdn Bhd v Tan*,[5] the Privy Council considered that a third party who assisted a trustee to commit a breach of trust, or procured him to do so, was liable to the beneficiaries for the resulting loss provided that the third party had acted dishonestly and not merely negligently. However, it was not necessary for the conduct of the trustee, whom the accessory assists, to have been dishonest or fraudulent.[6] It followed that it must be established that the accessory had knowledge that the transaction was in breach of a fiduciary obligation importing a trust.[7] On the facts of the case, however, this was hardly an issue as the accessory was the managing director and controller of the company, which was, in fact, the trustee in breach. It could not be contended, therefore, as an officer and controller of the company that he did not have the requisite degree of knowledge. Perhaps more interestingly, their Lordships expressed the view that a third party would owe a duty of care to the beneficiary in certain cases in the light of the particular facts.[8] This imports the notion that, in appropriate cases, the standard of liability would be objective, not just in regard to the state of mind, as indeed it is even in regard to culpability, but also in relation to scienter. There would seem, in certain recent cases, an interesting interplay between accessory liability and the duty of care.[9] In the present discussion, however, the issue of negligence is likely to be relevant only where there is a pre-existing duty. In most cases of accessory liability, there will not be a pre-existing relationship between the accessory and those entitled to the declaration or remedy. The relationship will be created by the transaction which involves the knowing assistance and the very lack of honesty on the part of the accessory. Insofar as this renders him, in contemplation of equity, a fiduciary – of sorts – he may well be then under a duty of care to the principal, but

---

1 See Alliot J [1987] 1 WLR 987 and May LJ [1989] 1 WLR 1340. See also Megarry V-C in *Re Montagu's Settlement Trusts* [1987] Ch 264.
2 See *supra* n 3 on p 33.
3 [1981] Ch 257. Vinelott J in deciding 'whether a derivative action can be brought against defendants who do not have voting control of the company on whose behalf the derivative claim is brought', held that an additional exception to the *Foss v Harbottle* rule should be allowed in 'the interest of justice', at 327. See *supra* n 2 on p 37 and accompanying text.
4 Millett, PJ, 'Tracing the Proceeds of Fraud' (1991) 107 *LQR* 71.
5 [1995] 2 AC 378.
6 [1995] 2 AC 378 at 392.
7 As was re-emphasised by Rimer, J in *Brinks Ltd v Abu-Saleh (No 3)* (1995) *The Times*, 23 October.
8 [1995] 2 AC 378 at 392.
9 *Bishopsgate Investment Management (in liquidation) v Maxwell (No 2)* [1994] 1 All ER 261.

he can hardly be said to owe a pre-transactional duty of care. In the *Tan* case, the situation was complicated by the fact that the accessory was a fiduciary officer of the trustee in breach, albeit in no relationship, according to conventional notions of company law, to the plaintiff. His domination over the activities of his company and his lack of integrity might, however, have indicated to their Lordships, the sort of relationship that existed in *Wallersteiner v Moir (No 2)*,[1] where the Court of Appeal was prepared to regard the corporation as little more than a cipher[2] for Dr Wallersteiner and his illicit activities. In any case, their Lordships' comments in the present case were *obiter dicta*, but nonetheless do point to an interesting avenue for developing personal liability in such cases.

As we indicated above, in their Lordships' view the state of knowledge was not always a good criterion to be employed, in determining whether a third party owed a duty to the beneficiary and the scale of knowledge referred to in the *Baden* case should be 'best forgotten'.[3] They thought that the third party's liability hinged on his dishonesty which was synonymous with 'a lack of probity' and which, in most part, 'equated with conscious impropriety', though acting in reckless disregard of others' rights or possible rights could be 'a tell-tale sign of dishonesty'.[4] Acting dishonestly or with a lack of probity 'meant simply not acting as an honest person would in the circumstances' and this was, in practice, an objective standard.[5] The standard of honesty does not hinge on a subjective standard of 'what the person actually knew at the time' and does not depend on 'the moral standards of each individual'. Their Lordships thought that in most situations, 'there was little difficulty in identifying how an honest person would behave. Honest people did not intentionally deceive others to their detriment or knowingly take others' property'. Thus, unless there was 'a very good and compelling reason', an honest person did not participate in a transaction if he knew it involved a misapplication of trust assets to the detriment of the beneficiaries.[6] Nor did an honest person, in such a case, deliberately close his eyes and ears, or deliberately not ask questions, lest he learnt something he would rather not know, and then proceed regardless.[7] Of course, it is necessary to enter the caveat, already mentioned, that in this case their Lordships were referring to a

---

1 [1975] QB 373.
2 But note the treatment of corporate personality and 'cipher' in company liquidation, *Re Pollypeck International plc (in administration)* [1996] 2 All ER 433. See also C Nakajima, 'Lifting the Veil' (1996) 17 *The Company Lawyer* 187, and *Re H (restraint order)* [1996] 2 All ER 391.
3 [1995] 2 AC 378, at 392, *per* Lord Nicholls. But note Clark, J in *Three Rivers District Council v Bank of England (No 3)* [1996] 3 All ER 558 at 581, while endorsing Lord Nicholls' *dictum* in the context of a third party's dishonest assistance in a breach of trust, nevertheless applied Peter Gibson J's scale of knowledge to the present case, which was concerned with the tort of misfeasance in public office. For a further discussion, see *infra* n 1 on p 44.
4 [1995] 2 AC 378 at 390.
5 *Ibid* at 389. Lord Nicholls distinguished this from 'dishonesty in criminal or other context' by referring to *R v Ghosh* [1982] QB 1053. See also *Secretary of State for Trade and Industry v Rogers* [1996] 4 All ER 854, in which the Court of Appeal held that where the summary form of procedure was used in applying for a disqualification order against a director, a judge was not entitled to make the finding of dishonesty if it formed no part of the statement of facts agreed between the parties; in other words, without the director's agreeing that his conduct had been dishonest.
6 *Ibid* at 389.
7 *Ibid*.

managing director and controller of a company that was the trustee in breach. It is highly questionable whether in a case not involving a person who can hardly deny, by virtue of his position, knowledge of the facts, that knowledge sufficient to base a determination of dishonesty can be so readily found.[1] In particular, in the case of financial intermediaries, while the law and good practice have, increasingly, imposed duties of inquiry, if not diligence, upon them, it is generally the case that bankers and financial intermediaries are entitled to assume the integrity of their clients and their transactions, unless they have grounds, albeit judged objectively, for suspicion.[2] Two further points arise out of their Lordships' observations in *Tan*. First, could 'a good and compelling reason' not be interpreted to include a situation whereby an intermediary, having reported its suspicion to the authorities, feels obliged to continue with the transaction? Secondly, it is submitted that, according to the second part of the observation, due diligence on the part of the intermediaries would, indeed, play a crucial part, if they did not wish to be accused of turning a blind eye, thereby being held liable as a dishonest third party. In deciding whether a person was acting honestly, a court would look at 'all circumstances known to the third party at the time . . . and . . . also have regard to his personal attributes, such as his experience and intelligence, and the reason why he acted as he did'.[3] Thus, the more experienced the third party is the higher the standard of diligence that may be required. Given the essentially objective determination that the court will be bound to make in such cases the existence of industry-wide practices and, in particular, guidance notes are likely to be of material significance.[4]

The shift from knowledge to dishonesty

This apparent shift of emphasis from knowledge to dishonesty, in deciding third party liability, is to be welcomed, particularly in the light of the conflicting duties imposed on the intermediaries by the criminal and civil law. It is important to emphasise, as the judges have repeatedly done, the critical significance of proof of want of probity. While reporting a suspicion may indicate knowledge, it is too draconian to attach a want of probity to a bank or financial intermediary that was conscientious and diligent enough to report its suspicion. It is submitted that the fact that a bank has reported its suspicion to the relevant authorities should be a good basis on which to establish its probity and honesty, and that it would be unjustifiable to impose on an intermediary liability to account personally for assisting a money launderer. This is particularly the case as it is against public policy[5] to expose banks to civil claims of constructive trust,

---

1 See, for example, *Brinks Ltd v Abu-Saleh (No 3)* (1995) *The Times*, 23 October, and *supra* n 7 on p 38 and accompanying text.

2 *Re David Payne & Co Ltd* [1904] 2 Ch 698. See also Millett J in *Macmillan Inc v Bishopsgate Investment Trust plc* [1995] 1 WLR 978 at 1014, stating, in the context of proprietary liability and liability in knowing receipt, 'account officers are not detectives . . . unless and until they are alerted to the possibility of wrongdoing, they proceed, and are entitled to proceed, on the assumption that they are dealing with honest men'. See also Gardner, S, 'Knowing Assistance and Knowing Receipt: Taking Stock' (1996) 112 *LQR* 56 at 82.

3 [1995] 2 AC 378 at 391.

4 See Conclusion, p 45.

5 For considerations of public policy, see *Swinney v Chief Constable of the Northumbria Police* [1996] 3 All ER 449.

thereby making them reluctant to acquire knowledge through due diligence procedures. The requirement of dishonesty, rather than mere knowledge, should help to prevent intermediaries from being held liable as a result of complying diligently with duties imposed upon them under the criminal law, while giving equity full power to take the profit out of crime[1] from those who deserve to be 'punished'.[2]

Doing more than mere compliance with the reporting obligations

While the author is minded to support the view of the Treasury's lawyers that a court would not be eager to impose crushing civil liability on an intermediary who had 'put its head into the noose' by reporting its suspicions, it is appropriate to highlight one very significant issue, which remains to be answered. As we have seen, it is the view of their Lordships that dishonesty may well be established by proof that the accessory acted in reckless disregard of the rights of another.[3] By the same token, merely complying with the reporting obligations imposed by the criminal law and Money Laundering Regulations, without also taking into account the rights of a person who might well be entitled to the money in question, would, according to their Lordships' view as expressed in *Tan*, be dishonest. It must be remembered that dishonesty or want of probity is a somewhat 'global' concept. While complying with the disclosure requirements for suspicious transactions would argue in favour of probity, it does not resolve the issue. In the same way, disclosure to the shareholders in general meeting and one's colleagues on the board does not, necessarily, place a director's self-dealing beyond the reach of a minority shareholder action.[4] Thus, while due compliance with the reporting provisions is indicative of good faith, it might well be advisable for the intermediary to take advice as to whether it should also, in some manner, seek affirmatively to protect the rights of those who, it knows or probably merely suspects, may be prejudiced by undertaking the transactions in question.[5] In *Finers v Miro*,[6] both Mummery J and the Court of Appeal

---

1 See, generally, Rider, BAK, 'Taking the Profit Out of Crime' in Rider, BAK and Ashe, TM (eds), *Money Laundering Control* (Dublin: Round Hall Sweet & Maxwell, 1996); Millett, PJ, 'Tracing the Proceeds of Fraud' (1991) 107 *LQR* 71; Birks, PBH (ed), *Laundering and Tracing* (Oxford: Clarendon, 1995).

2 However, ascertaining who deserves such 'punishment' remains fraught with difficulty, particularly in the light of the recent development of the law of restitution, which endeavours to award an equitable remedy so as to make the defendant 'disgorge a profit made or presumed to have been made out of the payment of a sum of money which should not have been made', as opposed to making such an award as 'a punishment', see Lord Woolf's *dicta*, not in the context of fraud but in regard to compound interest, in *Westdeutsche Landesbank Girozentrale v Islington London Borough Council* [1996] AC 669 at 723.

3 See *supra* n 4 on p 39.

4 *Cook v Deeks* [1916] 1 AC 554.

5 In respect of a third party exercising his rights over the property, which has become the subject matter of a restraint order, and a potential contravention of such an order, the court stated thus, 'the bank might be able to exercise rights without resorting to the court. However, . . . all banks will still consider it prudent to apply to the court for a variation [of the restraint order] for the avoidance of doubt and when no assurance has been given by the Crown Prosecution Services that any point averse to them will be taken'. See *Re K (restraint order)* [1990] 2 All ER 562 at 568–569, *per* Otton J.

6 [1991] 1 WLR 35.

thought that, in similar circumstances, the appropriate course of action was for the possible accessory to notify those whom he considered may be entitled to the funds in question. This fits uneasily with the offence of tipping-off.[1] It might, therefore, be prudent for an application to be made, in appropriate cases, for instructions to the court, or, in extreme cases, to place the money under protection, even in escrow, as is increasingly the practice in the US.

LOCUS STANDI

We have already raised the issue as to who might be competent to bring a civil action against an intermediary and it is now appropriate for us to explore this important issue in more depth. It would be inequitable to allow the wrongdoers to successfully sue the bank or intermediary. But it is not clear who a 'wrong-doer' is in this context. Certainly, the courts would not permit the person who has made profits out of criminal activity to sue. The common law doctrine of illegality on the grounds of public policy might well intervene to render a contract unenforceable, if its purpose is directly or indirectly to facilitate the commission of a crime or some act which is clearly against the public interest.[2] A contract to engage in conduct which is illegal in a friendly state, but which may not be so in England, may well be unenforceable on the basis that it is in the public interest to promote and facilitate good relations with friendly powers. Therefore, it has been held that contracts designed to evade exchange control regulations in other friendly states or smuggle contraband, in such circumstances, are unlawful at common law.[3] It follows that a contract to engage in the laundering of proceeds of a crime committed outside the UK might well be unenforceable in the English courts, although the point has never been taken. A contract to launder the proceeds of a crime committed within the jurisdiction of English law, would be illegal and unenforceable. The party seeking to utilise the arrangement to launder money could not, in any way, enforce the transaction. Whether the intermediary or a third party could enforce against the launderer, would depend very much on their state of knowledge. Generally speaking, provided the contract in question was not expressly forbidden, which is most unlikely, and therefore the illegality lies in its performance, and provided the intermediary or third party is ignorant of the illegal purpose and is not tainted, then they may well be able to enforce against the launderer.[4] Although the

---

1 Section 53 of the Drug Trafficking Act 1994 and s 93D of the Criminal Justice Act 1988, as amended by s 32 of the Criminal Justice Act 1993.

2 See, for example, *Scott v Brown Doering McNab & Co* [1892] 2 QB 724, in which the Court of Appeal held the contract to engage in stock market manipulation illegal.

3 See, for example, the Court of Appeal, in *Foster v Driscoll* [1929] 1 KB 470, held that an agreement to smuggle whisky into the US during the Prohibition was illegal.

4 See *Re K (restraint order)* [1990] 2 All ER 562, holding that a restraint order, made under s 8 of the Drug Trafficking Offences Act 1986, did not alter vested rights, including the contractual right of set-off, of the bank, who had acted in good faith and in ignorance of the tainted source of the deposited money. But, given the anti-money laundering procedures that financial intermediaries are now required to have in place, it may well be considerably harder to establish that the bank had acted in good faith and in ignorance of the source of the deposited money. See also *Re R (restraint order)* [1990] 2 All ER 569, in regard to the landlord whose tenant was under a restraint order.

general law relating to illegal and unenforceable bargains is beyond the scope of this discussion, it is important to raise the issue, which has, in practice, faced intermediaries in the US, albeit there are no reported court decisions; namely the extent to which a contract may be enforced once knowledge of its illicit purpose has been brought to the attention of the hitherto innocent counterparty. This might well be a problem in the case of option-related transactions or revolving contracts. It would seem that the position in civil law is that the time at which knowledge operates on the validity of the contract is at the time of contract, rather than execution. The English cases would tend to support this view and it is certainly not in the public interest to penalise an innocent counterparty. This is particularly so when the effect of holding the obligation unenforceable might be to allow the launderer to escape with the benefit of the transaction without having to submit to its burden. Obviously, much depends upon the facts of the case and the nature of the transaction. Concern has also been expressed in the US in regard to intermediaries and in particular advisers, including attorneys taking fees for work relating to the activities of a money launderer, once it has become apparent that there is a good chance that the sums in question are drawn from funds, directly or indirectly, which may be the proceeds of crime. While in England, provided value has been given and the transactions were entered into in good faith, it is hard to see that there would be a real risk of civil liability, although, on the wording of the relevant criminal offences, there may well be criminal liability. In such circumstances, a report should be made to the authorities thereby activating the procedures that we have already discussed.[1] In the US, the Justice Department and other relevant agencies, including the Securities and Exchange Commission, advise intermediaries to consult with the relevant District Attorney, and secure a release in regard to the funds in question, thus, in practice, achieving a similar result to the English law.

Restitutionary liability

Turning to the question of restitutionary liability, a man should not be allowed to benefit by his own wrong and the 'clean hands' doctrine in equity would be a satisfactory means of preventing such a person asserting a 'right' of an equitable nature.[2] However, it is not so clear that this principle could always be relied upon in regard to successors in title to the 'illicit profit', or third parties who may have some sort of equitable proprietary interest, perhaps arising by a right of security over the money in question. Equity will always protect its 'darling', namely the bona fide purchaser or provider of services for value, who has no notice of the wrongdoing. Of course, this issue is more relevant in the context of the so-called 'knowing receipt' cases, which is beyond the remit of this essay, rather than in relation to accessory liability, but where an intermediary offers services, the question may arise. The problem here is that we have to confront yet another notion of knowledge, which may well involve a rather different standard than in the imposition of liability. It is, generally, thought that to render a purchaser or provider of services for value not in good faith, it is sufficient

---

1 See *supra* n 6 on p 23 *et seq* and accompanying text.
2 *Attorney-General for Hong Kong v Reid* [1994] 1 AC 324.

that they have constructive notice. This means knowledge of facts which would put an ordinary reasonable person, in their position, on notice that something was up. As we have seen, this part subjective and part objective test is not likely to be the appropriate one for finding constructive liability. There, the degree of knowledge must be sufficient to found a basis for a determination of personal dishonesty, albeit judged objectively. To compound the problem, the provisions of section 35A of the Companies Act 1985 which, *inter alia*, allow counterparties to transactions, which would have been *ultra vires* or beyond the authority of a corporate agent, to enforce the contract against the company, provided they acted in good faith, have been interpreted as providing due protection unless it can be shown that there is subjective knowledge of the true facts. As we have already seen,[1] in other areas of the law, the courts have interpreted the notion of *mala fide* as importing not only knowledge, but also an element of malice possibly akin to the notion of reckless disregard for another's rights, as expressed by the Privy Council in the *Tan* case.[2] It would make sense, both in law and in practice, if the same notion of good faith was all pervading, and it is likely that, in a given case, the courts will attempt to iron out any present inconsistencies that exist, and bring the law into line with that set out in the cases on constructive liability. This would certainly make sense in regard to company law and, in particular, section 35, although it would involve, arguably, a more exacting standard than has hitherto been thought to be the case in regard to purchasers without notice. However, the more exacting the standard the greater degree of protection afforded to third parties, and this is, seemingly, in line with current judicial thinking.[3]

The balance of probity

The courts have been prepared to be quite searching in determining the relative equities and will deprive a claimant of his cause of action if there is evidence of an 'imbalance' of probity. Indeed, it has been argued that probity is a prerequisite to asserting a restitutionary claim in the first place although this is almost certainly not the case. While it is said he who comes to equity must have clean hands, probity would seem to be an issue only when contested. In other words, it is a factor in the exercise of the judge's discretion whether to award an equitable remedy or make available the powers of the court to enforce a bargain,[4] rather than a prerequisite for *locus standi*. Of course, outside the area of illegality and public policy, the common law has always been rather more robust and the culpability of the claimant would not necessarily be a factor in standing or judgment for the court, although, of course, it might well go to mitigation. Notwithstanding the uncertainty over what is meant by a 'wrongdoer' in this context, it is at least arguable that it is in the public interest that the position of

---

1 See, for example, *Three Rivers District Council v Bank of England (No 3)* [1996] 3 All ER 558 and *Melton Medes Ltd v Securities and Investments Board* [1995] Ch 137. See also *supra* n 3 on p 39.
2 See *supra* n 4 on p 39 and *Royal Brunei Airlines Sdn Bhd v Tan* [1995] 2 AC 378, at 390.
3 See *Re K (restraint order)* [1990] 2 All ER 562, and *Re R (restraint order)* [1990] 2 All ER 569.
4 In *Chase Manhattan Equities Ltd v Goodman* [1991] BCLC 897, a contract in breach of the Company Securities (Insider Dealing) Act 1985, was held unenforceable, on the ground that to enforce it with the powers of the court would be to enforce an objectionable transaction. This was despite the express provision under the Act that no contract was to be 'void or voidable' by reason of the breach of the insider dealing prohibition.

an intermediary, who has made an honest and conscientious attempt to comply with the law and best practice, should be protected. It is clearly in the public interest that those who are genuinely suspicious should be encouraged to bring their concerns to the attention of the authorities. Of course, it goes without saying that where the notification is made out of malice or without due care, then those damnified, whether the client or third parties, should have the right to expect compensation. Obviously, the line is a thin one, and there is a very real danger, in practice, that any uncertainty as to the risk of liability will persuade intermediaries to exercise excessive caution. At present, it would seem that the balance is tilted firmly in favour of excessive disclosure, and there is a perception that intermediaries are inclined to disclose information without adequate sifting. The Money Laundering Regulations 1993 do make it clear that the intermediary should exercise discretion in evaluating its own suspicions,[1] but given the inherent uncertainty which exists, it is hard to blame intermediaries for 'passing the buck' in this manner. Of course, as intermediaries become more aware of the very real risks that they may run under the civil law for indiscriminate reporting, or for even proper disclosures, the balance may well tilt the other way. In practice, for a large financial intermediary, it is rather more likely that a liquidator will come after them than the Crown Prosecution Service will prosecute. Thus, the balance of advantage, in the present uncertain state of the law, may well be in favour of not knowing too much about one's customers and their transactions – an objective that those responsible for the criminal law would hardly wish to foster. There is also the risk that unscrupulous intermediaries will seek to hide behind the uncertainty as a justification for failing to comply with the disclosure obligations.

CONCLUSION

Notwithstanding those potential problems, it is unlikely that there will be an opportunity for the Treasury to prepare revising legislation in the near future to address them. Suitably worded provisions in the proposed Guidance Notes may be of assistance and thought is being given to revision of the Money Laundering Regulations.[2] However, it is clear from the Law Commission's reports on the relationship of traditional fiduciary principles with the rules promulgated under the authority of the Financial Services Act 1986, that fundamental principles of law cannot be altered by such expedients.[3] Of course, judges may be influenced by such rules in determining the operation of basic principles of liability, such as whether a requisite standard of conduct has been met or what an ordinary reasonable person would do in the circumstances,[4] but there are distinct limits as to how far the courts can go in this regard. As we have already discussed, it is arguable that the English provisions are at variance with the European Directive on Money Laundering which, at least at first sight,

---

1 See regulation 14.
2 At the time of writing, the contents of the revision remain confidential.
3 Law Commission, *Fiduciary Duties and Regulatory Rules* Law Com No 236 (London: HMSO, 1995), and *Fiduciary Duties and Regulatory Rules* Consultation Paper No 124 (London: HMSO, 1992).
4 See *supra* n 4 on p 40.

seems to contemplate complete protection for financial intermediaries, who duly report their suspicions to the authorities, although the true extent of protection is uncertain.[1] Given that the courts in the UK would be bound to interpret and apply UK law so as to give proper effect to the Directive,[2] financial intermediaries in the UK may well be able to rely on this provision in the Directive as a defence to the imposition of such liability. Nevertheless, this issue remains an area of pure conjecture, as, in most other jurisdictions bound by the Directive, such liability would not even arise, given their very different legal tradition, which did not see the development of equity. Therefore, the Directive could not have been drawn up with the possibility of such liability in mind.

---

1 See *supra* n 4 on p 28 *et seq* and accompanying text.
2 See Rider, BAK and Ashe, TM, *Insider Crime* (Bristol: Jordans, 1993), at p 15, in respect of insider dealing regulation. See also *Marleasing SA v La Commercial International de Alimentacion SA* [1992] 1 CMLR 305; *Von Colson v Land Nordrhein Westfahlen* (1984) ECR 1891; *Lister v Forth Dry Dock and Engineering Co Ltd* [1990] AC 546; *Pepper v Hart* [1993] 1 All ER 42.

Chapter 3

OPEN-ENDED INVESTMENT COMPANIES —
A NEW BOTTLE FOR OLD WINE

Eva Z Lomnicka[1]

BACKGROUND

Collective investment through the pooling of investment capital has obvious benefits, particularly for the private investor: the spreading of risk, economies of scale and expert management of the pool. Until recently, in the UK, collective investment by the retail sector was achieved through either the unit trust or the investment trust company. The investment trust company appeared on the scene first, soon after the introduction of the registered company.[2] Its name, 'investment *trust*', is rather misleading — at least to a lawyer — as it does not take the form of a trust, in the true legal sense, but it is an ordinary registered company whose business it is to make profits through trading in other companies' securities. Being registered under the relevant Companies Act,[3] its share capital is necessarily fixed and it is subject to the usual restrictions on such companies redeeming their own shares.[4] In consequence, it cannot be an 'open-ended' investment vehicle in the sense of a company whose share capital varies as it buys back (and sells) its own shares. Thus, investors in an investment trust company must sell their shares through a stock market and cannot deal in its shares with the company itself. And it follows that the price of the shares — and hence the value of their investment — depends on market demand and is not a direct function of the net asset value of the pooled fund.[5] These two features of an investment trust company — the fact that realisation of the investment has to occur through a stock exchange and the fact that the value of the investment does not directly reflect the net asset value — account for its relative unpopularity with private investors.[6]

An alternative collective investment vehicle was devised in the 1930s, this time a vehicle utilising the trust: the unit trust. Here investors pool their capital and acquire 'units' in the pooled fund which is held by trustees and invested as advised by expert managers. Units may be bought and sold directly from and to the manager and the price of the units is based directly on the net asset value of the invested fund. Unit trusts are, therefore, a more 'user friendly' investment

---

1 Professor of Law, King's College London.
2 By Gladstone's Joint Stock Companies Act 1844.
3 Of 1985, or its predecessors. See the special provisions for investment trust companies in the Companies Act 1985 (hereafter 'CA 1985'), ss 265–266.
4 See, generally, the maintenance of capital provisions in CA 1985, Part V, ss 117–181, especially Chap IV (reduction of share capital), Chap VII (redemption of shares).
5 Although, clearly, the share price is related to the performance of the underlying investments.
6 Thus it is not subject to any special investor protection regime (cf unit trusts, considered below and see n 4 on p 51).

vehicle than the investment trust company and they soon became the more popular.

Elsewhere in the world, the benefits of collective investment were, generally, being achieved more simply through an open-ended corporate vehicle.[1] Investors can buy and sell their shares in a company which holds and manages investments, directly from and to the company, whilst the value of their investment is closely related to the net asset value of the fund invested by it.

As long as the UK retail collective investment market remained, essentially, dominated by on-shore, domestic institutions, the unit trust remained a satisfactory — if somewhat esoteric — collective investment vehicle. But when the fund management industry began to 'go global', UK unit trust companies found themselves at a competitive disadvantage. In seeking to penetrate overseas retail investment markets, they found the esoteric nature of the unit trust — especially in civil law countries where the trust concept was virtually unknown — a handicap. Moreover, the dual pricing mechanism adopted by unit trusts[2] was baffling to investors familiar with the single-pricing system operated by most open-ended investment companies. And overseas — especially off-shore[3] — funds in the open-ended corporate form were penetrating the UK market and providing an investment vehicle which was more readily understood by the ordinary UK investor. The advent of the single market for collective investment schemes in transferable securities in consequence of the EC UCITS Directive[4] further highlighted the disadvantages that UK unit trusts were under when they tried to utilise their single market 'passport' by marketing elsewhere in Europe.

Unsurprisingly, the UK collective fund investment industry began to lobby the UK government for the introduction of open-ended corporate collective investment vehicles for UK-based investment institutions. Although, originally, the driving force was the enhancement of competitiveness abroad (especially in the single market), the industry now sees the advent of open-ended investment companies ('OEICs') also as an opportunity to modernise and rationalise the domestic investment fund industry.[5] For example, the potential legal liability of the trustee in the unit trust context is regarded as problematic in some circumstances and, therefore, the corporate vehicle is, apparently, more attractive than the trust for collective investment in assets such as real property and derivatives.[6] Moreover, the corporate form is generally more flexible, for example in

---

1 For example, the SICAV (société d'investissement à capital variable), familiar on the Continent of Europe.
2 Whereby there is a difference between the sale and redemption price of units. This is now being reconsidered in the light of the introduction of on-shore open ended investment companies (OEICs) with single-priced shares, see below.
3 Collective investment vehicles from the Channel Islands and the Cayman Islands have been particularly successful in penetrating the UK market.
4 Directive on Undertakings for Collective Investment in Transferable Securities (85/611/EEC), as amended by Council Directive 88/220. It was anticipated by the regulatory regime of the Financial Services Act 1986 (hereafter 'FSA 1986') applicable to collective investment schemes (see below), see especially FSA 1986, s 86.
5 See *Open ended investment companies: The Next Generation, A Consultation Document* (HM Treasury, November 1996) (hereafter '*HMT Document 1996*'), para 12.
6 See *ibid*, paras 157–158 and Annex B, para 19. Thus, OEICs investing in such assets may be more successful than their unit trust counterparts have been.

the types of 'units' (ie shares) it may make available to investors.[1] It also entails (at least in theory) a greater degree of accountability of managers to investors in that investors are shareholders of the company with a potential role in its governance.[2] Thus, as such, they have the right, through shareholders' meetings, to hold their investment managers to account.

INTRODUCING OEICs

In view of the inappropriateness of much of the CA 1985 to open-ended corporate collective investment vehicles — especially the maintenance of share capital provisions — it was clear that significant legislative innovation was going to be necessary to make domestic OEICs possible. Given the well-known preference of government to avoid primary legislation — ostensibly in order to save on Parliamentary time — it was not surprising that a means was devised for making the necessary changes by secondary legislation. However, this has resulted in a complex, two-phase regime.

The first phase of the introduction of OEICs was achieved by means of regulations under the European Communities Act 1972.[3] This was possible because the regulations could be regarded as giving effect, in part,[4] to the EC UCITS Directive. Unfortunately, the Directive only applies to a limited range of collective investment schemes:[5] those investing in transferable securities (ie listed securities and warrants) and corresponding umbrella schemes. Thus, the regulations could only be used to introduce OEICs with the relatively narrow investment powers which fall within the scope of that Directive. In consequence, the Open-ended Investment Companies (Investment Companies with Variable Capital) Regulations 1996 ('the ECA Regulations')[6] made under the Act, which came into force on 6 January 1997, only permit the formation of OEICs investing in transferable securities. After much agonising,[7] the term in brackets in the title to the ECA Regulations, 'invest-

---

1 *Ibid*, Annex B, para 20.

2 See below in relation to the new on-shore OEICs.

3 Section 2(2). However, the legislative vires is limited (see Sch 2, para 1(1)). Thus, for example, the fraudulent trading provision in reg 58 of those regulations has a lesser penalty than the corresponding CA 1985, s 458 — although it will be increased by primary legislation at the earliest opportunity: *Open ended investment companies: A Second Consultation Document* (HM Treasury, April 1995) (hereafter '*HMT Document 1995*'), para 327. The Treasury had consulted previously: *Open ended investment companies: A proposed structure* (HM Treasury, December 1993).

4 As regards unit trusts, the UCITS Directive was anticipated by the FSA 1986, see especially Part 1, Ch VIII (and n 6 on p 51).

5 Moves to extend the UCITS Directive to undertakings with a wider range of investment powers have floundered.

6 SI 1996/2827, laid before Parliament in draft in July 1996 and passed in November after the usual (for legislation under the 1972 Act) affirmative resolution procedure. See n 3 on this page for the consultation documents which preceded the regulations.

7 See the list of the eight alternatives in *HMT Document 1995*, para 81 and *ibid*, Annex B, p 54 as to the 16 possible suffixes.

ment companies with variable capital',[1] is the technical term used[2] for OEICs which are formed under the ECA Regulations and which, therefore, enjoy automatically the single market UCITS 'passport' enabling them to be marketed throughout the EU. Thus they are also sometimes[3] termed 'UCITS OEICs' — a term which will be used in this essay.

In order to widen the scope of possible OEICs — in particular, to enable OEICs to invest in the same range of investments as domestic authorised unit trusts — the government decided to use another useful power to legislate by statutory instrument, that under the Deregulation and Contracting Out Act 1994, s 1.[4] At the time of writing, this second phase is well under way,[5] but not yet completed and a DCOA Order is expected soon which will enable non-UCITS OEICs — OEICs with investment powers beyond those provided for in the UCITS Directive (but in line with those of authorised unit trusts[6]) — to be established. Thus, just as there are UCITS and non-UCITS authorised unit trusts,[7] there will soon be both UCITS and non-UCITS OEICs. The intention is[8] that the non-UCITS OEICs will be incorporated and will operate and be regulated in the same way as the UCITS OEICs, except that their investment powers will be wider. Consequently, this discussion will concentrate on the corporate regime established by the ECA Regulations for UCITS OEICs, as it is expected that the regime under the DCOA Order will be very similar.[9]

Only *authorised* unit trusts (and their overseas equivalents, as far as investor protection is concerned[10]) may be marketed to the public in the UK.[11] There are, presently, no plans to provide for the creation of domestic OEICs with powers of investment that go beyond those available to authorised unit trusts.[12] However, as it is possible to create unregulated collective investment schemes (such as unit trusts) with unrestricted investment powers — although with very restricted marketing rights[13] — the Treasury has said it is open to persuasion that OEICs with such wide powers of investment should eventually also be provided for.[14]

---

1 The term is used in the Second EC Company Law Directive (77/91/EEC) and that directive's capital structure requirements may be (and in the UK have been) disapplied in the case of such companies. Consequently, those documents listed in Art 4 of the First Directive (ie letters and order forms) and used by such companies need to contain the words 'investment company with variable capital'.

2 In the FSA 1986 (see s 207(1), as amended by the ECA Regulations) and the ECA Regulations themselves (see regs 2(1), 3(2)).

3 See *HMT Document 1996, passim.*

4 The deregulation envisaged is the 'reliev[ing of the] specific burden in . . . s 716 of the Companies Act 1995': *ibid*, paras 53–54.

5 The requisite consultation process was completed in January 1997.

6 Thus, OEICs corresponding to money market funds, funds of funds, feeder funds, property funds (investing in land and related investments), derivatives funds and related umbrella funds will be possible.

7 Although non-UCITS authorised unit trusts, in fact, form a tiny fraction of the retail market.

8 See *HMT Document 1996*, paras 16, 104 and *passim.*

9 *Ibid, passim*, especially paras 59–65, 104.

10 For instance, collective investment schemes 'recognised' under FSA 1986, ss 86–88.

11 FSA 1986, s 76.

12 See *HMT Document 1996*, para 69 and Annex F. Thus, in so far as authorised unit trusts are presently unable to invest in, for example, commodities, neither will OEICs.

13 See n 11 on this page.

14 See *HMT Document 1995*, para 165.

The regime established by the ECA Regulations merely sets out the framework for the creation and operation of UCITS OEICs. Detailed regulation of OEICs, addressing investor protection concerns (including investment and borrowing powers), is found (and will be found in relation to non-UCITS OEICs when they eventually come into existence) in detailed Regulations made (or to be made in the case of non-UCITS OEICs) by the SIB.[1] This has the added advantage of enabling this detail to be amended easily and rapidly,[2] in response to market and investor protection needs. In this essay, these Regulations will be termed 'the SIB Regulations'.

THE UK REGULATORY CONTEXT

Before looking more closely at this new framework for OEICs, it must not be forgotten that, like authorised unit trusts, OEICs are, essentially, corporate vehicles for collective investment by private investors.[3] Like unit trusts,[4] they are 'collective investment schemes' for the purposes of the FSA 1986[5] and thus subject to that Act's investor protective regulatory provisions. These operate at a number of levels.

First, the FSA 1986 has special provisions for the authorisation and regulation of domestic authorised unit trusts[6] and corresponding provisions are enacted in the ECA Regulations for the authorisation and regulation of UCITS OEICs as products.[7] Moreover, the ECA Regulations[8] enable the SIB to make detailed regulations (termed 'the SIB Regulations' in this essay), equivalent to the Regulated Schemes Regulations made by the SIB under the FSA 1986[9] in relation to authorised unit trusts, concerning the investor protection aspects of OEICs. The stated aim of the SIB is to ensure similar investor protection for both OEICs and authorised unit trusts[10] and, therefore, the SIB's OEICs regulations reflect those already applicable to authorised unit trusts.[11]

---

1 In relation to UCITS OEICs, under reg 6 of the ECA Regulations. They are the Financial Services (Open-ended Investment Companies) Regulations 1997 (dated January 1997). For the consultation documents preceding these, see SIB's Consultative Paper 93 on *Open-ended Investment Companies* (October 1995); SIB's *Proposed Regulations for Open-ended Investment Companies* (October 1996) (hereafter, '*SIB's OEIC Proposals 1996*').
2 As the SIB Regulations are, technically, not statutory instruments. However, matters outside the SIB's legislative powers have to be provided for by the ECA Regulations.
3 As noted above, OEICs with powers of investment beyond those available for authorised unit trusts are not yet possible.
4 But unlike investment trusts: see FSA 1986, s 75(7).
5 Section 75(8). And see ECA Regulations, reg 10(11) (as to the requirements UCITS OEICs must satisfy in relation to the rights of participants referred to in s 75(8)(b)).
6 See especially FSA 1986, Part I, Chap VIII, ss 77–85.
7 See especially ECA Regulations, regs 7–27.
8 Regulation 6.
9 The Financial Services (Regulated Schemes) Regulations 1991 (as amended), made under FSA 1986, s 81 (constitution and management) and s 85 (scheme particulars).
10 See *HMT Document 1995*, para 10; *SIB's OEIC Proposals 1996, passim.*
11 And it is expected that the two sets of regulations will develop in tandem: *SIB's OEIC Proposals 1996, passim.*

Secondly, as well as the OEIC itself having to be authorised by the SIB as a product,[1] persons involved in the operation of the OEIC are carrying on 'investment business' for the purposes of the FSA 1986 and thus need to be 'authorised persons'.[2] Thus the depositary[3] and the ACD[4] have to be 'authorised persons'[5] and, as such, are subject to the regulatory regime — including conduct of business rules and capital adequacy requirements — of their regulator.[6] Moreover, as an OEIC — unlike a unit trust — has a separate legal existence, it carries on investment business in the UK itself[7] and so also needs to be an 'authorised person'.[8] However, as persons running the company and holding the company's investment capital are invariably 'authorised persons' and so already regulated as such, automatic authorised person status[9] is conferred on the OEIC itself by the FSA 1986.[10]

Finally, shares in OEICs are 'investments' for the purposes of the FSA 1986.[11] Therefore, certain activities in relation to them will constitute 'investment business'[12] and thus persons engaging in these activities in the UK, for example, persons advising on the purchase of OEIC shares, will also need to be 'authorised persons'.

These investor protection aspects of OEICs are not the subject of this essay. However, passing reference to them will need to be made as they shape the nature of OEICs and impose considerable constraints on how OEICs operate.

A NEW CORPORATE CODE

General

Given the flexibility of UK corporate law, it would have been possible to provide for OEICs under the CA 1985, duly modified — in particular, in relation to its maintenance of share capital requirements. However, after consultation, it was

---

1 For instance, an authorisation order under the ECA Regulations needs to be made. As noted below, the OEIC is also, automatically, an 'authorised person' (for the purposes of carrying on investment business) under FSA 1986, s 24A. The use of the word 'authorised' in these two different senses (authorised as a *product* and authorised as a *person*) causes confusion to the unwary.

2 FSA 1986, s 3.

3 See below.

4 See below.

5 See FSA 1986, Sch 1, para 16 (as amended by SI 1996/2958) which renders their activity 'investment business' and the ECA Regulations, reg 10, which requires the depositary and the ACD (if a sole director) to be authorised.

6 Which will normally be IMRO.

7 FSA 1986, Sch 1, para 16.

8 As well as having to be authorised as a *product* under the ECA Regulations, see n 1 on this page. It will be regulated directly by the SIB unless (as is likely) it joins IMRO. Thus, if all are members of it, IMRO will regulate (and coordinate the regulation of) the ACD, the depositary and the OEIC itself.

9 Not to be confused with 'authorisation' by reason of the authorisation order, see n 1 on this page.

10 FSA 1986, s 24A, added by ECA Regulations, reg 75 and Sch 8, para 11. Note also the consequential amendments to the FSA 1986 made by Sch 8 to the ECA Regulations.

11 FSA 1986, Sch 1, para 6.

12 See FSA 1986, Sch 1, paras 12–15. And note the restrictions on advertising in FSA 1986, s 57.

decided that this would require 'significant violence to the [CA 1985] require-ments about capital maintenance [and] . . . extensive textual amendment',[1] resulting in an untidy mess. Moreover, the future development of OEICs might have been inhibited by the constraints of the existing (albeit amended) compa-nies legislation. Therefore, it was decided to promulgate a free-standing, spe-cial purpose corporate code outside the Companies Acts.[2] This is a far tidier solution, easier for all to grasp[3] and conducive to further revision as the need arises.

This new special purpose corporate code under which OEICs operate is of spe-cial interest to company lawyers. It draws on many provisions of the CA 1985[4] and of insolvency law. In particular, it provides for the creation of a separate legal entity, owning capital subscribed by shareholders (the investors) to whom it issues (and, unlike ordinary companies, from whom it can repurchase) shares.[5] Its affairs are managed by directors,[6] who are in a similar legal position to directors of registered companies.[7] Moreover, there are provisions corre-sponding to CA 1985, ss 35–35B,[8] protecting third parties dealing with the company, whilst retaining the duty on directors, nevertheless, to abide by limi-tations as to capacity and authority which they are under. The directors are, to some extent, answerable to the shareholders. Thus, relevant general principles of company law established by the case law will, where appropriate, apply.[9]

However, the OEIC corporate code contains some special features. The main obvious difference is that OEICs, necessarily, are not subject to the usual main-tenance of share capital restrictions, although there are restrictions on the issue, redemption and pricing of their shares.[10] There are also significant differences in corporate governance.[11] The process of incorporation and related matters are also specific to OEICs.[12] Moreover, as required by the UCITS Directive, the corporate assets must be vested in a depositary for safekeeping.[13] Finally, as mentioned above and largely outside the scope of this discussion, OEICs oper-ate within a strict regulatory environment established under the ECA

---

1 See *HMT Document 1996*, para 56.

2 Additionally, the form of company accounts can now follow a different and more appropriate model from that in the CA 1985 — ie that established by the SIB for authorised unit trusts.

3 '[T]han a plethora of amendments scattered through the text' of the CA 1985: *HMT Document 1996*, para 57.

4 Indeed, by ECA Regulations, reg 2(4), expressions in the regulations which are also used in the CA 1985 (or FSA 1986) 'have the same meanings as in that Act'.

5 The shares are eligible for listing (although special exchange arrangements are necessary due to the fact that the shares are single-priced, close to net asset value) to make them attractive to those obliged to invest in listed securities. Moreover, they are eligible for paperless transfer under CREST.

6 ECA Regulations, reg 28(4), see further, below.

7 See below, especially n 3 on p 59.

8 And ss 322A and 711A, see ECA Regulations, regs 32–36, 38. These are considered further below.

9 See *HMT Document 1995*, para 49: 'the Treasury expects that a court would be likely to take account of any relevant precedents in the company law field' and *ibid*, para 215.

10 See the ECA Regulations, regs 39–46 and the SIB Regulations, Part IV.

11 See below.

12 See below.

13 See below.

Regulations and the SIB Regulations made thereunder, reflecting the fact that OEICs are, essentially, investment vehicles for the public at large. It is at this level that the OEIC begins to resemble an authorised unit trust, for example being an authorised vehicle and so regulated as a product by the SIB and having to vest its assets in a depositary — hence the market term 'a unit trust in a corporate wrapper'.[1]

The fact that OEICs operate in the context of a regulatory regime has enabled the new corporate code primarily to adopt regulatory sanctions[2] rather than the less effective and out-moded criminal sanctions which pervade the Companies Act. However, some criminal sanctions remain.[3]

Some of these special features of OEICs will now be considered.

Incorporation

The process whereby an OEIC is created differs substantially from the creation of a registered company under the CA 1985. The differences stem primarily from the involvement of the SIB. As noted above, domestic OEICs — like domestic authorised unit trusts[4] — need to be authorised as collective investment schemes by the SIB.[5] Yet they also need to satisfy the First EC Directive[6] as to the registration of certain documents. Therefore, a one-stop procedure has been devised whereby the conferment of authorisation by the SIB, rather than the registration of the constitutional documents with the relevant Registrar, is the act which incorporates the OEIC.[7] However, in common with ordinary companies, the constitutional document(s) must be lodged with the relevant Registrar of companies and registered by him[8] and thus is open to inspection.

In addition, the constitutional documents differ. Instead of two documents — a memorandum and articles — an OEIC has a single 'instrument of incorporation',[9] which is comparable to the 'deed of trust' in the case of a unit trust. Its minimum[10] contents requirements are set out in Schedule 3 to the ECA

---

1 Which is particularly apposite if there is a sole director — the ACD, see below.

2 See especially ECA Regulations, reg 66 and n 3 on p 49 on the limited powers of ECA Regulations.

3 See ECA Regulations, regs 7(5), 26(7), 58, Sch 6, paras 3(3), 19(1).

4 Unit trusts that are not authorised may be created but, unless they are from overseas and are 'recognised' under ss 86–88, cannot be marketed to the public: FSA 1986, s 76. As noted below, OEICs which are not authorised by the SIB cannot (as yet) exist.

5 The authorisation procedure and the conditions the proposed OEIC has to satisfy are set out in ECA Regulations, regs 7–12. For revocation of authorisation, see regs 16–17. Note especially reg 10 (criteria for authorisation – corresponding to FSA 1986, s 78) and reg 12 (UCITS Certificate may be issued).

6 EC Council Directive 68/151/EEC.

7 ECA Regulations, reg 3(1). For the procedure, which is a single-step process as far as the promoters are concerned and which involves close liaison between the SIB and the Registrar, see regs 13–14 (registrar receives documents before authorisation); reg 4 (registration by registrar); Sch 1 (Application of Part XXIV of CA 1985 (which concerns the Registrar)).

8 *Ibid*, reg 4 and Sch 1. The OEIC cannot commence business until its constitutional document has been registered: reg 4(3).

9 *Ibid*, reg 4(5). The term 'instrument of incorporation' is taken from UCITS Directive. Despite its name, it does not *confer* corporate status on the OEIC.

10 The SIB Regulations set out further requirements.

Regulations which also specify if and how alterations to it may be made.[1] The AUTIF,[2] in collaboration with the SIB, has produced a 'model' instrument of incorporation for its members and, therefore, domestic OEICs, in practice, have standardised instruments of incorporation.

There are two provisions hidden in Schedule 3 which are of interest to company lawyers. First, in contrast to the tortuous wording of CA 1985, s 14, there is a simple paragraph which merely states that 'the provisions of a company's instrument of incorporation shall be binding on the officers and depositary of the company and on each of its shareholders'.[3] Thus, given this simple wording, it is unlikely that the courts will transplant the difficult case-law on CA 1985, s 14[4] if they are ever called upon to construe this provision. Secondly, lest anyone be tempted to argue that the *Houldsworth* principle[5] is applicable to OEICs, there is another paragraph which makes clear that a shareholder is not, by reason of being such, debarred from obtaining damages or other compensation from an OEIC.[6]

Prospectus requirements

The prospectus requirements of UCITS OEICs differ in some respects from those applicable to ordinary registered companies and resemble those of authorised unit trusts — although the company law term 'prospectus', rather than the unit trust term 'scheme particulars', is used to describe the requisite document.[7]

The detailed requirements are to be found in the SIB Regulations.[8] Thus, the directors[9] must produce a prospectus complying with the contents requirements of Schedule 1 to the SIB Regulations[10] and, before marketing the OEIC shares in the UK, send copies of it to the SIB and the depositary.[11] Shares may not be sold in the EU unless a copy of the prospectus in the relevant official language is available to investors.[12] However, there are no restrictions on the distribution of 'mini' or 'sub-fund' prospectuses — as long as the full prospectus is available.

---

1 See ECA Regulations, Sch 3, para 5(1) (unalterable provisions); para 5(3) (provisions alterable with consent of shareholders); para 5(2) (alterable provisions). All 'significant' alterations must be approved by the SIB: reg 15. See also SIB Regulations, reg 10.1.

2 The Association of Unit Trusts and Investment Funds.

3 Schedule 3, para 6(1).

4 See, for example, the notorious *Hickman* principle, taken from *Hickman v Kent and Romney Marsh Sheep-Breeders' Association* [1915] 1 Ch 88, and subsequent case-law and commentaries thereon.

5 From *Houldsworth v City of Glasgow Bank* (1880) 5 App Cas 317 (now reversed by CA 1985, s 111A).

6 Schedule 3, para 6(2).

7 ECA Regulations, reg 6(2). See also the prospectus requirements of the UCITS Directive, Arts 27–33.

8 Made under ECA Regulations, reg 6(1), applying FSA, s 85 (which enables regulations as to 'scheme particulars' to be made in relation to authorised unit trusts) to UCITS OEICs. See Part 3 of and Sch 1 to the SIB Regulations.

9 The ACD (see below) must draw up the prospectus and the board (if there is one) must approve it: SIB Regulations, reg 3.01.1.

10 *Ibid.*

11 *Ibid*, reg 3.02.1(iii).

12 *Ibid*, reg 3.02.1(b) (UK); reg 3.02.2(b) (elsewhere in EU). The prospectus has to be offered to the investor if marketing is effected face to face or by telephone. Otherwise, it must be provided if the investor asks for it.

Unlike an ordinary registered company, an OEIC issues and redeems shares continuously and, therefore, the prospectus remains an important document throughout the life of the OEIC. Therefore, there are detailed provisions in the SIB Regulations as to the periodic revision of the prospectus. Thus, immediate revision of the prospectus is required 'upon the occurrence of any materially significant change' affecting its contents[1] and, in any event, the prospectus must be reviewed annually.[2] There are no specific requirements as to the revised form of the prospectus, although the date on which revisions are made must be clearly stated.[3] Thus, a completely new version may be issued or a mere supplement provided. Shareholder approval[4] is needed for certain specified changes to the prospectus, for example, a change in investment objectives and policy, or payments out of scheme property (including increased remuneration of the ACD).[5] Moreover, the ECA Regulations give the SIB a power of veto, exercisable within three months, in relation to any 'significant' proposed alterations to the prospectus, which, therefore, need to be notified in advance to the SIB.[6]

There are prospectus liability provisions in the SIB Regulations which are similar to those applicable in relation to ordinary company offer documents.[7] Thus, 'persons responsible' for the prospectus are identified,[8] obligations are imposed on them to ensure the prospectus is accurate[9] and liability, in the usual terms, is imposed on them for false or misleading statements in it,[10] with the usual defences available.[11] Moreover, there is also a general requirement that there must not be a significant departure, in the management of the scheme property, from the statements as to investment objectives and policy stated in the prospectus.[12]

Corporate governance

Ordinary registered companies are, in principle, free to adopt whatever structure they desire for the purposes of conducting the affairs of the company.[13] However, provision is invariably made in the articles of association for

---

1 *Ibid*, reg 3.04.1(a).

2 *Ibid*, reg 3.04.1(b).

3 *Ibid*, reg 3.04.2.

4 Or, in the case of a change only affecting certain shareholders, those shareholders' approval: *ibid*, reg 3.05.1.

5 An extraordinary resolution (ie one requiring a 75 per cent majority) is required for these changes (but not others): *ibid*, reg 3.05.2.

6 ECA Regulations, reg 15(1)(b);(3). The SIB intends to issue Guidance as to which alterations it regards as 'significant'.

7 See (in relation to securities listed on the London Stock Exchange) FSA 1986, ss 150–152 and (in relation to unlisted securities) the Public Offers of Securities Regulations 1995, SI 1995 No 1537 ('POS Regulations'), regs 13–15.

8 SIB Regulations, reg 3.03.2 (cf FSA 1986, s 152 and POS Regulations, reg 13).

9 *Ibid*, reg 3.03.1(a) – this obligation has no direct counterpart in the FSA or POS regime.

10 *Ibid*, reg 3.03.1(b) – in addition to any other liability (cf FSA 1986, s 150 and POS Regulations, reg 14).

11 *Ibid*, reg 3.03.4–3.03.5 (cf FSA 1986, s 151 and POS Regulations, reg 15).

12 *Ibid*, reg 3.05.4.

13 Although a plc must have at least two directors and a secretary.

management of the company affairs to be conducted by the board of directors or their delegates, subject to a degree of control by the shareholders' meeting.[1] In contrast, the ECA Regulations,[2] supplemented by the SIB Regulations,[3] contain significant constraints on the management structure of UCITS OEICs.[4]

A UCITS OEIC may choose to have either a single director[5] or a board of directors, who must each be a 'fit and proper person to act as directors of an investment company with variable capital'.[6] In either case, it must have an 'authorised corporate director' or 'ACD',[7] who must be a corporate body and an 'authorised person' under the FSA 1986.[8] If it has a single director, then this must be the ACD. If it has a board of directors, then one of its number must be designated the ACD.[9] The ACD undertakes the day-to-day business of the OEIC, including investment management and the selling and buying of the OEIC's shares. Being an FSA authorised person (usually by virtue of membership of the self-regulating organisation IMRO), the ACD is subject to a strict regulatory regime. Moreover, there are detailed provisions in the SIB Regulations[10] as to the appointment and termination of the appointment of the ACD. Thus, the ACD corresponds to the management company of a unit trust. If there is a board of directors, then the SIB Regulations contain detailed provisions as to the allocation of functions between the ACD and the board. In essence, the board must ensure that the ACD is acting properly and in accordance with the broad strategic policy determined by the board.[11] The board, the combination of whose 'experience and expertise must be such as is appropriate'[12] may, but need not,[13] contain non-executive directors — although it must[14] do so if the OEIC wishes to be listed on the Stock Exchange.

Mention should also be made of the depositary — required by the UCITS Directive[15] and corresponding to the trustee of a unit trust. As noted above, the

---

1 Adopting or modifying the relevant provision in Table A. See especially Art 70.
2 See especially reg 10(4)–(7) (criteria for incorporation) and Part III, *passim.*
3 See especially Part 6.
4 As well as those discussed below, another point of difference is that alternate directors are *not* permitted: SIB Regulations, reg 6.01.5. And there is no need for an OEIC to appoint a secretary.
5 ECA Regulations, reg 10(4). Originally (see *HMT Document 1995,* paras 122, 256) it was proposed that all OEICs have a minimum of three directors.
6 This is one criterion for the making of the OEIC's authorisation order: ECA Regulations, reg 10(5).
7 The term is in the SIB Regulations: see Sch 3 (Glossary).
8 SIB Regulations, regs 6.01.1, 6.01.2 and see ECA Regulations, reg 10(6) (if sole director, must be an authorised person). See FSA 1986, Sch 1, para 16, n 5 on p 52.
9 SIB Regulations, reg 6.01.2.
10 Part 6, s D.
11 See Part 6, s A.
12 ECA Regulations, reg 10(7). It is expected that the board may comprise 'foreign marketing associates; major [institutional] investors; or respected individuals': *HMT Document 1996,* Annex B, para 12.
13 A proposal that it be mandatory for OEICs to have independent directors was rejected in view of the oversight responsibilities of the depositary, see *HMT Document 1995,* paras 119–121 and *ibid,* Annex B, pp 57–58.
14 As a result of the listing requirements in the Yellow Book.
15 Article 7.1 (unit trusts); Art 14.1 (investment companies).

corporate assets[1] must be 'entrusted for safekeeping'[2] to an independent[3] depositary. However, in contrast to the position in the case of a unit trust where the trustee holds the scheme property on trust *for the unitholders*, the depositary holds the scheme property *for the company*, the shareholders having no interest in it. The depositary must again be a corporate body and an 'authorised person' under the FSA 1986.[4] Again, the ECA Regulations,[5] as amplified by the SIB Regulations,[6] set out the rights and duties of the depositary. In essence, as well as acting as custodian of the scheme property,[7] it has significant oversight functions in the interests of investor protection,[8] in particular to ensure that the regulatory obligations are fulfilled by the ACD and OEIC generally, which funcations are spelt out in the SIB Regulations.[9] In order that it may perform this role, Schedule 2 to the ECA Regulations confers rights on the depositary to attend, speak at and even convene shareholders' meetings and to receive information from the directors, in particular the board papers.[10] The OEIC's annual report to its shareholders[11] must contain a report from the depositary on the compliance of the board with the OEIC's constitution and regulatory regime.[12]

As for shareholders' meetings, it was decided[13] that the corporate code should follow normal principles of company law in requiring shareholders to meet annually and so enabling them to hold the directors to account. Thus, provision is made in the ECA Regulations for obligatory AGMs[14] (but without any criminal sanctions[15]) and the directors must lay copies of the annual report (containing the accounts of the company and auditors' report)[16] before the general meeting.[17] The SIB Regulations contain further provisions as to shareholders' meetings,[18] some of which replicate provisions in the CA 1985 and Table A, for example, in enabling the usual proportion of shareholders to requisition a meeting.[19]

---

1   Called the 'scheme property': ECA Regulations, reg 2(1). The SIB Regulations may exclude some of the OEIC's property (eg its premises) from this requirement.
2   ECA Regulations, reg 5 and see Sch 2. Delegation of this function is possible (for example, to a global custodian), with the depositary remaining responsible: reg 5(2)(b). The SIB Regulations make further provision for depositaries.
3   ECA Regulations, reg 10(8)(a),(f). The degree of independence caused some controversy, see *HMT Document 1995*, paras 131–137. See now SIB's Guidance Release 1/97: *Independence of Depositaries of Open-ended Investment Companies* (January 1997).
4   *Ibid*, reg 10(8)(d). Reg 10(8) sets out the criteria a depositary must satisfy in order for the OEIC to be authorised. See FSA 1986, Sch 1, para 16, n 5 on p 52.
5   See especially regs 5,10(8) and Sch 2.
6   See especially Part 6, sections B & C.
7   See SIB Regulations, reg 6.06–07.
8   It must only act in the interests of shareholders: *ibid*, reg 6.05.4.
9   *Ibid*, especially reg 6.05.1. It also has the power to appoint an ACD (subject to subsequent confirmation by the general meeting) if the OEIC ceases to have any directors.
10 Schedule 2, para 4. See also Sch 2, paras 5–6 (statement by depositary ceasing to hold office).
11 Required by ECA Regulations, reg 60. See also the provisions as to the half-yearly reports.
12 SIB Regulations, Sch 2, Part III.
13 After some controversy, see *HMT Document 1995*, paras 137–142; Annex B, p 62.
14 See reg 31(1).
15 As there are regulatory sanctions, see reg 66.
16 ECA Regulations, reg 61.
17 *Ibid*, reg 60(3).
18 See Part 10 thereof.
19 Regulation 10.01.3 (cf CA 1985, s 386).

Directors and unauthorised activities

Apart from being subject to special requirements imposed in the cause of investor protection,[1] the directors of an OEIC are, in other respects, treated very much like the directors of an ordinary registered company.[2] Thus, the new corporate code replicates — with some variations — the relevant provisions of the Companies Act 1985[3] (and occasionally, Table A).

As in the case of a registered company, the shareholders in general meeting appoint the board[4] — although the SIB has a power of veto over proposed replacement directors.[5] There is an express provision vesting all powers of the company in the director(s),[6] in particular, the power to manage the business.[7] This is in contrast to the more complex position in conventional companies, where, at least historically, the general meeting was regarded as the ultimate repository of any residual powers of the company although, in practice, the articles vest managerial control in the directors.[8]

As also mentioned above, there are provisions in the new corporate code which correspond to CA 1985, ss 35–35B, 322A and 711A. The draftsmen have taken the 1985 provisions, rearranged them slightly[9] and embellished them further to take into account the significant limitations on OEIC's activities in the ECA and SIB Regulations. The result is statutory provisions which are even more complex than those in the CA 1985.

ECA reg 32(1), like CA 1985, s 35(1), in effect precludes the plea of *ultra vires* (in the narrow sense[10] of lack of capacity[11]) being raised as a ground for invalidating any act of an OEIC.[12] However, the provision enabling a shareholder to restrain such activity (corresponding to CA 1985, s 35(2)) and the provision as

---

1 See, for example, ECA Regulations, reg 10(5) (each director to be 'fit and proper'), the requirement of the ACD to be an authorised person (see n 8 on p 57) and for the board (if any) to have appropriate expertise (*ibid*, reg 10(7), n 12 on p 57).

2 A conspicuous omission in the corporate code is any provision corresponding to Part X which concerns 'fair dealing' by directors. The reason is that OEIC directors are subject to control under the investor protection regulatory regime established by the other provisions of the ECA Regulations and the SIB Regulations.

3 See, for example, the equivalent of CA 1985, s 309 in ECA reg 29 (requiring directors to 'have regard' to the interests of company employees) and of CA 1985, s 318 in ECA reg 29 (inspection of contracts). And see reg 55(1) (corresponding to CA 1985, s 36C), reg 56 (corresponding to CA 1985, s 310), reg 57 (corresponding to CA 1985, s 727).

4 ECA Regulations, reg 28(2).

5 *Ibid*, reg 15(1)(e) — and (by virtue of its authorisation power) the initial directors.

6 'Subject to the provisions of the [ECA] Regulations, SIB Regulations and the company's instrument of incorporation . . .': *ibid*, reg 28(5).

7 *Ibid*, reg 28(4).

8 Table A, reg 70.

9 Thus, ECA Regulations, regs 32 and 33 correspond to CA 1985, ss 35(1) and 35A(1)–(3) respectively, whilst reg 36 corresponds to ss 35(2)–(3) and 35A(4)–(5).

10 See *per* Slade LJ in *Rolled Steel Products (Holdings) Ltd v British Steel Corporation* [1986] Ch 246, CA.

11 '[B]y reason of anything in [the ECA] Regulations, SIB Regulations or the company's instrument of incorporation' (cf 'by reason of anything in the company's constitution': the wording of CA 1985, s 35(1)).

12 See also reg 47, corresponding to CA 1985, s 3A(b), whereby a UCITS OEIC has 'power to do all such things as are incidental or conducive to the carrying on of its business'.

to directors' liability (corresponding to s 35(3)) are moved to another regulation,[1] considered below.

Similarly, ECA reg 3, like CA 1985, s 35A(1)-(3), operates '[i]n favour of a person dealing in good faith' with the OEIC and renders the exercise of certain powers free of any limitations in the OEIC's 'constitution'. However, there are significant differences in the detail.

First, although the powers covered are, like those in s 35A(1), those which seek 'to bind the company, or authorise others to do so', they extend beyond the power of directors[2] to the power of the general meeting.[3] This extension in respect of the general meeting is necessary as, unlike the case in a conventional company where the general meeting, in practice, has a very limited role, the general meeting, in the case of OEICs, has been given an enhanced function. Moreover, the provision in relation to the powers of the directors, instead of using the wording of s 35A(1) ('the power of the *board of directors* to bind . . .'[4]), talks of 'the power of the directors . . . (whether or not acting as a board) to bind . . .'. The wording in brackets, '(whether or not acting as a board)', avoids the difficulties that the wording of s 35A gives rise to in deciding if the activities of anyone other than the board — for example, the managing director — are covered. Despite the plural in reg 33 ('directors'), the intention appears to be to cover the activities of an ACD acting alone, whether or not it is the sole director.[5] *Secondly*, limitations under the OEIC's 'constitution' are stated[6] to include not only (as is the case under s 35A(3)) limitations deriving from shareholders' meetings,[7] but also limitations deriving from the ECA and SIB Regulations.[8] However, there is no mention of shareholders' agreements,[9] no doubt because, in practice, these will not arise in the case of OEICs. *Thirdly*, the provisions as to the 'good faith' requirement are even more convoluted than those in the CA 1985, although there is still no attempt actually to define the term.[10] There are provisions[11] corresponding to CA 1985, s 35A(2)(b) and (c), amplifying the application of the 'good faith' criterion, yet those provisions are expressly disapplied[12] in the case of limitations deriving from the ECA and SIB

---

1 Regulation 36. But ECA Regulations, reg 32(2) confirms that the duty of the directors to observe any limitations on their powers is not affected (cf the opening words of CA 1985, s 35(3)).

2 ECA Regulations, reg 33(1)(a).

3 *Ibid*, reg 33(1)(b).

4 My emphasis.

5 As the ECA Regulations contemplate the possibility of a sole ACD (see above) and, therefore, reg 33 must be intended to cover the activities of such a person. See *HMT Document 1995*, para 275.

6 In ECA Regulations, reg 33(3).

7 For instance, 'from a resolution of the company in general meeting or of a meeting of any class of shareholders' (cf s 35A(3)(a)).

8 Of course, limitations in the instrument of incorporation are clearly limitations under the OEIC's 'constitution'.

9 As there is in CA 1985, s 35A(3)(b).

10 There is considerable controversy as to what it means. The requirement is derived from the First EC Directive (68/151/EEC), Art 9 which has been used as an interpretive aid to the predecessor of s 35A (see *International Sales v Marcus* [1982] 3 All ER 551).

11 ECA Regulations, reg 33(2)(b) and (c). And see reg 33(2)(a) which corresponds to s 35A(2)(a).

12 By *ibid*, reg 33(4).

Regulations (only)[1] where the third party either (a) 'has actual knowledge';[2] or (b) 'has deliberately failed to make enquiries in circumstances in which a reasonable and honest person would have done so'.[3] The result is that, in such a case, there is no presumption of 'good faith'[4] (and so the burden of proving good faith remains on the third party) and the third party cannot take advantage of the provision[5] that states that he is not to 'be regarded as acting in bad faith by reason only of his knowing' the activity in breach of the ECA or SIB Regulations has occurred. Thus, in such a case, the court is left to decide if the third party has discharged the burden of proving 'good faith' without any guidance as to what that term means. If such a person has 'actual knowledge',[6] then, presumably, he will not be able to establish that he was in 'good faith'. If he has 'deliberately failed to make such enquiries' as a reasonable and honest person would have made,[7] then it would seem likely that again he will not be able to establish 'good faith' — although it is conceivable that a court might take the view that such a person may still be in good faith if a purely subjective definition of that term is adopted.[8] Why the legislature did not simply state that a person is deemed not to be in good faith if he has actual knowledge or unreasonably fails to make enquiries as to limitations in the ECA or SIB Regulations, but left the matter to be decided by the courts, is baffling. Yet the fact that it did not do so suggests that there may be occasions where the court is free to find 'good faith' in such circumstances. The position is further complicated by ECA reg 34. This corresponds to CA 1985, s 35B, so that a third party is, generally, not bound to make enquiries as whether any activity is *ultra vires*[9] or unauthorised.[10] However, reg 34 is expressed to be subject to the provision as to failure to make enquiries in the case of ECA or SIB Regulations, discussed above.[11] Thus, generally,[12] failure to make enquiries does not preclude a finding of 'good faith'. *Finally*, there is a provision[13] which corresponds to CA 1985, s 711A(1)–(2) and, therefore, a third party is not deemed to have notice of any document just because it is available for inspection — although a person may be deemed to have notice if he failed 'to make such enquiries as ought reasonably to be made'. This raises similar problems to those existing, potentially,[14] under the CA 1985 as to the relationship between this 'deemed notice' provision and the other

1 *Ibid*, reg 33(4)(a) — thus this disapplication does not apply if the limitations on powers are in the instrument of incorporation or a shareholders' resolution.
2 *Ibid*, reg 33(4)(b)(i).
3 *Ibid*, reg 33(4)(b)(ii).
4 In that reg 33(2)(c) is disapplied.
5 In reg 33(2)(b).
6 For instance, is within reg 33(4)(b)(i).
7 For instance, is within reg 33(4)(b)(ii).
8 See *Barclays Bank Ltd v TOSG Trust Fund Ltd* [1984] BCLC 1 at 17, where Nourse J (commenting on the predecessor to s 35A) regarded 'good faith' as a subjective concept. Yet the requirement that there be a 'deliberate' failure to inquire renders it very unlikely that such a person will be regarded as even subjectively in 'good faith'.
9 For instance, not 'permitted by [the ECA] Regulations, SIB Regulations or the company's instrument of incorporation': reg 34(a).
10 For instance, subject to 'limitations on the powers' referred to in reg 33: reg 34(b).
11 For instance, reg 33(4)(b)(ii), n 3 on this page.
12 Except in the case of limitations in ECA or SIB Regulations: reg 33(4)(b)(ii).
13 ECA Regulations, reg 35.
14 CA 1985, s 711A is not yet in force.

'good faith' provisions. It would seem that, when reg 34 applies (and it does not apply in the case of limitations in ECA and SIB Regulations[1]), it cannot be argued that it is 'reasonable' to make enquiries as to a document available for inspection. Otherwise, it would seem that, if it is reasonable to make inquiries, the third party will be deemed to have notice and therefore may not be able to establish 'good faith'.

The ECA corporate code brings together, in one regulation,[2] the provisions as to restraining *ultra vires*[3] or unauthorised activity[4] and ratifying it. The provisions largely[5] replicate the corresponding ones in the CA 1985.[6] Thus, a shareholder may bring proceedings to restrain an *ultra vires* or an unauthorised act unless the company is already under a legal obligation to perform it.[7] Moreover, the company in general meeting may ratify the activity 'by resolution' (ie ordinary resolution[8]) and a separate resolution is needed to absolve the directors from liability.[9] This is in contrast to the position under CA 1985, s 35 where *special* resolutions are required in relation to the *ultra vires* acts of an ordinary company. However, such resolutions have no effect on the powers of the regulators to bring actions under FSA 1986, s 61 or of investors to bring personal claims under FSA 1986, s 62.[10]

---

1 It is 'subject to regulation 33(4)(b)(ii)', see above.
2 Regulation 36.
3 For instance, activity covered by reg 32, see above.
4 For instance, activity covered by reg 33, see above.
5 But not quite, see below.
6 Viz: s 35(2)–(3); s 35A(4)–(5).
7 Regulation 36(1),(3) (re: reg 32); reg 36(2),(3) (re: reg 33). Regulation 36(2), like s 35A(4), does not actually confer any right in respect of unauthorised activity but preserves any right to bring proceedings which exists at common law.
8 Regulation 36(4) (cf s 35(3); s 35A(4)).
9 Regulation 36(5) (cf s 35(3) – there is no corresponding provision in s 35A because the common law already determines whether ratification by resolution is possible).
10 Regulation 36(6).

Chapter 4

THE LEGAL REGULATION OF DERIVATIVE INSTRUMENTS IN ANCIENT GREECE AND ROME

Ned Swan[1]

INTRODUCTION

The use of what we call today 'derivative instruments' originated in ancient Mesopotamia and, by about 500 BC, had spread throughout the Middle East.[2] An examination of the legal histories of ancient Greece and Rome shows how derivatives came to Europe.

ANCIENT GREECE

Compared to the thriving commercial states of Mesopotamia and the 'middle-man' nations, the economic development of Greece was slow, awkward and unfriendly to mercantile profit. As a recent commentator has written:

> 'It has always been a cause for puzzlement as to why the Greeks, intellectual pathfinders in every branch of pure science, should have revealed so stubborn a streak of tribal naïveté when it came to economics.'[3]

Some blame for this can be placed on the heroic ideal to which the Greeks aspired, which saw the training of the body for war and agricultural work as the highest pursuit.[4] The Homeric ideal had little praise for the merchant.[5] As Aristotle wrote:

> 'But . . . as I have already said, the means of life must be provided beforehand by nature; for the business of nature is to furnish food and that which is born, and the food of the offspring is always what remains over from that which is produced. Wherefore the art of getting wealth out of fruits and animals is always natural . . . necessary and honourable, while that which consists in exchange is justly censured; for it is unnatural and a mode by which men gain from one another.'[6]

Consequently, there was little commercial imagination exercised in Greek trade. The most advanced stage of Greek commercial policy seemed to be 'buy

---

1 Partner, Banking & International Finance Group, Cameron McKenna.
2 See Swan, Edward J, *The Development of the Law of Financial Services* (London: Cavendish Publishing, 1993), pp 1–33; Swan, Ned, 'Derivatives in the Beginning' (1996) *The Futures & Derivatives Law Review*, vol 3, no 4, pp 41–78.
3 Peter Green, *Alexander in Actium* (London: Thames & Hodson, 1990).
4 Xenophon, *Oeconomicus*, in vol 4 of Goold, GP (ed), Marchant, AC (trans), *Xenophon in Seven Volumes* (London: William Heinemann, 1979), pp 409–411.
5 Green, p 362.
6 Aristotle, *Politica*, Book I, 10.

cheap and sell dear'.[1] Trading for profit was sneered at as ungentlemanly and unathletic and if this attitude was prevalent in Athens, it was even more pronounced in Sparta, where a military élite was supported by an underclass of agricultural serfs.[2] The economic model with which Homer provided Greek culture consisted of barter for a few desirable luxury goods and conquest to obtain whatever else was needed. Greek trade was somewhat more sophisticated than this, but the ideas remained a model for Greek life, so that the kingdoms of the Near East appealed to the Greeks and Macedonians more as objectives for conquest and loot than wealthy and skilful trading partners.[3]

The legal position of futures contracts

It is generally accepted that the cash sale was the basic principle of Greek commerce. Ownership and possession of the item sold generally had to occur at the time of the exchange.[4] Pringsheim points out that Greek law 'did not know consensual contracts'.[5] As he said: 'Sale is for the Greeks identical with the exchange of money against goods'.[6]

The development of early Greek law to promote contracts for the future delivery of goods was far less commercially encouraging than the laws of Mesopotamia. As Pringsheim wrote:

> 'Greek sale implies transfer of ownership. Unascertained goods cannot be transferred and therefore cannot be sold and bought. Their transfer is possible only in the future after they have been specified. Liabilities for future performance are not compatible with the Greek conception of sale.'[7]

One of the earliest known Greek law-givers, believed to have lived in about the 7th century BC, was Charondas of Catana, whose laws were transmitted originally in early Athens orally, in verse form. His laws specifically forbade transactions in commodities for future delivery. Contracts for commodities were legally enforceable only if the commodities were paid for and delivered on the spot. Contracts that included any provision of credit were unenforceable. Charondas believed that any merchant extending credit caused himself loss suffered by delay in completion. It is thought that the principal reason for this regulation was to reduce litigation (and the costs to the government) by restricting the class of enforceable commercial contracts.[8] This view is reflected in a passage from Plato's *Laws,* which reads:

> 'When one person makes an exchange with another by buying or selling, the transfer shall be made by handing over the article in the appointed part of the market

1 Green, p 367.
2 Green, p 365.
3 Green, pp 362–363.
4 McDowell, Douglas P, *The Law in Classical Athens* (London: Thames & Hudson, 1978), p 138.
5 Pringsheim, Fritz, *The Greek Law of Sale* (Nachfolge: Hermann Bohlaus, 1950), p 47.
6 Pringsheim, pp 90–91.
7 Pringsheim, p 268. Pringsheim points out that Talmudic and Islamic law also only recognised 'sale for ready money'.
8 Gagarin, Michael, *Early Greek Law* (Berkeley: University of California Press, 1986), pp 52–75.

place and nowhere else, and by receiving the price on the spot; and no *delay in sale or purchase is allowed*. If a person exchanges something in any other place or under any other agreement, trusting the other party to the exchange, he must do so on the understanding that there is *no legal redress* regarding things not sold according to the laws set down.'[1]

There is, of course, the argument that Plato may have been talking about an 'ideal' rather than actual Greek laws. However, Pringsheim examines Plato's comments in comparison to those of Aristotle and Theophrastus, and concludes that Plato's statements of commercial risk were probably reflections of actual Greek law in many cities.[2] However, he recognises that these may have been subject to less stringent enforcement in more commercially oriented cities such as Athens.

Strict interpretation?

It is difficult to gauge how strictly prohibitions against contracts for future delivery were enforced. Athenian law court speeches seem to regard legal technicalities as arguments rather than immutable determinants of legal relations. Arguments principally make appeals to fairness. The main intention of the Athenian dispute resolution process seems to have been preservation of community solidarity (*koinonia*) rather than rigid satisfaction of legal requirements.[3] Consequently, the true attitude towards deferred delivery could have been more relaxed than legal writings make it seem. In any case, as time passed, the Greeks made some accommodations to the needs of expanding trade.

Bottomry exception

By the 5th century BC, sea-borne international trade was a crucial part of the commercial life of Greece. Some accommodations were made to promote trade in goods for future delivery, but the laws governing this type of commerce were strict. In Athens, speculative loans at high rates of interest to finance contracts for future delivery of some vital commodities were permitted. These were commonly called 'bottomry' loans. For example, loans on badly needed imported grain were permitted. The lender was permitted to loan the costs of the importation of grain at annual rates of between 10 and 48 per cent, depending on the length and consequent risk of the sea voyage required. If the grain was lost during the voyage, the borrower owed nothing. If the voyage was successful, the lender got principal and interest.

There were strict laws to protect the lender from any fraud by the borrower and other laws restricting these loans as to type of commodity eligible (grain), quantity of commodity to be imported (50 'loads'), and the destination of importation (Piraeus only).[4] However, grain was an exceptional commodity in ancient Greece because of the continuing need to secure adequate supplies to feed the population.[5]

---

1 Quoted in Millett, Paul, 'Sale, credit and exchange in Athenian law and society', in *Nomas: Essays in Athenian law, politics and society* (Cambridge: Cambridge University Press, 1990), p 186, emphasis added.
2 Pringsheim, pp 126–137.
3 Pringsheim, pp 178–179.
4 Toutain, Julian, *The Economic Life of the Ancient World* (London: Kegan Paul, Trench, Trubner & Co, 1930), pp 74–77.
5 Millett, pp 192–193.

Arrah

There was not much expansion of the Greek law of sale to accommodate sales of commodities for future delivery beyond this strictly limited class of loan arrangement.[1] However, a few rare references to *arrah* have been cited by scholars. In ancient Greece, *arrah* was a deposit, earnest money, or option fee committing both parties to a contract to a sale to be completed in the future. It was both a good faith payment and an incentive to complete in the future. Although a number of sources, including Aristotle and Theophrastus, refer to *arrah*, the only concrete example found is to *arrah* paid for the purchase of funerary equipment.[2]

Hellenistic synergy

There is, however, an area in which Greek law advanced beyond the limits discussed above and that is in Hellenistic Greek law. The conquests of Alexander gave Greek law a window on other systems of law and commercial relations, which appear to have influenced it in the Far East.

The conquests of Alexander of Macedon and the Hellenistic empires founded by his followers did nothing to substantially change Greek laws, but the new Greek rulers of Middle Eastern lands did not, necessarily, seek to impose Greek law on their new subjects. The Hellenistic rulers either left the laws of the countries they ruled in place, or, such as in the case of Alexandria, only applied the law of Greece in certain circumstances. Such a combination of systems moved toward tolerance of the more creative commercial laws previously existing in the Middle East.[3]

Ancient Mesopotamian systems of law had remained virtually unchanged for millennia. As Pringsheim says:

> 'More than once authors familiar with Babylonian law have been struck by its astonishing constancy, its iron stability. With some qualification, it seems true that there was little development in the forms of contracts, that a conservative oriental tendency preserved not only the old ideas, but even the contractual clauses; that little freedom was left for individual shaping and adapting; that through more than two millennia, Babylonian documents remained the same. So far as any development in the drawing of contracts can be observed, it seems to lead not to progress, but only to more elaborate expression. This monotonous uniformity is striking in a system, the survival of which can be observed in a unique way for several thousand years.'[4]

Ptolemaic Egypt

After the conquest of Egypt by Alexander, there does not appear to have been an immediate unification of law between the Ptolemaic Greek rulers and their Egyptian subjects. The Hellenistic Greeks conducted their private affairs according to principles of Greek law, but the Egyptian population, apparently, continued to operate under their own legal principles:

---

1 Millett, pp 167–174.
2 Millett, pp 175–176.
3 Rostovtzeff, M, *The Social and Economic History of the Hellenistic World,* vol 2 (Oxford: Clarendon Press, 1961), pp 1067–1068
4 Pringsheim, pp 503–504.

'The two streams of legal tradition touched and crossed each other at several points, but never did they merge.'[1]

Although the Hellenistic Middle East was ruled by the Greek successors of Alexander, many of the ways of doing business remained governed by the traditional legal relationships of the Middle East, including the long-lived contractual forms of cuneiform contracts about which Pringsheim speaks. Prominent among these are sales for future delivery. In Ptolemaic, Roman and Byzantine Egypt, there are a number of examples of contracts in which a party contracts to pay for goods to be delivered in the future.[2]

From a base in Alexandrian Egypt, it is easy to see how the ancient Middle Eastern methods of business relations could have influenced the world of the Greeks and Romans. From the earliest times, Egypt was a principal centre of importing grain into the Greek world.[3] Later, Alexandria was the principal trade partner of Italy.[4]

There is evidence that the Greek rulers of Alexandria, and their Roman successors, made little attempt to impose a universal system of law on the commerce of the city. It is thought that the city was, in fact, a collection of different communities, some based along ethnic lines, where commercial disputes were determined by the community's own internal judges, according to the community's own rules of commercial relations.[5] This would have made it easier for the merchants operating in Alexandria to adopt those commercial methods which were the most compatible with their business, without regard to the basic principles of Greek law.

Certainly, Egyptian law continued to operate not only during the Hellenistic period but during the Roman era.[6] During the Ptolemaic era, particularly with respect to contracts, it was decreed that the governing law would be the language of the contract.[7]

It is also true that, with respect to a number of issues under the law of obligations, Hellenistic documents written in Greek adopted Egyptian forms. Consequently, a number of Egyptian, and other Middle Eastern forms of agreement, made their way into Hellenistic business documents.[8]

This modification of European law by Eastern principles continued during Roman rule. For example, slaves in the Middle East were entitled to own property and, indeed, often engaged in business on their own account. Under

---

1 Wolff, Hans Julius, 'Law in Ptolemaic Egypt', *Essays in Honour of C Bradford Wells* (New Haven: American Society of Papyrologists, 1966), pp 68–77.
2 Bagnall, Roger S, 'Price in Sales on Delivery', *Essays in Honour of C Bradford Wells* (New Haven: American Society of Papyrologists, 1966), pp 85–96; Greene, Kevin, *The Archaeology of the Roman Economy* (London: BT Batsford, 1986), p 64.
3 Fraser, PM, *Ptolemaic Alexandria* (Oxford: Clarendon Press, 1972), p 133.
4 Fraser, p 151.
5 Alberro, Charles Ariel, 'The Alexandrian Jews During the Ptolemaic Period' (Michigan State University, PhD Thesis, 1976), pp 125–141.
6 Taubenschlag, Raphael, *The Law of Greco-Roman Egypt in the Light of the Papyri*, 2nd edn, rev (Warsaw: Panstwowe Wydawnictwo Naukowe, 1955), pp 3–4.
7 Decree of King Euergetes II (118 BC). Taubenschlag, pp 19–20.
8 Taubenschlag, pp 25–27.

Roman law, slaves were incapable of owning property, but in Hellenistic Egypt this was often disregarded.[1]

This influence was particularly important with respect to contracts for sales for future delivery. As stated above, this was a common practice in Hellenistic Egypt, and indeed in earlier Pharonic Egypt.[2] It is interesting to note here that such contracts usually contain penalties for failure to deliver, such as the so-called 'double' or a penalty of double the amount of the value of the goods. The penalty of the 'double' was frequently used in later medieval contracts and, possibly, shows the influence of the Middle East on the development of derivative contracts in Europe.

Under Greek Hellenistic law, future sales were expressly forbidden. However, in Hellenistic Egypt, the contracts found there showed that this was frequently disregarded.[3]

Also, in Hellenistic Egypt, is found another key characteristic of modern derivatives, the assignment of obligations.[4]

In order for the legal forms that originated in ancient Mesopotamia to have their place in forming the commercial law of Europe, it is important to show the continued existence and influence of these ancient forms at points of contact between the Middle East and Europe. From some of the comments previously stated, it can be seen that this is an idea supported by scholars of ancient documents. Another support is found in a series of Aramaic papyri found on the island of Elephantine on the Upper Nile.[5] These consist of legal documents and letters written by Jewish mercenaries employed by the Persian rulers of Egypt.[6]

With respect of legal papyri of this type, the conclusion of scholars is that they are strongly influenced by the cuneiform legal tradition, particularly the Syrian-Canaanite part of that tradition.[7] As Muffs points out, the ancient Middle East was 'characterised by a remarkable cultural continuity'. Sumerian legal and religious traditions were preserved by later Babylonian (Akkadian) traditions. As Akkadian was replaced by languages such as Aramaic, the legal traditions of the cuneiform clay tablets found their way into Aramaic, Persian and demotic papyri.[8] Thus, the legal traditions and formulations of ancient cuneiform continued to be preserved in Egyptian and Syrian documents, and awaited the arrival of the ancient Greeks and Romans.

Between about 300 and 250 BC, some Ptolemaic papyri were written near the east bank of the Nile which referred to a number of commercial transactions for future delivery. These are demotic papyri from Hibeh.[9]

---

1 Taubenschlag, p 46.
2 Taubenschlag, p 336.
3 Taubenschlag, p 338.
4 Taubenschlag, pp 417–418.
5 Muffs, Yochanan, *Studies in the Aramaic Legal Papyri From Elephantine* (Leiden: EJ Brill, 1969), p 1.
6 Muffs, p 1. The earliest known Aramaic legal papyrus from Elephantine is dated about 495 BC, and the oldest known Aramaic legal papyrus in Egypt is dated about 515 BC.
7 Yaron, Reuven, *The Law of the Aramaic Papyri* (Oxford: Clarendon Press, 1961), pp 114–128.
8 Muffs, pp 12–14.
9 Grenfell, Bernard P and Hunt, Arthur S, *The Hibeh Papyri: Part I*, (London: Egypt Exploration Fund, 1906).

There are a number of letters relating to future deliveries of oil and grain.[1] Slightly later (about 194 BC) there are demotic[2] papyri from Ptolemaic Egypt which detail grain loans (and are actually transfers of rights to the future production and delivery of grain) in forms remarkably similar to those nearly 2000 years older in ancient Mesopotamia. One such is as follows:

> '[Statement of year and invocation of the gods]
> [Identification of the seller]
> [Identification of the buyer]
> There belongs to you [a certain quantity of wheat and a certain quantity of barley] . . . which is owed by me in respect of the wheat and barley which you gave to me.
> I shall return it by year 7, first month of the season of Shemu, day 30, (being) wheat (and) barley, it being free from the expenses of freightage and haulage, without adulteration (or) chaff;
> While it will be measured, transported and consigned to your hand. Your representative (in) your house shall send
> the measure in which you measured it for me. However, much of the wheat (or barley) I shall not have given to you
> By year 7, first month of the season of Shemu, day 30, the aforementioned date (of payment), I shall give to you [date of delivery repeated]
> I shall not be able to give to you another date (of payment) for them. All the possessions of every kind which I have and which I shall acquire
> (will be) security for every word above until I act in conformity with them. Your representative is the one who is authorised regarding
> every word which he will address to me in the name of every word which (is written) above. I shall execute them according to his instructions without any force (being applied).
> [List of 5 witnesses].'

This document is interesting for the continuity it indicates between the forms of ancient cuneiform and the demotic papyri only about 200 years before the time of Christ. A grain loan is given, in exchange for rights for future delivery of commodities, or other payment, and witnesses are provided.[3]

A group of Greek and demotic papyri from a single family drawn between about 134 and 89 BC include a number of commercial transactions.[4] One such was a loan of grain which results in a future delivery of grain at a later date.[5] In the first century BC, another set of Greek papyri from Egypt contained commercial transactions for the future delivery of commodities, particularly grain.[6] One dating from 93 BC is a contract for the sale of wheat to be delivered six months after the date of the contract:[7]

> 'In the reign of Ptolemy surnamed Alexander, the god Philometor, the 22nd year, the priest of Alexander and the rest being as written at Alexandria, the 9th of the

1 Grenfell and Hunt, pp 183–211.

2 The word used to describe the popular form of written Greek used in Egypt at this time.

3 Andrews, Carol AR, *Catalogue of Demotic Papyri in the British Museum*, vol 4 (London: British Museum, 1990), pp 57–58.

4 Adler, Elkan Nathan, Tait, John Gavin, Heichelheim, Fritz M and Griffith, Francis Llewellyn, *The Adler Papyri* (Oxford: Oxford University Press, 1939).

5 Adler, Tait, Heichelheim, Griffith, pp 36–37.

6 Grenfell, Bernard P, Hunt, Arthur S, Smyly, J Gilbart, *The Tebtunis Papyri: Part I* (London: Henry Frowde, 1902).

7 Grenfell, Hunt, Smyly, pp 468–469.

month Peritius which is the 9th of Choiak, at Kerkeosiris in the division of Polemon of the Arsinoite Nome. Dionysius also called Petosiris, son of Theon also called Thonis Persian of the Epigone, and his wife Athenais, also called Athermouthis, daughter of Apollonius also called Pres Retis, Persian, with her guardian Dionysius, her husband, the aforesaid, have sold to Petesuchus, son of Marres, Arsinoite, three artabae of wheat at the price of 2000 drachmae of copper for each artaba, the whole price of the three artabae being one talent of copper coins; which sum the aforesaid have received from Petesuchus forthwith from hand to hand out of his house. Dionysius and Athenais shall pay Petesuchus or his agents in the month of Pauni of the 22nd year in wheat that is new, pure, and unadulterated in any way, by the 6th-Choenix measure of the dromos of the temple of Suchus at the aforesaid village by just measurement, delivering it to Petesuchus at the said village at their own expense; or if they fail to pay it as stated, the aforesaid that forfeit to Petesuchus . . . one and a half times its value. The aforesaid are themselves sureties to each other . . . Petesuchus . . . shall have the right of execution upon (the sellers), upon one or each or whichever he chooses and upon all their property, as if in accordance with a legal decision.'[1]

Another document from the group, but dated about AD 128 (by this time, Egypt was under Roman rule) is a contract for the future sale of a crop.[2]

Muffs cites a document which he translates as being an agreement for delivery of a consignment of barley and lentils to government officials. It says:

'You have consigned to us barley (amount given)
and our heart is satisfied therewith. We will deliver this grain.
We will render an account before the company commander and the authorities of
the Government House and the clerks of the Treasury.
If we do not deliver all of the grain that is yours in full,
We shall be liable to you for the sum of (a penalty amount).'[3]

The explanation of the above text states that the above phrase 'our heart is satisfied' means that the speakers agree that they have received an adequate payment of a specific performance in return for giving up some right.[4] The right given up in this case is claims against the owner of the lentils and barley that consign the goods to them. The statement that their hearts are satisfied is a concession that they have checked the goods and that they tally with the amount they are supposed to deliver. In other words, they are admitting that if the goods delivered are less than the goods they are supposed to deliver, the fault is not with the consigner of the goods, but with those who agreed to complete the delivery.[5] Thus, the right given up is a relinquishment of certain claims.[6]

Seleucid contracts
Only about 400 economic texts from the Hellenistic period have been published to date, so it is useful to look not only at Ptolemaic texts, but also at texts from the Seleucid area, which included parts of ancient Middle East (including

---

1 Grenfell, Hunt, Smyly, p 469.
2 Grenfell, Bernard P, Hunt, Arthur S, Goodspeed, Edgar J, *The Tebtunis Papyri: Part II* (London: Henry Frowde, 1907), pp 223–224.
3 *AP2* (484 BC), Muffs, p 52.
4 Muffs, p 56.
5 Muffs, p 58.
6 Muffs, p 58.

Babylonia) from which cuneiform documents originated.[1] In the Seleucid lands, cuneiform was still being used for some transactions including disposal of slaves, houses and prebend rights. Other transactions seem to have been done on parchment or papyrus.[2]

One type of derivative from this era is the sale of prebend rights. A prebend was a common concession in ancient times under which an individual or a group was entitled to purchase a share of the revenue of an institution, such as a temple, in exchange for providing something of value, such as the bread needed by the temple, etc.

Prebend sales are fascinating transactions from a number of points of view. First, they are by their nature bilateral promises. They are usually framed in terms of the purchaser receiving a portion of a temple's future revenues (such as one sixth of every twentieth day's revenues) in exchange for providing a promised service such as a supply of bread to the temple. Secondly, it appears to be the case that prebends were sometimes purchased by families or other syndicates which consisted of a number of shareholders. Thirdly, these prebend rights appear to be freely transferable by purchasers. Fourthly, women were important traders in the ancient Middle East and entitled to contract as principals in their own right.

An example of a prebend sale of the Seleucid era is fascinating because it shows both the similarities to ancient times and the changes wrought from the interaction of Greek and earlier Middle Eastern legal forms. One given by McEwan is translated as follows:

> 'Etirtu, [a woman, stated to be daughter and wife of certain people] has sold of her own free will one sixth of a day in day 20, her baker's prebend before [a list of gods and temples] monthly for the whole year . . . offerings and whatever appertains to one sixth of one day, this baker's prebend which is held with [another name listed] and the shareholders for . . . *mina* and two *shekels* of pure silver, *staters* of Antiochos, in good condition, for the full price, to [name of buyer] in perpetuity. [The seller then agrees to "clear" the title along with her husband.]'[3]

An interesting point about this sale is the fact that the woman seller signs a provision at the end agreeing to act jointly with her husband (who is, apparently, not an owner of the prebend) in clearing any future possible claims that may arise to the prebend. According to McEwan, this represents a phase in the transition of the status of women during the time of Hellenistic rule. Prior to the Hellenistic period, women were entitled to act in commercial transactions in their own name. After the imposition of Greek rule, the status of women began to be diminished. In the prebend sale above, the woman has to act jointly with her husband even though she is, apparently, the owner of the concession. In times that followed, women ceased to act in commercial transactions at all and all dealings on their behalf were conducted by male relatives. Attitudes towards slaves and real property also changed under Hellenistic rule. In general, there was a regressive restriction on the freedom of individuals to act, based on sex and status.[4]

---

1 McEwan, Gilbert JP, *Texts from Hellenistic Babylonia in the Ashmolean Museum* (Oxford: Clarendon Press, 1982), p 1.
2 McEwan, p 1.
3 McEwan, pp 7–8.
4 McEwan, p 8.

A few documents for future delivery also survive on papyrus from the Palestine ruled by the Ptolemies. One from February in 258 BC records instruction to complete a future delivery of wheat and barley.[1]

Regional interchange

Records of this time also show transactions in wheat between Syria and Egypt, which indicate an interchange of business transactions (and presumably forms of business transactions) between the two regions at that time.[2] Another papyrus in the same archive (called the 'Xenon Archive') refers to a transaction for the future delivery of wine and honey.[3]

Continuity in the Roman era

In the Roman era, the continued use of such contracts is shown by a number of papyri found in Egypt which are contracts for the future delivery of commodities.[4]

Changes under Greek law

Greek law, in and of itself, made little contribution to complex commercial transactions in general, and to the use of derivative contracts in particular. If any significant contribution can be said to have been made, it was the contribution of the expansionism of the Greek peoples and the penetration they made from Europe to the Middle Eastern lands they conquered.

The conquest and assimilation that occurred under Alexander, and his successors, brought the European Greek world into contact with the commercial forms of the Middle East. Rather than attempting to replace the ways of doing business they found, they acceded to the continuation of those forms to promote the prosperity of the kingdoms they had conquered. This had two long term impacts for Western culture. First, it began the process of merger of European markets with Middle Eastern business forms, particularly contracts for future delivery and other derivatives, which had long been a part of Middle Eastern commerce and proved to be a valuable contributor to Hellenistic commerce. Secondly, the conquests of the Macedonians opened the way for the future expansion of Rome into the Middle East. Indeed, it was the Roman conflict with the Seleucid Empire of the second century BC which prompted the physical expansion of Roman rule into Asia.[5] The Greek adoption of Middle Eastern business forms in the Middle Eastern lands they ruled may well have influenced changes in Roman law which led to a wider use of futures contracts and other derivatives in the Roman Empire of later years.

However, the intrusion of Greece into the Middle East had negative consequences for commerce as well. There was less emphasis on the value of using

---

1 Skeat, TC (ed), *Greek Papyri in the British Museum*, vol 7 (London: British Museum, 1974), pp 11–12.
2 Skeat, p 12.
3 Skeat, pp 16–17.
4 Grenfell, Bernard P and Hunt, Arthur S, *The Oxyrhynchus Papyri: Part II* (London: Egypt Exploration Fund, 1899).
5 Green, pp 414–432.

clever trading methods and less upon the value of the contributions of all sectors of society to commercial prosperity in Greek culture. In particular, the commercial position of women and slaves was reduced in that they could not trade or own property in their own right under Greek law. Apparently, Greek culture relied more upon the power of its warrior caste to acquire property than on the clever trading of its people to acquire the goods needed by society. Consequently, there was less need for the intellectual and commercial contributions of women and slaves. As a result, Greek law restricted their rights to contribute through the medium of trade. This was a step backward for the expansion of sophisticated forms of commerce in general, and for the acquisition of property through peaceful commercial means in particular. This reversal was not entirely corrected under subsequent Roman rule, as will be shown below.

ROME

The Roman economy

'All roads lead to Rome' is not merely a comment of the thoroughness of Roman engineering; it is an accurate description of the economy of the Roman Empire. In Julius Caesar's time, Rome's population was around 900,000; by the 2nd century, it was well over 1 million.[1] It had to import almost all of its food, clothing, furniture and building materials from all over the Empire. Very little was exported from Rome. In addition, it was the Empire's centre of wealth and power. In short, Rome was the principal destination for all the Empire's commodities.

The Roman emperors always regarded it as their task to supply grain to the population of Rome at reasonable prices (or sometimes freely) and the annual grain needs were enormous. The government needed 3,600,000 bushels a year just to distribute to public employees and the needy.[2] The general public's needs were even greater. It is estimated that Rome needed at least 10,000,000 bushels of grain a year to feed its population, by the time of Augustus.[3] Egypt supplied Rome with 5,000,000 bushels annually, Africa with 10,000,000, and Sicily with 2,000,000. This grain was under direct imperial control in that it was sent to Rome as an annual tax called 'tribute.' The excess was distributed to other parts of Italy, stored or sold on the open market to private dealers of firms or bread bakers. It took more than 6,000 ox-drawn barges a year to haul tribute grain from the harbour at Ostia to Rome.[4] Consequently, the report of Tacitus that 200 grain ships in the harbour at Ostia were destroyed by a storm and 100 more accidentally burned on the Tiber in a single day, and the emperor Nero still refused to raise prices, is consistent with such a volume.[5]

Wine was also imported into Rome in tremendous volumes. By the second century, 25,000,000 gallons a year were supplied by Italy and 25,000,000 gallons a

---

1   Frank, Tenney, *Rome and Italy of Empire*, vol 5 in *An Economic Survey of Ancient Rome* (Baltimore: Johns Hopkins Press, 1940), p 218.
2   Frank, pp 218–219.
3   Rickman, G, *The Corn Supply of Ancient Rome* (Oxford: Clarendon Press, 1980), p 10.
4   Frank, pp 219–220.
5   Tacitus, *The Annals of Imperial Rome* rev edn (Grant, Michael (trans)) (London: Penguin, 1989), 15.18.2, p 353.

year by Spain.[1] About 1,500,000 million gallons of olive oil were brought in annually.[2] Building materials were needed. The Colosseum alone is estimated to have used 200,000 tons of travertine and 200,000 tons of other tufa, brick and concrete. The Claudian Aqueduct used 100,000 tons of stone and the Forum of Trajan needed 50,000 tons of marble for the columns of one basilica.[3]

The economy of Rome was not limited to basic goods and commerce ranged far beyond the Empire to fill the desire of the Romans for exotic imported goods. Pliny reports that trade with India, China and Arabia required outflows of cash from Rome of 100,000,000 sesterces a year and he was concerned about this trade deficit.[4]

Much of the economy was state controlled. Tribute, in the form of needed commodities,[5] was collected and distributed by the *Fiscus* (imperial treasury), which provided warehouses and markets for the conduct of trade. The Fiscus was an important participant in trade by the time of the Emperor Vespasian controlling the marketing of such things tribute as grain, metals, pearls, exotic woods from Africa, wool, ivory from India, and glass made in Egypt.[6] Involvement in marketing included setting prices for commodities including grain, which given its impact on the popularity of the emperor, was the object of concern. Tiberius and Nero, in order to quell popular agitation over the price of grain, reduced the price.[7]

The fact that there was a great deal of state intervention in the Roman economy, at times much more than others, does not mean there was not a great deal of private participation in commodity trade. It simply meant that its scope was limited by state regulation and competition. Rome auctioned contracts for the transport of provincial grain to private merchants and the emperors often offered incentives to encourage private merchants to trade.[8] Tribute grain constituted only about one third of the grain available for export from Africa and Egypt,[9] and there were other agricultural areas of the Empire. Consequently, parallel with the state involvement in marketing, there was a great deal of trade by private merchants. Private merchants were called *negotiatores,* with descriptions often containing identifications as to type and geographical origin. For example, a *negotiator cretarius Britanniciannus* was a trader in British ceramic goods.[10] Merchants were frequently of humble background[11] and, curiously,

1 Frank, p 220.
2 Frank, p 221.
3 Frank, p 221.
4 Frank, p 282, citing Pliny, 6.101 and 12.24.
5 Including wax which was stored in a warehouse called the *Horrea Candelaria*. Frank, p 234, citing Pliny 21.77.
6 Frank, pp 231–232.
7 Tacitus, *The Annals of Imperial Rome*, Loeb Classical Library, p 363.
8 For example, the Emperor Claudius (AD 41–54) offered to indemnify for any losses incurred in carrying grain to Rome and special incentives to merchants who could make shipments of over 75 tons.
9 Silver, p 80.
10 Greene, Kevin, *The Archaeology of the Roman Economy* (London: BT Batsford, 1986), pp 166–167.
11 Wax tablets dating from 40 AD from a suburb of Pompeii record two freedmen in the grain importing trade, Silver, p 80.

the vast majority of merchants involved in importing commodities to Rome were foreigners from Asia, Africa, Egypt, Spain, and Syria, etc.[1]

Yet, despite the enormous and extensive trade in commodities that the Roman Empire required, the sophistication of its economic structures did not keep pace. Under the Republic, the Romans' outlook, like that of the Greeks they admired, was agrarian and militaristic.[2] Their behavioural models were Achilles and Cincinnatus.[3] As Cato the Censor wrote in about 160 BC:

> 'It is true that to obtain money by trade is sometimes more profitable . . . On the other hand it is from the farming class that the bravest men and the sturdiest soldiers come, their calling is most highly respected, their livelihood is most assured and is looked on with the least hostility, and those who are engaged in that pursuit are least inclined to be disaffected.'[4]

However, some speculation in grain is reported and bottomry loans of the kind used in Athens (p 65 above) were employed.[5]

After the Republic, the early emperors, such as Augustus and Tiberius, initially paid little attention to commerce, allowing a *laissez-faire* mercantilism to run its course.[6] In time, emperors such as Vespasian and Diocletian tried to regulate the Roman economy, but their policies consisted largely of rigid state intervention in the mechanics of business rather than flexible policies to encourage the growth of commerce.[7] For example, Rome tried to run its complicated economy without public debt, on a cash basis. Shortages of public money were met by increasing taxes, debasing the coinage or both. To some extent, the ruinous financial burdens imposed by heavy taxes and inflation from adulteration of coined money contributed to the ultimate collapse of Rome.

These shortcomings are puzzling because there were ways in which Rome was financially sophisticated. Its unified system of coinage was one of the things that helped tie the Empire together.[8] Banking also reached a reasonable level of sophistication with banks taking deposits, lending at interest, and using written

---

1 Frank, p 242.
2 Frank, p 295.
3 A leading citizen of the 5th century BC who, according to tradition, left his farm to lead the Romans to victory over an invading enemy and then returned to finish his ploughing.
4 Marcus Cato, *On Agriculture*, Loeb Classical Library, p 3. It is hard to imagine that any Roman could have embodied a combination of agrarian and militaristic impulses better than Cato the Censor. Better known than his well-regarded treatise on agriculture, from which the above quotation is taken, is his repeated demand to the Senate *'Delenda est Carthago'* (Carthage must be destroyed) which helped precipitate the Third Punic War (149 to 146 BC) ending with the destruction of Carthage, Rome's leading military and commercial rival.
5 Broughton, TRS, 'Roman Asia Minor', chapter in *An Economic Survey of Ancient Rome*, vol 4 (Baltimore: Johns Hopkins Press, 1938).
6 Frank, pp 267 and 295.
7 The Edict of Diocletian (AD 301) was a comprehensive attempt to regulate prices and wages which had adverse effects on agriculture and trade.
8 One of the curious things about finding buried treasure in modern England is that hoards of Roman coins nearly 2,000 years old are far less rare than British coins of a few hundred years ago. This is because far more Roman coins were minted. To the emperors, coins were not only money, but advertising. They confronted the emperor's subjects with portraits of who was in charge, every time money was handled.

directions to transfer money without the need to carry cash. However, the Roman system of commodity trading may not have, generally, reached the level of sophistication necessary for commodity futures contracts to become part of the ordinary course of business of the Empire.

Futures contracts in Rome

There is evidence of some use of commodity futures contracts in Rome in the middle of the 1st century BC. At that time, Pompey[1] played an active role in securing Rome's grain supply. He understood that long-term planning was necessary to secure the food supply of a large population. He improved that supply by letting out contracts to private grain merchants for periods of years, with the initial period being three years.[2]

Some *de facto* speculation in future commodity prices was also present in tax collection. In the 2nd century BC, companies of Roman businessmen, called *publicani*, were given the right to contract to collect taxes in Roman Asia. Successful bids for these contracts were paid in Rome, in cash, for contracts lasting five years. These companies did not deal directly with the taxpayers themselves, but subcontracted this work to agents called *pactiones*. The taxes or tithes actually collected by these subcontractors were often paid in commodities. The practice was that these commodities were immediately sold and the cash was credited to the *publicani*. This entailed a commodity price change risk between bid for the contract and sale of commodities representing payment of taxes.[3]

Other evidence about commodity sales that has come down to us points to the sale of large quantities of commodities being made on the spot. For example, records of private grain sales in Lower Egypt during Roman rule show that three-quarters of the sales took place during the five months from September to January. This indicates that most farmers sold their grain shortly *after* the harvest rather than before, which would not have been the case if they had been selling to grain dealers under contracts for future delivery.[4]

However, there are a number of documents that have survived from the era of Roman rule in Egypt and the Middle East which show use of derivative contracts and, indeed, secondary assignment of such agreements. In AD 308 and 309, a number of sales of beans for delivery in the future are recorded. In 314, a future sale of vegetable seed is recorded.[5]

Other documents of future sales of wine and other commodities, dating from the 4th through to the 6th centuries, show that the use of these futures contracts continued right through the Roman era and into the Byzantine era

---

1 Julius Caesar's son-in-law and one-time partner in power. Caesar's crossing the Rubicon caused a break between them which ended with Pompey's assassination in Egypt in 28 BC.

2 Rickman, G, *The Corn Supply of Ancient Rome* (Oxford: Oxford University Press, 1980), p 57.

3 Rickman, pp 38–43.

4 Duncan-Jones, Richard, *Structure and Scale of the Roman Economy* (Cambridge: Cambridge University Press, 1990) pp 148–149.

5 Boak, Arthur, Youtie, Herbert (eds), *B Archive of Aurelius Isidious* (Ann Arbor: University of Michigan Press, 1960), pp 326–338.

following the Fall of Rome.[1] Later in the Roman era, in the 3rd and 4th centuries, there are also a number of contracts for future delivery of wine and other commodities.[2] A contract from Egypt, dated 21st January 261, for the future delivery of wheat, is held in Uppsala, Sweden.[3]

As shown above (see p 72), there were various kinds of futures contracts being used in Egypt during the Roman period. Grain 'Loan' futures contracts resembling those of early Mesopotamia were used. Indeed, there is even evidence of a kind of secondary market existing for commodity futures contracts in the form of 'credit notes for grain' which circulated.[4]

Derivatives and Roman law

Rome has had tremendous influence on futures trading and regulation for centuries, up to the present day. However, Rome's most important contributions to commodity futures trading were not economic but legal. Roman law has provided the framework of commodity futures regulation from the early Middle Ages. It has provided the civil law basis for all of the important regulatory systems of Western Europe and the United States: canon law, the law merchant, the English common law and various European codes of law, including the Code Napoleon.[5]

The essential contribution of Roman law to the regulation of Western futures trading was in its definition of different elements of the law of sale and the law of contract. In the development of the Roman law of sale, all the stages of contract law necessary to promote futures trading evolved: spot sales, sales of commodities for future delivery, and finally, assignment of contracts.[6]

However, Roman law was slow to develop these tools for commerce such as futures contracts. Rome is thought to have been founded around 750 BC and to have been organised as a Republic around 550 BC.[7] At the beginning of the Republic, agriculture and cattle raising appeared to have been the main occupations. Rome had no coinage and did not have an extensive trade. An alphabet had just been introduced.[8]

Early Roman law was extremely formal and, consequently, not suited to the needs of fast moving commercial transactions. Initially, Roman law, like the

---

1 Bell, HI (ed), *Greek Papyri in the British Museum*, vol 5 (London: British Museum, 1917), pp 222–223, 275.

2 Hunt, Arthur S, *The Oxyrhynchus Papyri: Part VII* (London: Egypt Exploration Fund, 1910), pp 209–211. See also Chambers, M, Cockle, WEH, Shelton, JC, Turner, EG, *The Oxyrhyncus Papyri: Volume 48* (London: Egypt Exploration Society, 1981), p 78. Jacobsen, A Bulow, Whiteorne, JEG, *The Oxyrhynchus Papyri: Volume 49* (London: Egypt Exploration Society, 1982), pp 249–250.

3 Frid, Bow, *Ten Upsala Papyri* (Bonn: Rudolf Habelt, 1981), pp 49–60.

4 Howgego, Christopher, 'The Supply and Use of Money in the Roman World 200 BC–AD 300' in *The Journal of Roman Studies*, vol 82 (London: Society for Promotion of Roman Studies, 1982), pp 1–31, 27–28.

5 Borkowski, Andrew, *Textbook on Roman Law* (London: Blackstone Press, 1994), pp 336–345.

6 Schulz, Fritz, *Classical Roman Law* (Oxford: Clarendon Press, 1951), pp 465–633.

7 Tellegen-Couperus, Alga, *A Short History of Roman Law*, rev edn (London: Routledge, 1993), p 5.

8 Tellegen-Couperus, p 9.

earlier Greek law, consisted of a series of norms handed down from generation to generation orally.[1] The application of this oral law was characterised by strict formulations of words, and specific required acts. The administration of this law, even in its civil applications, was overseen by a group of civic priests called *Pontifices* (pontiffs).[2] Only fragments of these early laws have come down to us and those fragments have no bearing on the subject of this essay.[3]

Knowledge of early Roman law improves from the time when the Romans began writing their laws down, about 462 BC. The Romans looked to Athens and other Greek cities for guidance and commissioned a group of citizens to record laws for Rome in about 451 BC. These were issued in the form of the Twelve Tables published in 449 BC.[4]

From the point of view of derivative contracts, the key development that led to their use in Roman law was Rome's evolution of a law of obligations. In Roman law:

'the law of obligations is concerned with situations where a person has incurred a personal liability for which he is answerable at law.'[5]

An obligation consisted of:

(1) A duty on the person incurring the obligation; and
(2) A right of the other party to enforce that duty at law, which could result in an award of damages.

Under Roman law, the person to whom the duty was owed thus possessed an asset or *res incorporalis*.[6]

Early history of Roman law and derivatives

The way that these future obligations were allowed to arise, so that they became agreements in the nature of modern derivatives, was a long process under Roman law. At first, Roman law, like Greek and Germanic law, was a law of rural communities based on the family unit with its principal concerns being family relationships, inheritance and the possession of land.[7]

The Twelve Tables divided the transfer of property into two classifications. The first was transfer of *res mancipi*, which meant things that could be transferred only in a formal ceremony in the presence of five witnesses. *Res mancipi* included Roman land, rights for the use of land, slaves, beasts of burden and cattle. The second was transfer of any other property, known as *res nec mancipi*, which was effected by simple delivery.[8]

---

1 Tellegen-Couperus, p 17.
2 Tellegen-Couperus, p 18. Zimmerman, Reinhard, *The Law of Obligations* (Oxford: Oxford University Press, 1996), p 83.
3 Tellergen-Couperus, p 19.
4 Tellegen-Couperus, pp 19–20.
5 Borkowski, p 241.
6 Borkowski, p 242.
7 Zimmerman, pp 1–2.
8 Promulgated in 451 and 450 BC, Crawford, MH (ed), *Roman Statutes* (III), vol 2 (London: Institute of Classical Studies, 1996), p 556.

At the time of the Twelve Tables, there was also a verbal form of agreement for the future delivery of commodities, which was called the *stipulatio*. This agreement was effected by a simple formula consisting of the question, 'Do you agree?' (*Dari spondes*), and a response, 'I agree' (*Spondeo*).[1]

As Roman commercial life developed, evolution of the laws of property transfer was needed. In about 367 BC, a body of magistrates, called *praetores urbani*, was established to administer justice in the city of Rome. Included within that magistrate's jurisdiction were disputes between Roman merchants. About 243 BC, another magistracy, the *praetores peregrini*, was created with jurisdiction over disputes where a foreigner was a party. After establishment of these 'praetors', private commercial law developed from the praetors' interpretations of legal principles and from their publication of the Edict,[2] which set forth additional legal principles on which their decisions would be based. In their cases, the *praetores peregrini* began to develop and apply a kind of international law called the *jus gentium*. The *jus gentium* was distinguished from the older civil law applicable to Roman citizens, the *jus civile*, in that it incorporated principles (sometimes borrowed from foreign law or customs) which the praetors considered to be universally recognised to be just.[3] This body of law had an important influence on the development of the law of contract.[4]

Roman law of sales and derivatives

By about 200 BC, a law of sale contracts had developed. The three essential elements required for validity of a sales contract (*emptio venditio*) were the agreement of the parties (however expressed), price, and a thing to be sold. There were no particular requirements of form.[5] The price was required to be fixed and stated in money. The object of the sale had to be some thing available for sale in commerce (*in commercio*). No valid sale contract could be made for a free man or public property, or for anything that it was not possible for the seller to posses (i.e. the moon, a hydra, a slave who died five years ago).[6] However, a contract for the sale of things which could come into the seller's possession in the future (*res futurae*) was valid. Contracts could be made for the future delivery of commodities such as unharvested wool, grapes, grain or olives.[7]

1   Borkowski, pp 277–283. Pugsley, David, *The Roman Law of Property and Obligations* (Cape Town: Juta & Co, 1972), p 65. It should be noted here that Pugsley makes a strong case that in early Roman law, *stipulatio* did not exist as a separate kind of binding transaction. His argument is essentially that if that were the case, *stipulatio* would have nullified the formal requirements on which the law of the early republican period is based. Consequently, he concludes that *stipulatio* must have been confined to certain kinds of *res mancipi* transactions discussed above. On the other hand, Borkowski thinks *stipulatio* may have pre-dated the Twelve Tables: Borkowski, p 277.

2   The Edict was amended from time to time. Hadrian ordered it to be unalterable in AD 130 with the publication of a restatement by the jurist Silvius Julianus entitled the *Edictum Perpetuum*.

3   Kunkel, Wolfgang, *Roman Legal and Constitutional History*, 2nd edn (Oxford: Clarendon Press, 1973), pp 75–77.

4   Tigar, Michael E and Levy, Madeline, *Law and the Rise of Capitalism* (New York: Monthly Review Press, 1977), pp 11–19.

5   Watson, Alan, *Roman Private Law around 200 BC* (Edinburgh: Edinburgh University Press, 1971), p 130. See also, Watson, Alan, *Legal Origins and Legal Change* (London: Hambledon Press, 1991), p 148; and Watson, Alan, *The Law of Obligations in the Later Roman Republic* (Oxford: Clarendon Press, 1965), pp 41–99.

6   Watson, *Legal Origins*, p 130.

7   Watson, *Legal Origins*, p 131, citing Cato, *On Agriculture*, pp 146–150.

A key contribution of Roman law to the development of derivative contracts was the recognition of 'consensual' contracts (*nudo consensu*). These could be entered into without the formal requirements of earlier Roman law. Nothing more than consent was required. No executed document or deed, no list of witnesses, no formal acts, no specific words and no delivery of any commodity or its price was required. A pure sale of promises entered into by agreement of the parties was all that was needed.[1] This represents a Roman liberalisation of derivative contracts beyond the formalities of Middle Eastern commerce, and, indeed even beyond the liberality of modern derivative commerce in the UK and the US, where the doctrine of 'consideration' might prove a bar to such a consensual agreement. A description of these consensual contracts is found in Sections 135 to 138 of the third book of *The Institutes of Gaius*.[2]

Gaius himself wrote in the middle of the 2nd century about 'deeds', but this type of contract is thought to have been recognised under Roman law in the second century BC because of the demands of international trade on Roman commerce which brought Roman law into contact with customs, procedures and forms of other cultures such as those of Egypt, Syria and the Middle East.[3]

Roman speculation and chance
By the 2nd century AD, the distinctions between the *jus civile* and the *jus gentium* were blurred. The *praetores urbane* were combined with the *praetores peregrini* when Roman citizenship was extended to the citizens of subject states (the *peregrini*) in 212. In the 2nd century AD, Sextus Pomponius wrote a 36 book commentary of the *jus civile* entitled *Ad Sabinum*.[4] In *Sabinus, book 9*, he identified and distinguished between two kinds of valid contracts for future delivery. The first type, *vendito re speratae*, included contracts which promised the future delivery of items such as future crops. The second, *vendito spei*, was, essentially, a sale of whatever proceeds a speculative venture returned. The important legal distinction between them was the first kind was void if the goods failed to materialise (no crop), but the second was valid without regard to whether the venture yielded any proceeds.[5] Pomponius wrote:

> 'There can be no sale without a thing to be sold. Nevertheless, future produce and offspring are validly purchased so that when the offspring is born, the sale is regarded as having been complete from the time of agreement. But if the vendor takes steps to prevent the birth or the growing of produce, he will be liable to the action on purchase.

---

1 Schulz, pp 524–526.

2 *The Institutes of Gaius*, Gordon, WM and Robinson, OF (eds) (London: Duckworth, 1968) pp 341–343.

3 *The Institutes of Gaius: Part II, Commentary*, De Zulueta, Francis (ed) (Oxford: Clarendon Press, 1985), pp 146–148. Sohm, Rudolph, *The Institutes*, 3rd edn (Oxford: Clarendon Press, 1907), pp 396–403. Macleod, Henry Dunning, *The Theory of Credit*, 2nd edn, vol 1 (London: Longman, 1893), pp 233–237, 276–289.

4 The title is a reference to the leading school of Roman jurists at the time, the Sabinians, who took their name from one of their early leaders Massurius Sabinus who lived during the first century. He wrote a highly regarded treatise on the *jus civile* and, consequently, many subsequent treatises on the same subject were, like Pomponius's, entitled *Ad Sabinum*. Tellegen-Couperus, pp 103–104. Borkowski, p 44. *Oxford Classical Dictionary*, p 859.

5 Buckland, WW, *A Text-Book of Roman Law From Augustus to Justinian*, 3rd edn, revised by Peter Stein (Cambridge: Cambridge University Press, 1963), p 483.

'. . . Sometimes, indeed, there is held to be a sale even without a thing, as where what is bought is as it were, a chance. This is the case with the purchase of a catch of birds or fish or of *largesse* showered down. The contract is valid even if nothing results, because it is a purchase of an expectancy and, in the case of *largesse*, if there is eviction from what is caught, no purchase proceedings will lie, because the parties are deemed to have contracted on that basis.'[1]

The second section, above, deals with the sale of chance as in, 'I sell all the fish from the next cast of my net' or, 'I sell all the money I can gather the next time some wealthy person throws silver to the mob'.[2] This section emphasises the point that the key ingredient of a valid contract was agreement of the parties. If parties wished to contract for the outcome of a gamble, that was fine, as long as they agreed to do so. The law would not judge the wisdom of the contract, it would simply enforce the intentions of the parties. This example makes it clear that speculation was a legally permissible pursuit from the point of view of contract law. Some historical Roman writers considered speculation unhelpful to the smooth functioning of the economy. Cicero condemned those Greeks and Romans who withheld grain from the market to speculate in the rise of grain prices that followed a crop failure in Sicily.[3] However, contracts based on speculative ventures were enforceable. In Rome, commodity futures contracts were enforceable, even if speculative.

Assignment of contracts

Evidence of any active secondary market in futures contracts in Rome is difficult to find. This may be due to a lack of commercial imagination, but it appears to be at least partly the result of slow development of the legal recognition of the right to assign commercial contractual rights and obligations.[4]

In early Roman law, an assignment of contractual rights and obligations was not enforceable. This was because a commercial contract was considered to bind the parties only (privity of contract). A third party could obtain no rights nor incur any obligations under it. Eventually, this changed, but the process had to go through several stages and may not have been complete before the Fall of Rome in AD 476.[5]

The first method of avoiding the problems entailed by the strict enforcement of privity of contract was by making a new contract (*novation*). Contracts of novation were recognised under Roman law and were not considered to be exceptions to the principle of privity of contract. A novation called for a new contract between one of the original parties and a third party, and for consent of all parties whose rights or duties were affected. For example, if a novation

1   *The Digest of Justinian*, vol 1, Mommsen, Theodor and Krueger, Paul (Latin text eds), Watson, Alan (English trans ed) (Philadelphia: University of Pennsylvania Press, 1985), pp 514–515.
2   This is what is meant by 'largesse' which is the accepted translation of the word *missilia* in the Latin original. Mackintosh, James, *The Roman Law of Sale* (Edinburgh: T & T Clark, 1892), p 25, n L 8.
3   Broughton, pp 554 and 550.
4   Watson, *Law in the Later Roman Republic*, pp 208–219.
5   Schulz, pp 626–629.

was intended to change the creditor of a previously contracted debt, the original creditor (A), after obtaining the consent of the original debtor (B), would make a contract with the new creditor (C) which transferred A's right to payment to C, and extinguished B's duties to A.[1]

However, as stated, a novation was not considered an exception to privity of contract. An exception did take place, in substance, by change of legal procedure allowed by the praetors. Substitution of parties to lawsuits was allowed. For example, if A transferred his right to a debt to C, and C had to bring an action to collect, C was permitted to bring the action in the name of A under a *mandatum* (mandate),[2] appointing C to bring the action in the name of A. The praetor would issue judgment according to the *formula Rutiliana*: 'If B owes A, condemn B to pay C.'[3] This device did not require the consent of the debtor. As a practical matter, this made it possible to transfer rights under contracts for the future delivery of commodities, because transfers would be enforced by the praetors.

However, this mandate had limitations due to the fact that the law still technically recognised A as the obligor. The mandate was revocable by A any time before the joinder of issue (*litis contestatio*), and the mandate ended with the death of either A or C. Also, at any time prior to joinder, B could legally extinguish his debt by agreement with A.[4]

The next stage in recognising the assignment of rights, without employing the fiction that the former obligor still had an interest in enforcing the contract, began to be reorganised under the Emperor Antoninus Pius.[5] Thereafter, the law was eventually changed so that assigned rights were enforced in the name of C (*actio utilis*) and could not be effected by A's revocation or the death of either A or C. The law was also modified to bar B from obtaining release once A or C had given B notice of the assignment.

It is generally agreed that, by the time Roman law was collected and organised in the *Corpus Juris Civilis* ordered by the Byzantine Emperor Justinian,[6] Rome had fully evolved a law of assignment.[7]

Derivatives in the late Roman Empire

The 'classical age' of the evolution of Roman law was between AD 100 and 250. By the time of the reign of the Emperor Constantine (306 to 337), both Roman law and Roman government were losing their flexibility. The development of law was becoming a process of collecting the codes and opinions of past writers rather than evolving new legal principles.[8] The culmination of this process was

---

1 Nicholas, Barry, *An Introduction to Roman Law* (Oxford: Clarendon Press, 1962), pp 199–201.
2 Also referred to as *procuratio 'in rem suam'* (for its own benefit). Nicholas, p 201.
3 Named after the Praetor Rutilius. Nicholas, p 200, n 2.
4 Nicholas, p 201.
5 The adopted son of Hadrian, he ruled from AD 138 until 161.
6 Emperor from 527 until 565. Borkowski, pp 50–57.
7 Nicholas, p 201. Buckland, WW, *A Manual of Roman Private Law*, 2nd edn (Cambridge: Cambridge University Press, 1953), pp 300–301. Zimmermann, pp 58–67.
8 Tellegen-Couperus, pp 134–136.

the promulgation of the Codex Theodosianus by the Emperor Theodosius II in 438. In 395, Theodosius I, the last Emperor of a unified Roman Empire died and, in 476, the last Roman Emperor, Romulus Agustulus was deposed. This is the date often given as the end of the Roman Empire.

The Code of Theodosius remained in effect in the West until the end of the Roman Empire, and, after 476, it continued to be followed in many parts of the former Empire and to be incorporated, at least in part, in codes of laws promulgated by the barbarian tribal kings that came to power in parts of the former Empire in Western Europe. In the Byzantine Empire, the Code of Theodosius was replaced by the 6th century Code of Justinian which was also a collection and restatement of ancient Roman law.[1] As is discussed below, these codes have had an important influence on the mercantile law which has regulated commodity futures trading since that time in Europe, the UK and the US.

One other legal development, commencing under the Roman Empire, which has been an important and continuing influence on the regulation of commodity futures trading was the development of the legal jurisdiction of the Roman Catholic Church. Beginning in the 3rd century, Christians submitted disputes to bishops for resolution. This prompted a development of a theologically influenced legal framework to serve as a basis for ruling on such questions. The first efforts to develop this framework were in the writings of Tertullian[2] and Cyprian[3] in the 3rd century. After 398, the Emperor gave bishops the legal jurisdiction over any civil cases where the parties consented to jurisdiction. The first organised body of canon law, the eight books of the *Constitutiones Apostolorum,* were written about 400. Subsequently, bishops were given general jurisdiction over the administration of justice within their dioceses. Canon law continued to develop after the Fall of Rome. With the growth of the Church's influence in Europe, it became an increasingly important determinant of commercial relations in those areas where it was conceded that the Church was entitled to exercise authority. Canon law was, during the Middle Ages, one of the principal regulators of commodity futures trading.

Roman derivatives trading policy

In the context of derivatives trading, Roman law seems more hospitable than Roman commerce to the use of derivatives. Legal regulation of commodity futures trading contracts, although such contracts existed in Roman commerce, do not seem to have played an important part in extending Roman control over natural resources. The principal tools of Roman commodity policy were the

---

1 Borkowski, pp 50–57.

2 He is thought to be the same person as the 2nd century Roman jurist Terullianus, author of a number of books of legal commentary. The son of a centurion, he converted to Christianity in 197 and wrote a number of theological works, part of the legacy of which (in addition to early canon law) are such vivid religious slogans as: 'The blood of the martyrs is the seed of the church' and 'It is certain because it is impossible'. Often at odds with orthodox Church teaching, he left the Church in 213 and, late in life, founded a sect known as Tertullianists. *Oxford Classical Dictionary* (III), 2nd edn (Oxford: Clarendon Press, 1970), pp 1046–1047.

3 A follower of Tertullian and bishop of Carthage (c 248). Martyred in 258, he was made a saint. *Oxford Classical Dictionary* (III), pp 305–306.

army and state control. In order to obtain the commodities needed, Rome conquered the area where they were produced (ie the grain of Sicily, Africa, Egypt; the wine of Italy and Spain, etc) and compelled regular shipment of large quantities of those commodities to Rome as tribute. Other commodities, those too distant or otherwise not appropriate for the use of military force (ie those from China, India and Arabia) were often purchased with state money.

However, contracts for the future delivery of commodities were permitted. In about 160 BC, Cato the Censor describes the terms of contracts for the sale of lambs to be born in the future.[1] By the 2nd century, Pomponius was writing of contracts for future commodities as being commonly accepted.

The principal policy that furthered Rome's control over natural resources seemed to be the facilitation of trade under Roman jurisdiction. As discussed above, the economy of the Roman government had two important needs to fill: commodities to feed, clothe, and house the population of Rome, and cash to run the Empire. Permitting the enforcement of contracts for future commodities of all kinds expanded the range of Roman commerce in ways that promoted both goals.

The ability to enter into futures contracts assisted merchants trading under Roman jurisdiction to gain a degree of commercial control over not only presently existing commodities, but commodities to be produced in the future. This gave them some assurance of continued prosperity in that it allowed traders to assure themselves of a supply of future goods, and allowed producers of commodities to realise a present cash value for commodities not yet ready for delivery. Legal encouragement of commodity futures contracts would have led to an increase in the total value of all commodity trades under Roman jurisdiction because not only present, but future commodities could be bought and sold. In terms of increasing the commodity supply to Rome, futures contracts would have certainly directed a certain quantity of future commodities toward the capital. However, this benefit was diluted in importance by the fact that many future commodities were already directed to Rome as tribute. The other benefit from future trade is that it would have put in commerce money in payment for future goods which increased Rome's tax base.

This provided a significant financial advantage over the regulatory policy of the Greek city states. In Greek law, the enforcement of contracts for future delivery was severely restricted. Consequently, commerce in such contracts would have made no significant contribution to the commercial income of Greek merchants or to the tax base of Greek cities. In Rome, the situation was different. Almost any sort of futures contract was enforceable and, consequently, a vehicle for adding income to the Roman economy and the tax base of Rome. Considering the scale of the Roman economy, it is hard to overstate the importance of allowing business in futures contracts to be conducted. Trade may not have been the calling which Roman writers considered the most admirable, but the obvious policy of Roman law was to facilitate its profitable conduct in virtually any form

---

1 Cato, *On Agriculture*, pp 135–136.

the traders found agreeable. Futures contracts increased Rome's wealth and Roman law acknowledged the benefits.

Roman legal disabilities

In general, the status of women was severely restricted under Roman law. Roman wives are said to have achieved a degree of emancipation that was the envy of married women under 19th century English law, but the commercial position of women was far inferior to that of ancient Mesopotamia. Under Roman law, even a mature woman was required to have a guardian. She was not entitled to act on behalf of others, for example, as a guardian. She was unable to own property and, generally, unable to make contracts.[1]

Slaves suffered from similar disabilities, in contrast to their position in ancient Mesopotamia. Although slaves in Roman society often held positions of trust and responsibility, they were not legally entitled to own property and, consequently, were not allowed the opportunity to gain control over their own destinies through commercial enterprise, as were the slaves of ancient Mesopotamia.[2]

CONCLUSIONS ON DERIVATIVES IN THE CLASSICAL AGE

The classical age of Greece and Rome, although often regarded as a beacon of enlightenment in Western Europe, represented something of a dark age in the history of commerce. If one regards the commercial success of a society as a function of the degree of its utilisation of the total human intellectual resources of the society, then the application of those resources was severely restricted in Greece and Rome. The principal channels of achievement and success were war and agriculture. The acquisition of goods by other means, principally those of successful trade through the diligent application of intellectual skill, was seen as an inferior profession and discouraged. As a corollary to this attitude, women and slaves, who held an inferior position in war and agriculture, were seen as inferior contributors to the prosperity of the nation. As a result, Greece and Rome made lesser efforts to draw upon their abilities than did the striving, trade-orientated city states of ancient Mesopotamia. As a result, it is fair to say that they hamstrung their own progress toward prosperity. Restricting achievement to those that possess a certain status diminishes the range and number of talents which are directed towards giving their best abilities to a society. This cannot but reduce the probability of any society's success. Despite the achievements in Greece and Rome, they undoubtedly could have done better if they had made the effort to utilise the best talents of a wider range of people in promoting their trade and commerce.

These limitations had an effect on the use of derivatives. Derivatives are an effective commercial tool for:

(1) securing future commodity supplies;
(2) financing future commodity production;

---

1 Borkowski, pp 94–95.
2 Borkowski, p 80.

(3) attracting trade; and

(4) serving as things to sell.

However, ancient Greece greatly restricted their legality and use, as well as restricting the classes of people who could enter into commerce. Hellenistic records show the model was there for them, but the Greeks failed to maximise its benefits.

The Romans also failed to maximise the benefits of derivatives, but less so as time progressed; they liberalised their law to the point where it is fair to say that they laid the legal foundations of modern derivatives trading. Indeed, Pomponius's writings indicate that their liberality in allowing freedom of derivative contracts may exceed that of the US and the UK today.

Chapter 5

THROWING CAUTION TO THE WIND — COMPANY FRAUD INVESTIGATION AND PACE 1984

Helen Parry[1]

'It is a regretful feature of commercial and corporate fraud in these modern times that the facilities are available for sophisticated fraudsters to prevent the trail leading to the unravelling of the fraud from being followed up. The secrecy provisions of some countries' corporate and banking laws operate to this effect. Nominee shareholdings in offshore companies do as well. There is often no alternative if frauds and dishonest stratagems are to be laid bare but to demand answers from those who are in a position to give them. This, in my opinion, is at least part of the statutory policy behind Pt XIV of the Companies Act 1985.'

Scott J in *Re London United Investments plc*[2]

INTRODUCTION

This policy of providing special powers abrogating the right to silence to particular agencies charged with investigating fraud sprang from the difficulties characterised so succinctly by Scott J above. The Police and Criminal Evidence Act 1984 (PACE), on the other hand, was born out of a determination to prevent miscarriages of justice, such as confessions in police custody prompted by violence or threats of violence on the part of police officers. These objectives are, in some respects, implacably irreconcilable. PACE, and the Codes of Practice promulgated under PACE, are predicated on the existence of a right to silence. Despite this, the various special inquisitorial investigative regimes found in the Companies Act 1985, the Insolvency Act 1986, the Financial Services Act 1986, the Banking Act 1987 and the Insurance Companies Act 1982,[3] omit to state expressly that the common law privilege against self-incrimination including, *inter alia*, the right to silence, has been abrogated. Neither do they deal expressly with the possible conflict with PACE. As a result, there is a potential conflict not only between statute and common law but also between statutes.

If Parliament had been prepared to confront these problems directly when agreeing all this legislation, then it is possible that a great deal of time and money (including taxpayers' money through the legal aid scheme) may have

---

1 Senior Lecturer in Law, London Guildhall University.
2 [1992] BCLC 91.
3 Companies Act 1985, ss 431–437 and 447; Insolvency Act 1986, s 236; Financial Services Act 1986, ss 94, 105, 177–178; Banking Act 1987, ss 41–44; Insurance Companies Act 1982, s 44.

been saved. These interpretative difficulties have proved a highly fertile ground for defence teams, fuelling a barrage of litigation instigated by defendants in high profile fraud cases. That this should have occurred is not surprising, given the extreme conjunction of draconian, inquisitorial powers and rich, articulate defendants who are used to being accorded respect and to wielding power and control in their lives.

In this essay, I propose to review the litigation addressing the particular conflict between such statutory powers and PACE, in particular PACE, s 67(9) and Code C.[1] Section 67(9) provides that:

> 'Persons (other than police officers) who are charged with the duty of investigating offences or charging offenders shall in the discharge of that duty have regard to any relevant provision of such a code.'

Codes are promulgated under PACE, s 66 and they deal with matters such as the administering of a caution.[2] The current form of the caution begins with the legendary 'You do not have to say anything', clearly presupposing the existence of a right to silence.

THE INTERPRETATION OF PACE, SECTION 67(9)

Apart from the general question of the overall relationship between PACE and the various special powers provisions, there are two questions which have been addressed by the courts. First, what is meant by 'charged with the duty of investigating offences'? Secondly, what is meant by 'shall have regard to'?

If it can be shown that an investigator is not so charged then the issue of 'having regard to' the codes need not be addressed. If an investigator is so charged, this may mean that such an investigator is bound to administer a caution, unless one takes the view that 'to have regard to' does not necessarily require compliance. This may be an appropriate interpretation if the caution provision is clearly in direct conflict with the special powers. Alternatively, one may simply decide that the two statutes are in direct conflict with each other and that the latter overrides the former.

THE GUINNESS AFFAIR — THE COMPANIES ACT 1985 AND PACE

Following a decision of Henry J in the first Guinness trial, the Court of Appeal decided that whether DTI inspectors appointed under s 432 of the Companies Act 1985 to investigate the Guinness affair were 'charged with investigating offences' was a question of fact, and that, as a matter of fact in that case, such inspectors were not so charged.[3] The Court of Appeal cited with approval Henry J's analysis of the issue:

1　Code of Practice for the Detention, Treatment and Questioning of Offenders (Code C) published by the Secretary of State pursuant to powers conferred by s 66 of PACE. Police and Criminal Evidence Act 1984 (Codes of Practice) No 2 Order 1990, SI 1990/2580. Paragraph 10, Cautions; para 16, Charging of a Detained Person.

2　Paragraph 10.

3　*R v Seelig and Another* [1991] 4 All ER 429.

'When one looks at the obligations on them under the Companies Act of 1985, their obligation is to investigate the affairs of the company and to report. In the course of such investigation, criminal offences will emerge but the fact that they do does not alter the duty of the inspectors. Their duty is to investigate the affairs of the company and to ascertain the facts; they are not conducting a trial. It is for others to investigate any criminal offences that may be uncovered by the inspectors. The inspectors may be required by the Secretary of State to provide under s 437(1) material that might point to the commission of a crime, but it is not for them to investigate whether that material constitutes an offence as such. Parliament, when setting out the duties of the inspectors in the 1985 Act, which was after the Police and Criminal Evidence Act 1984, in my judgement chose their words carefully, and therefore the codes do not apply.'[1]

The Court of Appeal agreed that whether a person was conducting an investigation under s 67(9) was a question of fact in each case and that Henry J could justifiably have reached such a conclusion.

The role of the DTI inspector

Since that decision was taken, the Court of Appeal, the European Commission on Human Rights and the European Court of Human Rights have considered various aspects of the Guinness investigation.

One of the grounds of appeal was based on the argument that the various agencies involved in the investigation, such the police, the DTI inspectors, the Serious Fraud Office (SFO) and the Crown Prosecution Service (CPS) colluded in order to order to keep the case with the DTI for as long as possible. The objective of so doing was to take maximum advantage of the fact that the DTI regime provides both for the abrogation of the right to silence and for evidence so obtained to be admissible in court. In replying to this argument, in the Court of Appeal action, the various agencies involved in investigating the affair disclosed correspondence, notes, minutes of meetings and internal memoranda including notes of conferences with prosecuting counsel. Lord Taylor, the Lord Chief Justice, referred to these disclosures, many of which he said would, normally, have been regarded as subject to legal professional privilege and possibly public interest immunity, as being 'wholly exceptional' and 'in most cases undesirable'.[2]

These disclosures revealed clearly that, from 1 January 1987, the DTI inspectors knew that there was 'the first concrete evidence of very substantial potential criminal transactions'.[3] Despite this fact, the police were not brought into the investigation until May 1987. Before this, the documents show that the inspectors were now 'much more optimistic about breaking Saunders completely' and, further, they noted that 'It is very important to pin these activities on Saunders'.[4]

---

1 *Ibid.* Watkins LJ, citing Henry J in *R v Saunders and Others*, the first Guinness trial, on 21 November 1989.

2 *R v Saunders*; *R v Parnes*; *R v Lyons*; *R v Ronson* [1996] 1 Cr App R 463.

3 *Ibid.*

4 *Ibid.*

When Saunders took his case to the European Court of Human Rights, Judge Repik, in his concurring judgment, commented that:

> 'By 12 January 1987, the Inspectors were in possession of concrete evidence that criminal offences had been committed. As early as 30 January 1987 the applicant was identified as one of the persons suspected of having committed those offences. At the conference on 25 January 1987 attended by members of the Crown Prosecution Service, it was noted that police inquiries were justified since a fraud had clearly been committed. However it was decided to delay commencing the inquiry because the police, unlike the inspectors, had little prospect of obtaining useful evidence from the potential defendants.'[1]

Kirk and Woodward addressed the point, with regard to the issue of PACE, s 67(9) and such DTI investigations, arguing that there may be circumstances where DTI inspectors could be considered to be investigating offences and where a caution would be required. Arguably, in the light of these later disclosures, the Guinness affair may have been such a case.[2]

The issue of the application of s 67(9) was however not specifically argued in the Court of Appeal in Saunders et al. The question, of relevance to this discussion, which was addressed, was whether the authorities had misused the inspectors as evidence gatherers because 'unlike the police they were not bound by PACE'. The Court of Appeal clearly was following the view taken by Henry J and the Court of Appeal in *R v Seelig*.[3]

THE *LONDON UNITED INVESTMENTS* CASE

The DTI comments revealed in Lord Justice Taylor's judgment, which referred to 'pinning' an offence on Ernest Saunders, echoed an accusation levelled at DTI inspectors in the case of *Re London United Investments plc*, when counsel for an individual accused of a $43m fraud, which had been the subject of a DTI investigation, submitted, with regard to DTI questions which his client had refused to answer, that:

> 'since a good deal about the missing $43 million was already known, the only purpose of the proposed question was to try and fix guilt on Mr Wilson.'[4]

Defence lawyers in this case, perhaps paying heed to the Seelig judgments, had challenged the DTI proceedings on different grounds. Seelig had co-operated with the DTI and answered their questions, seeking subsequently (unsuccessfully) to have these answers excluded as evidence under s 78 of PACE, on the grounds that it would be unfair given (*inter alia*) the absence of a caution'.[5]

---

1 Case of *Saunders v UK* (1997) 23 EHRR 1313.
2 Kirk, DN and Woodcock, AJJ, *Serious Fraud Investigation and Trial*, 1st edn (London: Butterworths, 1992), p 23. See also the evidence of John Wood, Director of the SFO, to the Trade and Industry Committee, House of Commons Session 1989–90 Third Report Question 557.
3 See n 3 on p 88 above.
4 See n 2 on p 87 above *per* Scott J at p 116.
5 'In any proceedings the court may refuse to allow evidence on which the prosecution propose to reply to be given if it appears to the court that, having regard to all the circumstances including the circumstances in which the evidence was obtained, the admission of the evidence would have such an adverse effect on the fairness of the proceedings that the court ought not to admit it' PACE, s 78(1).

However, Wilson, in *Re London,* refused to answer the DTI questions. When the DTI proposed to take enforcement action against him under s 436(3) of the Companies Act, for failing to co-operate in this way, he sought judicial review to challenge the validity of the appointment of the inspectors.[1]

Counsel for Wilson claimed that the appointments were *ultra vires* the power of the Secretary of State because it was not open to him to appoint inspectors to try and establish the guilt or innocence of an individual of a criminal offence related to a company. He predicated this line of argument on the *dictum* of Lord Denning MR in *Re Pergamon Press Ltd,*[2] when he commented that: 'inspectors are not a court of law . . . they decide nothing, they determine nothing . . . they only investigate and report'.

In response to this argument, counsel for the inspectors argued that, while it was true that they determined nothing and decided nothing, they were supposed to reach conclusions on the evidence they had heard and on the facts that they discovered, and that their report may well disclose facts and draw inferences which, if well founded, would establish guilt or innocence of criminal offences in other proceedings.

It was further proposed on behalf of Wilson that, in all the circumstances, the inspectors' questions were unfair and that, therefore, the court should exercise its discretion not to take action against him under s 436(3). This the court declined to do.

The contrasting of the inspectors' duty to investigate and report with a court of law in *Re Pergamon Press* is reminiscent of the dichotomy drawn by Henry J in *Seelig* where he, initially, characterised the duty of inspectors as being to 'investigate the affairs of a company and to ascertain the facts. They are not conducting a trial'.[3] This dichotomy between investigation and trial omits several possible stages of the process, such as those of investigating offences and of prosecution.

SAUNDERS V THE UNITED KINGDOM[4]

This distinction between DTI investigatory functions and the adjudicative process can also be found in the judgment of the European Court of Human Rights, in *Ernest Saunders v The United Kingdom,* although not with regard to the specific issues of PACE, s 67(9) cautions or the validity of the appointment of DTI inspectors. The ECHR case was focused on the fairness of the criminal trial

---

1 Under s 436, inspectors appointed to investigate the affairs of companies may certify to the Companies Court the refusal of a person to comply with a requirement imposed upon him. The court may then inquire into the case and, after hearing evidence, punish the offender. In practice, what often happens is that, when the court regards a refusal to co-operate as unjustified, the offender is given the opportunity to appear again before the inspectors, and comply with their requirements before it is decided he will be punished. A similar system operates for insider dealing investigations. See FSA 1986 s 178. Arlidge, A, Parry, J, Catt, I, *Arlidge and Parry on Fraud,* 2nd edn (London: Sweet & Maxwell, 1996), p 438.

2 *Re Pergamon Press Ltd* [1970] 3 All ER 535 at 539.

3 See n 1 on p 88 above.

4 See n 1 on p 90 above.

itself and considerable efforts were made by the Court to distinguish between the investigatory and adjudicative stages. The Court concluded that Article 6(1) of the European Convention on Human Rights was not applicable to the inspectors' investigative proceedings.[1] They further held that such investigations did not involve the determination of a criminal charge. It based its views concerning the Companies Act regime on the earlier ECHR decision, *Fayed v The United Kingdom,* where the Court held that the inspectors' function was 'essentially investigative in nature' and that 'their purpose was to ascertain and record facts which might subsequently be used as the basis for action by other competent authorities, prosecutory, regulatory, disciplinary or even legislative'.[2]

In his concurring opinion, Judge De Meyer, however, expressed serious reservations about this approach, commenting that:

> 'for prosecution purposes there is no real or practical difference between information so obtained (from DTI inspectors) and information obtained by the police or the judiciary in the course of a criminal proceeding *stricto sensu.* In the system of the Act concerned, each of these categories of information is part of the evidence to be considered in the determination of the criminal charge and thus the "administrative" or "preparatory" investigation performed by the Inspectors is part of the criminal procedure. The right to silence and the right not to incriminate oneself must apply to the preliminary investigation.'[3]

This approach contrasts sharply with that of the Lord Justice Taylor in the Court of Appeal in *Saunders et al* when he remarked on the very different regime of interviews of DTI inspectors compared with that of interviews by the police and the SFO. He describes the DTI inspections as 'investigatory: unlike the police and the SFO they are not prosecutors or potential prosecutors'.[4]

It may be argued that many of these arguments concerning the role and function of the DTI inspectors are artificial and, in some cases, hard to justify. In the *London United* and *Guinness* affairs, the DTI inspectors were at least very close to investigating offences. If it is considered desirable for them to investigate offences expressly then it may be preferable if the legislation could be amended in such a way as to allow them to do so without raising the possibilities of challenges, based on the absence of a caution, of the validity of the appointment of the inspectors.

PRIVATE INVESTIGATORS AND PACE

The High Court has adopted a more robust approach to the question of whether persons other than police officers are investigating offences, in the context of video piracy. In *Joy v Federation Against Copyright Theft Ltd*, Kennedy LJ, while applying the *Seelig* judgment, generally, to the effect that it was a question

---

1   'In the determination of . . . any criminal charge against him, everyone is entitled to a fair . . . hearing . . . by an independent and impartial tribunal', European Convention on Human Rights, para 6 (1).
2   Judgment of 21 September 1994, Series A no 294–B p 47.
3   See n 1 on p 90 above at p 30.
4   See n 2 on p 89 above.

of fact in each case, rejected arguments to the effect that PACE, s 67(9) only applied to those acting under a quasi-official or statutory power to prosecute. He decided that the court at first instance would probably have decided (if the right question had been asked) that a private investigator working for the Federation Against Copyright Theft (FACT) was a 'person (other than a police officer) charged to investigate offences', and therefore should have administered a caution. The investigator was so charged under the terms of his contract of employment. FACT also has developed the practice of proceeding in appropriate cases to instigate private prosecutions for offences involving video piracy.[1]

THE WALLACE DUNCAN SMITH AFFAIR — PACE AND THE BANKING ACT 1987

The *Joy* and *Seelig* judgments both figured in a preliminary skirmish in the notorious case of *Wallace Duncan Smith*, the merchant banker whose bank was wound up and who was convicted of offences involving fraudulent trading and deception in the wholesale money markets.[2] In the torrent of litigation which soon followed, one can see parallels with the *Guinness* affair.

Smith, Seelig and Saunders all gave evidence to regulatory authorities and then sought, subsequently, to have their answers excluded from their trials, under PACE, s 78.[3] Smith was seeking to exclude answers that he had provided during an interview with Mr Reeves, a member of the Supervision Division at the Bank of England. The relevant statute in this case, the Banking Act 1987, contains a specific provision, s 42, which deals explicitly with the investigation of offences: 'Where the Bank has reasonable grounds for suspecting that a person is guilty of contravening s 3 or s 35 above, the Bank . . . may by notice require that person or any other person to provide information, to produce documents and attend and answer questions'.[4]

However, Mr Reeves, in his evidence, stated that there was a specific department of the Bank dedicated to carrying out such investigations. He did not work for that department and was not carrying out a s 42 investigation when he interviewed Mr Smith. The court was satisfied that the duty imposed on Mr Reeves was to ensure that the criteria for authorisation under Schedule 3 of the Act were maintained.[5] This duty fell well short of a duty to investigate offences. It was found that if an offence came to his notice, he had to have regard to it, but in carrying out this function he was not investigating an offence.

The court did, however, admit that there was sometimes a 'fine line' between making preliminary inquiries about an offence, on the one hand, and actually

1 *Joy v Federation Against Copyright Theft Ltd* [1993] Crim LR 589, QBD.
2 For a discussion of the Wallace Duncan Smith affair, see 'Wallace Duncan Smith: Conman or Victim?' Parts I and II, Helen Parry *FT Fraud Report,* February and March 1997.
3 *R v Smith (Wallace)* [1994] 1 WLR 1399; *R v Saunders and Others* at n 1 on p 89 above; *R v Seelig* at n 3 on p 88 above.
4 The Banking Act 1987, s 42(1).
5 The Banking Act 1987, Sch 3, para 1(1).

investigating that offence, on the other.[1] The evidence from this interview was, in fact, excluded by the judge, exercising his discretion under PACE, s 78, but this was because of the fact that Mr Reeves had received a telephone call from a director of the bank in question. The caller had accused Wallace Duncan Smith of defrauding the bank. Mr Reeves failed to inform Smith of the phone call and that he was interviewing him, *inter alia,* to try to ascertain whether there was any truth in the accusation of fraud. Smith had instigated the meeting himself and had volunteered to come and talk to Reeves, concerning some losses involving alleged non existent certificates of deposit and the possible effect that this could have on the markets. He was not aware of the fact that he was under suspicion of fraud when he was answering Mr Reeves' questions.

Neill LJ held that, although s 67(9) did not apply to this situation, nevertheless regard should still be had to the principles of fairness in the Code of Practice. There had been elements of unfairness here and the evidence was excluded.[2]

MONEY LAUNDERING — *THE BANK OF ENGLAND V RILEY*[3]

Section 42 powers were subject to judicial scrutiny in a bizarre case concerning a small Midlands based charity devoted to helping women with legal problems. This charity somehow became the target of an unlikely cast of characters, involving the former Philippines President Ferdinand Marcos, and was accused of being used as a front for laundering hot money from around the globe.

However, in *The Bank of England v Riley*, the Court of Appeal was concerned principally with an analysis of the relationship between s 42 powers and the common law privilege against self incrimination. Riley, like Wilson in *Re London,* had refused to co-operate with the inquisitorial regime, although at a different stage from that of Wilson. She had been the subject of a s 42 investigation, but the questions that she refused to answer came from a court order requiring her to answer interrogatories designed to ascertain whether she had assets within or outside the jurisdiction. She, like Wilson, was also facing enforcement action against her for non-compliance.

The statutory basis for this action was s 42(4) of the Banking Act 1987, which provides that:

> 'any person who without reasonable excuse fails to comply with a requirement under this section shall be guilty of an offence and liable on summary conviction to imprisonment for a term not exceeding six months.'

Riley argued that the privilege against self incrimination was such a 'reasonable excuse'. The issue of cautions was not raised in this case, and so it provides no light on the question as to whether such a caution would have been required by those exercising s 42 powers, which was the implication of the judgment in *Smith*.[4]

---

1 *R v Smith* at n 3 on p 93 above *per* Neill LJ at p 1405.
2 *Ibid.*
3 *The Bank of England v Riley and Another* [1992] Ch 475.
4 See n 3 on p 93 above at p 1404.

However, Ralph Gibson LJ did make short shrift of the notion that the privilege against self-incrimination constitutes a 'reasonable excuse'. Such an interpretation would in his view 'emasculate' the objective of the provision, and he confined the notion of what would be a 'reasonable excuse' to physical and practical matters such as: 'physical inability to comply with a requirement for information arising from illness or accidental destruction of the relevant documents, and did not extend to the privilege of self incrimination'.[1]

Once again, as with the Companies Act, the statutory regime was held to have implicitly abrogated the privilege. The *Riley* case holds a peculiar interest for the author. I knew of the charity when it first started in Stoke-on-Trent, having been informed about it through an acquaintance, who had helped to form a small self-help group targeted at the mothers (and, in a few instances, fathers) of children who had been abducted overseas by non-UK partners. I did attend a few meetings of this group in the capacity of law lecturer at a local institution and so it was with no little amazement that I followed the subsequent extraordinary developments in the case, which came to resemble a plot from a Hollywood movie, acceptable to even the most jaded conspiracy buff, involving allegedly, in addition to the Marcos millions, the Stalker affair, freemasonry, and international organised crime.[2]

'REASONABLE EXCUSE' AND THE CRIMINAL JUSTICE ACT 1987

The notion of 'reasonable excuse' which figures in the Banking Act 1987 can also be found in another piece of legislation enacted in the same year. The Criminal Justice Act 1987 (CJA 1987) was the seminal piece of legislation which set up the SFO and the inquisitorial regime operated by that office. Reference to a 'reasonable excuse' for non co-operation can be found in s 2(13).[3] This section has been subjected to judicial scrutiny on several occasions in connection with both *Guinness* and *Smith*, and more recently in connection with the Maxwell pensions fraud affair.

In *R v The Director of the Serious Fraud Office, ex parte Saunders*,[4] the question of the effect of the section on the inquisitorial regime as it affects parties other than the defendant was raised. Additionally, and controversially, the question of how the regime should operate after a defendant had been charged was raised. The SFO was created during the Guinness affair, and the police did transfer the case to the new agency after Saunders had been charged with many criminal

---

1 *Ibid.*

2 'Hot Money Link in Stalker Report', Penrose, B and Connett, D (1986) *Sunday Times*, 17 August; 'Taxman Probes Town's Elite / Inland Revenue to Investigate Investors in 2 Million Pound Charity in Stoke on Trent', Dyer, C (1985) *Sunday Times*, 21 July.

3 For a full discussion of CJA 1987, s 2(13) see Arlidge, A, Parry, J, Catt, I, *Arlidge and Parry on Fraud*, 2nd edn (London: Sweet & Maxwell, 1996), p 438.

4 *R v The Director of the Serious Fraud Office, ex parte Saunders* [1988] Crim LR 837 (*ex parte Saunders*).

offences. The SFO, using its powers under s 2(3),[1] sought some documentation relating to the case, not from Saunders himself, but from the company. However, Guinness was engaged in a civil action against Saunders and was, at that time, subject to a court undertaking not to disclose such information. This was done to avoid the risk of prejudicing the impending criminal trial. Guinness sought to have the undertaking overturned so that it could comply with the SFO order. The case went to judicial review.

The court decided that, in contrast to the legislative regime in statutes, such as the Exchange Control Act 1947, whose structure provided for a separate regime to operate *after* a defendant had been charged, no such differentiation was apparent in the CJA 1987, and it was possible for documents to be disclosed post charge. Nevertheless, the existence of the court undertaking would provide a 'reasonable excuse', not non co-operation. The court went on to provide some further guidance on these issues. The remarks were technically *obiter*, because, as a matter of fact, at the time of the hearing the SFO notice had actually lapsed.

PACE, CAUTIONS AND THE CRIMINAL JUSTICE ACT 1987

The court further advised that a s 2(2)[2] notice could be sent to a defendant post charge, because the investigation did not cease on charge. However, given that the CJA 1987 was 'subject to PACE 1984', the notice should be accompanied by a caution and questioning should be restricted to that category of question allowed for, post charge, under para 16.5 of the Code of Practice.[3]

The DTI regime post charge

This limited victory for Ernest Saunders echoes an earlier small victory concerning the inspectors' right to question him post charge. In early January 1990, the High Court held a *voire dire* to consider an application by Saunders to exclude DTI transcripts of their eighth and ninth interviews with him, which took place after he had been charged. Henry J duly exercised his discretion under PACE, s 78 to so exclude those transcripts. He decided that it could not be

---

1 A written notice must be served on either 'the person under investigation' or on any other person to 'produce at such place as may be specified in the notice and either forthwith or at such time as may be so specified any specified documents which appear to the Director to relate to any matter relevant to the investigation, or any such documents of a specified description which appear to him so to relate' CJA 1987, s 2(3).

2 CJA 1987, s 2(2) provides that a written notice must be given to the person under investigation or to any other person 'whom he has reason to believe has relevant information that they must answer questions about the investigation either at a specified time and place or forthwith'.

3 'Questions relating to an offence may not be put to a person after he has been charged with that offence, or informed that he may be prosecuted for it, unless they are necessary for the purpose of preventing or minimising harm or loss to some other person or to the public or for clearing up an ambiguity in a previous answer or statement, or where it is in the interests of justice that the person should have put to him and have an opportunity to comment on information concerning the offence which has come to light since he was charged or informed that he might be prosecuted. Before any such questions are put he shall be cautioned in the terms of paragraph 10.4 above'. Code C para 16.5.

said to be fair to use material obtained by compulsory interrogation after the commencement of the accusatorial process.[1] Clearly, the DTI has greater powers than the SFO to use evidence in court. The SFO is restricted by the provisions of s 2(8) in its use of evidence obtained by means of the CJA 1987 regime, whether such evidence is obtained pre or post charge.[2]

Wallace Duncan Smith and post charge section 2 notices

The guidance given in *R v The Director of the Serious Fraud Office, ex parte Saunders* was later pressed into service on behalf of Wallace Duncan Smith. Smith ventured forth once more into the fray, seeking judicial review of a post charge CJA 1987, s 2(2) notice.[3] In this action, Nolan LJ felt unable to depart from the *ex parte Saunders* judgment that such a notice could be sent post charge, with a caution and subject to the Code, para 16.5 restriction.[4] He distinguished between the situation pre and post charge. Pre charge, a s 2(2) notice would *override* any caution previously administered by the police or other agency, but in the post charge situation he found:

> 'We regard it as almost unthinkable that Parliament should have authorised the Serious Fraud Office to continue the exercise of inquisitorial powers against the accused, not merely after he had been charged, but also throughout the trial.'[5]

PACE, the CJA 1987 and cautions

In her affidavit, the Director of the SFO acknowledged the difficulty caused by the conflict between PACE and the CJA 1987. The SFO has, clearly, been set up precisely to investigate offences and so the option of arguing, as in *Seelig* and *Smith,* that the investigation was not governed by PACE was certainly not available here. The question had to be confronted directly. How can one reconcile the apparently irreconcilable?

In her affidavit, the Director focused on the meaning of 'to have regard to', as follows:

> 'I and my designated members made every attempt to have regard to and where possible and appropriate to comply with the Code of Practice save where the provisions are in conflict with the requirements of the CJA.'[6]

So it appears from this judgment that the CJA 1987 is subject to PACE and, therefore, some regard must be had to the codes. Compliance is possible only when there is no conflict. The Director indicated that a form of caution was used by the SFO (although there was no requirement to do so). It begins thus:

1 Ruling of 29 January 1990, discussed in the ECHR judgment *Saunders v UK* at p 7.
2 CJA 1987, s 2(8) provides that s 2 answers may not be given in evidence in criminal proceedings except:
    (a) where proceedings are brought under s 2(14) for giving false information either deliberately or recklessly; or
    (b) where the individual makes a statement inconsistent with it. For a discussion of this inconsistency between CJA powers and others, see Kirk and Woodcock above at n 2 on p 90 at p 21
3 *R v Director of the Serious Fraud Office, ex parte Smith* [1992] 1 All ER 730 (*ex parte Smith*).
4 See n 3 on p 96 above.
5 *Ibid* at p 738.
6 *Ibid* at p 739.

'During this interview you will be asked to provide information to assist the SFO in an investigation into suspected serious or complex fraud. You are obliged by law to answer truthfully . . .'[1]

Nolan LJ agreed with the Director that this was appropriate as a means of reconciling the two statutes pre charge, but felt compelled to follow *Saunders* post charge, adding, however, a further refinement to the *Saunders* approach. Pondering the troublesome issue of how the special powers could be prefaced by a caution as decided in *Saunders*, he hit upon the notion of using 'reasonable excuse' in s 2 (13):

'The answer as it seems to us must be that the court regarded the enhanced right of silence which common law and statute law traditionally conferred upon a person once he has been charged as providing him, in the language of s 2(13) with a "reasonable excuse" for failing to comply with the requirement.'[2]

The *Riley* approach to the meaning of the phrase was not cited in this case, perhaps not surprisingly as it would not have proved helpful. There is more of an analogy to be found with the approach in *ex parte Saunders* to the issue in the context of third party refusal to provide documents as a result of being the subject of a court undertaking which was considered to be a 'reasonable excuse' for non compliance. In *ex parte Saunders* and in *ex parte Smith*, the excuse was predicated successfully on a legal as opposed to a physical impediment, the sole category allowed for specifically in *Riley*. In *Saunders*, the legal problem could be characterised in the form of a conflicting legal *duty* to fulfil an undertaking given to a judge in another court arising from a civil trial which pre dated the criminal trial. This undertaking was demanded in order to protect the defendant's right not to have his criminal trial unfairly prejudiced by an earlier civil action. Conversely, in *ex parte Smith*, the legal problem took the form of a conflicting *right* enjoyed by the defendant under both common law and PACE.[3]

After wrestling with these knotty problems, the court in *Smith* proposed the following form of words to be presented to a recipient of a post charge s 2 notice to the effect that 'he was not obliged to answer such questions, but if they were answered . . .'.

The statement then went on to outline the position regarding the admissibility of evidence in court under s 2(8).

Smith at the House of Lords

This was, however, a short-lived victory for Smith. A few months later, the decision in the Divisional Court was comprehensively reversed by the House of Lords in a highly controversial judgment.[4]

One 'striking feature' of this appeal was that counsel for the respondent, in the words of Lord Mustill, had not pressed with any vigour 'either of the grounds upon which the Divisional Court found in his favour'.[5]

---

1 *Ibid.*
2 *Ibid* at p 742.
3 *Ibid* at p 740.
4 *Smith v The Director of the Serious Fraud Office* [1992] 3 All ER 456 (*Smith*).
5 *Ibid* at p 469.

The House of Lords decided that if the Director was empowered to compel answers then the administering of a caution would be a self contradictory formality which Parliament could not possibly have intended. This decision could not diverge more widely from that of Nolan LJ, who would have found such a view 'almost unthinkable'.[1] He also read Parliament's intention very differently pointing out that the Code of Practice, promulgated in 1990, post dated the CJA 1987 and was duly approved by both Houses of Parliament with full knowledge of the CJA 1987, and that there was nothing in CJA which expressly removes the protection of PACE.

Lord Mustill continued to argue that:

> 'conversely if the Director had no power of compulsion after charge, then the issuing of yet another caution would make no difference. The words of the caution could only make sense if the Director could not compel an answer, in which case there would be no logic in treating the existence of a further caution as a reasonable excuse for not answering, for the words of the caution would make sense only if the Director could not compel an answer, in which case no excuse, reasonable or otherwise, would be necessary as compliance could not be required.'[2]

Smith, however, had moved his ground, simply claiming that the SFO had no right to interview post charge, with or without a caution. He further claimed that the statutory conflict with Code C and with a long established common law right to silence was so acute that the CJA 1987 regime should be considered to be subject to an implied exception in the case of persons who had been charged.

Lord Mustill, delivering the judgment of the House of Lords, rejected this proposition, arguing that the only interpretation conceivable which could produce that solution was to say that when a person was charged he ceased to be a person whose affairs were to be investigated and so there could no longer be any 'matters' relevant to the investigation.

Furthermore, there was an issue over whether the special powers are concerned with the 'affairs' of a subject, which, in Lord Mustill's view, must extend beyond the matters which caused the charge to be laid.[3]

Returning to matters which were addressed at the beginning of this essay, Lord Mustill went on to draw a comparison between a DTI investigation where the disclosure of evidence is a by product of 'an investigation directed to other ends' as opposed to the SFO's objectives which he characterised as being to 'extract material which will lead to a conviction'.[4]

---

1 See n 5 on p 97 above
2 See *Smith* at n 4 on p 98 above at p 470.
3 'Under ss 2 and 3 of the CJA 1987 the Director has the power to:
   (1) require the person whose affairs are to be investigated to answer questions and furnish information with respect to any matter relevant to the investigation;
   (2) require the person whose affairs are to be investigated (a) to produce documents appearing to relate to any matter relevant to the investigation, or account for their absence, and (b) to provide an explanation for any such document; and
   (3) require any other person to answer questions and furnish information with respect to any matter relevant to the investigation;
   (4) require any other person (a) to produce documents appearing to relate to any matter relevant to the investigation, or account for their absence, and (b) to provide an explanation for any such document.' Lord Mustill at p 471.
4 *Ibid* at p 472.

It is fascinating to note that, when Lord Mustill characterised the role of a DTI investigation, he did so in terms which create the widest possible gulf between investigation of the DTI's utterly vague 'other matters' and the very specific and final description of the SFO's objective as 'extracting material which will lead to a conviction'. Anyone reading these remarks in isolation from the literature would be given the impression that these modes of investigation are as different as it is possible for investigations to be. This is a picture which does not necessarily accord with the actual investigation into the Guinness affair, described so clearly by Lord Justice Taylor in the Court of Appeal[1] and in the judgment of the European Court of Human Rights in *Saunders v the UK*.[2]

Lord Mustill, in *Smith*, went on to address the issue of the origins of the PACE regime, indicating that the special restrictions on questioning post charge actually originated in a nineteenth century practice to abstain from questioning a defendant who had been taken into custody. This was not considered to have been a universal practice. He further posited that the true origins of the Code lay in the general rule excluding involuntary confessions. This he claimed meant that these post charge restrictions were not applicable to this situation, because the question of the admissibility of evidence was not an issue in the *Smith* case.

Again, one could contrast this with the earlier *Saunders* case, when DTI post charge evidence was excluded under PACE, s 78 precisely because the DTI, unlike the SFO, can use the evidence obtained under compulsory powers in court, a power which was an issue in the case. In this sense, one can see that there is some consistency between this *Smith* judgment at the House of Lords and Henry J's *voire dire* in the High Court, concerning the Saunders affair.

Finally, in *Smith*, the Lords applied the maxim *generalibus specialibus non derogant*, a maxim of interpretation meaning that general things do not derogate from special things, and that, therefore, the more general provisions of Code C yield to the particular provisions of the CJA 1987. This maxim is considered to be an exception to the general principle of implied repeal (*leges posteriorer priores contrarias abrogant*). The doctrine of implied repeal provides that when a later enactment does not expressly repeal an earlier enactment, but the provisions of the later enactment are contrary to those of the earlier, the latter, by implication, repeals the former. The exception arises, however, when the more specialist statute pre dates a later general provision. In this case, although the *primary* legislation, (PACE), pre-dated the CJA 1987, the *secondary* legislation, Code C post dated the CJA 1987.[3]

The maxim *generalibus specialibus non derogant* was applied in the later Court of Appeal judgment, *Re Arrows (No 4)*, when the Court found that provisions of the Insolvency Act 1986 which were in conflict with the CJA 1987 were overridden by the later statute.[4] This would seem, however, to be more accurately described as an application of the more general doctrine of implied repeal.

---

1 See n 2 on p 89 above.
2 See n 1 on p 90 above.
3 Craies, *Statute Law*, 7th edn (London: Sweet & Maxwell, 1971), p 366 and Cross, *Statutory Interpretation*, 2nd edn (London: Butterworths, 1987), p 204.
4 *Re Arrows (No 4)* [1993] BCLC 1247.

Lord Mustill, in *Smith,* pointed out reasonably that any fundamental criticism of the law must be directed at Parliament for creating it, and not at the courts for applying it.[1] One may have been forgiven for thinking that *Smith* had laid this particular matter to rest (at least as far as the English courts were concerned), but such a view would underestimate the ingenuity of defendants and their lawyers in high profile fraud cases.

THE MAXWELL AFFAIR AND THE CJA 1987 — A CHALLENGE TO THE HOUSE OF LORDS

In *R v Stipendiary Magistrate, ex parte The Director of the Serious Fraud Office,*[2] the Director moved for judicial review of a decision of the Metropolitan Stipendiary who had dismissed a charge brought under the CJA, s 2(13) against Larry Trachtenberg. In June 1992, Mr Trachtenberg had been charged with offences arising from the SFO investigation into the Maxwell affair. On 26 June, the Director of the SFO issued a s 2 notice. Mr Trachtenberg attended, but refused to answer any questions or furnish information, claiming that he had a 'reasonable excuse' under s 2(13). The Director then issued a summons alleging that he had failed to comply. Among the issues to be decided was whether the Stipendiary had been wrong in his interpretation of s 2.

Underlying Trachtenberg's argument was the proposition that *Smith* was wrongly decided, and that the issue could only be resolved in the House of Lords. The court decided that the magistrate was wrong, both in his decision and the reason he gave for the decision.

Trachtenberg had argued that Lord Mustill, in *Smith,* had not considered properly the meaning of 'reasonable excuse'. This issue had, however, already been addressed by the Court of Appeal in *Re Arrows (No 4).*[3] Mr Trachtenberg was a director of two Maxwell companies. Like Saunders and Smith, he had received a post charge s 2 notice. Mr Trachtenberg argued that he had a reasonable excuse not to comply because he had been charged with a criminal offence and had the right not to disclose his defence at least until after he had received the full prosecution case statement under CJA 1987, s 9.

Mr Trachtenberg further proposed that *Smith* had been decided *per incuriam,* without a proper analysis of the CJA 1987, which contained two stages — an investigation stage including s 2, and a prosecution stage, which takes over when the person has been charged. Alternatively, he argued that, on the basis of *Pepper v Hart,*[4] the intention of Parliament, as shown by the speech of the Minister in charge of the Bill in the House of Lords, was that the person being examined would be at most a 'suspect'. This, he argued, meant a person who had not been charged, or witnesses who were not under suspicion.[5]

---

1 See *Smith* at n 4 on p 98 above at p 475.
2 *R v Stipendiary Magistrate, ex parte Director of the Serious Fraud Office* (1994) *The Independent* 24 June, QBD.
3 *Re Arrows (No 4)* [1993] BCLC 1247.
4 [1993] AC 593.
5 Reference to the speech of the Earl of Caithness, *Ibid* at p 1249.

Steyn J, in *Re Arrows*, declined to accept this argument, holding that the Lords in *Smith* had not overlooked a fundamental distinction between investigative and accusatorial powers in the CJA 1987. The Act, clearly, allowed for both to be exercised at the same time. He further decided that there was no ambiguity, obscurity or absurdity warranting a resort to the *Pepper v Hart* doctrine.

It must be at least arguable, however, that an area of statutory interpretation that has produced such wildly different interpretations, particularly concerning the intention of Parliament, would be a prime candidate for a *Pepper v Hart* approach. With regard to the question of 'reasonable excuse', Steyn J revisited *Riley*.[1] In particular, in the context of a s 2(3) notice concerning documents, he held that Mr Trachtenberg's interpretation:

> 'emasculates the extensive inquisitorial powers entrusted to the Director by Parliament . . . In the context of s 2(13) reasonable excuse is plainly a defence intended to cover particular circumstances such as physical inability to comply with the notice or accidental loss or destruction of the transcript and the like. The fact that a charge has been laid does not create a defence under s 2(13).'

Rose LJ disposed of Mr Trachtenberg's point concerning CJA 1987, s 9. The section, which empowered a Crown Court judge to require case statements after the transfer, did not inhibit the Director's very wide investigative powers.

The High Court agreed with the Court of Appeal in *Re Arrows* that the magistrate had been wrong both in his decision and in the reason for his decision, but by the time this case had come to court the SFO was no longer seeking a remedy.

INSIDER DEALING, PACE AND 'REASONABLE EXCUSE'

Inspectors may be appointed under s 177 of the FSA 1986 to investigate suspected cases of insider dealing. Kirk and Woodcock suggest that, in contrast to the inspectors appointed under the Companies Act 1985, they are charged with the duty to investigate offences, and that, therefore, they are subject to PACE and should issue a caution before questioning suspects.[2] The FSA 1986 also includes a provision to allow for non-compliance which has arisen due to a 'reasonable excuse'. In *Re an Inquiry under the Company Securities (Insider Dealing) Act 1985*, both the Court of Appeal and the House of Lords held that if an interviewee (in this case a financial journalist who refused to reveal his sources concerning an insider dealing story) can point to a recognised head of privilege, such as in this case the statutory privilege contained in the Contempt of Court Act 1981, s 10, he would have a 'reasonable excuse'.[3]

A similar line was taken in *Re Arrows (No 4)* with regard to the question of whether public policy immunity, or other head of public policy justifying non-disclosure, such as national security, could amount to a 'reasonable excuse'.[4]

---

1 See n 3 on p 94 above.
2 They are required to 'establish whether or not a contravention' of the insider dealing law has occurred and to report the results of their investigation to the Secretary of State, FSA 1986, s 177(1). See also Kirk and Woodcock p 228.
3 [1988] AC 660.
4 See n 3 on p 101 above.

CONCLUSION

After examining this wealth of litigation on the conflicting provisions of PACE, Code C and statutes providing for inquisitorial regimes, I would like to take issue with at least part of Lord Mustill's judgment in *Smith*. While, characterising, uncontroversially, the legislative techniques used in drafting the various statutes containing inquisitorial regimes as 'unsystematic', and the area of law in general as 'contentious', he goes on to conclude that he does not believe that 'anything is to be gained by analysing the reported cases' (except the few cited in the judgment).[1] I would like to suggest, on the contrary, that an analysis of the case-law in this field is very useful, in that it does provide an insight into the difficulties that the courts have faced when confronted with the uncomfortable juxtaposition of unsystematic and contentious legislation and very litigious defendants, highly sensitive to the issue of their human rights. In the area of fraud investigations, the importance of producing legislation which is as clearly expressed as is possible is paramount.

Perhaps the legislature was shy of introducing bills to Parliament which confronted in clear and explicit language the fact that the right to silence was being removed. I note that in the early Guinness litigation, Seelig, who was being interviewed by the DTI inspectors not long after the Companies Act 1985 had come into force, stated that neither he nor his lawyers realised that the Act did, by implication, remove the right to silence, and provide for such potentially self incriminating material to be used as evidence against him in court.[2] This assertion was rejected by the Court.

If the statute had removed the right to silence expressly much of the subsequent litigation may have been avoided. In any event, the European Court of Human Rights has now made it difficult for evidence such as that of Saunders and Seelig to be used in court in future and so a partial reform of the law may soon be inevitable, at least with regard to admissibility.

Agencies such as the Securities and Investments Board (SIB) also operate inquisitorial regimes. When conducting investigations, for example under s 105 of the FSA 1986, the SIB needs to know if and when a caution needs to be administered. Currently, I understand the position to be that if they are using these powers to investigate a matter that may involve a criminal offence, such as theft or deception, they do, but otherwise they do not administer a caution.

Similarly, the DTI now operates a split system of investigation, administering cautions as the possible criminal offence becomes more apparent. On the basis

---

1 *DPP v Ellis* [1973] 2 All ER 540;
   Hammond v Commonwealth of Australia (1982) 152 CLR 188;
   Lam Chi- Ming v R [1991] 3 All ER 172;
   R v Brown, R v Bruce (1931) 23 Cr App R 56, CCA;
   R v Director of the Serious Fraud Office, ex parte Saunders (1988) 138 NLJ 243;
   Rees v Kratzmann (1965) 114 CLR 63 Aust, HC.

2 'According to Seelig, if he had appreciated all that, he would have risked contempt proceedings rather than provided answers which might incriminate him.' Watkins LJ in *R v Seelig* at n 3 on p 88 above.

of *Smith*, however, it could be argued that the inquisitorial regimes under specialist statutes, such as the Companies Act 1985 and the FSA 1986, override PACE and Code C.

I propose that Parliament should take action and legislate to clarify the situation so that all those who are charged with exercising special powers to investigate fraud have clear statutory guidance on the requirement to administer a caution.

Chapter 6

SOME BRIEF REFLECTIONS ON THE STATE OF COMPANY LAW

John Birds[1]

When writing in honour of a distinguished academic and co-author, it seems appropriate, given that Tony Boyle has contributed to the whole area of company law,[2] to offer some modest thoughts as to the state of the subject in general, with some specific reference to a topic which has been a special concern of his, namely the question of shareholder remedies especially for breach of company directors' duties. It must be acknowledged that many other people have, in recent years, made worthwhile contributions to the subject; in many cases from a broader perspective than, perhaps, this writer is qualified to adopt. This essay does not pretend to rank with such perspectives and aims to do no more than offer some broad-based reflections.[3] Further, apologies are offered to other authors, and, indeed, to more traditional company law scholars whose thoughts may have influenced the writer but to whose work express reference is not made.[4]

The timing of this contribution also seems apt for some general reflections. Britain has recently elected a new government after 18 years of Conservative rule during which time there have been many changes in company law. These changes have been influenced, in particular, by developments in Europe and, if there has been a domestic theme, it has to be that of deregulation and 'lifting the burden on business'. However, the nature of legislative reform has, for many years, been, generally, piecemeal. Despite the efforts of some commentators, there does not appear to have been much overall reflection, and it is the view of many that the general state of the companies legislation is, quite simply, shocking.[5] We have not had a body, such as the company law committees of past years, whose remit has been to look at the subject in the round.[6] A government which is

---

1 Professor of Law, University of Sheffield.
2 Especially in his general editorship of *Gore-Browne on Companies*. His other writings also range widely.
3 Many of the other contributors to this book offer much more rounded perspectives on the subject.
4 I would single out for particular mention Parkinson's *Corporate Power and Responsibility* (Oxford University Press, 1993), but all company lawyers owe a debt to Jim Gower for writing one of the most lucid legal textbooks ever: *Principles of Modern Company Law*, 5th edn (London: Sweet & Maxwell, 1992). Tom Hadden's *Company Law and Capitalism* was also a very stimulating book, the long-expected update of which is awaited with high expectations. The new text by Cheffins, *Company Law: Theory, Structure and Operation* (Oxford University Press, 1996) is also an excellent contribution.
5 Even if one does not agree with the details of all of Len Sealy's criticisms (especially in *Company Law and Commercial Reality*), his forceful critique of the general state of company law, at least as embodied in the legislation, is surely unanswerable.
6 Although *quaere* whether they always really did so.

clearly determined to bring a fresh look to at least some aspects of the law affecting business, for example as regards the regulation of financial services, may be persuaded that a similar job can be done with regard to company law.

The more constructive approach to the European Union, which the Labour Government has already espoused, may also offer some hope. British company law is now inevitably European in nature, while reflecting, at the same time, the traditions of a common law system based on notions of contract and equity. The programme for harmonisation must surely be concluded, and a major part of this ought to include agreed sensible rules on the basic way in which companies are governed and the mechanisms which the law adopts to ensure honest and capable governance.[1]

However, the question has to be asked whether or not such a review can be undertaken without taking a very basic look at the variety of forms of company which exist and the rules which do and should govern the operation of that variety of forms. Company law is a rich invention but it consists of a vast number of complex and, perhaps, unwieldy rules. What those rules should be is surely not just a matter of facilitating business. As Tony Boyle has said,[2] company law is part of the law of institutions and not simply a part of commercial law in the sense of the law of transactions in which businesses engage. To look at the rules of company law simply from a perspective of facilitating business may not be appropriate when we consider that the company forms an absolutely vital part in the lives of individual citizens, whether as investors, employees or customers. Before we rush into enacting another piece of legislation affecting companies, whether that be a major statute introducing a wide range of changes which may be desirable in themselves, or yet another statutory instrument making minor (in legal terms) but perhaps quite significant (in practice) changes to the operation of companies, perhaps we should take a more fundamental look at what the company, as a legal creature, does and whether or not its various forms should, perhaps, be regulated differently in some ways.

It would probably be futile to attempt to change the basic philosophy of the law which, for well over a century and a half, has made the registered company form available with relative ease and relatively little cost, and for at least 100 years has sanctioned its availability for the smallest of concerns.[3] The business and legal community is simply too accustomed to that state of affairs and can be expected to resist any attempt to restrict incorporation, even if that were desirable. It would also be an extraordinarily complex task to unravel many group arrangements if, for example, one were to restrict the registered company, in a strict sense, to bodies satisfying minimum requirements.[4] The registered company form is not used just for business and it is not suggested that the position should be otherwise. Indeed, there may be a case for yet more, simple, forms of registered company, whether to accommodate such as the professional

---

1 The valuable work, in this respect, of such as the Cadbury Committee and the Royal Society of Arts' *Tomorrow's Company Inquiry* (1996) is acknowledged, but their contributions do, perhaps, have their limitations, not least because of their 'self-regulatory' nature.

2 *Boyle & Birds' Company Law* 3rd edn (Jordans, 1995), p 31.

3 *Salomon v Salomon & Co Ltd* [1897] AC 22.

4 There is still, perhaps, a case for a more structured look at the realities of the group of companies.

partnership or the small unincorporated association, which survives by the application of various rules of the general law. The emphasis of this essay, though, is on the company as a form of business association. It assumes that the limited company form will survive and survive in large numbers.

Yet even here, as many other writers have pointed out,[1] there are at least three forms of business association all of which, in practice, have to, or may, adopt the registered company form, but which, in many respects, are as different as chalk and cheese. These are, first, the 'large' public company, at least some of whose shares are offered widely to the public and traded on some form of stock market; secondly, the business, which may be large in economic terms but without much, if any, public involvement in terms of share ownership; and thirdly, the small private company, running what is, of course, in reality an incorporated partnership or a one person business. Yet all the rules of 'company law' apply *prima facie* to all these different types. Of course, there are exceptions and qualifications; but much of the complexity of company law exists because it attempts at first to do one job, and then proceeds to do several, and has to legislate accordingly.[2]

To illustrate this theme and to support the argument that a more fundamental examination of the company than we have had for very many years, perhaps if ever, is desirable, it is proposed to examine briefly the rules relating to a few different areas of company law, and to examine their appropriateness in the context, in particular, of the two extremes of the different types of association mentioned above, namely the large public company and the small incorporated partnership. As already suggested, no one now could, in reality, propose scrapping a system which allows the registration of an association as a company with relative ease. However, one then has to ask — on what basis does the law recognise this association as a valid legal person? Whatever the type of company, the answer, of course, is that the law is giving a special status to what is still regarded fundamentally as a contract. The basic constitutional documents of any company, its memorandum and articles of association, are deemed to be a contract,[3] and their registration is the fundamental requirement for incorporation. This, of course, still reflects the historical origins of the company, based on notions such as deeds of settlement and partnerships. One cannot blame our ancestors for building on this by legislating that the registration of the appropriate documents was, fundamentally, all that was required, but it must be asked whether this is appropriate for all types of company today.

As regards the small private company, the answer may be that it remains a sensible starting point. After all, many companies are incorporated to take over an existing business run by one, or two, or a few people, or to commence such a

---

1 Notably, perhaps, Tom Hadden, *op cit*, n 2 on p 105.

2 This is not to deny that, of course, there are some real differences between public company law and private company law, especially since 1980 following implementation of EC Directives, particularly the Second and Fourth Directives. Some notable concessions have been granted to private companies (in capital maintenance rules and in terms of 'deregulation') and to 'small' and 'medium-sized' private companies (in terms of accounting and auditing requirements). However, the basic starting point is still that there is one registered company to which all the rules, *prima facie*, apply, and this certainly is the case in respect of fundamental questions of corporate structure and the control of management.

3 Companies Act 1985, s 14.

business, although the contract concept appears strange in respect of the company with but a single real member, sanctioned formally in British law in recent years,[1] yet a fact of business life (and legal sanction[2]) for much longer. However, even in respect of the incorporated quasi-partnership, the notion of contract often appears odd. The terms of much of that contract are, in practice, contained in statutory rules (Table A, etc — although, oddly, the current Table A was drafted with the public rather than the private company in mind), and may be much constrained by statutory provisions. This seems inevitable, to an extent. Assuming that some degree of protection from liability for the members of an incorporated small business must remain, as politically it could hardly be otherwise, statute must limit the freedom of the members to derogate from rules designed to protect those dealing with the business. However, it may not be necessary to do so by blanket rules such as those providing procedures for such a company to alter its capital structure in a way that does not impinge on any outsider. Is there really anything wrong in upholding a freely negotiated agreement, binding the company itself, by all the members of a company that there will not be any increase in the capital of that company? The law, currently, does not allow this,[3] but it is not easy to see the moral, rather than the legal, justification for such a prohibition, save that, as our law now stands, it may be necessary because there has to be one rule applicable to all shapes and sizes of company.[4] In addition, one may ask whether it is not an indictment of the rules of company law that shareholders' agreements have long been felt necessary to supplement the deficiencies in the statutory model.

The contract analogy breaks down in other ways, most notably, perhaps, in that body of the law which governs exactly what is the subject-matter of, and who are the parties to, and who can enforce, the statutory contract. Much creative writing has been devoted to attempting to reconcile cases which, in reality, are surely in part irreconcilable.[5] These concern both substantive and procedural questions. Are any, and if so what, 'outsider' rights contained in the memorandum and articles of association enforceable against the company? When does an individual member of the company have locus standi to enforce provisions of the articles whether they concern 'outsider' or 'membership' rights?[6] What should be the scope of any special dispute resolution mechanism for addressing problems in small incorporated companies? Surely, a fundamental problem in finding appropriate legal solutions to these questions lies in the fact that, as things are at present, it seems to be the case that an answer for the small incorporated company has to be applicable also to the largest public listed company. This does not, with respect, seem sensible. If the small company association really is a contract, why should its terms not be binding on all participants, irrespective of strict legal

---

1 The Companies (Single Member) Private Limited Companies Regulations 1992, SI 1992/1699, implementing the Twelfth EC Directive.
2 *Salomon v Salomon & Co Ltd*, n 3 on p 106.
3 *Russell v Northern Bank Development Corporation* [1992] 1 WLR 588.
4 If there is misuse, the likes of the Insolvency Act 1986, s 214 can be used to attribute proper responsibility.
5 For example, Wedderburn [1957] CLJ 194, Goldberg (1972) 35 MLR 362, Gregory (1981) 44 MLR 526, Drury [1986] CLJ 219.
6 A question which is surely as important as the substantive question: see *Boyle & Birds, op cit*, 3.18.

distinctions between their capacities,[1] save, of course, where there are standard grounds for interfering with freedom of contract.[2] One facet of this problem, namely the question of enforcement, is at the time of writing being considered by the Law Commission.[3] Of course, its provisional conclusions consider the question of the enforceability of 'contract' rights in a small company, but they do not raise one further question which perhaps they might — are any of the traditional forms of litigation, whether by way of personal, representative or derivative action, really necessary for the small private company? Might it not be more sensible to have a procedure (a revamped s 459 of the Companies Act 1985) under which all such disputes can be raised and settled, perhaps initially even outside the traditional confines of the Chancery Division? Further comment on these matters will be made below.

Whatever the issues regarding small private companies, surely it is time to break the contract link in respect of the large public company. Recent years have seen a growing body of commentary directed at the issue of what the company is,[4] which, in reality, is concerned with bodies which are far removed from small concerns. Of course, different political and economic perspectives may produce different answers to the question of what a company is, but it seems to be widely accepted now that 'tomorrow's company' has to be concerned with more than the traditional principal concerns of company law, namely the rights and obligations of the 'owners' of the company, the shareholders, as regards those entrusted with its governance.[5] As presently constituted, the law says that the relationship between shareholders and between shareholders and directors is governed primarily by contract. As a result of any lack of real recognition that interests other than those of shareholders are the ultimate test of validity of corporate decisions, the duties and responsibilities of company directors continue to be framed by a body of law derived from property law and equity; this naturally looks at ownership and trust. This may often be appropriate, whatever one's views about a wider body of 'constituents'; for example in terms of rules which penalise directors from abusing the trust placed in them, but many would argue that the governance of the large corporation must reflect the fact that, in many respects, the management of the large public company is a matter of genuine public concern. If we were to divorce the constitution of such companies from the traditional contract base, this might lead to more sensible solutions to problematic areas of company law. To consider this further, it seems appropriate to pick up on points made earlier and look in a little more detail at what, for many, is one of the most fascinating and intractable areas of company law, namely the question of shareholder remedies.

As we know, based on notions of Victorian democracy, company law dictates that, in respect of all types of company, the general meeting of shareholders is the ultimate arbiter, even if, by contract, the powers of that body can be restricted where legislation does not otherwise provide.[6] The general meeting

1 For example, *Beattie v E & F Beattie Ltd* [1938] Ch 708.
2 Misrepresentation, duress, undue influence, etc.
3 Consultation Paper No 142, 1996. See now Report No 246, 1997.
4 Notably, from a lawyer's perspective: see Parkinson, *op cit*, n 2 on p 105.
5 See, especially, the RSA Inquiry, n 1 on page 106.
6 Table A, reg 70.

receives the directors' annual report as to their stewardship and decides, in theory, whether or not to entrust that stewardship to them for a further period. Yet we also have long known that, in large companies, the general meeting is in almost every case more of a public relations exercise than a real decision-making body.[1] In small companies, it is possible to dispense with much of the formality altogether.[2] Resolutions may, nonetheless, be put to the general meeting and, of course, have to be so put in a wide range of areas. When voting on such resolutions, the law says, in general, that shareholders can vote in their own interests and are not bound by any fiduciary or quasi-fiduciary principles, because a share is an item of property and the traditional common law approach is that people can use their property as they think fit.[3] Sometimes, however, this approach breaks down. When voting for alterations of the articles, and perhaps on other resolutions, shareholders have to act in good faith for the benefit of the company,[4] although this principle is easier to state than to apply in cases when real bad faith cannot be shown.[5] However, in respect of small companies, disputes over such matters are hardly likely now to be litigated by reliance on any such general principle, but by way of allegations of unfairly prejudicial conduct under s 459 of the Companies Act 1985. In a large company with a widely-owned share capital, is that general principle of any real applicability? Directors' control of the proxy-voting machinery, shareholder apathy, etc. mean that legal challenges to shareholder resolutions are not likely to take place. Dissatisfied shareholders will simply sell their shares or the company may become vulnerable to a take over bid. The market for corporate control[6] is, clearly, often a more potent control mechanism than the threat of litigation. It is surely not without significance that virtually all, if not all, the decided cases involving challenges to alterations of the articles concern companies that, in effect, were incorporated partnerships, but the attempts to analyse and rationalise them tend to assume that the principles apply to companies of all types. No doubt this is legally correct, but is it appropriate in practice?

Indeed, it might be argued that the pressures and opportunities of the market place can deal effectively with shareholders in large companies who are unhappy with decisions taken by directors or majority shareholders and where traditional company law doctrines are often thought to be lacking. If such a shareholder does not agree with, for example, a special resolution to alter the articles or a resolution altering class rights, should the resolution itself be capable of challenge at all provided the shareholder can find a ready market for his shares at a fair price or there is a mechanism to compel the company to give him a fair price? *A fortiori*, perhaps, if the law recognises the company as more than simply the interests of its shareholders. As long as the investor receives a fair return and has the opportunity to move his investment to seek to secure that,

---

1 Although occasionally, of course, the large institutional investors will flex their muscles. See, generally, Farrar, *Company Law* (London: Butterworths, 1991), chapter 34.

2 Under the provisions introduced by and under the Companies Act 1989, ss 113–117.

3 *Pender v Lushington* (1877) 6 Ch D 70, *North-West Transportation Co Ltd v Beatty* (1887) 12 App Cas 589, *Northern Counties Securities Ltd v Jackson & Steeple Ltd* [1974] 1 WLR.

4 *Allen v Gold Reefs of West Africa Ltd* [1900] 1 Ch 656 and the subsequent line of cases culminating in *Greenhalgh v Arderne Cinemas Ltd* [1951] Ch 286.

5 See *Boyle & Birds, op cit*, 3.27 to 3.30.

6 See, especially, Bradley, 'Corporate Control: Markets or Rules' (1990) 53 MLR 170.

the question may be raised as to whether he retains the exclusive right to sanction decisions on altering the corporate constitution or its capital structure.

It is thought, though, that different considerations should apply when the dissatisfaction arises because of alleged wrongdoing by directors. If powers have been abused, if decisions go beyond legitimate risk-taking and become mismanagement, if directors make unjustified personal gains from their position, does not any rational and moral approach dictate that the law must provide effective mechanisms for these wrongs to be remedied so that responsibility falls properly on miscreant directors? It is surely not a satisfactory answer to leave this to the vagaries of government or other regulatory powers or to the market place.[1] Outside the powers which government already has,[2] but which it cannot realistically be expected to use except in fairly extreme cases, what can these mechanisms be?

It is, primarily, in this context that the Law Commission has reviewed shareholder remedies. Their very valuable and learned Consultation Paper[3] led to a formal Report in October 1997.[4] In brief, it seems fair to say that they have recommended a clarification of the circumstances in which a minority shareholder may bring a derivative action, hardly a fundamental change to the basic law. The traditional factors, such as ratifiability and wrongdoer control would still be considered, although the legal framework would be clearer and more accessible. As far as the primary statutory remedy for shareholders, namely s 459 of the Companies Act 1985, is concerned, they first thought that a new more streamlined statutory remedy should be created to deal with the most common allegations of unfairly prejudicial conduct, principally exclusions from management; that additional regulations should be inserted into the current Table A in order to provide shareholders in smaller companies with contractual methods of resolving disputes so that they do not have to go to court; and that there should be changes in the management of those disputes which do go to court, so as to reduce the length and cost of proceedings. In the final Report, the Commission has withdrawn from suggesting a wholly separate remedy for exclusions from management, preferring instead that s 459 contain presumptions of unfair prejudice in this context. They also, quite properly, lay great stress on case management in s 459 proceedings, mirroring the Woolf Report recommendations,[5] and on alternative dispute resolution, in an attempt to reduce the enormous length and cost of many such pieces of litigation.

The suggested changes in respect of s 459, which the Commission's survey showed is used overwhelmingly in small private companies, seem a valuable step forward. But one may, perhaps, question whether the whole thrust of their provisional conclusions, and especially those on the derivative action, are not

---

1 Cf *Prudential Assurance Co Ltd v Newman Industries Ltd* [1982] Ch 204.

2 Companies Act 1985, Part XIV.

3 See note 3 on p 109. For a much fuller and more reasoned critique of the Law Commission's Consultation Paper, see the learned chapter by David Sugarman in this collection: chapter 11, below. See also the September 1997 issue of *The Company Lawyer* for other useful comments.

4 Cm 3769, Law Com No 246. This brief chapter was written before publication of the Report, but a few additions to take account of the final Report have been made at proof stage.

5 July 1996.

rooted too firmly in the contract model of the company. Setting out the requirements for such an action in modern rules of court will certainly make it easier for parties to understand them, but is there any guarantee that the court will not look to the history of the rule in *Foss v Harbottle*[1] to determine the type of case where a minority shareholder's action should be allowed to proceed? Will this take us any further? Will the judges, on their own initiative, recognise the essentially different nature of the large company and adopt the view that wrongs in that sort of company should be capable of redress free from historical notions about what this sort of company really is? Without going very far at all in terms of recognising the range of interests that the modern large corporation should serve, is there not a case for saying that a shareholder who holds a certain percentage of the shares should have an automatic right at least to initiate a claim? This is, essentially, what has long been proposed in the Fifth EC Directive, yet it is hardly considered by the Law Commission.[2]

It is respectfully submitted that the fundamental problem here lies again in the real refusal of English law to separate out the different types of company, and that this is a trap into which the Law Commission has fallen. This is, perhaps, not surprising, as it can be argued that the courts, the legislature and many writers of textbooks have fallen into the same trap on many occasions in the past. Perhaps the Jenkins Committee did the same when, in attempting to recognise the problems surrounding the derivative action, they simply recommended that a specific remedy be tagged on to what subsequently became section 459. Rather than treating the problems of shareholder remedies as largely common in all types of company, it might be better to examine each type of company separately and examine the problems in respect of each type, then legislate for each in a quite distinct way. Of course, the solutions might in the end, in part, be not dissimilar, although it is thought that in this way, as already indicated, small company disputes might be completely separated and dealt with by some form of more appropriate dispute resolution machinery, whether they involve the most common problem of exclusion or whether they involve allegations of breaches of such as traditional directors' duties. Further, the judges interpreting and applying any new provisions ought to be clearer as to the context in which they are operating.

On the other hand, and to be fair to the Law Commission, this is not what they were asked to do, and, indeed, it was no doubt a task beyond the small team available to do the task they were set. It may be thought that we need a proper Company Law Committee which can review the whole of the subject and place the rules in their proper context. As has already been indicated, there have been many instances in recent years of 'tinkering around' with the rules of company law for particular purposes, often those perceived as having short-term political gains. Surely, we deserve better than that. We should be arguing for an

---

1 (1843) 2 Hare 461, explored classically by, among others, Wedderburn [1957] CLJ 194 and [1958] CLJ 93 and Boyle (1965) 28 MLR 317.
2 In the final Report, this proposal merits only a rather dismissive footnote (n 23 on page 73). The Law Commission was far more concerned to draw on the changes made to shareholder remedies by other common law jurisdictions, which is perhaps curious given the European flavour of much of our company law today; see also my final comment on this page.

examination of the proper place and responsibilities of the large corporation, a proper recognition of the context in which it operates and a proper mechanism for the redressing of wrongs done to it in the context of our membership of the European Union, but with due regard also to our history and the lessons learnt by other common law jurisdictions.[1]

---

1 As Mads Andenas points out (Chapter 16, below), a rather more constructive approach to Europe has been a trademark of much of Tony Boyle's writing: see especially Boyle (1991) 13 *Company Lawyer* 6.

Chapter 7

SHADOW AND DE FACTO DIRECTORS IN THE CONTEXT OF PROCEEDINGS FOR DISQUALIFICATION ON THE GROUNDS OF UNFITNESS AND WRONGFUL TRADING

Geoffrey Morse[1]

INTRODUCTION

Section 6 of the Company Directors Disqualification Act 1986 requires the court to make a disqualification order against a person if it is satisfied that he is or has been a *director* of a company which has at any time become insolvent and that his conduct *as a director* of that company makes him unfit to be concerned in the management of a company.[2] Susceptibility to such an order, therefore, depends initially upon whether a person is or has been a director of a company and his unfitness as such is then to be judged by reference to his acts as a director.[3] Given those parameters, the prevalence of applications for disqualification orders on the grounds of unfitness following an insolvency under section 6 has inevitably raised the question as to who exactly is to be regarded as a director of a company for this purpose. This in turn has led the courts, almost for the first time, to consider the width of the concept of 'directorhood', albeit within the context of disqualification.

Almost contemporaneously, the same question has also been raised in connection with the application of another statutory development relating to insolvency. Under s 214 of the Insolvency Act 1986 the court may make an order against a person who is or has been a director of a company that such a person contributes towards the assets of the company if it finds that the person concerned has been guilty of wrongful trading in relation to that company.[4] The

---

1 Professor of Company Law and Head of the Department of Law at the University of Nottingham. I am grateful to my colleagues Stephen Girvin and John Armour who read this essay in draft and made several helpful comments.

2 If those conditions exist then, unlike the other grounds for disqualification in that Act, the court has no discretion as to whether an order should be made. See *Secretary of State for Trade and Industry v Gray* [1995] 1 BCLC 276 where it was said that the policy behind this was to improve standards. Other cases, both before and since that decision, have emphasised that the protection of the public is the primary purpose of the section, sometimes framing that in terms of abuse of the privilege of limited liability.

3 Although those appear to be distinct questions, the latter seems to have been used by the courts to determine the width of the former. See p 120 below.

4 Wrongful trading arises where the company concerned has gone into insolvent liquidation and the director ought to have concluded before then that there was no reasonable prospect that that could have been avoided. See, generally, *Re Produce Marketing Consortium Ltd (No 2)* [1990] BCLC 520 and *Re Sherborne Associates Ltd* [1995] BCC 40.

intention behind s 214 has always been clear — directors should not be allowed to continue trading and so incur corporate debts which they ought to have known would in all reality not be paid.[1] If that happens, the directors concerned in effect lose the privilege of limited liability with regard to those debts.[2] Again, the potential of this liability has caused the courts to consider the question, in that context, as to the categories of those who can be regarded as directors and so liable to contribute to the assets of the company concerned.

In answering that question, the courts have applied the same criteria whether the context has been wrongful trading or disqualification. It is the purpose of this essay to examine those criteria, both as to the potential categories of those who can be included as directors and the further definition of those categories, and to consider whether in fact they should be identical in relation to both sections. There is no reason, other than a natural desire for consistency, why they should be the same. As Browne-Wilkinson VC said in *Re Lo-Line Electric Motors Ltd*:[3] 'The meaning of "director" varies according to the context in which it is to be found'.

POTENTIAL CATEGORIES OF DIRECTORS

Section 282 of the Companies Act 1985 requires every private company to have a director and every public company to have two. Section 741(1) of that Act defines a director as *including* any person[4] occupying the position of director, by whatever name called.[5] It is immediately clear, therefore, that a director not only includes properly appointed persons operating under the title of director (so called *de jure* directors) but others occupying that position under another title. The width of that inclusive wording is, however, not entirely clear.

In *Re Eurostem Maritime Ltd*,[6] Mervyn Davies J held that it was wide enough to include all those, whether properly appointed or not, who are actively concerned in the management of a company since they would be occupying the position of director. As such, it would include at a stroke anyone not properly appointed as a director[7] but who nevertheless could be said to be occupying the position of director. This category of individuals are referred to as *de facto* directors. In *Re Lo-Line Electric Motors Ltd*,[8] however, Browne-Wilkinson VC disagreed with this wide interpretation of s 741(1). In his opinion, the wording is

---

1 See the Cork Committee Report on Insolvency Law and Practice, 1982 Cmnd 8558.
2 Such conduct is also relevant to the question of unfitness for the purposes of a disqualification order.
3 [1988] BCLC 698 at 706.
4 Thus including corporate directors of other companies.
5 See also s 251 of the Insolvency Act 1986 and s 22(4) of the Company Directors Disqualification Act 1986, where the same wording is used.
6 [1987] PCC 190.
7 Or anyone who had been properly appointed but whose appointment had ceased to be valid. A distinction between those never validly appointed and those whose appointment had ceased to be valid was made, however, in *Morris v Kanssen* [1946] AC 459 (HL) in relation to what is now s 285 of the Companies Act 1985. That section was held not to validate the acts of those who had never been appointed but only of those whose appointment had ceased to be valid.
8 [1988] BCLC 698.

simply concerned with the title given to a person who is nevertheless a *de jure* director in the sense of being properly appointed[1] and does not as such expressly apply to non-appointed *de facto* directors. Such an interpretation requires that the words 'occupying the position' of director in s 741(1) be taken to mean the position of a *de jure* director and that the operative words are 'by whatever name called'.[2]

It is not immediately clear why an interpretation of s 741(1) should limit the words 'occupying the position of director' to *de jure* directors as distinct from *de facto* directors. After all, *de facto* directors are, by definition, occupying the position of director. The answer is to be found in the need to vary the meaning of the word 'director' according to the context. Thus, it is argued, the meaning of director must be limited to *de jure* directors in the context of the formal requirements of the Companies Act, such as s 282 (the need for a minimum number of directors, referred to above) and s 288 (the register of directors).[3] Given that, the statutory definition in s 741(1) needs to be capable of limitation to *de jure* directors if the need arises. That would not be the case if the inclusive words of that section encompassed *de facto* directors automatically.

However, the point is that the definition in s 741(1) is inclusive only so that it is open to the courts to extend the definition of director if the circumstances warrant it and they have done so in relation to both wrongful trading and disqualification for unfitness so as to include *de facto* directors.[4] The reasons for those decisions and the criteria which have been used to define such individuals will be discussed below.[5] For the present, it is enough to note that it has been done without using the statutory definition in s 741(1) as to 'occupying the position of a director'.

In sharp contrast to *de facto* directors, the definition of a director is expressly extended in certain statutory provisions so as to include a shadow director. This is the case with both section 6 of the Company Directors Disqualification Act 1986[6] and s 214 of the Insolvency Act 1986.[7] The concept of a shadow director, unlike a *de facto* director, does have an exhaustive statutory definition. That

---

1 The example given in the case is where the company's articles provide that the conduct of the company's affairs is committed to governors or managers.

2 A similar point was taken by Croom-Johnson J in *IRC v Heaver* [1949] 2 All ER 367. Referring to the equivalent provision in the 1929 Companies Act, the judge said that the definition only applied to those lawfully discharging directorial functions in accordance with the company's constitution, whatever that individual is called.

3 See [1988] BCLC 698 at 706 per Browne-Wilkinson VC. Other sections which would require this restricted definition include s 291 (directors' share qualification) and section 293(2) (age limits). Note, however, s 285 (validity of acts), discussed at n 5 on p114, above, where it was held that *de facto* directors were included in the definition but only if they had at one time been *de jure* directors.

4 As to disqualification, see *Re Eurostem Maritime Ltd* [1987] PCC 190; *Re Lo-Line Motors Ltd* [1988] BCLC 698; *Re Richborough Furniture Ltd* [1996] 1 BCLC 507; *Secretary of State for Trade and Industry v Laing* [1996] 2 BCLC 324 and *Secretary of State for Trade and Industry v Hickling* [1996] BCC 678. On wrongful trading, see *Re A Company* (1988) 4 BCC 424; *Re Tasbian Ltd (No 3)* [1991] BCLC 792 and *Re Hydrodam (Corby) Ltd* [1994] 2 BCLC 180.

5 See p 117 below.

6 Section 22(4) of that Act.

7 Section 214(7).

definition is found in s 741(2) of the Companies Act 1985, s 251 of the Insolvency Act 1986 and s 22 of the Company Directors Disqualification Act 1986. For all practical purposes, these definitions are the same.

Thus, the definition of a shadow director in the Insolvency Act says that it means:[1]

> 'a person in accordance with whose directions or instructions the directors of a company are accustomed to act (but so that a person is not deemed a shadow director by reason only that the directors act on advice given by him in a professional capacity).'

The use of the word 'person', rather than 'individual', makes it clear that a company can also be regarded as a shadow director if the circumstances are correct. There are limited exceptions to this in the application of the definition to certain provisions of the Companies Act 1985 so that in those cases a holding company will not be regarded as being a shadow director of its subsidiary company.[2] But this does not apply to liability under either s 6 of the Disqualification Act or s 214 of the Insolvency Act.[3]

Thus, the courts have to consider three categories of persons when considering who is a director for the purposes of disqualification and wrongful trading applications. These are *de jure*, *de facto* and shadow directors. It is equally clear that these categories are regarded as being quite distinct from each other. Despite attempts by counsel to confuse the issue, Browne-Wilkinson VC, in the *Lo-Line* case, was clear that for the purposes of disqualification for unfitness *de facto* directors included not only those persons who had never been *de jure* directors (who might be described as 'pure' *de facto* directors) but also those who had been *de jure* directors but who had ceased to be such (who might be described as 'converted' *de facto* directors).[4] As such, there is a clear division between *de jure* and *de facto* directors. Either the individual is properly appointed under the company's constitution whatever he is called, or he is not.

Nor, it is said, is there any overlap between the judge-made concept of a *de facto* director and the statutorily defined shadow director. In *Re Hydrodam (Corby) Ltd*, Millett J expressed the point forcibly:

> 'I would interpose at this point by observing that in my judgement an allegation that a defendant acted as a de facto or shadow director, without distinguishing between the two, is embarrassing. It suggests — and counsel's submissions to me support the inference — that the liquidator takes the view that de facto or shadow directors are very similar, that their roles overlap, and that it may not be possible to determine in any given case whether a particular person was a de facto or a shadow director. I do not accept that at all. The terms do not overlap. They are alternatives, and in most and perhaps all cases are mutually exclusive.'[5]

---

1 Rather than includes, so that the definition is exhaustive.
2 See s 741(3) of the Companies Act 1985 for the list of the sections so affected.
3 See, eg *Re Hydrodam (Corby) Ltd* [1994] 2 BCLC 180.
4 [1988] BCLC 698 at 707. Of course in other contexts the distinction between pure *de facto* directors and converted *de facto* directors is of importance. See, eg *Morris v Kanssen*, n 7 on p 114 above, and *IRC v Heaver Ltd*, n 2 on p 115 above.
5 [1994] 2 BCLC 180 at 182. That point was expressly endorsed by Evans-Lombe J in *Secretary of State v Laing* [1996] 2 BCLC 324 at 347.

Millet J went on in that case to suggest definitions of both a *de facto* and a shadow director. Although, as we shall see, those definitions are open to criticism, particularly in relation to the intentions of the person involved, the basic point which he made as to the general distinction between the two concepts remains valid. A *de facto* director is acting as if he were a director; a shadow director, on the other hand, is not so acting, he is directing others. As Millett J put it, he does not intend to be seen as director — he 'lurks in the shadows, sheltering behind others, who he claims, are the only directors of the company to the exclusion of himself'.[1] It is less clear, however, as to whether these two distinct categories can never overlap. But, before returning to that issue at the end of this essay, it is important to define exactly what is involved in these two categories.

DE FACTO DIRECTORS

It is now quite clear that whatever is meant by *de facto* directors, the liability for disqualification as a director on the grounds of unfitness and for wrongful trading extends to them. In *Re Lo-Line Electric Motors Ltd*,[2] Browne Wilkinson VC held, as a matter of construction, that the liability for disqualification[3] applied to anyone merely *de facto* acting as a director. This was because the substantive provision required the courts to have regard to the defendant's conduct as a director and there was no reason to suppose that Parliament had intended that the decision to disqualify should turn on the validity of a person's appointment.[4] This reasoning has since been followed expressly in *Re Richborough Furniture Ltd*,[5] *Secretary of State v Laing*[6] and *Secretary of State v Hickling*.[7]

Similar reasoning compelled Millett J, in *Re Hydrodam (Corby) Ltd*,[8] to extend the liability for wrongful trading to *de facto* directors:

> 'Liability for wrongful trading is imposed by the Act on those persons who are responsible for it, that is to say, who were in a position to prevent damage to creditors by taking proper steps to protect their interests. Liability cannot sensibly depend upon the validity of the defendant's appointment.'[9]

In *Re Lo-Line* and *Re Eurostem*, there was no serious dispute that the defendants had been acting as *de facto* directors so that only general statements were made

---

1 [1994] 2 BCLC 180, 183 per Millett J.

2 [1988] BCLC 698.

3 Under s 300 of the Companies Act 1985, which became s 6 of the Company Directors Disqualification Act 1986.

4 This had also been the view of Mervyn Davies J in *Re Eurostem Maritime Ltd* [1987] PCC 190 based on two earlier decisions: *Re Canadian Land Reclaiming and Colonizing Co* (1880) 14 Ch D 660 (liability for misfeasance) and *Re New Par Consols Ltd* [1898] 1 QB 573 (liability to submit statement of affairs on a winding up). In the former case, *de facto* directors were equated with directors *de son tort*. In the latter case, it was held that the purpose of the provision as to statements of affairs was to get at the persons with the information. Mervyn Davies J based his decision on this general policy ground in addition to his interpretation of s 741(1) of the Companies Act 1985. See text relevant to n 4 on p 114 above.

5 [1996] 1 BCLC 507, 524 per Timothy Lloyd QC.

6 [1996] 2 BCLC 324, 329 per Evans-Lombe J.

7 [1996] BCC 678, 691 per Judge Weeks QC.

8 [1994] 2 BCLC 180.

9 *Ibid* at 182.

as to what would constitute a person a *de facto* director, in either its pure or converted form. In *Re Hydrodam*, the case was actually decided on the issue as to whether the defendants were shadow directors, but Millett J ventured the following definition of *de facto* directors as part of his comparison with shadow directors:

> 'A de facto director is a person who assumes to act as a director. He is held out as a director by the company, and claims and purports to be a director, although never actually or validly appointed as such. To establish that a person was a de facto director of a company it is necessary to plead and prove that he undertook functions in relation to the company which could properly be discharged only by a director. It is not sufficient to show that he was concerned in the management of a company's affairs or undertook tasks in relation to his business which cannot properly be performed by a manager below board level.'[1]

Those words were adopted and applied expressly by Evans-Lombe J in *Secretary of State v Laing*.[2] In that case, the judge decided that neither of the defendants could be regarded as *de facto* directors because, on the facts, neither had done anything which could unequivocally point to their assumption of the role of director. They had been involved in varying degrees in the management of the company but, applying the Millett test, that was insufficient. The judge added that in respect of one of the defendants, even if on one occasion he had held himself out as being a director, there had been no further such incidents, and one incident did not make a person a *de facto* director for ever. It would be a question of fact as to how long that status prevailed — termination cannot, by definition, be a formal process.

The Millett definition, adopted by Evans-Lombe J, can be seen to consist of two elements: (i) an intentional holding out by the company or the defendant that he is a director; and (ii) proof of his undertaking functions which could only be performed by a director and not by a senior manager or equivalent person. In *Re Richborough Furniture Ltd*,[3] Timothy Lloyd QC regarded the Millett test as being neither correct nor exhaustive. His principal criticisms related to the necessity of a holding out, by self or company, for the definition to apply. This must be correct. If a person has actually been acting as a director in such a way that he has responsibility for the wrongful trading or is unfit to be concerned in the management of a company, the purposes of the two provisions under consideration, protection of the public and creditors, cannot depend upon whether there has been a holding out. Such concepts are designed primarily for contractual liability not public policy protection. It is fair to say that Millett J's definition was given in the context of highlighting the difference between shadow directors ('lurking in the shadows') and *de facto* directors ('purporting to act as such') and that he never had to apply his own definition in that case.

Timothy Lloyd QC substituted his own definition of a *de facto* director, which amounts, in effect, to a reworking of the second, evidential, part of the Millett definition:

1　[1994] 2 BCLC 180, 183.
2　[1996] 2 BCLC 324, 338.
3　[1996] 1 BCLC 507.

'It seems to me that for someone to be made liable to disqualification under section 6 as a de facto director, the court would have to have clear evidence that he had either been the sole person directing the affairs of the company (or acting with others all equally lacking a valid appointment, as in *Morris v Kanssen*) or, if there were others who were true directors, that he was acting on an equal footing with the others in directing the affairs of the company. It also seems to me that, if it is unclear whether the acts of the person in question are referable to an assumed directorship, or to some other capacity such as a shareholder or, as here, consultant, the person in question must be entitled to the benefit of the doubt.'[1]

This test, which was followed in *Secretary of State v Hickling*,[2] carries echoes of the liability which can attach to trustees *de son tort*.[3] Under that doctrine, a person who is neither a trustee nor having authority from a trustee and who takes upon himself to intermeddle with trust matters or to do acts characteristic of a trustee, will be liable as if he were a trustee and accountable to the beneficiaries as such.[4] Thus, where solicitors appointed by a sole trustee to invest funds, sold those investments and reinvested the funds after the death of that trustee and before the appointment of new trustees, they were held to be accountable personally for the loss caused by that transaction.[5]

Clearly, acting where there are no *de jure* directors will also be the most cogent case for acting as a *de facto* director. But where there are *de jure* directors in place it will, under the Lloyd definition, be more difficult to establish liability as a *de facto* director. This is because it will be necessary to show that the defendant was acting on an equal footing with the other directors. Yet not all *de jure* directors act on an equal footing with each other.[6] Further, even if his acts could amount to being a director, that will not be enough if they could equally be referable to his acting in some other capacity. The defendant must be given the benefit of the doubt. Why should this be so?

The practical application of this test, in the two cases in which it has been applied, has been that those involved have escaped liability for disqualification, not on the grounds that they were not unfit to be directors but because they were not *de facto* directors. In the *Richborough* case, the defendant's actions were categorised as being equally appropriate to a consultant or a shareholder, even though he had been actively involved in financial discussions and in day-to-day matters which were ordinarily matters of management for the board. In the *Hickling* case, the defendant was excused because his acts were equally referable to his role as the company secretary or an employee. These acts included the giving of cash forecasts to the board and his attendance at board meetings, where he himself always stated that he was 'in attendance'.[7]

---

1 [1996] 1 BCLC 507, 524.
2 [1996] BCC 678.
3 It should be remembered that the earlier cases on directors refer to directors *de son tort*.
4 See *Mara v Browne* [1896] 1 Ch 199 at 209, *per* A L Smith LJ.
5 *Blythe v Fladgate* [1891] 1 Ch 337. Modern terminology might put this liability in terms of a constructive trust, but the principle is the same.
6 Otherwise, many of the factual situations in petitions under s 459 of the Companies Act 1985 or s 122(1)(g) of the Insolvency Act 1986 would never have arisen.
7 There is some suggestion in the judgment that another reason why the defendant was not a *de facto* director was that he had never been represented as such.

One of the reasons why the test for establishing a *de facto* director in the context of disqualification for unfitness is so limited is that a person can only be judged unfit under s 6 in connection with his activities as a director. Thus, it is said those activities must be unequivocally those of a director. Another possible reason for giving the benefit of the doubt to the defendant in these cases is that disqualification is in effect a penal process and must be construed strictly. But this is to miss the point of what disqualification proceedings are all about.

In both cases the defendants were doing things which could have been done by a director in the normal course of events, ie they were involved in the running of a company, and that company became insolvent. The real question is whether their conduct as such made them unfit to be concerned *in the management of a company* as required by the section. The section does not say 'unfit to be directors'. Further, if a disqualification order is made against a person he is disqualified not only from being a director but also from being 'in any way, whether directly or indirectly . . . concerned or [taking] part in the . . . management of a company'.[1] Thus, in the *Richborough* case, the judge considered that although the defendant was not a *de facto* director, his activities were very close to a breach of a similar prohibition as to involvement in management imposed upon him as an undischarged bankrupt under section 11 of the Act.

If the purpose of disqualification orders for unfitness is to raise standards and/or to protect the public, surely it is better that someone who has been involved in the management of a company and whose conduct as such has made them unfit to be so concerned should be liable to disqualification. To extend the definition of a *de facto* director for this purpose so as to include those undertaking directorial functions, ie those which it would not be unusual for a director to undertake, would achieve the purpose of the section. Nor would it distort the language of the section. Such a person is acting as a director.[2] To insist on concepts of equal footing and unequivocal acts distorts the picture. Being regarded as a *de facto* director does not mean that a person will be disqualified, it must still be shown that he is unfit because of it. The current test looks at the picture from the wrong angle.

What should the position be in relation to wrongful trading? Again there is no reason why the criteria for establishing a de facto director should necessarily be the same as for disqualification orders. If the width of who is a director can vary with the context so, presumably, can the meaning of a *de facto* director.[3] The purpose of liability for wrongful trading is to encourage realism amongst those managing a company's affairs by making them liable personally for debts which were incurred by the company after the time when they ought to have realised that those debts would not in all reality be repaid. Given that *de facto* directors are subject to that liability, there is no doubt that those who fall within the first part of the Lloyd definition (ie where there are no *de jure* directors) should be liable.

In this context, it is arguable that the restrictions on the definition of *de facto* directors imposed in the second part of the Lloyd definition (where there are

---

1 Company Directors Disqualification Act 1986, s 1.
2 Which is the factor which distinguishes him from being a shadow director.
3 See n 2 on p 115 above.

de jure directors) can properly be justified. Wrongful trading is triggered, not by failures of management generally, but by the failure to put the company into liquidation early enough. On that basis, it could be argued that the liability should only apply to those who are acting on an equal footing with the *de jure* directors, ie those who could affect that decision, and that defendants should be given the benefit of the doubt. On the other hand, culpability for wrongful trading is based on the defendant's conduct in relation to 'the functions as are carried out by that director in relation to the company',[1] so that liability depends upon the defendant's role within the company, which would no doubt take into account the equal footing point. It seems strange, therefore, to exclude defendants from all potential liability on that basis.

Further, there is also the point that there is a defence to liability for wrongful trading under s 214(3) of the Insolvency Act 1986. If, after the time when liability for wrongful trading began,[2] the defendant can show that he took every step to avoid the potential loss to the creditors as he ought to have taken, he will not be liable. If, therefore, the person concerned was involved in the management of the company in terms of doing things which it would not be unusual for a director to do, the fact that he is not on an equal footing with the *de jure* directors could well be taken into account in deciding the steps he ought to have taken under s 214(3), just as it would be with a 'junior' director. Thus there seems, once again, to be no compelling reason why the definition should be so restricted.

SHADOW DIRECTORS

Liability to wrongful trading and to disqualification on the grounds of unfitness extends to shadow directors simply because, in each case, the statute says so.[3] Unlike the situation in relation to *de facto* directors, there is an exhaustive definition of who can be a shadow director which applies in both cases:

> '"**shadow director**" in relation to a company, means a person in accordance with whose directions or instructions the directors of a company are accustomed to act (but so that a person is not deemed a shadow director by reason only that the directors act on advice given by him in a professional capacity).'[4]

Initially, the question which arose in connection with this definition concerned the boundary to be drawn between those giving advice in a professional capacity and shadow directors. This arose where the advice also involved some control over part of the company's affairs, although in neither case did the issue actually fall to be decided. In *Re A Company*,[5] the company had reached its overdraft limit with the bank. The bank investigated the company and prepared a report. Various steps were then taken by the board, under pressure from the

---

1 See s 214(4)(a) of the Insolvency Act 1986. By s 214(5), this also includes functions which have been entrusted to him even if he does not actually carry them out.
2 The point when the defendant ought to have realised that there was no reasonable prospect of avoiding an insolvent liquidation: section 214(2)(b).
3 Insolvency Act 1986, s 214(7); Company Directors Disqualification Act, s 22(4).
4 Insolvency Act 1986, s 251; Company Directors Disqualification Act 1986, s 22(5).
5 (1988) 4 BCC 425.

bank, to implement several recommendations in the report. On that basis, it was claimed that the bank had become a shadow director and so potentially liable for wrongful trading. The issue arose only in respect of an application by the bank to strike out the petition on the basis that the bank could not possibly be a shadow director. Knox J refused to do so — the claim was not obviously unsustainable.

Subsequently, in *Re Tasbian Ltd (No 3)*,[1] on an application to rescind an order granting leave to bring disqualification proceedings out of time, Vinelott J had to consider whether the defendant could be regarded as a shadow director so as to allow the petition to proceed. The defendant was originally the company's adviser, but subsequently became a paid consultant. He was put into the company by a major creditor, in a capacity known as a 'company doctor'. The nature of the defendant's involvement with the company was in dispute, but it was at least arguable that he had been involved in a restructuring, although it was counter-argued that his control was purely negative. The judge held that the dividing line between a watch-dog or adviser imposed by an outside investor and a shadow director was a narrow one and there was a serious question as to whether the defendant had, at some stage, crossed the line.[2]

Those cases really only raised the potential difficulties in defining a shadow director. They did, however, suggest that, potentially, it was very wide since in both cases, the matter was allowed to proceed to trial. In *Re Hydrodam (Corby) Ltd*,[3] however, the issue came for a full determination, not in the context of professional advice but as to the question of the liability of directors of a holding company as shadow directors of a subsidiary. Millett J, having carefully separated the categories of *de facto* and shadow directors, set out the following criteria which had to be proved in order to establish the latter category:

> '(1) who are the directors of the company, whether de facto or de jure; (2) that the defendant directed those directors how to act in relation to the company or that he was one of the persons who did so; (3) that those directors acted in accordance with such directions; and (4) that they were accustomed so to act. What is needed is first, a board of directors claiming and purporting to act as such; and secondly a pattern of behaviour in which the board did not exercise any discretion or judgment of its own, but acted in accordance with the directions of others.'[4]

Applying those criteria to the facts of the case, the judge held that, even assuming that the parent company was itself a shadow director of the subsidiary, a director of the parent company was not as such a shadow director of

---

1 [1991] BCLC 792
2 Vinelott J also considered that the question as to whether the defendant was a *de facto* director or not had the same narrow divide. He does not seem to have distinguished between the two categories. It is impossible to tell from the report whether the defendant was acting as a director or telling the board what to do, although the inference is more towards the latter, so that he would have been liable as a shadow director. In the *Richborough Furniture* case, as noted above, a similar situation was fought by reference to the *de facto* director category. Each case must depend upon the role assumed by the defendant.
3 [1994] 2 BCLC 180.
4 [1994] 2 BCLC 180, 183.

the subsidiary simply by taking part in board meetings of the parent company.[1] Any directions they gave to the subsidiary would be as agents for the parent company, which would consolidate the position of the parent company as a shadow director, but would not make them such as individuals. They would have had to have given individual and personal instructions to the subsidiary to be liable personally in that way.

Of course, a parent company or anyone who comes within the Millett criteria would be a shadow director for the purposes of wrongful trading or disqualification. The four specific criteria set out by the judge would seem to be a fair analysis of the statutory definition but his subsequent explanatory gloss would seem to go beyond that definition in imposing additional limitations beyond the wording of the statute.

First, all that the statute requires is there are directors who can be directed how to act, not that there are such persons purporting or claiming to act as directors. Thus, although there must be one or more *de facto* or *de jure* directors before there can be a shadow director, all that is required is that these are persons acting as directors. There does not seem to be any question of intention involved. This point mirrors the discussion above on Millett J's definition of *de facto* directors as to whether any element of holding out is necessary.[2] The point is important because if there are no directors, *de facto* or *de jure*, to be directed the defendant cannot be a shadow director and since, by definition, he is not a *de facto* director, he would escape liability altogether. This is another reason why the definition of a *de facto* director should not be unduly confined.

The second point is that the statute requires the directors to be accustomed to act on the instructions of the defendant. It does not say that this must be the case on every occasion or that they can never exercise any discretion or judgment of their own. If Millett J is correct in this, it would mean that if a board had on one occasion acted on its own initiative on perhaps some trivial matter there could be no shadow directors, even though on every other occasion the board had done as instructed. Nor would such a person be a *de facto* director if he was careful never to do anything personally which might be construed as acting as a director. Neither does being accustomed to act in accordance with instructions mean being obliged to do so. The fact that the board can exercise a discretion does not mean that they are not accustomed to act on instructions, either because, in fact, they have no real choice in the matter or they are impressed/unduly influenced by the instructor.

This question of discretion was considered in *Re PFTZM Ltd*,[3] a case which arose, not on wrongful trading or disqualification but on whether the defendants could be regarded as shadow directors for the purposes of having to answer questionnaires in an insolvent liquidation. The case does, however, directly relate to the issue in hand. Two officers of a consortium which had

---

1 The judge expressly rejected a submission that the directors of a parent company which was a shadow director of its subsidiary were automatically shadow directors themselves. He did say, however, that where there were only titular directors of a company there was a strong inference that there were shadow directors somewhere.
2 See p 118 above.
3 [1995] BCC 281.

financed the company attended weekly management meetings with the board for over two years after the company became financially troubled. Their attendance was a condition of the continuance of the company's credit. His Honour Judge Paul Baker QC rejected the claim that they had become shadow directors in the following terms:

> 'The central point, as I see it, is that they were not acting as directors of the company; they were acting in defence of their own interests. This is not a case where the directors of the company . . . were accustomed to act in accordance with the directions of others, i.e. the applicants here. It is a case here where the creditor made terms for the continuation of credit in the light of threatened default. The directors of the company were quite free to take the offer or leave it.'[1]

The fact that the applicants were acting in defence of their own interests does not seem to be an automatic reason for denying them status as shadow directors. It is a good reason for denying them status as *de jure*[2] directors[3] — but the fact that they were creditors protecting their interests does not mean that the board could not be accustomed to act on their instructions. There is nothing inherently incompatible with the statutory definition of a shadow director and a creditor protecting his interests.[4] There must be protection for banks seeking to safeguard their interests in a constructive manner but simply because they are acting as such should not be an automatic exclusion from all liability.

Nor is it clear to what extent the directors in that case had a real choice as to whether to take the offer or leave it. If the only alternative is immediate insolvency, what discretion does the board have in any real sense of that word? In any event, the board had exercised that discretion by acting in accordance with the applicant's instructions for two years — is that not enough to establish that they were accustomed to act in that way? The bottom line is that the applicants 'ran' the board of directors and so the company for two years. Given the public and creditor protection policy aspect of the liability in that case and the areas considered in this essay, surely they should be accountable. Yet again, as with *de facto* directors, the courts are approaching the situation from the wrong angle.

CONCLUSIONS

Given the purpose behind liability for wrongful trading and susceptibility to disqualification proceedings, both those provisions apply not only to *de jure* directors, but also to *de facto* and shadow directors. *De jure* directors are those who are appointed properly under the company's constitution, by whatever name they

---

1 *Ibid* at p 292.
2 And possibly as *de facto* directors, depending upon what they actually did.
3 A similar problem in partnership law was solved by the House of Lords in *Cox v Hickman* (1860) 8 HL Cas 268 where it was held that creditors taking money from a firm in an attempt to recover their debts did not make them partners in the true sense of the word. Taking a share of profits of a business was not, without more, evidence of a partnership. See also Partnership Act 1890, s 2(3).
4 The Cork Committee sought to exclude banks, etc. from liability for wrongful trading 'where their acts are unreflected in the carrying out of the offending business': 1982 Cmnd 8558 para 187. My point is that where their acts do stray over into carrying out the business then there should be liability.

operate. *De facto* directors are those who act as directors; it should not matter whether they intend to do so or not; nor should it be necessary for them to be acting on an equal footing with other *de jure* or *de facto* directors. If there are no other directors, *de jure* or *de facto*, that point does not, of course, arise.

Shadow directors are those who direct the directors, *de facto* or *de jure*, as to how to act, provided that the directees are accustomed to act in accordance with those directions. It should not be necessary for the directees to intend to act as directors, provided that they do so, nor should it be necessary to show that they never exercised any discretion or that they had no, even theoretical, choice in the matter.

The distinction between shadow directors and *de facto* directors is clear. The first category requires directing the directors, whilst the second requires acting as a director. If there are no directors, *de facto* or *de jure*, there cannot be shadow directors. But this does not mean that a person can never be both a shadow director and a *de facto* director. Suppose there are *de jure* directors of a company and X, who is not a *de jure* director, instructs those directors how to act, etc. and also undertakes directorial functions of his own. On what basis is X not to be regarded as being both a shadow and *de facto* director? The distinction made by Millett J in the *Hydrodam* case is based on X's intention; ie does he hold himself out as a director or does he lurk in the shadows pretending that he is not one. But that element of his definition of a *de facto* director has been criticised in subsequent cases and there is no suggestion of it in the statutory definition of a shadow director. Of course, in most cases, there will be a clear distinction between the two, but although distinct the two categories are not mutually exclusive.

Chapter 8

CAN A RECEIVER BE NEGLIGENT?

Harry Rajak[1]

INTRODUCTION

It is an honour to be associated with a publication which honours Tony Boyle and, in particular, his substantial contribution to the study of Company Law. I am indeed fortunate to be one of the many beneficiaries of Tony's profound grasp of this noble subject, of his ever-available advice and assistance, and of his friendship.

THE ORIGINS OF COMPANY RECEIVERSHIP

The law of company receivership springs from the ancient form of receivership developed by the Courts of Equity to assist landlords in ensuring, as far as possible, the stipulated return on the tenanted property and, where necessary, recovery of the property itself. This ancient institution was adapted in the late Victorian period to assist lenders in recovering their loan and any unpaid interest. It is clear that here we exist in a world of unsuccessful tenants and debtors who have tumbled into bankruptcy, with the inevitable consequence of being unable to pay either the rent or the interest, and unable, successfully, to exploit the property or to repay the capital sum borrowed. Despite the comparative strength of the landlord vis-à-vis the tenant or the mortgagee vis-à-vis the mortgagor, the need developed for the protection of the landlord or mortgagee and receivership was the means by which this protection was effected.

Why did the mortgagee need protection? The story is well told in one of the best known Court of Appeal dissenting judgments of the late Victorian period — that of Rigby LJ in *Gaskell v Gosling*,[2] a dissenting judgment which was upheld by the House of Lords.[3] Despite, apparently, holding the whip hand, the mortgagee might find himself unable, without severe penalty, to recover the property from an impecunious mortgagor and to use the income derived from the property to satisfy any arrears of rent. 'The mortgagee', according to Rigby LJ,[4]

> 'could only make the income available for keeping down the interest on his security by entering into possession. This entry into possession by a mortgagee was always considered a strong assertion of his legal rights, since he did not come under any

---

1 Professor of Law, University of Sussex and Director of the Centre for Legal Studies, University of Sussex; a version of this essay was delivered at the annual conference of the Insolvency Lawyers' Association on 8 February 1997.
2 [1896] 1 QB 669.
3 [1897] AC 575.
4 [1896] 1 QB at p 691.

obligation to account to the mortgagor except in a suit for redemption. He was accordingly treated with exceptional severity in a suit for redemption and made to account, not only for what he actually received, but for what he might without wilful default have received. . . . Still greater were the risks and less desirable the possession when the mortgaged property consisted of or included, as it might do, property embarked in trade and subject to the vicissitudes of commercial business. It follows of course from the almost penal liabilities imposed upon a mortgagee in possession that Courts of Equity were very slow to decide that possession had been taken. . . . The Courts also favoured any means which would enable the mortgagee to obtain the advantages of possession without its drawbacks.'

Alternatively, a mortgagee or others with an interest in the property might be faced with the prospect of the rapid diminution in the value of that property on account of fraud or mismanagement. In the early case of *Evans v Coventry*,[1] where the plaintiffs sought the winding up of two societies in one of which they held life insurance policies and, in the other, cash deposits, they needed remedies in addition to the winding up. 'The defendants', observed Knight Bruce LJ, (in the Court of Appeal),[2]

'are persons or include persons, who owed duties to those represented by the Plaintiffs in respect of the funds of the society, for the purpose of care and protection. Those duties appear to have been abandoned in a manner deserving, as it would at present appear, the strongest observation. This has led to a grievous loss, which has been sustained by persons of small means and in humble circumstances, who are ill able to bear it. These same defendants have now under their control, or in their power, a poor remnant of the property which they have so ill-cared for. Whatever may be the specific allegations, . . . this remnant of property is in danger.'

And it was, of course, the institution of receivership which provided the remedy on each of these occasions. It was the office of receiver which commended itself to the Court of Equity as an acceptable device to enable a mortgagee to exercise control over the property without going into possession and it was, of course, the receiver who could be appointed to take charge of the property where, otherwise, the risk of the disappearance of that property was too great. The adaptation of this remedy of receivership to serve the interests of a person who had advanced money to a borrower for trading purposes brought with it a startling and dynamic innovation — the possibility of the management of the debtor.

As is well known, this adaptation occurred in the last quarter of the nineteenth century, during which, at some magic moment, the floating charge was born and with it, before long, the receiver and manager, who unlike his limited forbear, the property receiver, whose ambit was limited to receiving the rents, selling the property and protecting the assets, soon acquired the powers and trappings of total managerial control. And, it was, of course, the fundamental concept of contract which acted as the midwife at the birth of this dynamic offspring.

Contract was also at the root of a further essential feature of this extraordinary remedy of receivership. A further step was necessary to ensure that the protection of the mortgagee was complete. It was all very well to take possession through another, but the well developed principles of commercial agency

---

1 (1854) 5 De GM & G 911 (43 ER 1125).
2 At 917 (1127).

would ensure that any default on the part of the receiver was visited upon the mortgagee as the receiver's principal. Not only was this a danger to the mortgagee where the receiver might have been guilty of wilful default, but in the case of the receiver and manager of a company debtor, the mortgagee might be vicariously liable for the damages suffered by a creditor whose contract with the company debtor was wrecked by the appointed receiver and manager.

Contract provided the answer in ensuring that the receiver was the agent not of the mortgagee but of the debtor. As puzzling as this agency has appeared to judges and commentators from time to time, it has stood the test of time. No matter that the receiver is appointed by the mortgagee (helped again by a contractual provision that the mortgagee simply acts as the debtor's or mortgagor's agent), no matter that the receiver is invulnerable vis-à-vis the debtor, the courts have never had any difficulty in upholding the invariable provision in the contract which declares the receiver so appointed to be the agent of the debtor. The steps in this aspect of the saga are, again, well captured by Rigby LJ:[1]

> 'Mortgagees began to insist upon the appointment by the mortgagor of a receiver to receive the income, keep down the interest on incumbrances, and hold the surplus, if any for the mortgagor, . . . Presently mortgagees stipulated that they themselves should in place of the mortgagor appoint the receiver to act as the mortgagor's agent. This made no difference in the receiver's position, and imposed no liability on the mortgagee appointing. Though it was the mortgagee who in fact appointed the receiver, yet in making the appointment the mortgagee acted, and it was the object of the parties that he should act, as agent for the mortgagor. . . . By degrees the forms of appointment of receivers became more complicated, and their powers of management more extensive; but the doctrine explained by Lord Cranworth . . . [in *Jefferys v Dickson*] was consistently adhered to, and it remained true throughout that the receiver's appointment, and all directions and powers given and conferred upon him, were supposed to emanate from the mortgagor, and the mortgagee, though he might be the actual appointor, and might have stipulated for all the powers conferred upon the receiver, was in no other position, so far as responsibility was concerned than if he had been altogether a stranger to the appointment.'

This agency has, of course, now acquired statutory respectability,[2] but its peculiarity has not gone unremarked. According to Peter Millet QC, as he then was, '[t]he so-called agency of the receiver is not a true agency, but merely a formula for making the company, rather than the debenture-holders, liable for his acts'.[3] Hoffmann J, as he then was, expressed a similar sentiment in the course of the *Gomba Holdings* litigation, when he said 'Although nominally the agent of the company, his [the receiver's] primary duty is to realise the assets in the interests of the debenture holder and his powers of management are really ancillary to that duty.'[4]

---

1 [1896] 1 QB at 691–693.
2 In the case of administrative receivers by s 44(1)(a) of the Insolvency Act 1986 and in the case of a Law of Property Act receiver by s 109(2) of the Law of Property Act 1925.
3 'The Conveyancing Powers of Receivers After Liquidation' [1977] 41 *Conv (NS)* 83, 88.
4 *Gomba Holdings UK Ltd & Others v Homan and Bird* [1986] 1 WLR 1301, 1304.

Whatever might be said about the development of receivership to protect land-lords from the consequences of wilful default, it cannot be denied that the ability of the receiver and manager to break the company debtor's existing contracts and to be able to do so without fear of personal liability or vicarious liability for the appointing debenture holder has been an essential part of the institution of receivership as a corporate rescue regime.

THE RELATIONSHIP BETWEEN THE RECEIVER AND THE APPOINTOR

The essential legal relationship is that between receiver and debtor, a relationship pushed uneasily into the principal/agent category. Indeed, the protection of the mortgagee may well depend on the absence of any significant contractual relationship between itself and the receiver. The mortgagee's position is jeopardised when it conducts itself in such a way as to be seen to direct the receiver in the carrying out, by the latter, of his duties, thereby constituting a real principal/agency relationship.[1] The mortgagee's position may also be rendered vulnerable if the debtor company goes into liquidation, although here the courts have, generally, been kind to mortgagees, first by protecting them against personal liability for transactions undertaken by the receiver after the coming into effect of the liquidation and, secondly, by ensuring the smooth running of the tail end of the receivership by enabling the receiver to continue to deal with and dispose of the debtor's property even though no longer the latter's agent.[2]

The principle that liquidation, while ending the principal/agent relationship between company and receiver, does not create automatically or presume rebuttably a principal/agent relationship between mortgagee and receiver was established in the 1890s, first by *Burt, Boulton & Hayward v Bull*[3] — where the court-appointed receiver was held personally liable for goods ordered after the liquidation — and *Gaskell v Gosling*,[4] where the House of Lords reversed the judgments at both first instance and in the Court of Appeal in absolving the appointors of the receiver from liability on contracts undertaken by the receiver after the company's liquidation. In the Court of Appeal, Rigby LJ, who dissented,[5] mused that had the receiver been sued personally for payment of the goods delivered, he may have been held liable personally, but the House of Lords, in upholding this dissenting judgment, was quite happy to contemplate that no one might be liable.

The legal relationship between receiver and appointor is, of course, most frequently conceptualised as one in which the receiver owes a primary duty to his appointor either to sell the debtor's assets to enable the appointor's debt to be paid, or to manage the debtor's assets also with a view to the

---

1 A recent example of this can be seen in *American Express International Banking Corporation v Hurley* [1986] BCLC 52.
2 See, for example, *Sowman v David Samuel Trust* [1978] 1 WLR 22.
3 [1895] 1 QB 276.
4 [1897] AC 575.
5 Above, see text associated with n 4 on p 127.

payment of the appointor's debt, but in accordance with a longer time scale. This is well expressed by the following statement of Jenkins LJ in *Re B Johnson (Builders) Ltd*:[1]

> 'The company gets the loan on terms that the lenders shall be entitled, for the purpose of making their security effective, to appoint a receiver with powers of sale and of management pending sale, and with full discretion as to the exercise and mode of exercising those powers. The primary duty of the receiver is to the debenture holders and not to the company. He is receiver and manager of the property of the company for the debenture holders, not manager of the company.... [T]he whole purpose of the receiver and manager's appointment would obviously be stultified if the company could claim that a receiver and manager owes it any duty comparable to the duty owed to a company by its own directors or managers.'

THE RELATIONSHIP BETWEEN THE RECEIVER AND THE COMPANY TO WHICH HE IS APPOINTED

Leaving aside the nature of the agency relationship between company debtor and receiver, the question arises as to whether any duty is owed by the receiver to the company. The uncompromising nature in which the receiver's duty to the appointor is sometimes expressed — as in *B Johnson (Builders)*[2] — leaves little room for any comparable duty, given the likely possibility of conflict between lender and company, especially where the latter is insolvent. And this would follow whether one sought to conceptualise such a duty in terms of equitable or common law principles, either a fiduciary duty to act in good faith or a duty of care to avoid negligence in the conduct of the company's affairs.

It is the case, however, despite the ritual utterance of the receiver's primary responsibilities towards the debenture holder, that a principle that the receiver does owe a duty of care to the company has crept into the law. Indeed, it is now possible to find authority which extends the ambit of such a duty to a guarantor of the company's debt. It is the development of this duty and its compatibility with the receiver's duty to the debenture holder that I shall explore in some depth shortly, but before doing so, I would like to discuss briefly the nature of the duty to act in good faith and the duty of care.

THE NATURE OF THE DUTY OF CARE

This common law duty is one of our most familiar. It may be variously expressed but it imports a duty to act reasonably and not negligently and, as such, implies an objective standard of behaviour against which the particular conduct under litigious scrutiny can be judged. A duty so expressed is, *prima facie*, boundless, but interpretation and rules as to causation have ensured that the class of beneficiaries of this duty (variously defined as those within the risk

---

1 ([1955] Ch 634, 661 (approved by Lord Templeman in the recent Privy Council decision of *Downsview Nominees v First City Corporation* [1993] AC 295).
2 *Ibid.*

or as neighbours), is sufficiently small so as to avoid the seriously damaging effects to society of an otherwise boundless liability for negligent conduct. Thus the extension of this duty to cover negligent misstatement[1] was restrained by the principle that such a duty only arose where it was within the business of the defendant to give such advice,[2] and extended only to those shown to have relied upon the correctness of the misstatement.[3] And the courts have also been concerned, in recent years, to ensure that the duty of care does not extend to pure economic loss.[4]

Despite these limitations, it is, of course, a trite observation that there is barely any objective human conduct which is incapable of being assessed in terms of reasonableness or negligence. This duty has thus been invoked on behalf of the victims of allegedly negligent actions by a vastly varied collection of people, from drivers, to sportsmen and women, to the actions and advice of professionals and trades people and so on. Company directors,[5] auditors[6] and trustees[7] have long been in the frame and there is no reason, in principle, why receivers should not be.

We need only turn to the simple facts of the recently decided *Knight v Lawrence*[8] to observe how obviously sensible it is that receivers be included within this duty. Here, a Law of Property Act receiver was held liable in damages to the owners (and mortgagors) of property which had been sold by the receiver at what was alleged to be a substantially reduced price, owing to the fact that the receiver had failed to serve rent increase notices on the tenants. The right to serve such notices had fallen due during the receivership and the court (Browne-Wilkinson VC) accepted expert evidence that it was 'one of the first functions of a receiver in a case like this to get solicitors or others to review the position of the rent review clauses and to take such steps as are necessary to ensure that the reviews take place'.[9] According to the judge, 'the duty of care arising from the position of a receiver is owed not only to his principal but also to those directly and immediately affected by his actions'.[10]

Before we pass on to the fiduciary duty, I would like to make three observations in relation to the duty of care owed by *company directors*. First, the courts have

---

1 *Hedley Byrne & Co Ltd v Heller & Partners Ltd* [1964] AC 465.
2 *Mutual Life Ltd v Evatt* [1971] AC 793.
3 *Weller & Co v Foot and Mouth Disease Research Institute* [1966] 1 QB 569.
4 *D & F Estates Ltd v Church Commissioners* [1989] AC 177, *Greater Nottingham Co-Operative Society Ltd v Cementation Piling and Foundations Ltd* [1989] QB 71, *Murphy v Brentwood District Council* [1991] AC 398.
5 *Dorchester Finance Co Ltd v Stebbing* [1989] BCLC 498 (which shows the extension of this duty to a non-executive director) although it is well to bear in mind the generally low standard of care expected by the courts of company directors, see, eg *Dovey v Cory* [1901] AC 477 and the difficulty which confronts attempts to seek compensation for any damage caused, see *Pavlides v Jensen* [1956] Ch 565.
6 *Caparo Industries plc v Dickman* [1990] 2 AC 605, *Al Saudi Banque v Clark Pixley (a firm)* [1989] 3 All ER 361, although note the restriction of the duty so as not to extend to a member of the public at large.
7 *Bartlett v Barclays Bank Trust Co Ltd* [1980] 1 All ER 139.
8 [1991] BCC 411.
9 [1991] BCC at 418.
10 At 417.

established a quite benign regime for directors requiring of the latter only minimal attention to their jobs to satisfy a standard of non-negligent conduct. A variety of principles, including the permitting of wide powers of delegation, have resulted in comparatively few instances of recorded negligent conduct for which company directors have been held liable. Secondly, the *procedural* obstacles to a successful suit against allegedly negligent company directors are sometimes quite daunting. Finally, both in the case of trustees and company directors, legislation empowers the court specifically to relieve the negligent defendant from the consequences of his negligence,[1] even if, somewhat peculiarly, the director or trustee is required to have been acting reasonably (as well as honestly) in order to come within the privileged class of those entitled to this magnanimity.

It may just be that underlying the principles of negligence, as applied to company directors, there is a policy that little or nothing should be done that might inhibit the entrepreneurial risk-taking commercial activity to which our society was committed by certain fundamental developments in the nineteenth century, especially that of the growth and extension of the principle of limited liability. In addition, judges have always been sensitive to the charge that they enjoy the luxury of hindsight when assessing the conduct of company directors undertaken in the heat of commercial battle. Either or both of these considerations may be relevant to receivers, especially if we have regard to receivership in its dynamic, corporate rescue mode. It must be said, however, that hitherto, the major attack on the idea that receivers are under a duty of care has been based on the proposition that the appropriate duty is one of good faith and that this is incompatible with the existence of a duty of care.

One illustration of the duty of care is whether or not appropriate advice has been sought. In each of two recent cases, a finding of negligence has been closely associated with a failure by the receiver (in one case) and a mortgagee (in the other) to take appropriate advice. In the former, *American Express International Banking Corporation v Hurley*,[2] where the receiver was appointed to a debtor which carried on a highly specialised business with highly specialised equipment, one reason why the receiver was held to be negligent was his failure to take advice as to the proper value of this specialised equipment.

In the other decision, *Tse Kwong Lam v Wong Chit Sen*,[3] a decision of the Privy Council on appeal from the Court of Appeal in Hong Kong, an award of damages against the mortgagee was based on the failure by the latter to take expert advice as to the proper value of the debtor's property, which was bought by a company with which the mortgagee was closely associated. Expert advice as to the price would have protected him against the allegation of a conflict between his duty to the mortgagor and his personal interest. In fact, the sale could not be set aside because the debtor had delayed too long in bringing the proceedings, but damages were awarded in lieu of rescission.

---

1 Section 61 of the Trustee Act 1925, s 727 of the Companies Act 1985.
2 [1986] BCLC 52.
3 [1983] 1 WLR 1349.

THE NATURE OF THE FIDUCIARY DUTY

The fiduciary duty, of course, is central to the position of trustee and has been extended to anyone whose position resembles that of a trustee. This duty can be contrasted with the duty of care by reference to the fact that it, typically, arises where there is already a close relationship between the person who owes the duty and the beneficiary of the duty and where the former enjoys ownership or control over assets belonging to the latter or where the former has a position akin to that of confidant or being in *loco parentis* to the other. It has, thus, been applied to agents, solicitors, partners, employees, even, recently, to local authorities, as well as, of course, to company directors and company promoters.

For the purposes of this essay, however, the significant extension is to mortgagees vis-à-vis (at least) their mortgagors. This extension is readily comprehensible. Mortgagees have a power of sale which it is comparatively easy to abuse. The sale of the mortgaged property at an undervalue to the mortgagee or his nominee would constitute an unacceptable abuse of power and the inclusion of mortgagees within the group of those owing a duty of good faith is of ancient vintage.[1] As Cross LJ put it, in the case of *Cuckmere Brick v Mutual Finance*[2] — and this much is certainly not in dispute — '. . . the sale must be a genuine sale by the mortgagee to an independent purchaser at a price honestly arrived at'.

It is also beyond dispute that a similar duty is owed by a receiver, who, of course, is in a very similar position to a mortgagee, at least in the material particular now under consideration, namely, being able to control another's property and, especially, being able to exercise a power of sale in relation to it. This was expressed by Jenkins LJ in *Re B Johnson (Builders) Ltd*[3] in the following terms:

> '. . . [H]is [the receiver's] power of sale is, in effect, that of a mortgagee, and he therefore commits no breach of duty to the company by a bona fide sale, even though he might have obtained a higher price and even though, from the point of view of the company, as distinct from the debenture holders, the terms might be regarded as disadvantageous.
>
> In a word, in the absence of fraud or mala fides . . . the company cannot complain of any act or omission of the receiver and manager, provided that he does nothing that he is not empowered to do and omits nothing that he is enjoined to do by the terms of the appointment.'

THE POSITION OF THE RECEIVER PRIOR TO *RE B JOHNSON*

This formulation by Jenkins LJ expresses the bold *ratio* of the decision, namely that the receiver is not subject to a duty of care to the company debtor. We will examine this decision in a little more detail in a moment, but I would here observe that, whatever else its faults, such a bold statement at least has the merit of eliminating the conflict inherent in subjecting a receiver both to a primary duty to the debenture holder to ensure the repayment of the latter's loan plus

---

1 See *Rushworth's* case [1676] 2 Freeman 14 (22 ER 1026).
2 [1971] Ch 949.
3 [1955] Ch 634 at 662.

interest and to a duty of care to the company debtor (which must, as a minimum, at least sometimes import the postponement of a sale where there is a strong indication that the value of the assets might increase).

Does *B Johnson* reflect faithfully the principles of the day, or does it ignore the existence of a duty of care to which a receiver had already become subject? Lightman and Moss, in their rightly praised monograph on receivers of companies,[1] level at *B Johnson* this very charge, in particular that it overlooked at least two previous decisions, *Wolff v Vanderzee*[2] and *McHugh v Union Bank of Canada*.[3] Lightman and Moss also support the proposition that the receiver does owe a duty of care, by reference to the case of *Tomlin v Luce*.[4] All these cases are the subject of a close analysis by Salmon LJ in the important decision of *Cuckmere Brick v Mutual Finance Ltd*,[5] where the judge begins by observing that:

> '[i]t is impossible to pretend that the state of the authorities on this branch of the law [the duties on a mortgagee in exercising the power of sale of the mortgaged property] is entirely satisfactory. There are some dicta which suggest that unless a mortgagee acts in bad faith he is safe. His only obligation to the mortgagor is not to cheat him. There are other dicta which suggest that in addition to the duty of acting in good faith, the mortgagee is under a duty to take reasonable care to obtain whatever is the true market value of the mortgaged property at the moment he chooses to sell it.'

and concludes:

> 'both on principle and authority . . . a mortgagee on exercising his power of sale does owe a duty to take reasonable precautions to obtain the true market value of the mortgaged property on the date on which he decides to sell it. No doubt in deciding whether he has fallen short of that duty the facts must be looked at broadly, and he will not be adjudged to be in default unless he is plainly on the wrong side of the line.'[6]

Lightman and Moss clearly rely heavily on this passage, but it should be noted that little is given away by Salmon LJ as far as the duty of care is concerned. There must be substantial leeway in assessing a mortgagee's conduct, first so as to avoid the hindsight problem and, secondly, to ensure that the latter's freedom to sell whenever he wishes remains unimpeded. These important *dicta* cannot, therefore, be relied upon for the wider proposition that would seek to restrict the power of sale where, for example, the price was likely — or even bound — to rise in the future, or even near future.[7] A further point should be observed. All the cases prior to *B Johnson*, and which Lightman and Moss criticise for overlooking, are cases of sales by mortgagees rather than receivers and this does raise the issue of whether the same principle does necessarily apply to both.

---

1 *The Law of Receivers of Companies*, 2nd edn (London: Sweet & Maxwell, 1994).
2 10 LT (NS) 353.
3 [1913] AC 299.
4 (1885) 51 Ch D 573.
5 [1971] Ch 949.
6 At 966–969.
7 Whether or not *Cuckmere Brick* is authority for the proposition that there is a duty of care on a mortgagee to the mortgagor and by extension on the receiver to the mortgagor and others related to the mortgagor, eg guarantors, is far from settled, see the views of Bently, 'Mortgagee's Duty on Sale – No Place for Tort?' [1990] 54 *Conveyancer & Property Lawyer* 431, discussed below, see text associated with n 6 on p 141.

I would argue that no such automatic extension can be made. Regard must be had to the peculiar tripartite nature of the relationship among debenture holder, debtor and receiver. The confused interweaving of legal and actual agency relationships is clearly of a different order than, say, mortgagee and mortgagor and this still leaves open the question as to whether even this very watered down form of a duty of care as identified in *Cuckmere Brick* can be extended to a receiver. The latter, it must also be remembered, is the subject of a primary responsibility to the debenture holder, something which does not exist in the case of the bilateral relationship between mortgagee and mortgagor.

THE RECEIVER AS KING — THE DECISION IN *RE B JOHNSON*

As I have already indicated, here is a decision uncompromising in its rejection of any imposition of a duty of care on the receiver. 'In this case', according to Lord Evershed MR:[1]

> 'in so far as the charges against the receiver involve the proposition that the receiver did not get the best price he could have got and should have got, equally those charges . . . rest upon a misapprehension of the elementary principle that a mortgagee, or a receiver exercising the mortgagee's power of sale, is under no such duty to the mortgagor to obtain the best possible price for the property charged.'

This was, of course, a bad case from the point of view of the debtor. The application against the receiver and manager, under what used to be section 333 of the Companies Act 1948,[2] was presented *seven* years after the receiver had been appointed, had closed down the business and disposed of the assets. The applicant complained of the failure of the receiver to preserve the goodwill of the business. It was a hopeless case but it is interesting not only for the *dicta* already quoted, but also for the jurisdiction under which the application was brought. Section 333 provided for a summary remedy against a past or present director, a manager or a liquidator or any officer of the company, where the latter 'has misapplied or retained or become liable or accountable for any money or property of the company, or been guilty of any misfeasance or breach of trust in relation to the company . . .'. In fact, the Court of Appeal held that the receiver was not within the class of potential respondents to a summons under this section, nor was an act of negligence (which was what was alleged) within the definition of misfeasance. According to Lord Evershed:

> 'a claim based exclusively on common law negligence, an ordinary claim for damages for negligence simply, would not be covered by the section. Nor is such a claim brought within the section by the mere expedient of adding epithets to the negligence charged, calling it "gross" or "deliberate". Nor, by that expedient without out more, can what in truth is mere negligence be converted into something else, namely, breach of trust.'[3]

---

1 [1955] Ch at 651.
2 Now s 212 of the Insolvency Act 1986.
3 [1955] Ch at 648.

The Court of Appeal attacked on two fronts, first as to jurisdiction in dismissing the idea that such a suit lay against a receiver at all and that misfeasance included negligent conduct and, secondly, that, anyway, there was no negligence. As we will see, *B Johnson* has not been left in control of this field. And it is also important to observe that, in the re-enactment of this statutory jurisdiction,[1] the summary procedure is now tenable specifically against an administrative receiver and that breach of the duty of care is included as one of the grounds on which it may be invoked.

THE WORLD TURNING UPSIDE DOWN?

This position, of course, changed in the 1980s. Lord Denning set the pace with his judgment in *Standard Chartered Bank v Walker*.[2] Strictly speaking, the issue was the procedural one of whether leave should be given to the directors to defend an action brought against them under a guarantee which they had given to the plaintiffs to secure the company's debt. The judge below had granted summary judgment to the plaintiffs under Order 14 of the Rules of the Supreme Court, but the Court of Appeal gave leave to the guarantor/directors to defend because the conduct of the receiver and manager, in disposing of the company's assets, raised an arguable plea that the latter was negligent and, if such negligence was established, it was eminently arguable that it caused or increased the guarantors' loss. Lord Denning clearly enjoyed himself. After quoting the *Cuckmere Brick* analysis, he made clear the extent of the duty of care that was being considered:

> 'This duty is only a particular application of the general duty of care to your neighbour which was stated by Lord Atkin in *Donoghue v Stevenson* and applied in many cases since [including, for good measure, *Anns v Merton*]. The mortgagor and the guarantor are clearly in very close proximity to those who conduct the sale. The duty of care is owing to them — if not to the general body of creditors of the mortgagor. There are several dicta to the effect that the mortgagee can choose his own time of sale, but I do not think he can sell at the worst possible time. It is at least arguable that, in choosing the time, he must exercise a reasonable degree of care.'[3]

And, as far as the receiver was concerned, he owed:

> 'a duty to use reasonable care to obtain the best possible price which the circumstances of the case permit. He owes this duty not only to the company, of which he is an agent, to clear off as much of its indebtedness to the bank as possible, but he also owes a duty to the guarantor because the guarantor is liable only to the same extent as the company.'[4]

This was one of the great preliminary proceedings, although not as great as *Donoghue v Stevenson*. Invested with all the mythology of the victory for the underdog, the good guy, it was soon confirmed in *American Express International Banking Corporation v Hurley*,[5] although, in the event, by way of *obiter dictum*,

---

1 By s 212 of the Insolvency Act 1986.
2 [1982] 1 WLR 1410.
3 At 1415.
4 *Ibid.*
5 [1986] BCLC 52.

owing to the confusing circumstances of that case, where the receiver was ultimately liable, but not by reason of any duty of care to the guarantor. The guarantor was liable under the guarantee, but owing to the receiver's negligence, the guarantor had a claim against the lender, who had become, by reason of intermeddling, the principal of the receiver. The receiver was, in turn, liable to the lender by reason of the contract under which he was appointed as the receiver.

Damages were awarded to the mortgagor in *Tse Kwong Lam v Wong Chit Sen*[1] by what can only be described as a duty of care route. Although the mortgagee was closely associated with the company which purchased the property, the debtor failed to have the sale set aside on a breach of good faith basis, owing to the fact that he delayed too long before bringing his claim. But in view of this close connection, the Privy Council (of whose Board Lord Templeman was a member) held that there was an onus on him to show that he had arranged for the best price in the circumstances and, on the facts, he had failed to discharge this onus. By the end of the 1980s, there seemed no doubt that both a mortgagor and a receiver were subject to a duty of care as well as a duty of good faith. And this seemed confirmed by the eminently sensible decision of *Knight v Lawrence*.[2]

THE WHITE KNIGHT TO THE RESCUE

We really had no reason to sit back and pretend that this confused situation had at last been resolved. We were dealing with an inherently unstable settlement. If the receiver does have a duty of care to the debtor, there will, inevitably, be circumstances when he will have to delay the sale of the property, or, indeed, proceed speedily with the sale of the property, despite the contrary wishes of the debenture holder to whom, we must accept, the receiver has a primary responsibility. This issue again came before the Privy Council (this time from New Zealand) in *Downsview Nominees v First City Corporation*.[3] Downsview was the assignee of a first debenture given by the debtor ('GEM'). A second debenture had been granted to First City Corporation ('FCC') and a receiver was appointed by Downsview. FCC offered to pay the full indebtedness of Downsview in order to be able to assume control of the debtor and carry out what seemed to be the only viable plan, the sale of the business. Downsview and its receiver rejected this offer and decided to try to trade the debtor out of its insolvency. This was one of the grounds on which the New Zealand courts held the receiver liable for breach of the duty of care.

Trading continued, the indebtedness grew and the New Zealand Court of Appeal upheld the decision below awarding substantial damages to FCC, calculated by reference to the difference between the loss that would have been incurred had FCC been permitted to carry out its plan for the debtor and the loss that was actually incurred under the receivership. The receiver was held to

---

1 [1983] 1 WLR 1349.
2 [1991] BCC 411 (see above, text associated with n 8 on p 134).
3 [1993] AC 295.

be in breach of his duty of care to FCC, the second debenture holder. The New Zealand Court of Appeal approved the following statement of the trial judge (Gault J):

> 'the proposition that a receiver will not be liable in negligence so long as he acts honestly and in good faith no longer represents the law of New Zealand . . . the authorities clearly indicate that on an application of negligence principles, a receiver owes a duty to the debenture holders to take reasonable care in dealing with the assets of the company.'[1]

It should be observed here that a duty to the debenture holders referred, in fact, to the second debenture holder, who stood in a direct line between the receiver appointed by the first debenture holder and the debtor. This statement is thus to be taken as expressing a duty of care by the receiver to the debtor. The Privy Council was having none of this. Basing itself both on *Re B Johnson (Builders) Ltd* and the *Cuckmere Brick* case, the Privy Council asserted that these left:

> 'no room for the imposition of a general duty to use reasonable care in dealing with the assets of the company. The duties imposed by equity on a mortgagee and on a receiver and manager would be quite unnecessary if there existed a general duty in negligence to take reasonable care in the exercise of powers and to take reasonable care in dealing with the assets of the mortgagor company.'[2]

The actual result did not differ from that below; it was the basis for that result which is of great significance in this decision.

CONCLUSION

The Privy Council has thrown down the gauntlet and declared, in effect, that the general duty of care in negligence has no place in the assessment of the relationship between mortgagee and mortgagor and between receiver and mortgagor. This has come in for much criticism, not least from Lightman and Moss.[3] It also seems to fly in the face of the eminently sensible decision in *Knight v Lawrence*.[4] Yet a persuasive analysis based largely on two recent decisions,[5] and published a year or so before the *Downsview* decision, argued in favour of the very result in that case.[6] The author expressed approval of the *Parker-Tweedale* approach, in which the Court of Appeal held that a mortgagee owed no duty of care to a beneficiary under a bare trust of the equity of redemption and quoted Nourse LJ that it is:

> 'unnecessary and confusing for the duties owed by a mortgagee to the mortgagor and surety, if there is one, to be expressed in terms of the tort of negligence. The authorities which were considered in the careful judgments of this court in

---

1 See [1993] AC 295 at 310.
2 See [1993] AC 295 at 315.
3 *Op cit*, pp 120–123.
4 [1991] BCC 411.
5 *Parker-Tweedale v Dunbar* [1990] 2 All ER 577 and *China & South Sea Bank Ltd v Tan Soon Gin* [1989] 3 All ER 839.
6 See Bently, 'Mortgagee's Duty on Sale – No Place for Tort?' [1990] 54 *Conveyancer & Property Lawyer* 431.

Cuckmere Brick Co Ltd v Mutual Finance Ltd demonstrate that the duty owed by the mortgagee to the mortgagor was recognised by equity as arising out of the particular relationship between them . . .'[1]

According to Bently, this result 'is solid because it rests on principle — namely that prior to the Judicature Acts all mortgagee actions would have taken place in Chancery, and that to apply tort principles to any of these relationships represents a "fusion fallacy"'.[2]

How then to attempt to reconcile two conflicting positions — the generalised existence of a duty of care and the exclusiveness of the application of the fiduciary duty in governing the conduct of mortgagees and receivers? To exclude the duty of care cannot be sustained in the light of the obvious correctness of *Knight v Lawrence*, where restricting the scrutiny of the receiver's conduct within the terms of the fiduciary duty would have yielded no remedy for the plaintiff. On the other hand, it is, with respect, surely correct to oppose the indiscriminate application of the duty of care to relationships which have a deep equitable foundation.

It is submitted that the clue for reconciling these conflicting positions lies in the careful formulation by Purchas LJ in his concurring judgment in the *Parker-Tweedale* decision:

> 'Where there is a direct contractual relationship the law will be slow to imply a duty greater than that created under the contract even if that contract is silent in a particular respect . . . Even where there is no direct contractual relationship but where there is a contractual context against which the parties came into a relationship short of a direct contractual one, again a duty in tort enlarging the rights enjoyed by the victim of the alleged tort beyond those provided for in the contractual context generally will not be imported . . .
>
> . . . The proposition put as a broad principle is that the mortgagee exercising the rights of sale of a property subject to a mortgage owes a duty to the beneficiary of a trust on which the mortgagor holds that property, of whose interest the mortgagee is aware. The duties on a mortgagee exercising a power of sale were considered in *Cuckmere Brick Co Ltd v Mutual Finance Ltd* . . . There is no room for the superimposition on that duty owed to the mortgagor of a further duty owed by the mortgagee directly to a beneficiary in these circumstances.'[3]

The first paragraph in the extract above expresses the importance of having regard to the actual legal relationship and counsels against the importation of another legal relationship to produce a contrary result to that dictated by the express relationship. In principle, at least, if a statute dictates result A, we should shy away from holding that equity would dictate B and then so holding. The second paragraph counsels against the superimposition of one duty upon another. In our typical case, where, in principle, the receiver owes a primary responsibility to the mortgagee, it is obviously confusing, as well as contradictory, to superimpose on the receiver another, general duty (the duty of care) to the mortgagor. The proper analysis, it is submitted, is to investigate whether, in his conduct, the receiver has been concerned to discharge the primary duty and whether he has, in fact, done so. If this is the case, *cadit quaestio*. The secondary

---

1 [1990] 2 All ER at 582.
2 Bently, *op cit* at 440.
3 [1990] 2 All ER at 587.

duty, that to the mortgagor (or, indeed, guarantor, even perhaps other creditors), should only be considered insofar as the receiver's conduct has not been in connection with the primary duty, or if so, has not discharged that duty. The secondary duty, thus, is not superimposed on the primary duty, but only comes into consideration if and when, consideration of the primary duty is irrelevant. This, it is submitted, would leave untouched the fiduciary duties of the mortgagee to the mortgagor, enable the receiver to carry out his primary responsibility to the mortgagee and limit the application of the duty of care to the area outside these two duties.

What, it may be conjectured, if the mortgagee urges the receiver to act to the detriment of the mortgagor; if, for example, the mortgagee, in *Knight v Lawrence*, had urged the receiver to refuse to serve notice of rent increase? In such circumstances, the mortgagee's interference will have reversed the receiver's agency and the latter will have become the agent of the mortgagor[1] and, in the absence of the primary duty, no conflict will arise with the breach of the duty of care.

Seeking to avoid the conflict of different duties is not merely a matter of principle. In the particular instance of the role of the receiver, the impact of a generalised duty of care would severely limit the role of administrative receivership as a corporate rescue mechanism. It would multipy conflict and, as a consequence, litigation, often at the insolvent debtor's expense to the detriment of the creditors. It is true that we have, so far, been much more successful than, say, the United States in keeping to a minimum futile litigation engaged in reassessing business decisions taken in the heat of the moment, but there is pressure to open up this area to litigation and a recent Consultative Document of the Law Commission would greatly increase the power of minority shareholders to challenge board decisions.[2]

Of course, we must ensure that proper remedies are available to shareholders, guarantors, mortgagors and others in pursuit of claims for compensation for loss caused by company directors, mortgagees, receivers and so on. Yet a blanket 'duty of care' lacks the subtlety required to ensure that such remedies are consistent with the prevailing entrepreneurial culture. If we are going to hold fast to the primacy of the floating charge and the present supremacy of the lender, the existence of a general duty of care on the receiver will simply provide a wasteful and delusionary means for challenging this supremacy.

---

1 See *American Express International Banking Corporation v Hurley* [1986] BCLC 52.
2 *Shareholder Remedies: A Consultation Paper* (Law Commission Consultation Paper No 142, 1996).

Chapter 9

ENFORCING WRONGFUL TRADING — SUBSTANTIVE PROBLEMS AND PRACTICAL DISINCENTIVES

Adrian Walters[1]

INTRODUCTION

A decade has passed since the wrongful trading provision in the Insolvency Act 1986, s 214 was introduced. Few cases have been reported and an air of dejection pervades writing on the subject. Commentators doubt whether s 214 provides effective protection for creditors of companies which continue to trade despite looming insolvency.[2] It would be a mistake to conclude that neglect is the only explanation for the dearth of authority on s 214. Empirical studies have shown that proceedings are commenced regularly which, presumably, settle out of court.[3] Several factors weigh in favour of settlement. A liquidator must judge whether the significant costs of proceeding to trial are justified given ordinary risks of litigation. Failure will have adverse costs implications. He may doubt whether the directors have sufficient resources to meet an order and pay his costs. Also, pursuit of an action to trial could prolong the liquidation which may be undesirable. Nevertheless, my purpose is to argue that s 214 *is* difficult to enforce, for two reasons. First, it lacks conceptual clarity. There is scope for differences of judicial opinion over what constitutes 'wrongful trading' and over how liability should be quantified. This creates problems of proof and makes it difficult for a liquidator contemplating proceedings to conduct rigorous cost-benefit analysis. Secondly, s 214 proceedings are proving difficult to fund, a problem exacerbated by recent decisions.[4]

PART ONE: THE POLITICS AND PRACTICE OF ENFORCEMENT

The Cork Report and the parliamentary debate

The Cork Committee ('Cork')[5] recommended the introduction of directors' civil liability for wrongful trading because of perceived deficiencies in the

1 Lecturer in Law, Nottingham Trent University, Solicitor. I am grateful to Janet Ulph for her comments on an earlier draft.
  References to statutory provisions are to the Insolvency Act 1986 unless otherwise stated.
2 See, eg Godfrey and Nield, 'The Wrongful Trading Provisions — All Bark and no Bite' (1995) 11 *ILP* 139; Schulte, 'Wrongful Trading: An Impotent Remedy?' (1996) 4 *JFC* 38.
3 Hicks, 'Wrongful trading — has it been a failure' (1993) *ILP* 134; Williams and McGee (1993) 7 *Insolvency Lawyer* 2.
4 *Re MC Bacon (No 2)* [1990] BCLC 607; *Re Oasis Merchandising Services Ltd; Ward v Aitken and others* [1997] 2 WLR 764, affirming HC [1995] 2 BCLC 493. See further, Part III on p 153.
5 Report of the Review Committee, *Insolvency Law and Practice*, Cmnd 8558, ch 44.

operation of the fraudulent trading provision then contained in the Companies Act 1948, s 332. This created both civil and criminal liability for fraudulent trading.[1] Consequently, judges tended to impose the criminal law standards of pleading and proof on a party applying for civil relief and refused to impose civil liability unless the applicant could establish fraudulent intent or 'actual dishonesty, involving real moral blame'[2] on the respondent's part. Cork proposed that the scope of civil liability should be expanded to encompass 'those who suffer foreseeable loss as a result, not only of fraudulent, but also of unreasonable behaviour'.[3] The subjectively honest director who knew that his company was insolvent but, unreasonably, caused it to soldier on, incurring fresh liabilities, should, along with the fraudster, stand to lose the protection of limited liability. Thus, directors should be judged according to an objective standard.[4] The provision was intended to target a variety of perceived abuses. Whilst Cork considered the essence of wrongful trading to be, 'the incurring of liabilities with no reasonable prospect of meeting them', directors of 'heavily under-capitalised' companies who carry on trading 'with insufficient share capital and reserves' were also in its sights.[5] To avoid civil liability for wrongful trading, the directors of an insolvent company would be expected to 'take immediate steps for the company to be placed in receivership, administration or liquidation'.[6] To allay fears that such corrective action might lead to the premature closure of businesses, Cork added that directors should be able to apply to court for anticipatory relief.[7]

At para 1805 of its report, Cork recognised that the proposal to proscribe wrongful trading involved a trade off between two policy objectives, on the one hand, pursuit of the national economic interest through 'enterprise', on the other, the need to raise standards of corporate governance and commercial probity:

> 'A balance has to be struck. No one wishes to discourage the inception and growth of businesses, although both are unavoidably attended by risks to creditors. Equally a climate should exist in which downright irresponsibility is discouraged and in which those who abuse the privilege of limited liability can be made personally liable for the consequences of their conduct. We believe that our proposals . . . strike a fair balance between those two conflicting needs.'

Cork's proposal was radical and infused with an instrumentalist spirit. It appears to have been driven more by a desire to deter irresponsible conduct than by any perceived need for an effective civil remedy which might benefit creditors. One commentator infers from para 1805 that the intention of Parliament 'was at least partly penal'.[8] Cork and the subsequent White Paper

---

1 A civil sanction for fraudulent trading is preserved in s 213 and a separate criminal provision appears in Companies Act 1985, s 458.

2 *Re Patrick and Lyon Ltd* [1933] Ch 786.

3 Cork Report, para 1777.

4 *Ibid*, paras 1782–1783.

5 *Ibid*, paras 1784–1785.

6 *Ibid*, para 1786.

7 *Ibid*, paras 1798–1803, a recommendation not included in the White Paper, *A Revised Framework for Insolvency Law*, Cmnd 9175. An attempt to re-introduce it was defeated in the Lords — see *Hansard*, HL Vol 462, cols 44–48. Oditah, 'Wrongful Trading' [1990] *LMCLQ* 205, 211 argues that the court nonetheless has inherent jurisdiction to grant anticipatory relief.

8 Dine, 'Wrongful Trading — Quasi-Criminal Law?' in Rajak, *Insolvency Law and Practice* (Sweet & Maxwell, 1993).

both put forward proposals to extend the statutory disqualification regime and it is hard to escape the conclusion that wrongful trading was seen as one of a series of measures, the overall aim of which was to deter irresponsible conduct. The structure of the Insolvency Act 1985 confirms this impression. The wrongful trading and disqualification provisions appear in a coherent block.[1] The two are linked explicitly as a court making a wrongful trading declaration against a director may disqualify him in the same proceedings.[2]

The parliamentary debate on what became Part II of the Insolvency Act 1985 focused more on deterrence and less on the reform's remedial potential. For the most part, the debate was couched in the generalising language of the public interest. A consensus emerged that steps to deter abuse of limited liability were desirable.[3] The government's view was that the wrongful trading provision would 'provide an even more powerful spur to proper conduct than our proposals on disqualification'.[4]

There was less consensus over how best to strike a balance between 'enterprise' and 'abuse'. Opinions differed over whether certain types or degrees of conduct should be stigmatised. The 'phoenix syndrome' aside, few specific abuses were identified.[5] Several MPs were concerned that the provision might act as a barrier to the establishment of small businesses, producing results which would fly in the face of the government's commitment to enterprise-led economic growth. Cork's hostility to the under-capitalised company[6] was not shared. As Peter Thurnham, MP put it during debate:

> 'We must accept the fact that in many businesses, trading on creditors' capital is all part of the business. One does not pay one's supplier until one has been paid by one's customer, where there is difficulty with the customer . . . there are under-capitalised companies . . . we should be able to help rather than . . . hinder them.'[7]

At the same time, others regarded 'robbing Peter to pay Paul' in this way as wrongful.[8] Many were concerned that directors might be frightened into taking precipitate action and that experienced businessmen, corporate 'doctors' and

---

1 Insolvency Act 1985, Chapter I of Part II (ss 12–19). On disqualification, see now Company Directors Disqualification Act 1986.

2 Company Directors Disqualification Act 1986, s 10.

3 The tone was set by Under-Secretary of State for Trade and Industry, Alex Fletcher, MP, during second reading:
'The provisions . . . are principally concerned with combating abuses of limited liability. Limited liability is an essential element of a successful commercial and financial system, but it is abused. The Government's view is that limited liability is a privilege. Any misuse of it, as a result of incompetence or of lack of concern for the interests of creditors, must be punished in the interest of consumers and the business community generally . . . [the Bill] will deter and punish those who take advantage of limited liability either by negligent conduct or by furthering their own interests at the expense of creditors.'
Hansard, HC Vol 78, cols 145, 153.

4 *Ibid*, col 147.

5 'Phoenix syndrome' denotes the practice whereby directors trade a company into insolvency and acquire its assets from a 'friendly' liquidator at a discounted price through the mechanism of a new 'phoenix' company having the same directors and shareholders as the old company and a similar name. The assets are re-cycled; the liabilities of the old company left behind.

6 *Supra*, n 5 on p144.

7 *Hansard*, HC Vol 78, col 163.

8 *Hansard*, HL Vol 458, col 915.

financiers might be discouraged from taking up non-executive directorships of ailing companies.[1] Section 214 draws no obvious line between legitimate and wrongful behaviour and there is thus every reason to suppose that the uncertainties and concerns described will resurface within the enforcement process.

The practice of enforcement

Only the liquidator of an insolvent company can commence proceedings.[2] Thus, a company must have entered either creditors' voluntary liquidation (by shareholders' resolution)[3] or compulsory liquidation (by court order)[4] before proceedings can be commenced. In voluntary liquidation, the creditors appoint a liquidator, who must be licensed to act in accordance with Part XIII of the Act.[5] When a court in England and Wales makes a compulsory winding-up order, a state-appointed official receiver becomes liquidator, usually on an interim basis, until a licensed insolvency practitioner ('IP') is appointed by either the creditors or Secretary of State.[6] The upshot, in practice, is that responsibility for enforcement rests almost exclusively with private IPs, figures who, whilst legally accountable to creditors and their own professional regulator, are equally concerned about the profitability of their own businesses. Naturally, an IP is more interested in whether s 214 provides a cost-effective remedy which will augment a company's assets available for distribution to creditors and less interested in deterrence. With this in mind, I consider in Part II the substantive problems which s 214 causes the IP.

PART TWO: WRONGFUL TRADING — SUBSTANTIVE PROBLEMS

To persuade the court to exercise its discretion under s 214(1) and make an order against a director, a liquidator must establish that:

(a) the company has gone into insolvent liquidation; and
(b) at some time before the commencement of the winding up of the company, the respondent knew or ought to have concluded that there was no reasonable prospect that the company would avoid going into insolvent liquidation; and
(c) that the respondent was either a director or shadow director of the company at that time.[7]

If these elements are established, the court may make an order, but is not bound to do so. A defence is available if the respondent establishes that having reached the state of knowledge referred to in (b), he took every step with a view to minimising the potential loss to the company's creditors as he ought to have

---

1 See, eg *Hansard*, HC Vol 78, cols 160, 191, 198–199.
2 Cork recommended that individual creditors should have *locus standi*, a proposal rejected by the government.
3 Section 84(1)(c).
4 Sections 122–124.
5 Section 100.
6 Sections 136–139. There is no equivalent of an official receiver in Scotland.
7 Paraphrasing subss (2), (7).

taken.[1] The applicable standard (for the objective test of knowledge in (b), and for determining whether the respondent took 'every step') is that of the reasonably diligent director having both the general knowledge, skill and experience that may reasonably be expected of a person carrying out the same functions as are carried out by that director in relation to the company, and the general knowledge, skill and experience that that director possesses. From the IP's perspective, this presents several difficulties.

'No reasonable prospect'

In deciding whether or not a director 'knew or ought to have concluded that there was no reasonable prospect that the company would avoid going into insolvent liquidation', the court is blessed with hindsight. The court knows that the company went into liquidation. Yet it must assess the respondent's conduct retrospectively on the basis of what he knew or ought to have concluded at some time *before* the company went into liquidation and, artificially, ignore the fact that liquidation did ensue subsequently. There is scope here for judicial policy-making, producing different outcomes according to the preferences of individual judges. A judge who is, on balance, both 'pro-enterprise' and 'pro-rescue' will take greater care in using hindsight and show greater willingness to give a director the benefit of any doubt than one who is 'pro-creditor'.[2] The former may well be reluctant to review, from the comfort of the courtroom, the decisions of a respondent taken in the heat of the commercial moment.[3] A liquidator must persuade the court to discount hindsight for proceedings to succeed, an implicit requirement which amounts to a subtle upwards adjustment of the standard of proof. Furthermore, this adjusted standard may itself vary according to the pre-disposition of each judge in relation to the issues of policy aired in Part I. The decision in *Re Sherborne Associates Ltd*[4] illustrates the point.

The case of *Re Sherborne Associates Ltd*

The first respondent, Squire, founded SAL early in 1987 to run an advertising agency. He invited the second and third respondents, Irving and Ellwood, to invest in SAL and join its board as non-executive directors. Squire was an experienced accountant who had a successful track record in business. Irving was a respected figure and former MP who had some experience of public relations. Ellwood ran his own business, which Squire had helped to make profitable. Of the three, none of whom had experience in advertising, Squire was the dominant figure. Squire recruited three executive directors who were experienced in advertising to manage SAL and generate business. SAL was never profitable and went into creditors' voluntary liquidation in 1989. The liquidator's case was that, by specified dates in January 1988, the three knew or ought to have

1 Section 214(3).
2 The labels 'pro-enterprise', 'pro-creditor' are admittedly simplistic. I use them to illustrate the provision's *spaciousness* and the room for manoeuvre within it.
3 There is room for tacit operation of variants of the so-called 'sunshine' defence which derived from Buckley J's observations in *Re White & Osmond (Parkstone) Ltd*, unreported, 30 June 1960, a fraudulent trading case.
4 [1995] BCC 40.

concluded that there was no reasonable prospect that SAL would avoid going into insolvent liquidation. Squire died before the proceedings reached trial.[1]

The judge dismissed the case against all three, a conclusion which appears perverse in the light of the evidence. SAL's own financial information showed that it was technically insolvent before the end of 1987. By January 1988, the board had acknowledged that SAL was doomed unless turnover could be increased substantially. The two surviving respondents admitted that, by January 1988, they had lost confidence in the executive directors' ability to produce realistic sales projections. SAL's capacity to generate increased turnover had been further hampered by the resignation of a key executive director. The judge summarised the evidence as to SAL's plight in January 1988 in these terms:

> 'A strong case can be made that Sherborne was then in, and could be seen to be in, a situation which could only end in . . . liquidation . . . The way forward to profitability could only be through a substantial increase of business. How could this be achieved? The executive directors said . . . they could do it. Yet by the end of January it was known that . . . the largest producer of business . . . was leaving and would take his clientele . . .'

The liquidator was only required to establish on the *balance of probabilities* that the respondents knew (actually or constructively) by January 1988 that there was no reasonable prospect that SAL would avoid going into insolvent liquidation. Yet his 'strong case' failed to persuade the court to discount what the judge described as, '. . . the danger of hindsight, the danger of assuming that what has in fact happened was always bound to happen . . .'. The sympathetic words used to describe the respondents ('responsible men, two of them at least with considerable achievements, who were applying themselves to the problem') suggest that the judge was anxious to avoid a conclusion which might deter experienced businessmen from supporting small companies whether as investors, non-executive directors or corporate doctors.[2] The liquidator may have fared better had it been possible to cross-examine Squire and had the case been pleaded more effectively.[3] Nevertheless, *Sherborne Associates* shows that a court concerned about the 'dangers of hindsight' may dismiss a good claim. In bringing proceedings, the IP faces the risk that the standard of proof may be raised.

Discounting hindsight — 'minimum standards'

Actions have succeeded in four cases.[4] No prominence was given in these cases to the 'dangers of hindsight'. In each, the respondents failed either to comply with statutory filing obligations or to introduce financial controls to their businesses. These cases show that s 214 imposes minimum standards of conduct

---

1   The judge held that the right of action survives a respondent's death and can be pursued against his estate.
2   It may be that judges consider it more appropriate to pursue deterrence through the Company Directors Disqualification Act 1986, s 6. See eg *Re Cargo Agency Ltd* [1972] BCC 388.
3   [1995] BCC 40, 47, 54.
4   *Re Produce Marketing Consortium Ltd (No 2)* [1989] BCLC 520; *Re DKG Contractors Ltd* [1990] BCC 903; *Re Purpoint Ltd* [1991] BCLC 491; *Re Fairmount Tours (Yorkshire) Ltd*, unreported, Huddersfield CC, 15 February 1989.

on directors and suggest that the court may be prepared to 'discount hindsight' if the respondent's conduct falls below the mark.

Re Produce Marketing Consortium Ltd (No 2) provides the earliest example of this approach. Here, PMC traded as a fruit importer, at first successfully. It made losses from 1981 onwards and, from 1984, could only continue trading with the bank's support. The position deteriorated further by mid-1986. PMC went into voluntary liquidation in October 1987 with a substantial deficiency. It had continued to enjoy the bank's support throughout its final two years' trading despite regularly exceeding its overdraft limit. PMC's directors had only managed to keep the bank happy by running up massive amounts of trade credit with one supplier. There was a history of late preparation and filing of accounts which proved significant. In particular, the accounts for year ending 30 September 1985 (showing reduced turnover of approximately 40 per cent and increased net liabilities of roughly 100 per cent compared with the previous year) were not signed off until February 1987.

Knox J held that PMC's two directors ought to have realised by July 1986 that there was no reasonable prospect that PMC would avoid going into insolvent liquidation. They were ordered to pay £75,000. The judge followed the wording of s 214(4) closely. Thus, the respondents were taken to have known in July 1986 that which was only revealed when the September 1985 accounts were eventually produced. The state of affairs revealed there would have been ascertained by July 1986 had PMC complied with its statutory obligations.[1] Knox J acknowledged that the standard was flexible with less being expected of the directors of small companies 'in a modest way of business with simple accounting procedures . . .' Nevertheless, he held that directors are required to meet certain minimum standards which apply regardless of the size of a company's business.[2] These include statutory financial reporting obligations.

This approach has been followed subsequently. The respondent was held liable in *Re Purpoint Ltd*, a case in which the company had failed to keep accounting records or establish rudimentary financial controls. The respondent's failure to ensure that the financial position of the company was ascertainable at a given moment weighed against him. Vinelott J's distaste for small, under-capitalised companies was thinly-concealed.[3] His judgment suggests that the court will not agonise over hindsight if the directors of such a company have failed to monitor its financial affairs. Similarly, a failure to appreciate the niceties of basic company law will weigh against a respondent. It was significant, in *Re DKG Contractors Ltd*, that the respondents, who were the company's only directors and shareholders, had treated its assets as their own. The fact that, in the judge's words, the respondent's 'own knowledge, skill and experience were hopelessly inadequate' for the task of running a limited company, was no protection.

Thus, in the case of a small company operating an unsophisticated business, the provision has been used to uphold basic provisions of company law. Often,

---

1 Companies Act 1985 Part VII, especially s 242.

2 The minimum standard can be varied upwards on the basis of subjective factors (s 214(4)(b)). More is expected of an experienced company director, a point not taken in *Sherborne Associates*.

3 [1991] BCLC 491, 498C.

however, the directors of such small, under-capitalised companies will not have the personal resources to meet an order. Equally, IPs would be unwise to draw too much substantive comfort from 'minimum standards' cases. In *Produce Marketing*, PMC's income derived from fixed commissions. Gross turnover levels were a direct indicator of profitability. Given its trading history, it was easy to show that PMC was never likely to have achieved the required increases in turnover. An admission in correspondence that the directors had concluded by February 1987 that PMC's liquidation was inevitable further enhanced the liquidator's prospects. In *Purpoint* and *DKG Contractors*, the liquidator succeeded on other grounds and the s 214 claims were 'add-ons'. In a case of greater complexity than 'minimum standards' cases, the IP must reconstruct the company's trading history and show that the respondent ought to have anticipated insolvency at a given point or points. To achieve this, he may need to conduct oral examinations of the directors under s 236 and develop sophisticated analyses of the company's financial information.[1]

Quantum

Even if liability is established, an order will not follow as of right. The wording of s 214(1) is flexible. The court '*may* declare that . . . [the respondent] . . . is to be liable to make *such contribution (if any)* to the company's assets *as the court thinks proper*'. This makes it difficult for the IP to predict the quantum of a successful claim.

In *Produce Marketing*, Knox J considered that the primary purpose of a s 214 order is to compensate creditors rather than penalise directors. Thus, he held that the sum payable should, generally, reflect the amount by which the company's net assets have been reduced as a result of the respondent's conduct. Equally, however, he was concerned not to restrict the court's room for manoeuvre:

> '. . . Parliament has . . . chosen . . . wide words of discretion . . . it would be undesirable to seek to spell out limits on that discretion . . . The fact that there was no fraudulent intent is not of itself a reason for fixing the amount at a nominal . . . figure, for that would amount to frustrating what I discern as Parliament's intention in adding section 214 to section 213 . . . but I am not persuaded that it is right to ignore that fact totally.'[2]

Professor Dine argues that, by focusing on the director's *culpability*, the courts have introduced a *punitive* element into the process of assessing quantum, a justifiable view given the width of the provision and the prominence accorded to deterrence during the parliamentary debate.[3] It is submitted, however, that Knox J's *dictum* cuts both ways. He could be read as suggesting that whilst the court should not, automatically, make a nominal order whenever it characterises conduct as *wrongful*, this lesser degree of culpability can be taken into account as a *mitigating* factor in determining the amount of the contribution. There is as much scope for the court to fix a contribution at an amount *falling*

---

1 Of the type discussed in Cooke and Hicks, 'Wrongful Trading — Predicting Insolvency' [1993] *JBL* 338.
2 [1989] BCLC 520, 553F.
3 *Supra*, n 8 on p 146.

below Knox J's compensatory measure, as for it to make a punitive order. The cases bear out this contention. In *Produce Marketing*, a contribution of £107,946 was sought. Knox J took into account the fact that there had been no deliberate wrongdoing and ordered the respondents to pay £75,000. In *Purpoint* and *DKG Contractors*, it was impossible for the court to quantify the impact of wrongful trading on the company's overall net asset position. The contributions ordered were equivalent to the debts incurred after the point at which the respondents ought to have concluded that there was no reasonable prospect of insolvent liquidation being avoided. This appears more generous than Knox J's compensatory measure and the respondents may have benefited from their failure to keep proper accounting records.[1] The discretion is wide enough to enable the courts to develop guidelines on mitigation. So if the facts of *Sherborne Associates* were to recur, the court might impose liability *and then* take into account the respondents' excellent track record when assessing quantum.[2] Unless the parties agree quantum early on, an IP cannot anticipate the precise amount which the respondent may be ordered to pay.

PART THREE: DISINCENTIVES TO FUNDING

An IP often faces a struggle to fund litigation which might benefit creditors. Use of corporate assets to fund litigation which is not guaranteed to succeed may be regarded as a bad risk. Equally, if a liquidator asks creditors to contribute to a fighting fund, only those with a particular axe to grind may want to risk throwing good money after bad. An IP will not want to risk substantial amounts of his own firm's resources on litigation without an indemnity from creditors.

Two additional disincentives to funding have arisen. The first concerns whether the liquidator can recoup the costs of unsuccessful proceedings from the company's assets as a liquidation expense; the second, whether the liquidator can freely assign a statutory right of action or its proceeds to a third party funder. These questions are not confined to the s 214 context. However, their impact as disincentives is a powerful one, the force of which is enhanced by the substantive difficulties discussed in Part II. Both turn on whether the right of action and/or its proceeds can be characterised as *the company's property* at the time of liquidation or later. The answer goes some way to determining whether the proceeds are caught by a debenture-holder's security or go entirely to benefit unsecured creditors and plays a dynamic part in shaping creditors' attitudes towards the funding and commencement of proceedings.

---

1 I work on the assumption that a company's assets as recorded in its balance sheet will decline in value as it approaches insolvent liquidation. Then, any increase in net current liabilities will exceed the total sum of the debts actually incurred.

2 Cases may arise in which the court accepts that the respondent took *some* steps to reduce potential loss to creditors but not *every step to minimise* loss so that a defence is not available. In such a case the court might give credit to the respondent for showing some concern for the creditors when assessing quantum.

Property of the company?

Knox J assumed, in *Produce Marketing*, that any payments made under an order would be caught by the bank's general floating charge.[1] For this assumption to be correct, it must rest on one of two conclusions about the legal character of wrongful trading proceedings. The right of action could be characterised as an unrealised asset of the company, in which case the proceeds are then simply proceeds of realisation of that corporate asset. Alternatively, whilst the right of action might be characterised as one vesting substantively in the liquidator, the proceeds could be treated as a separate fund characterised as after-acquired property of the company.[2] Knox J appears to have taken the first view, regarding the right as an enhanced version of the company's right to sue its directors for breach of duty and therefore derivative in nature.[3] Either way, the proceeds would fall within the compass of a general floating charge, a result justified by the wording of the section which requires any contribution ordered to be made '*to the company's assets*'.

Statutory wording notwithstanding, most commentators take the view that the right of action is not a corporate right and that any proceeds go exclusively to benefit unsecured creditors, with the result that a company cannot grant a charge over either right or proceeds.[4] Those who support this view regard Knox J's assumption as incorrect because it threatens to frustrate what they perceive to be the primary objective of s 214, namely, enhancement of unsecured creditors.[5] It now receives support from the decisions in *Re MC Bacon (No 2)* and *Re Oasis Merchandising Services Ltd*.[6] Nevertheless, as Professor Prentice and Dr Wheeler acknowledge,[7] this does not mean that, for unsecured creditors, all in the garden is rosy. Logically, there is no incentive for secured credi-

---

1 [1989] BCLC 520, 554A. By 'general floating charge' I mean a floating charge over the entire assets and undertaking of the company present and future.

2 'Property' is defined in s 436 to include future property.

3 [1989] BCLC 520, 553A. This is the accepted view of the legal nature of misfeasance proceedings under s 212. See Oditah, 'Misfeasance Proceedings Against Company Directors' [1992] *LMCLQ* 207.

4 Sealy, 'Insolvent Company — Wrongful Trading' [1989] *CLJ* 375; Prentice, 'Creditor's Interests and Directors' Duties' [1990] *OJLS* 263; Oditah, *supra*, n 7 on p 144; Hicks, 'Advising on Wrongful Trading' (1993) 14 *The Company Lawyer* 16, 55; Wheeler, 'Swelling the Assets for Distribution in Corporate Insolvency' [1993] *JBL* 256. For an opposite view supporting an analogy between wrongful trading and misfeasance, see Schulte, *supra*, n 2 on p 143; Simmons, 'Funding actions in insolvency' (1995) 8 *Insolvency Intelligence* 57.

5 A policy objective not articulated systematically during parliamentary debate. The issue was confronted directly only once during debate in full house when an amendment to subs (1) was tabled which would expressly have earmarked the proceeds for distribution to unsecured creditors. The government's position was that the amendment would prevent preferential creditors from sharing the proceeds. This was considered undesirable as it would encourage rogue directors to pay off non-preferential creditors and trade on at the expense of preferential creditors. The government concluded that, 'the proceeds of wrongful trading should be for the generality of creditors' which, given the context, I take to mean *all* creditors whatever their status. See *Hansard*, HC Vol 83, cols 559, 567. Note also that s 175 provides for preferential debts to be paid from either '. . . assets of the company available for payment of general creditors . . .' or from any property the subject of a floating charge in priority to the chargee. For preferential creditors to participate, the proceeds would have to be treated as a corporate asset.

6 *Supra*, n 4 on p 143.

7 *Supra*, n 4 on this page.

tors to assist in funding proceedings if the proceeds do not feed their security. A major potential source of finance for litigation is ruled out and unsecured creditors are left to 'self-fund'.

The case of MC Bacon (No 2)

One question to be determined in *MC Bacon (No 2)* was whether the costs of unsuccessful proceedings against a bank could be treated as a liquidation expense payable in priority to the bank out of assets the subject of its own floating charge. The liquidator established at an interlocutory stage that an action could lie against the bank as a shadow director,[1] but abandoned the claim at trial and was ordered to pay the bank's costs personally. He claimed reimbursement of the bank's and his own costs from assets which were the subject of the bank's floating charge, on the ground that these were liquidation expenses.

Generally, liquidation expenses are payable from floating charge assets in priority to all claims. Rule 4.218 of the Insolvency Rules 1986 (SI 1986/1925) determines what can be regarded as an expense and the order in which expenses are to be paid. The liquidator argued that the costs should be treated as 'expenses properly chargeable or incurred by . . . the liquidator in preserving, realising or getting in any of the assets of the company' within rule 4.218(1)(a). In Millett J's judgment, s 214 proceedings are not brought for the purpose of realising or getting in *corporate assets*, which he took to mean assets belonging to the company when liquidation commences.[2] He held that the proceeds of action are held on trust by the liquidator for 'the general body of creditors' and neither the company nor any floating chargee can claim them.[3] Millett J declined to make a similar order under the court's inherent jurisdiction.[4]

This has several consequences. First, a liquidator is liable personally for the costs of s 214 proceedings and although the court has power to allow him to recoup them out of assets available for distribution to unsecured creditors, such an order will rarely be of practical use. Secondly, it is not, generally, possible to fund proceedings from floating charge assets and an IP is, therefore, unlikely to bring proceedings without financial backing from unsecured creditors. In the light of the discussion in Part II, it may be difficult to persuade unsecured creditors who have already lost their shirts, to part with their trousers as well!

One cannot quibble with the result in *MC Bacon* itself. Millett J was anxious to avoid subordinating the bank's floating charge to the costs of unsuccessful proceedings against the bank (which included the costs of an unsuccessful challenge to the charge's validity). However, in an ordinary case against a director,

---

1 *Re a company (No 005009 of 1987), ex parte Copp* [1989] BCLC 13.

2 [1990] BCLC 607, 613G, 615D.

3 *Ibid*, 612. Although this part of Millett J's judgment deals with the position in relation to a preference action under s 239, it is clear that his analysis, based on *Re Yagerphone Ltd* [1935] Ch 392 also applies to s 214.

4 *Ibid*, 614–616. The court has inherent jurisdiction to determine questions of costs. This is not fettered by the Insolvency Rules (see rule 4.220(2)).

the IP and unsecured creditors are left to pursue the remedy, and uphold the wider cause of deterrence, at their own risk.[1]

The case of *Oasis Merchandising*

In response to the problems raised in *MC Bacon*, IPs have explored the possibility of funding litigation with outside assistance. As *Oasis Merchandising* shows, specialist commercial funders do exist who have shown a willingness to finance s 214 proceedings. However, as *Oasis Merchandising* also shows, there is a danger that the court will stay an action financed with outside support on the ground that the financing arrangement constitutes champertous maintenance of legal proceedings.

The facts were as follows. OMS's liquidator commenced s 214 proceedings against five individuals. He had entered previously into a funding agreement with London Wall Litigation Claims Ltd ('LWL'), a self-styled provider of specialist litigation support services for IPs. The liquidator agreed to sell a share of any proceeds to LWL, who, in return, agreed to finance the action and indemnify him against any liability for costs provided that the action was conducted at LWL's direction. The respondents applied to stay the action on the ground that LWL was maintaining it under a champertous agreement. A brief excursus to the law of champertous maintenance is required to complete the picture.[2]

Maintenance is defined in *Halsbury's Laws* as:

> '. . . the giving of assistance or encouragement to one of the parties to litigation by a person who has neither an interest in the litigation nor any other motive recognised by law as justifying his interference.'[3]

Champerty is a species of maintenance. An agreement is champertous if, under its terms, the maintainer is promised a share in the proceeds of the litigation in consideration for providing funds. Criminal and civil liability for maintenance were abolished in 1967. However, the law still treats a funding arrangement tainted by unlawful maintenance as an illegal contract, void on grounds of public policy,[4] and the court can, therefore, stay proceedings the subject of a champertous agreement as an abuse of process.[5]

Maintenance and champerty were evolved to redress abuses peculiar to medieval society, at a time when administration of justice was hampered by lack

---

1 Millett J added, *obiter*, that the costs of an unsuccessful attempt to recover a *corporate asset* cannot be treated as an expense under rule 4.218(1)(a) because nothing is recovered. This applies to the costs of a failed misfeasance action under s 212 where, as the right of action is derivative and its proceeds would feed a general floating charge, there appears to be no objection to the liquidator being allowed, under the inherent jurisdiction, to recoup costs which he is ordered to pay from floating charge assets. He may also be able to recoup his own legal costs under r 4.218(1)(n). Even then, the liquidator may still 'carry the can' if asset realisations do not cover costs.

2 For a full survey, see Walters, 'Foreshortening the shadow: maintenance, champerty and the funding of litigation in corporate insolvency' (1996) *The Company Lawyer* 165 and 'A modern doctrine of champerty?' (1996) 112 *LQR* 560.

3 4th edn, Volume 9, para 400.

4 Criminal Law Act 1967, s 14(2).

5 *Grovewood Holdings Plc v James Capel & Co Ltd* [1995] Ch 80. See, however, the recent case of *Abraham v Thompson*, unreported 24 July 1997, in which the Court of Appeal expressed some doubt as to whether it is appropriate to stay maintained proceedings as an abuse of process.

of impartiality. A study of the mischiefs targeted by medieval statutes suggests that the operation of the contemporary legal system reflected closely the hierarchical relationships of power inherent in the feudal system. Royal officials and influential nobles, habitually, took assignments of spurious claims, using their position to secure a favourable result in return for a share of the spoils. Rival feudal nobles took sides in disputes between members of their retinues; support which, commonly, led to warfare. Thus, champerty was evolved both to enhance the administration of justice and as a public order measure. Although lacking in any mischief on this scale, the agreement in *Oasis Merchandising* was *prima facie* champertous as it provided for division of proceeds.

Halsbury's definition suggests that, if the maintainer demonstrates a legitimate interest which justifies his support, then the arrangement is valid. This century has witnessed a gradual expansion of the categories of justifiable maintenance as the desirability of both trade unions' and insurance companies' support for litigation have been recognised.[1] The zenith of a modern approach, which seeks to re-evaluate champerty in the light of modern conditions, is marked by the House of Lords decision in *Giles v Thompson*.[2] Here, the court upheld arrangements under which hire firms provided the victims of road accidents with replacement vehicles free of charge and then maintained negligence actions commenced in the victims' names on the basis that damages awarded for loss of use would go to pay the hire charges. Following this modern approach, the court should be slow to strike down a funding agreement as champertous if the party in receipt of support would be denied access to justice as a result.[3]

Concern for access to justice has not, as yet, embraced litigation involving the IP. There is, nevertheless, a line of authority[4] conferring an exemption on the IP based on the statutory power of sale,[5] which can be used to justify the champertous assignment of rights of action to third parties. In *Oasis Merchandising*, the argument focused on this line of authority. The key question was whether the proceeds were corporate property. If so, the liquidator was free to assign a share to LWL as the price for its support, using his power of sale.[6]

Robert Walker J construed the liquidator's power of sale narrowly and stayed the action. He followed *MC Bacon*, holding that the proceeds were not corporate property and did not fall within the scope of the power of sale which only enables a liquidator '. . . to sell any of the *company's property*'. Whilst it appears that a liquidator can freely assign a corporate right of action and/or its proceeds without fear of champerty, the same cannot be said of his statutory right under

---

1 See, eg *Hill v Archbold* [1968] 1 QB 686. Creditor support has long been regarded as legitimate — *Guy v Churchill* [1880] 40 Ch 481. Maintenance is justifiable if the maintainer has a genuine commercial interest in the maintained litigation — *Trendtex Trading Corporation v Credit Suisse* [1982] AC 679.
2 [1994] 1 AC 142.
3 See, eg Sir Thomas Bingham MR's approach in the Court of Appeal, [1993] 3 All ER 321, 348J.
4 *Seear v Lawson* (1880) 15 Ch D 426; *Re Park Gate Waggon Works Co* (1881) 17 Ch D 234; *Ramsey v Hartley* [1977] 1 WLR 686, cited with approval in *Stein v Blake* [1996] AC 243; *Bang & Olufsen UK Ltd v Ton Système Ltd* [1993] CAT 834.
5 Schedules 4, 5; s 436.
6 It was conceded that the right of action could not be assigned outright as only a liquidator has *locus standi*. See further, *Re Ayala Holdings Ltd (No 2)* [1996] 1 BCLC 467.

s 214. The approach in *MC Bacon* was approved by the Court of Appeal. Delivering the leading judgment, Peter Gibson LJ sought to harden the distinction between corporate rights and statutory rights vesting exclusively in the liquidator:

> 'The scheme of the 1986 Act suggests that only [a corporate right] falls within "the property of the company" which [a] . . . liquidator can sell. Thus a right of action against directors for misfeasance which the liquidator . . . can enforce under section 212 . . . and the fruits of such an action are property of the company capable of being charged[1] . . . because the right of action arose and was available to the company prior to the winding up . . . with this can be contrasted the right of action by a liquidator and the fruits of such an action, for . . . preference or fraudulent or wrongful trading, which are not the property of the company . . .'

A submission that the liquidator's act was a valid exercise of the power in Schedule 4, para 13 '. . . to do all such other things as may be necessary for winding up the company's affairs . . .' was also rejected.

The Court of Appeal's judgment is disappointing. It contains no real attempt to grapple with questions of policy. We are left to wonder how, in the late-twentieth century, an agreement which shifts risk from one private operator (albeit one licensed under the Act) to a second, identified private operator who falls within the scope of the court's jurisdiction as to costs,[2] can possibly be regarded as a threat to administration of justice. Arguably, the court should follow the modern approach to champerty developed outside the insolvency context (epitomised by *Giles v Thompson*), and give due weight to the fact that, without outside support, an IP may not have the resources to pursue good claims. Liquidators regularly assign corporate rights of action outright to third parties (usually directors) who then proceed with the benefit of legal aid. Such assignments are usually entered into on the basis that any proceeds will be shared between the company and the assignee. Companies are ineligible for legal aid. The courts routinely uphold a dubious practice which drives a coach and horses through the legal aid legislation as a legitimate exercise of the power of sale[3] and yet object to the type of funding arrangement contemplated in *Oasis Merchandising*. We must now draw a distinction for funding purposes between misfeasance and wrongful trading proceedings. The right of action under s 212 and/or its proceeds are treated as corporate property. A liquidator is free to assign the property in misfeasance under the power of sale to anybody on any terms. He can look more readily to secured creditors and commercial funders for support. There is a perverse incentive to 'overload' misfeasance and bring actions under section 212 which test the outer parameters of directors' duties at common law[4] when claims may fall squarely within s 214. This seems absurd.

---

1 And, by extension, freely assignable under the power of sale.
2 Supreme Court Act 1981, s 51; *Aiden Shipping Co Ltd v Interbulk Ltd (The Vimeira)* [1986] AC 965.
3 See, eg *Norglen Ltd v Reeds Rains Prudential Ltd* [1996] 1 WLR 864; *Circuit Systems Ltd v Zuken-Redac (UK) Ltd* [1996] 3 All ER 748. Although, see now the Civil Legal Aid (General) (Amendment) (No 2) Regulations 1996 which came into force on 1 June 1996 and are likely to curb this practice.
4 Directors' fiduciary duties are expanding to encompass creditors' interests. See, Prentice, *supra* n 4 on p 152; Sealy, 'Directors' Wider Responsibilities' (1987) 13 *Monash LR* 164; Grantham, 'The Judicial Extension of Directors' Duties to Creditors' [1991] *JBL* 1.

It is clear from Peter Gibson LJ's judgment that a liquidator can, *personally*, sell the fruits of s 214 proceedings provided that the terms of sale confer no right on the purchaser to influence the conduct of proceedings.[1] In particular, any terms inconsistent with the liquidator's statutory right to apply to court for directions[2] should be avoided. Sub-sales by the purchaser should also be expressly prohibited.[3] One wonders whether commercial funders will be prepared to support actions on this basis. Whatever their position, it is unfortunate that a distinction between derivative and non-derivative rights has to be drawn to decide whether a funding arrangement is champertous or not in the first place.

PART FOUR: CONCLUSION

I have sought to examine the dynamics of enforcement with reference to s 214. If we take the issues raised in Parts II and III as a whole, it is no surprise that so few claims are brought to trial. However, while offering this assessment, I remain content to leave others to lament what they perceive to be an unhappy state of affairs. We should not conclude automatically that the provision is a dead letter just because there is a lack of *visible* enforcement. We do not know to what extent the IP is able to use the threat of proceedings to concentrate directors' minds and force quick settlements. It is a fair bet that there are at least some directors who will prefer to settle because of the risk that if they lose the court might disqualify them in the same proceedings.[4] Whilst this places considerable strain on the idea that s 214 can operate as a deterrent, it is too soon to rule out its effectiveness as a remedy completely. Also, it is clear that the enactment of the objective minimum standard of care is leading to a culture-shift within the common law. Until recently, the courts were reluctant to impose liability on directors for loss caused by managerial carelessness or error of judgement. The courts now favour a more interventionist approach in which the director is judged according to the objective standard contained in s 214(4).[5] The idea that directors should be subject to a professional standard is gaining ground. We should be slow to write off a provision which, in setting new benchmarks, may serve to sharpen directors' awareness of their legal responsibilities.

The problem remains that, if we are serious about the use of section 214 as a *deterrent*, then visible enforcement is needed for that deterrent to remain

---

1 A re-statement of the *ratio* in *Glegg v Bromley* [1912] 3 KB 474. Here, the court established that future proceeds of a right of action in tort are property assignable in equity even though the right of action is a bare right, incapable of assignment. The court would not have upheld the assignment in *Glegg* if it had conferred any right on the assignee to influence conduct of the action. Note, however, that, no objection was raised in *Giles v Thompson, supra,* n 2 on p 155 to an agreement reserving the assignee's right to appoint its own solicitor to pursue an action in the assignor's name. Arguably, a liquidator would need the consent of unsecured creditors to this type of assignment in relation to s 214 as it follows from *MC Bacon* and *Oasis Merchandising* that the fruits are caught by the statutory trust.

2 Sections 112(1), 168(3).

3 *Trendtex, supra* n 1 on p 155.

4 *Supra* n 2 on p 145.

5 *Norman v Theodore Goddard* [1991] BCLC 1028; *Re D'Jan of London Ltd* [1993] BCLC 646, and Professor Boyle's own reflections on this development at (1996) 17 *The Company Lawyer* 83.

credible. Yet, IPs will only proceed against worthwhile targets,[1] and then only if someone can be persuaded to fund the action. A liquidator can now engage legal representation on the basis of a conditional fee.[2] However, it is too early to judge the impact of this development. Several City law firms have indicated a general willingness to enter into conditional fee arrangements. However, one doubts whether these firms will be keen to carry the risks associated with large-scale wrongful trading litigation.[3] As the law stands, it appears that the future of s 214 will be shaped as much by the attitude of unsecured creditors as by the attitude of the courts.[4]

---

1 Respondents may make more attractive targets if they hold directors' and officers' liability insurance. However, a liquidator will then find himself up against a well-resourced opponent. One cannot be sanguine about a liquidator's prospects in relation to other 'deep pockets', eg banks. See Bhattacharyya, 'Shadow directors and wrongful trading revisited' (1995) 16 *The Company Lawyer* 313 and Professor Morse's essay in Chapter 7 of this collection.

2 Conditional Fee Agreements Order 1995, SI 1995/1674, Conditional Fee Agreement Regulations 1995, SI 1995/1675.

3 Oasis Merchandising's liquidator, ultimately, resolved his funding difficulties by entering into a conditional fee arrangement with a large and reputable solicitors' firm. Whether this influenced the court's decision is a matter of conjecture.

4 The unreported decision in *Katz v McNally*, 22 May 1997, a case on s 239 proceedings, provides an interesting postscript. Here, an unsecured creditor agreed to indemnify the company against its liability for costs in return for the company granting a first charge over any recoveries in the creditor's favour. The Court of Appeal held that this arrangement was lawful and in so doing expressed some doubt as to the correctness of *MC Bacon (No 2)* on the question of whether the costs of a *successful* wrongful trading action can be recouped from recoveries. This is of some comfort to creditors as is Lindsay J's refusal to make a non-party costs order against a creditor-funder in *Eastglen Ltd v Grafton* [1996] 2 BCLC 279, and see further, Walters, 'Creditor-Funded Litigation in Corporate Insolvency [1997] CFILR 126. However, there is nothing in English law which allows a funding creditor to receive, as a right, a higher proportion of recoveries than non-funding creditors to reflect his added risk. This contrasts with the position in Australia under the Corporations Law, s 564. As such, the future of s 214 is left very much in the hands of unsecured creditors with a particular axe to grind and money to spare.

Chapter 10

RATIFYING DIRECTORIAL WRONGDOING — THE LEGAL FICTION OF SHAREHOLDER CONSENT IN ENGLAND

John P Lowry[1]

INTRODUCTION

It is a basic principle of the law of trusts that in an action by a beneficiary against a trustee for breach of trust, the trustee may plead by way of defence that the breach in issue was committed with the consent of the beneficiary.[2] In the company law context, this is translated into the notion of 'shareholder ratification' whereby a miscreant director may avoid liability (for example, for breach of the fiduciary duties) where it can be shown that the company ratified the wrongdoing either antecedently or subsequently.[3] Typically, such breaches arise where company directors engage in self-dealing, thereby violating the no-conflict rule which lies at the core of fiduciary responsibility. Although the fiduciary duties of directors are strict, the process of shareholder ratification, as it currently operates, can be seen as immunising company directors from the consequences of breach.[4] It therefore

---

1 Senior Lecturer in Law, Department of Law, Brunel University. The author owes a debt of gratitude to Rod Edmunds of the University of Sussex and to Professor Frank Simonie of Fairleigh Dickinson University, New Jersey for their typically incisive comments on earlier drafts of this essay. The usual caveat applies.

2 The classic statement of the rule was made by Romer LJ in *Fletcher v Collis* [1905] 2 Ch 24 at 27, who said: '[a] beneficiary who knowingly consented to the breach could not, if of full contracting age and capacity, and in the absence of special circumstances, afterwards be heard to say that the conduct of the trustee in committing the breach of trust was, as against him the particular beneficiary, improper . . .' See, also, *Nail v Punter* (1832) 5 Sim 555; *Re Pauling's Settlement Trust* [1964] Ch 303; *Re Bucks Constabulary Widows' and Orphans' Fund Friendly Society (No 2)* [1979] 1 WLR 936; *Swan v Perpetual Executors and Trustees Association of Australia Ltd* (1897) 23 VLR 293; *Spellson v George* (1992) 26 NSWLR 666. See further, Oakley, *Parker & Mellows: The Modern Law of Trusts* (London: Sweet & Maxwell, 1994) at p 598 *et seq;* Hanbury and Martin, *Modern Equity* (London: Sweet & Maxwell, 1997) at p 644 *et seq;* Meagher and Gummow, *Jacobs' Law of Trusts in Australia* (Sydney: Butterworths, 1997) at p 647 *et seq.*

3 *Winthrop Investments Ltd v Winns Ltd* [1975] 2 NSWLR 666 at pp 679, 680–689. See *Regal (Hastings) Ltd v Gulliver* [1967] 2 AC 134n, [1942] 1 All ER 378 (references hereafter are to the official report only), considered further at n 4 on p 162, *infra.*

4 But where the profiteering directors are fraudulent and in a position to control the voting of the company, a shareholder may bring a derivative action. The one true exception to the principle of majority rule, as encapsulated by the rule in *Foss v Harbottle* (1843) 2 Hare 461, is where a fraud has been perpetrated by those who 'hold and control the majority of shares in the company and will not permit an action to be brought in the name of the company', *per* Lord Davey in *Burland v Earle* [1902] AC 83 at 93. See also, *Dominion Cotton Mills v Amyot* [1912] AC 546 (PC); *Cook v Deeks* [1916] 1 AC 554 (PC); *Foster v Foster* [1916] 1 Ch 532; *Estmanco (Kilner House) Ltd v GLC* [1982] 1 WLR 2; *Atwool v Merryweather* (1867) LR 5 Eq 464n. See further, *Boyle & Birds' Company Law* (Bristol: Jordans, 1995), ch 15.

follows that adherence to strict rules of disclosure of all material information surrounding the breach of duty becomes all the more necessary if the fiduciary duties of directors are not to be diluted by some conditional duty of disclosure.

The first part of this essay will outline the current regime for the ratification of directorial breaches of fiduciary duties. It will be demonstrated that while the duty of disclosure cast upon directors was formulated originally along strict lines, the modern judicial tendency has been to adopt a more equivocal view of the duty. It will be posited that the Law Commission's Consultation Paper No 142, *Shareholder Remedies*,[1] which excluded shareholder ratification expressly from its purview,[2] represents a missed opportunity for an authoritative, critical review of the process. It will be seen that the current judicial view of the disclosure requirement of directors is, fundamentally, deficient and, as such, may be seen as undermining the prophylactic basis of the fiduciary duties.[3] The second part of this essay considers the disclosure standard formulated by the Delaware Chancery Court and the Delaware Supreme Court. It will be argued that if the concept of 'informed consent' to directorial breaches of duty is to acquire legitimacy in England, the mechanism for shareholder ratification should be reformed at its root, using the Delaware model as its matrix. The possibility of accommodating the Delaware approach on this side of the Atlantic, through the vehicle of *uberrimae fides* (with consequent strict liability for failure to disclose all material information to the shareholders' meeting), is considered. Such a solution would, at least, remedy the tempering effect which the current ratification process has upon the fiduciary duties of company directors.

THE RATIFICATION PROCESS IN ENGLAND

In England, two parallel bodies of law govern the ratification process, namely common law principles and the statutory provisions contained in the Companies Act 1985. Directors who, in breach of their fiduciary duty to avoid a conflict between their duties to the company and their personal interests, profit personally by availing themselves of information acquired through their position as directors, may avoid liability by obtaining shareholder ratification.[4] On the other hand, where a director has, fraudulently, expropriated a company

---

1 Consultation Paper No 142 (London: The Stationery Office), published 22 October 1996, (hereafter referred to as the LCCP).

2 Para 5.2. See *infra* n 1 on p 168 and associated text.

3 See further, Lowry, 'Directorial Self-Dealing: Constructing A Regime Of Accountability' (1997) 48 *NILQ* 2.

4 In *Regal (Hastings) Ltd v Gulliver*, *supra* n 3 on p 161. Lord Russell stated, at 150, that the directors 'could, had they wished, have protected themselves by a resolution (either antecedent or subsequent) of the Regal shareholders in general meeting'. The effect of antecedent shareholder ratification of a director's breach was explained by Vinelott J in *Movitex Ltd v Bulfield* (1986) 2 BCC 99, 403 at 430. He said: 'The resolution in general meeting protects the director not because it operates to release him from the consequences of a breach of the self-dealing rule but because, to the extent that the company in general meeting gives its informed consent to the transaction there is no breach; the conflict of duty and interest is avoided'. See also, *Canada Safeway Ltd v Thompson* [1951] 3 DLR 295.

asset, the breach of duty is non-ratifiable and the director may be impeached by a shareholder instituting a derivative action.[1]

At common law, shareholder ratification of directorial breaches of duty is achieved by the relatively straightforward process of obtaining an ordinary resolution of the shareholders in general meeting whereby the transaction in question is ratified.[2] The notice convening the shareholders' meeting must state, in explicit terms, the purpose for which the meeting is being called, insofar as it must provide a 'fair, candid, and reasonable explanation' of the business proposed.[3] Failure to comply with this requirement will result in the resolution, if passed, being held ineffective as against those shareholders who dissented or who were absent from the meeting.[4] Further, it was held by Kekewich J, in *Tiessen v Henderson*,[5] that the notice calling the extraordinary general meeting in which ratification is to be sought must disclose all facts necessary to enable the shareholder receiving it to determine in his own interest, whether or not he ought to attend the meeting. He concluded that the pecuniary interest of a director in the matter of a special resolution to be proposed at the meeting is a material fact for this purpose.

The common law requirement of shareholder ratification has been relaxed by the Companies Act 1985 with respect to transactions between a company and a director. Section 317(1) of the Companies Act 1985 lays down the duty of disclosure, which is mandatory in effect. It provides that a director who is in any way interested in a contract with the company must declare the nature of his interest to the board. Failure to comply with this requirement renders the director liable to an unlimited fine on conviction on indictment.[6] Such a contract is voidable, and the company can call upon the director to account for the gains he has made.[7] It has been held that compliance with this provision requires disclosure to a duly convened and constituted board

---

1 See, for example, *Cook v Deeks, supra* n 4 on p 161, in which the Privy Council held that where directors misappropriate corporate assets which they are regarded as holding in equity on behalf of the company, they cannot by using their votes cause the company to ratify the breach. See also, *infra* n 2 on p 168 and associated text.

2 *Benson v Heathorn* (1842) 1 Y & CCC 326; *Aberdeen Rly Co v Blaikie* (1854) 1 Macq 461; *North-West Transportation Co Ltd v Beatty* (1887) 12 App Cas 589, *per* Sir Richard Baggallay at 593–594. A breach of duty is equally ratifiable by obtaining the informal approval of *every* member who has a right to vote on such a resolution: *Re Duomatic Ltd* [1969] 2 Ch 365; *New Zealand Netherlands Society Oranje Inc v Kuys* [1973] 1 WLR 1126; *Queensland Mines Ltd v Cropper* (1978) 18 ALR 1, noted Sullivan (1979) 42 *MLR* 71 who comments that the decision in *Queensland Mines* 'suggests that many such breaches can now be forestalled or condoned by the simple expedient of obtaining the consent of boardroom colleagues who are often little more than ciphers'.

3 *Kaye v Croydon Tramways Company* [1898] 1 Ch 358. See further, *Boyle & Birds' Company Law, op cit,* n 4 on p 161 at 360 *et seq.*

4 *Ibid* at 370 (Kekewich J).

5 [1899] 1 Ch 861.

6 Companies Act 1985, s 317(7).

7 *Hely-Hutchinson v Brayhead Ltd* [1968] 1 QB 549. However, in *Guinness plc v Saunders* [1990] 2 WLR 324, Lord Goff was of the view that breach of the duty of disclosure triggers only the criminal sanctions provided for in s 317 and does not *per se* give rise to any civil consequences.

meeting, a function which cannot be delegated to a sub-committee of the board.[1]

Importantly, Article 85 of Table A, if adopted, allows for the duty to obtain shareholder ratification of transactions between the company and a director to be avoided, retaining only the s 317 requirement of disclosure to the board of directors. Although Article 85 underpins s 317 insofar as the requirement for disclosure of 'the nature and extent of any material interest' is preserved, it goes on to relieve the director from his liability to account for any gains made and provides that 'no such transaction or arrangement shall be avoided on the ground of any such interest or benefit'.[2] Against this, it should be noted that Article 94 goes on to prohibit a director of the company voting at any board meeting, or a committee of the board, on any resolution concerning a matter in which the director, or a person with whom the director is connected, has a material interest. It has been held that such a director cannot be counted in the quorum for such a resolution.[3] However, the general prohibition contained in Article 94 does not extend to cover director/members voting on a resolution at a company's general meeting.[4]

The inherent weakness of the disclosure requirements laid down in the model Articles becomes particularly apparent where a director who has an interest in a transaction with the company has a dominant position on the board. The deficiencies of the Table A provisions have received some statutory recognition insofar as the Companies Act 1985 reinforces the common law requirements of disclosure with respect to two categories of transaction where the possibility of conflict is manifest. First, ss 320–322 require substantial property transactions with directors to be approved in advance by the company in general meeting. A 'substantial property transaction' is defined as arising where the market value of the asset exceeds the lower of £100,000 or 10 per cent of the company's net

1 *Guinness plc v Saunders* [1988] BCLC 43 (Browne-Wilkinson J). The issue was not directly addressed in the House of Lords decision. Fox LJ, in the Court of Appeal, opined that even if all the members of the board had known of a contract this would not validate payments made thereunder, (see [1988] 1 WLR 863 at 868). However, a director need not disclose interests to a duly convened board which are patently obvious, such as his interest in his own service contract which is generally known to his colleagues: *Runciman v Walter Runciman plc* [1992] BCLC 1084, noted Lowry, [1993] *JBL* 279. For the purposes of the section, there can be a directors' meeting in the case of a sole directorship. In *Neptune (Vehicle Washing Equipment) Ltd v Fitzgerald* [1995] BCC 474, it was held that when holding the meeting alone, a sole director had to make the declaration to himself and record the declaration in the minutes.
2 It is also common practice to adopt Article 86, which provides for disclosure of a continuing interest to the board.
3 *Re Greymouth Point Elizabeth Rly & Coal Ltd* [1904] 1 Ch 32; *Re North Eastern Insurance Co Ltd* [1991] 1 Ch 198. See now the exceptions specified in Article 94. Note also, Article 96 whereby the members may, by ordinary resolution, suspend or relax the prohibition either generally or in respect of any particular issue. It is common for small private companies not to adopt Article 94, thereby permitting their directors to vote on resolutions on contracts in which a director has an interest.
4 *NW Transportation Co v Beatty, supra* n 2 on p 163; *Burland v Earle, supra* n 4 on p 161 at 93; *Re Express Engineering Works Ltd* [1920] 1 Ch 466.

asset value if more than £2,000.[1] These provisions were designed to respond to an alarming number of cases involving fraudulent asset stripping by directors.[2] Secondly, subject to certain exceptions, ss 330–344 impose a general prohibition on companies making loans to directors or entering into any guarantee or providing any security in connection with a loan to a director of a company or a director of a holding company. The regulation of such loans dates back to the Companies Act 1948 and was severely tightened in the 1980 Act in order to address the growing problem, identified in a series of DTI investigations, of directors filtering money under the guise of loans on highly favourable terms from their companies.[3]

THE SHIFTING BOUNDARIES OF THE DISCLOSURE DUTY

The orthodox rule embodying the duty of disclosure was stated by Moss JA in *Earle v Burland*,[4] who stressed that the duty cast upon directors not to profit secretly from their position is strict unless such profit is made after obtaining 'the unanimous consent of all the shareholders, given after full explanation of all the circumstances and full knowledge of the position.'[5] In *Imperial Mercantile Credit Association (Liquidators) v Coleman*,[6] Lord Cairns opined that:

> 'A man declares his opinion or his intentions when he states what his opinion is, or what his intentions are, not that he has an opinion or that he has intentions; and so, in my opinion, a man declares his interest, not when he states that he has an interest, but when he states what his interest is.'[7]

This early formulation reflected the strict view of equity in adopting a prescriptive approach towards the issue of consent in the trustee/beneficiary context. In this respect, a series of principles have evolved against which the apparent consent of beneficiaries to any breach of trust is tested.[8] For example, the need for unanimity of consent, if a trustee is to avoid liability completely, was recognised by Wilmer LJ in *Re Pauling's Settlement Trusts*.[9] Those beneficiaries who dissent can still bring an action for breach. The point was made by Fry LJ in

---

1 Transactions exempted from the requirement of approval in general meeting are laid down in s 321. The two principal exceptions are (a) inter-group transfers when the property is to be acquired by a holding company from one of its wholly owned subsidiaries, or vice versa, or by one wholly-owned subsidiary from another wholly owned subsidiary of that holding company: s 321(2)(a); and (b) arrangements entered into by a company which is being wound up otherwise than by a members' voluntary winding up: s 321(2)(g).
2 HC Official Report, SCA, 2 July 1981, col 425.
3 See the White Paper, 'The Conduct of Company Directors' (Cmnd 7037, 1977).
4 (1900) 27 AR 540. See also, *Baillie v Oriental Telephone & Electric Co Ltd* [1915] 1 Ch 503 CA; *Grant v United Kingdom Switchback Railways Co* (1888) 40 Ch D 135 CA; *Imperial Mercantile Credit Association (Liquidators) v Coleman* (1873) LR 6 HL 189.
5 *Ibid* at 561. See also, *Furs Ltd v Tomkies* (1936) 54 CLR 583 at 602, in which Starke J stated that disclosure 'requires [the director] to make a full disclosure of all information which is then or may thereafter during the currency of the agreement be within his knowledge or power'.
6 (1873) LR 6 HL 189.
7 *Ibid* at 205.
8 See, for example, Hanbury & Martin, *Modern Equity* (London: Sweet & Maxwell, 1997), p 645 *et seq.*
9 [1964] Ch 303, at 335.

Re Massingberd's Settlement[1] that passive assent is insufficient: 'Consent is not a mere formality. It is a judgment of a person who is interested'.[2] Further, the consent must be freely given by an adult who is *sui juris*,[3] and it must be fully informed insofar as the beneficiary 'fully understands what he is concurring in . . .'[4]

However, it is apparent that, in the company/business law context at least (as distinct from the law of trusts), a more benevolent approach is emerging towards the issue of directorial disclosure and shareholder consent. This tendency is discernible in recent *dicta* which suggest that some conditional duty of disclosure will suffice. For example, in *NZ Netherlands Society v Kuys*,[5] Lord Wilberforce stated that a fiduciary will not be in breach if he can show that the information withheld would not, in any case, have affected the beneficiaries' decision. His Lordship remarked: 'But the appellant was quite unable to point to any matter relevant . . . which, had it been disclosed, would have affected the society's decision . . .'[6] This approach is mirrored by Hutley JA in *Walden Properties Ltd v Beaver Properties Ltd*,[7] who said:

> 'The court of equity has always been a jealous guardian of the rights of the person entitled to the benefit of the performance of fiduciary duties. However, where the fiduciary duty is to provide information, and the information can be shown by the fiduciary to be incapable of affecting the result, I consider that the beneficiary cannot take advantage of the breach of duty.'[8]

It is suggested that these more recent formulations of the duty can be interpreted as representing an erosion of the disclosure standard. They, seemingly, depart from the unequivocal language used by Moss JA, in as much as there is a significant shift in emphasis. Taking a literal view of Lord Wilberforce's formulation, those charged with giving information to shareholders can themselves decide what is a material fact. Only in the event of a subsequent legal challenge will the immateriality of the non-disclosed fact in issue have to be established. Given the evidential complexities which arise in this respect, it is arguable that Moss JA may well have had in mind the simpler solution of a presumption that *all* information surrounding the making of the secret profit should be deemed material. Only thus can it truly be said that the shareholders received a 'full explanation of all the circumstances'. The advantage of this approach lies in its simplicity. It avoids the situation whereby the court is put in the position of speculating whether or not a non-disclosed fact would have affected the shareholders' vote. As Lord Chelmsford LC observed in *Smith v Kay*:[9]

---

1 (1890) 63 LT 296.
2 *Ibid* at 299.
3 *Adye v Feuilleteau* (1783) 3 Swan 84n; *March v Russell* (1837) 3 My & Cr 31 cf *Overton v Bannister* (1884) 3 Hare 503.
4 *Per* Wilberforce J at first instance in *Re Pauling's Settlement Trusts* [1962] 1 WLR 86 at 108, approved by the Court of Appeal in *Holder v Holder* [1968] Ch 353 at 394, 399 and 406.
5 [1973] 1 WLR 1126.
6 *Ibid* at 1135.
7 [1973] 2 NSWLR 815.
8 *Ibid* at 846–847.
9 (1859) 7 HL Cas 750.

'can it be permitted to a party who has practised a deception, with a view to a particular end, which has been attained by it, to speculate upon what might have been the result if there had been a full communication of the truth?'[1]

Yet the apparent erosion of the disclosure standard discernible in the language used by Lord Wilberforce and Hutley JA has received implicit statutory endorsement. The Companies Act itself is framed in terms which envisage a lower standard of disclosure than that envisaged by Moss JA. The duty under s 317(1) to disclose 'the nature of' the director's interest falls short of anything amounting to a full and frank disclosure of all circumstances surrounding the contract with the company in which the director is interested.

However, this dilution of the disclosure standard is not being replicated in all Commonwealth jurisdictions. For example, in *Canada Safeway Ltd v Thompson*,[2] Manson J, citing Lord Davey's opinion in *Burland v Earle*,[3] stated that: 'In my view, nothing less than a unanimous resolution of its shareholders consenting to the buy after full disclosure . . .' would suffice to relieve the directors from their liability to account.[4] A strict view of the disclosure requirement was also taken by the New Zealand Court of Appeal in *Witten-Hannah v Davis*,[5] a case involving a solicitor's breach of the fiduciary duty of loyalty to his client. The client had not been advised independently in respect of a financial arrangement she had entered into with the solicitor in which she had suffered loss. Richardson J stated that:

> 'In discharging fiduciary responsibilities a solicitor cannot have a personal interest in a transaction unless the client is fully informed of all the facts and of all the implications for the client and then freely consents. In some circumstances and because of the insidious potential for conflict of interest, the discharge of that responsibility can only be established by ensuring that the client is independently advised. Ensuring independent advice is not a separate fiduciary duty but rather a means of discharging the responsibility of ensuring that the client is fully informed and freely consents to her solicitor's participation in the transaction.'[6]

It is evident that, in Richardson J's view, the issue of whether or not the fiduciary in question has done all that is necessary to obtain the genuine consent of the 'beneficiary' is synergistic with the discharge of the fiduciary duty in question. Further, the duty does not end with disclosure of material facts without more, but extends to explaining the implications which ratification, if granted, would give rise to.[7]

Against this background of judicial and statutory liberalisation of the disclosure requirement (by the Privy Council and the New South Wales courts) the Law

---

1 *Ibid* at 759. In *Re Imperial Mercantile Credit Association* (1869) LR 9 Eq 223 at 225–226n, James VC said that: 'I do not think a Court of Equity is in the habit of considering that a falsehood is not to be looked at because if the truth had been told the same thing might have resulted'.

2 *Supra* n 4 on p 162.

3 *Supra* n 4 on p 161.

4 [1951] 3 DLR 295 at 299.

5 [1995] 2 NZLR 141. See also, *Haira v Burbery Mortgage Finance & Savings Ltd (In Receivership)* [1995] 3 NZLR 396, CA.

6 *Ibid* at 149.

7 In reaching his conclusion, Richardson J was mindful of the statement of Lord Chelmsford LC in *Smith v Kay, supra* n 9 on p 166 and of the observation of James VC in *Re Imperial Mercantile Credit Association, supra* n 1 on this page. See further, n 3 on p 174, *infra* and associated text.

Commission summarily dismisses the opportunity to subject the ratification process to examination, stating that it 'is outside the scope of this project to consider in depth the conditions necessary for effective ratification'.[1] Why this issue is not considered further is unclear. Perhaps the Commission was mindful of the difficulties of accommodating the focus of its remit within the current debate surrounding corporate governance. Clearly, there is the fundamental problem of embarking upon a systematic review of the apparatus for corporate decision-making within a system wedded to the unitary board. Nevertheless, the issue of shareholder consent is critical, and manifestly so when viewed from the perspective of whether or not the mechanism for ratification achieves genuine shareholder exculpation of directorial wrongdoing.[2] While it is self evident that ratification is supposedly founded upon the notion of fully informed consent (based upon knowledge of all material facts surrounding the director's breach),[3] the disclosure requirement formulated by Lord Wilberforce is singularly lax as a means of achieving this objective. Since the ratification process has a pivotal role in the overall regime for remedying wrongs to the company, the failure of the Commission to subject the effectiveness of the current mechanism to examination represents a major lacuna in its review. Its failure in this respect means that an opportunity for legislative reform has been lost.

Given the mire in which the ratification process now stands, it is evident that a regime needs to be constructed which addresses the need for impartial deliberation of a director's self-dealing and the need for effectively protecting the company's interests. Such a regime should also perform, within this framework, its preordained prophylactic role. For if the fiduciary standard is to retain its vigour as commercial practice and ethics enter the twenty-first century, then those breaches of duty that are ratifiable must be subject to full and proper scrutiny.

THE CASE FOR ENLIGHTENED DESPOTISM — DISENFRANCHISING THE INTERESTED DIRECTOR

It has long been settled that a director may, *qua* shareholder, exercise his voting rights to protect his own interests even though his personal interests may be tangentially opposed to those of the company. The right to participate in such a vote can be traced to the principle that 'the shareholder's vote is a right of property, and prima facie may be exercised by a shareholder as he thinks fit in his

---

1 Paragraph 5.2. Where, however, a director has expropriated company property fraudulently, the breach of duty is non-ratifiable and the director may, of course, be impeached by a shareholder instituting a derivative action. The principle underlying ratification was explained by Vinelott J in *Movitex Ltd v Bulfield* (1986) 2 BCC 99, 403 at 430 when explaining the effect of antecedent release from liability: 'The resolution in general meeting protects the director not because it operates to release him from the consequences of a breach of the self-dealing rule but because, to the extent that the company in general meeting gives its informed consent to the transaction there is no breach; the conflict of duty and interest is avoided'. See, also, *Canada Safeway Ltd v Thompson, supra* n 4 on p 162.

2 See further, *Guinness plc v Saunders* [1990] 2 AC 663; *Runciman v Walter Runciman plc* [1992] BCLC 1084.

3 See *Burland v Earle, supra* n 4 on p 161 and associated text.

own interest'.[1] This freedom is unfettered, except where the director's voting power is exercised in order to perpetrate a fraud, or to oppress the minority.[2] In *North-West Transportation Co Ltd v Beatty*,[3] the resolution of a general meeting to purchase a vessel at the vendor's price was held to be valid, notwithstanding that the vendor himself JH Beatty held the majority of the shares in the company, and the resolution was carried by his votes. Sir Richard Baggallay, who delivered the principal opinion of the Privy Council, said:

> 'But the constitution of the company enabled the defendant JH Beatty to acquire this voting power; there was no limit upon the number of shares which a shareholder might hold, and for every share so held he was entitled to a vote; . . . [the defendant] had a perfect right to acquire further shares, and to exercise his voting power in such a manner as to secure the election of directors whose views upon policy agreed with his own, and to support those views at any shareholders meeting; . . .'[4]

The position which allows a director (admittedly voting *qua* member), to participate in a vote ratifying a breach of fiduciary duty has given rise to judicial frustration on the basis that directorial franchise deprives the process of impartiality. Commenting on the inability of the court to order that such resolutions be put to the vote of independent shareholders, James LJ observed in *Mason v Harris*,[5] that:

> 'It has been suggested that the Court has some means of directing a meeting to be called in which the corrupt shareholders shall not vote. If the Court had any such power that mode of proceeding might furnish the best remedy in cases of this nature, but I cannot see how any directions for holding such a meeting could be given.'[6]

Apart from cases involving allegations of fraud, it seems that the only situation where some prohibition on directorial voting does exist is where the very validity of the shares in question is being challenged.[7] In *Hogg v Cramphorn Ltd*,[8] the directors of the defendant company, which was the subject of a take over bid,

---

1 *Carruth v Imperial Chemical Industries Ltd* [1937] AC 707 at 765, *per* Lord Maugham.
2 Where this results in conduct which unfairly prejudices the minority, the appropriate course of action for them is to petition the court under s 459 of the Companies Act 1985.
3 *Supra* n 2 on p 163. See also *Burland v Earle, supra* n 4 on p 161 at 94; *Northern Counties Securities Ltd v Jackson & Steeple Ltd* [1974] 1 WLR 1133 at 1146. Cf *Prudential Assurance Co Ltd v Newman Industries Ltd (No 2)* [1982] Ch 204 at 309–310 (*per* Vinelott J). See further, Boyle (1981) 2 *Co Law* 264.
4 (1887) 12 App Cas 589 at 601.
5 (1879) 11 Ch D 97. For a detailed analysis of these decisions, see Rixon, 'Competing Interests And Conflicting Principles: An Examination Of The Power Of Alteration Of Articles Of Association', [1986] *MLR* 446.
6 *Ibid* at 109. For a contrary view, see Sealy, (1970) 86 *LQR* 413 at 415–416 who argues that disallowing the votes of interested shareholders would be tantamount to restricting the 'parliamentary franchise . . . to those who pay no taxes and receive no pension'.
7 The situations where the holders of 'interested' shares are prohibited *expressly* from participating in a vote are severely limited, for example, ss 164(5) and 174(2) of the Companies Act 1985, which concern resolutions by a company to repurchase a member's share. But these provisions do not prohibit the holder of the shares from voting, they merely disfranchise the shares that are affected. See further, Sealy, *Cases and Materials in Company Law* (London: Butterworths, 1992) at p 125. See also, Wedderburn, (1967) 30 *MLR* 77. Professor Sealy has remarked that no principle of general application can be developed from these cases, see (1970) 86 *LQR* 413 at 416.
8 [1967] Ch 254. See also, *Atwool v Merryweather* (1867) LR 5 Eq 464n.

issued 5,707 shares with special voting rights to known supporters in an attempt to forestall the bid and protect their position on the board. They were acting in good faith throughout, but it was held that they had used the power to allot shares for an improper purpose. However, the breach of duty was capable of ratification by the members in general meeting, provided the new share issue was not counted in the vote on the resolution. Buckley J stated:

> 'Had the majority of the company in general meeting approved the issue of the 5,707 shares before it was made, even with the proposed special voting rights attached (assuming that such rights could have been so attached conformably with the articles), I do not think that any member could have complained of the issue being made; . . . Before setting the allotment and issue of the 5,707 shares aside, therefore, I propose to allow the company an opportunity to decide in general meeting whether it approves or disapproves of the issue of the shares . . .'[1]

Nevertheless, the apparent regret expressed by James LJ at the general impotence of the court to call such meetings whenever the interests of the company so require seems to have been met with a degree of sympathy in more recent decisions. In *Smith v Croft (No 2)*,[2] Knox J took the view that, when considering whether or not to allow a minority shareholder's action by way of exception to the rule in *Foss v Harbottle*,[3] the court should have regard to the views of those shareholders who are not involved in the proposed action either as defendants or as persons connected with them. He said:

> 'Ultimately the question which has to be answered in order to determine whether the rule in *Foss v Harbottle* applies to prevent a minority shareholder seeking relief as plaintiff for the benefit of the company is, 'Is the plaintiff being improperly prevented from bringing these proceedings on behalf of the company?' If it is an expression of the corporate will of the company by an appropriate independent organ that is preventing the plaintiff from prosecuting the action he is not improperly but properly prevented and so the answer to the question is 'No'. The appropriate independent organ will vary according to the constitution of the company concerned and the identity of the defendants who will in most cases be disqualified from participating by voting in expressing the corporate will.'[4]

The view of Knox J in favouring independent assessment of whether a breach of duty should be litigated is attractive. The situation whereby, in the absence of fraud, directors are permitted to vote to ratify their own self-dealing,[5] clearly does strip the ratification process of impartiality. If the paramount concern is the welfare of the company, it is arguable that the court, as the ultimate arbiter of the company's interest, should be empowered to summon a general meeting

---

1 *Ibid* at 269–270. In *Bamford v Bamford* [1970] Ch 212, the Court of Appeal approved and applied Buckley J's approach where, on facts which were strikingly similar to those in *Hogg v Cramphorn* above, the directors obtained shareholder ratification of the share issue as soon as court proceedings were initiated. Harman LJ stated at 237–238: 'It is trite law . . . [that] directors can, by making full and frank disclosure and calling together the general body of the shareholders, obtain absolution and forgiveness of their sins . . .'

2 [1988] Ch 114. See, also, *Prudential Assurance Ltd v Newman Industries (No 2)*, *supra* n 3 on p 169.

3 *Supra* n 4 on p 161.

4 *Supra* n 2 on this page at 185.

5 This is achieved by severing their role as directors from their capacity as shareholders whose vote is seen as a property right, see *North-West Transportation Co Ltd v Beatty*, *supra* n 2 on p 163; *Carruth v ICI Ltd*, *supra* n 1 on p 169.

of the company. It would seem to follow that the conduct of such a meeting should be under the direction of the court, and those who have a personal interest in the vote, should be disenfranchised. Yet this solution, which at first sight appears to meet the need, has not escaped significant criticism. For example, Professor Parkinson has questioned the ability of the courts to construct 'a truly impartial vetting body' out of the shareholders at large.[1] He argues that, to achieve true impartiality, it would be necessary not only to disenfranchise the interested directors, but also those shareholders with whom they have some connection. Identifying connected or nominee shareholders, if at all possible, would be a Herculean task. In any case, the effectiveness of shareholders as monitors of the board is questionable.[2] More particularly, a shareholder who decides to litigate on the company's behalf will face the major hurdle of obtaining sufficient information about the irregularity which will allow the action to be launched. The right of shareholders to information beyond that which must be statutorily disclosed is limited. The contents of the directors' report and the audited accounts will, generally, be of little help. While the auditors are required by s 237(1) of the Companies Act 1985 to include in their report details not disclosed in the accounts of loans to directors and other transactions in which the directors have an interest, the auditors are not required to police the company to detect breaches of duty.

Given these central concerns surrounding the viability of constructing an independent organ of shareholders, perhaps the obvious route for reform lies with the disclosure standard itself. Such an approach would go some way towards strengthening the position of shareholders seeking to challenge the conduct of directors. For this, it is valuable to take stock of the approach adopted to this issue by the courts in Delaware, which have, traditionally, taken a strict view towards the question of directorial disclosure. As such, the Delaware cases stand in stark contrast to the emerging benevolence seen in England and Australia.[3]

LESSONS FROM DELAWARE — THE REQUIREMENT OF 'COMPLETE CANDOR'

In Delaware, the duty cast upon directors and officers of corporations when communicating information to stockholders is premised upon the notion of 'complete candor'. As a matter of state law the standard of disclosure is

---

1 Parkinson, *Corporate Power and Responsibility – Issues in the Theory of Company Law* (Oxford: Clarendon Press, 1993) at p 216 *et seq*.

2 See Riley, 'Controlling corporate management: UK and US initiatives' (1994) 14 *LS* 226, who observes at p 246, that obtaining shareholder approval is 'largely a mere formality; management's control of the corporation, and particularly the proxy voting process, in the face of dispersed shareholdings enables it to procure almost any shareholder sanction it requires'.

3 See nn 5 and 7 on p 166, *supra* and associated text.

symbiotic with the general fiduciary duties imposed upon corporate directors.¹ In framing the duty, the resonance of insurance law decisions relating to the insured's duty of disclosure is clearly discernible.² For example, in *Empire Southern Gas Co v Gray*,³ the Court of Chancery, holding that the scope of the duty extends to misleading proxy statements issued with a view to soliciting proxies, observed that:

> 'The accepted and desirable tendency has been to place the burden of candor upon those who would communicate with stockholders rather than to require the stock-holders to be eternally vigilant.'⁴

An obvious point of comparison lies in the realistic view, implicit in the court's statement, to the effect that, as with insurers, shareholders are in a particularly weak position *vis à vis* those charged with the disclosure of information to them.⁵ And so, a strict view of the duty is justified. Thus, in *Gerlach v Gillam*,⁶ an action was brought challenging the company's ratification of contracts that would have, personally, benefited its dominant director. The court granted an injunction on the basis that the shareholders' ratification was induced by a proxy statement which failed to disclose the dates of the contracts in question, how they were negotiated and the dominant director's role in the negotiations. It is noteworthy that the court asserted that company directors owe a duty of 'complete candor' to shareholders *whenever* information is being provided.⁷

This approach has been followed and refined in a line of cases. For example, in *Kelly v Bell*,⁸ Chancellor Duffy (as he then was) noted that 'directors owe a duty to honestly disclose all material facts when they undertake to give out statements about the business to stockholders'.⁹ Significantly, the Delaware

---

1 The rule is that directors of a Delaware corporation will be in breach of a fiduciary duty to their shareholders when they misrepresent or omit material information. See, for example, *Rosenblatt v Getty Oil Co* 493 A2d 929 at 944 (Del 1985); *Weinberger v OUP Inc* 457 A 2d 701 at 710 (Del 1983); and *Lynch v Vickers Energy Corp* 383 A 2d 278 at 281 (Del 1977), discussed *infra*; and *Re Anderson, Clayton Shareholder Litig* 519 A 2d 680 at 689–690 (Del Ch 1986). The position in Delaware is in marked contrast to that in England, where the traditional view is that the fiduciary duties of directors are owed to the company only, not to the shareholders: *Percival v Wright* [1902] 2 Ch 421. However, in certain circumstances a duty may be owed to shareholders, see *Coleman v Myers* [1977] 2 NZLR 225; *Allen v Hyatt* (1914) 30 TLR 444, PC. See further, *Boyle & Birds'*, *op cit* n 4 on p 161, ch 14.

2 See *infra* nn 2–5 on p 174 and associated text.

3 46 A 2d 741 (Del Ch 1946).

4 *Ibid* at 746.

5 In the insurance context, the duty of disclosure is justified on the basis that the insured has the advantage of information. See, for example, *Re Yager* (1912) 108 LT 38 at 45 where Channell J said that: 'The special facts upon which the contingent chance is to be computed lie most commonly in the knowledge of the insured only; the underwriter trusts to his representation, and proceeds upon confidence that he does not keep back any circumstance . . .' See further, Clarke, *The Law Of Insurance Contracts* (London: LLP, 1994) at p 549 *et seq*.

6 139 A 2d 591 (Del Ch 1958).

7 *Ibid* at 593. See, also, *Eisenberg v Chicago Milwaukee Corp* 537 A 2d 1051 (Del Ch 1987). In *Stroud v Milliken Enterprises Inc* 552 A 2d 476 at 480 (Del 1989), the Delaware Supreme Court stressed that a board's 'duty of complete candor to its shareholders to disclose all germane or material information applies as well to matters of corporate governance as to corporate transactions'.

8 254 A 2d 62 (Del Ch 1969).

9 *Ibid* at 71.

Supreme Court stated, in *Singer v Magnavox Co*,[1] that '[i]t is settled Delaware law
. . . that corporate officers and directors . . . owe their corporation . . . a fiduciary obligation of honesty, loyalty, good faith and fairness.'

Delineating the true extent of the disclosure standard has met with a mixed
response in the Delaware courts. The leading decision is *Lynch v Vickers
Energy Corp*.[2] Lynch was a former shareholder of a company which had
been acquired by Vickers, its majority shareholder, by way of a tender offer.
He sued for damages on the basis that there had been less than full and frank
disclosure of the value of the company's assets, with the result that the
company's minority shareholders had been coerced to sell their shares for a
grossly inadequate price. The Delaware Supreme Court took the view that in
determining whether the duty of 'complete candor' had been discharged, its
function was limited to determining whether the defendants had disclosed
'all information in their possession *germane* to the transaction in issue'.[3] The
Court defined 'germane' as 'information such as a reasonable shareholder
would consider important in deciding whether to sell or retain stock'.[4] On
the facts, this translated into the duty to disclose precise information, not
generalities, so that:

> 'when, as here, management was in possession of two estimates from responsible
> sources — one using a "floor" approach defining value in terms of its lowest worth,
> and the other a more optimistic or "ceiling" approach defining value in terms of its
> highest worth — it is our opinion that complete candor required disclosure of both
> estimates. If management believed that one estimate was more accurate or realistic
> than another, it was free to endorse that estimate and to explain the reason for
> doing so; but full disclosure, in our view, was a prerequisite.'[5]

More recently, the court has criticised its use of the term 'germane' on the basis
that it lacked precision. In *Rosenblatt v Getty Oil Co*,[6] Moore J said that it 'has no
well accepted meaning in the disclosure context'.[7] In its stead, the court
endorsed the test of 'materiality' formulated by the Supreme Court of the
United States in *TSC Industries Inc v Northway Inc*:[8]

> 'An omitted fact is material if there is a substantial likelihood that a reasonable
> shareholder would consider it important in deciding how to vote . . . It does not
> require proof of a substantial likelihood that disclosure of the omitted fact would
> have caused the reasonable investor to change his vote. What the standard does

1 380 A 2d 969 (Del 1977).
2 383 A 2d 278 (Del 1977).
3 *Ibid* at 281. Italics supplied.
4 *Ibid*.
5 *Ibid*.
6 493 A 2d 929 (Del 1985).
7 *Ibid* at 944. In fact the term 'germane' seems to have now lost favour with the Delaware
   Supreme Court. In *Bershad v Curtiss-Wright Corp* 535 A 2d 840 (Del 1987), the Court did not cite
   Lynch in its determination of whether the duty of candor had been breached, relying only upon
   Rosenblatt and *Smith v Van Gorkom* 488 A 2d 858 (Del 1985). However, the Chancery Court
   continues to cling to the terminology, see, for example, *Weinberger v Rio Grande Industries Inc* 519
   A 2d 116 (Del Ch 1986). Quillen J has expressed the view, extra-judicially, that *Rosenblatt* should
   replace *Lynch* as Delaware's leading authority on the disclosure rule, see (1985) 10 *Del J Corp
   Law* 465. See, further, Pease, 'Delaware's Disclosure Rule: The "Complete Candor" Standard,
   Its Application, And Why Sue in Delaware' (1989) 14 *Del J Corp Law* 445.
8 426 US 438 (1976).

contemplate is a showing of a substantial likelihood that, under all the circumstances, the omitted fact would have assumed actual significance in the deliberations of the reasonable shareholder.'[1]

The breadth of the duty stated by the US Supreme Court stands as the antithesis of that which has been seen to be the current position in England. In the USA, the duty does not require proof that the actual decision of the shareholders in general meeting would have been different.[2] All that is required is that the omitted fact would have been of relevance (assessed objectively) to the decision-making process, irrespective of whether or not the result of the vote would have been different had it been disclosed. This expression of the duty is, in fact, in accordance with the traditional view of the English judiciary as it stood some 60 years ago. In *Brickenden v London Loan & Savings Co*,[3] Lord Thankerton examined the scope of the disclosure duty and said:

> 'When a party, holding a fiduciary relationship, commits a breach of his duty by non-disclosure of material facts, which his constituent is entitled to know in connection with the transaction, he cannot be heard to maintain that disclosure would not have altered the decision to proceed with the transaction, because the constituent's action would be solely determined by some other factor . . . Once the Court has determined that the non-disclosed facts were material, speculation as to what course the constituent, on disclosure, would have taken is not relevant.'[4]

RECONSTRUCTING A STRICT REGIME FOR DISCLOSURE IN ENGLAND

As has been seen, the central issue which lies at the very foundations of the ratification process is the degree of disclosure required before the company's consent can be properly described as 'fully informed'. To achieve this objective, the appropriate analogy to be applied is the doctrine of *uberrimae fides* as it operates in insurance law. Importing this doctrine into the realms of the contemporary company law requirements governing ratification of directorial misconduct would be relatively straightforward, as demonstrated by *Brickenden*. In fact, the merits of such an approach have received judicial endorsement. For example, Lord Denning MR, in *Hely-Hutchinson v Brayhead Ltd*,[5] commented that: 'It seems to me that when a director fails to disclose his interest, the effect is the same as non-disclosure in contracts *uberrimae fide* or non-disclosure by a promoter who sells to the company property in which he is interested'.[6]

---

1 *Ibid* at 449.
2 Cf *NZ Netherlands Society Oranje Inc v Kuys*, (Lord Wilberforce) *supra* n 5 on p 166 and *Walden Properties Ltd v Beaver Properties Ltd*, (Hutley JA) *supra* n 7 on p 166.
3 [1934] 3 DLR 465.
4 *Ibid* at 469. This passage has since been applied in New Zealand in *Farrington v Rowe McBride & Partners* [1985] 1 NZLR 83 and in *Witten-Hannah v Davies, supra* n 5 on p 167 and in Australia in *Commonwealth Bank of Australia v Smith* (1991) 102 ALR 453 and in *Wan v McDonald* (1992) 105 ALR 473.
5 [1968] 1 QB 549.
6 *Ibid* at 585. For a fuller analysis of this line of reasoning see Lowry, 'Directorial Self-Dealing: Constructing A Regime Of Accountability' (1997) 48 *NILQ* 211.

It is noteworthy that the tenor of the language adopted currently by the Delaware courts when deciding the scope of the disclosure duty of directors echoes resoundingly that of the English courts in insurance law cases where the central issue has been the test of materiality. Section 18 of the Marine Insurance Act 1906 lays down the general duty of disclosure applicable to all classes of insurance. In essence, s 18(1) provides that the assured must disclose to the insurer 'every material circumstance which is known to the assured . . .' Materiality is defined by s 18(2), which states: '[E]very circumstance is material which would influence the judgment of a prudent insurer in fixing the premium, or determining whether he will take the risk'.[1] The meaning of 'influence' for the purposes of this provision has received extensive judicial consideration. In *Container Transport International Inc v Oceanus Mutual Underwriting Association (Bermuda) Ltd*,[2] the Court of Appeal held that an insured is bound to disclose those material facts which *might* influence the judgment of a prudent insurer in deciding whether or not to accept the risk or in setting the premium.[3] This approach was endorsed by the House of Lords in *Pan Atlantic Insurance Co Ltd v Pine Top Insurance Co Ltd*,[4] which rejected the argument that materiality should be measured by reference to whether its 'influence' on the prudent insurer's judgment was 'decisive'. Lord Mustill took the view that the expression denotes an effect upon the thought processes.[5]

Transplanting the doctrine of *uberrimae fides* into the ratification process would result in a requirement of full disclosure of all information surrounding the transaction in which the director is interested, without qualification by reference to whether or not the non-disclosed fact would have influenced the decision of the shareholders in deciding whether or not to ratify the breach.[6] Accordingly, as is patently evident from the US Supreme Court's formulation of the duty in *TSC Industries Inc v Northway Inc*,[7] the question of materiality should lie with the shareholders, not the miscreant director, so that whether or not information should be discounted as being irrelevant to their decision must rest within the shareholders' exclusive province. Any formulation of some lesser conditional duty of disclosure only serves to compound the difficulties faced by shareholders in monitoring directorial wrongdoing.

CONCLUSION

Any attempt at limiting the extent of the duty of disclosure by reference to a 'decisive influence' test would strike at the foundations of the fiduciary

---

1 Against this background, note that in *Kahn v Lynch Communication Systems Inc* 669 A 2d 79 at 88 (Del 1995), the Court stated that materiality is 'determined from the perspective of the reasonable shareholder, not that of the directors . . . who undertakes to distribute information'.

2 [1984] 1 Lloyd's Rep 109.

3 See also, *Highlands Insurance Co v Continental Insurance Co* [1987] 1 Lloyd's Rep 109; *Zurich General Accident and Liability Insurance Co Ltd v Morrison* [1942] 2 KB 53.

4 [1995] 1 AC 501.

5 *Ibid* at 531. See also 517 (Lord Goff).

6 In contrast to the view expressed by Lord Wilberforce, see n 6 on p 166, *supra* and associated text. This approach would, therefore, accord with the Supreme Court's view of the duty as formulated in *TSC Industries Inc v Northway Inc*, *supra* n 8 on p 173 and associated text.

7 *Supra* n 8 on p 173 and that of Lord Thankerton in *Brickenden v London Loan & Savings Co*, *supra* n 3 on p 174.

standard. If the fiduciary principle is to retain its prophylactic role, the defence of consent must be founded upon full knowledge of all the circumstances surrounding the director's breach. Herein lies the weight of the doctrine's preventative value. Information not considered necessary to the shareholders' decision can be discounted by them as appropriate. But the question of materiality must lie with the shareholders, not the self-dealing director. Any judicial formulation of a conditional duty of disclosure merely compounds the existing difficulties faced by shareholders in policing directorial wrongdoing. While Lord Wilberforce and Hutley JA may be motivated by a desire to mitigate the harshness of equity by limiting the disclosure requirement, such attempts are potentially destructive. If the fiduciary principle is to continue to fulfil its preordained task, there can be no scope for covering the simplicity of its orthodoxy under a crepuscular haze of conditional disclosure. Put simply, the fiduciary duties were designed to protect the vulnerability of a company from the unconscionable practices which may tempt its directors. In this respect, the duties represent the cornerstone of the fiduciary relationship. Although conceived in the eighteenth century, the fiduciary standard has not lost its potency with the passage of time, particularly when viewed in the light of recent events in England, and beyond, surrounding the Maxwell affair, Blue Arrow, the collapse of the Bond or Qintex empire, and Tricontinental. Against this backdrop, compliance with the fiduciary standard should remain unconditional, and notions directed towards their relaxation are unsustainable in the modern commercial world.[1]

The re-adoption of a strict duty of directorial disclosure in England is also an attractive and simple solution when viewed from an evidential perspective. In Delaware, it is settled law that the plaintiff is not hindered by either *scienter* or negligence in a claim for non-disclosure.[2] The point was stressed by the Chancery Court in *In re Anderson, Clayton Shareholders' Litigation*,[3] that:

> '[T]he question whether shareholders have, under the circumstances, been provided with appropriate information upon which an informed choice on matter of fundamental corporate importance may be made, is not a decision concerning the management of business . . .'[4]

Accordingly, unlike the so-called business judgment rule, the plea of due care and good faith is not available to the defendant directors.[5] Perhaps more significantly, however, the unflinching manner with which this duty strikes can be seen by the fact that there is no 'reliance' requirement in a claim for breach of the duty of disclosure.[6] This departs from the basic rule, under the general law

1 See the judgment of Swan J in *Irving Trust Co v Deutsch* 73 F 2d 121 (1934) at 124 who proceeded on the basis that, if equity did not maintain a harsh and constant surveillance, then infidelity would be all the more tempting. This view would seem to have coloured Lord Templeman's approach in *Attorney-General for Hong Kong v Reid* [1994] 1 AC 324.

2 See, for example, *Arnold v Society for Savings Bancorp Inc* 678 A 2d 533 (Del Ch 1996); *Williams v Geir* 671 A 2d 1368 at 1379 (Del 1996); and *In re Santa Fe Pacific Corp Shareholder Litigation* 669 A 2d 59 at 66 (Del 1995).

3 519 A 2d 669 (Del Ch 1986).

4 *Ibid* at 675.

5 See *Estate of Detwiler v Offenbacher* 728 F Supp 103, 150 n 18 (SDNY 1989), in which it was held, *inter alia*, that the business judgment rule is inapplicable to allegations of misrepresentations or omissions in a proxy statement.

6 *In re Tri-Star Pictures Inc* 634 A 2d 319 at 327 (Del 1993).

that a misrepresentation will not render a contract voidable unless it induced the contract. In consequence, the only defence available to the defendant is that the non-disclosed information was immaterial. In other words, once the plaintiff establishes the materiality of the non-disclosed information or of the misrepresented fact, liability is thereby triggered. Such an uncompromising solution to the disclosure duty when seeking shareholder ratification of directorial misconduct will at least go some way towards achieving the notion of 'fully informed' consent. It would also reinforce the prophylactic rationale underlying the fiduciary duties. Treating the duty of disclosure as synergistic with the fiduciary duty of loyalty, as in Delaware, would seem to be the logical step if these objectives are to be achieved.

Chapter 11

RECONCEPTUALISING COMPANY LAW — REFLECTIONS ON THE LAW COMMISSION'S CONSULTATION PAPER ON SHAREHOLDER REMEDIES

David Sugarman[1]

INTRODUCTION

The rules surrounding the standing, pleading and proof of corporate litigation in English company law are notoriously convoluted.[2] Towering over this area, like Frankenstein's monster, stands the legacy of *Foss v Harbottle*.[3] Whilst not a Gothic novel, it has nonetheless generated its own horror stories of unfulfilled rights and ruinous litigation.[4] Fortunately, there have been a few lights to lead us through this murky maelstrom, one of whom has been Tony Boyle. Taking his inspiration from the study of Anglo-American corporate law, Tony's work on shareholder remedies has made a signal contribution to the understanding and rationalisation of this notoriously bewildering but important field of company law.[5] It is, perhaps, fitting that this essay should also address the reform of

---

1 Professor of Law, Law Department, Lancaster University. This essay is a revised version of a paper first presented at a symposium on the Law Commission's, *Shareholder Remedies: A Consultation Paper* organised by the Society of Public Teachers of Law (SPTL) Company Law Section on 13 December 1996 at the Institute of Advanced Legal Studies, London. I am grateful to Leonie Sugarman for her helpful comments. An earlier version of this essay was published in *The Company Lawyer* (1997) vol 17, nos 8 and 9. Since this essay was completed, the Law Commission has published its response to the consultation paper discussed in this essay: namely, The Law Commission (Law Com No 246), *Shareholder Remedies* (London: HMSO, Cm 3769, October 1997). This essay draws upon my forthcoming study of company law in a post-modern world: see, also, Sugarman, D, 'Corporate Groups in Europe: Governance, Industrial Organization, and Efficiency in a Post-Modern World' in Sugarman, D and Teubner, G (eds), *Regulating Corporate Groups in Europe* (Baden Baden: Nomos, 1990) 13.

2 See Sealy, LS, 'Problems of Standing, Pleading and Proof in Corporate Litigation' in Pettet, B (ed), *Company Law in Change* (London: Stevens, 1987) 1; and Prentice, DD, 'Shareholder Actions: the Rule in *Foss v Harbottle*' (1988) 104 *LQR* 341.

3 (1843) 2 Hare 461. See, generally, Sealy, LS, 'Problems of Standing, Pleading and Proof in Corporate Litigation' and Prentice, DD, 'Shareholder Actions: the Rule in *Foss v Harbottle*'.

4 See, for example, Bartlett, AF, *Power, Prejudice and Pride* (London: AF Bartlett, 1982), which describes the experience of being involved in the modern leading case on *Foss v Harbottle*: namely, *Prudential Assurance Co Ltd v Newman Industries Ltd (No 2)* [1982] Ch 204.

5 This is evident from his earliest research, such as 'The Minority Shareholder in the Nineteenth Century: A Study in Anglo-American Legal History' (1965) 28 *MLR Review* 317, 'The Derivative Action in Common Law' (1967) *JBL* 120, and his *The Shareholders' Derivative Action in Anglo-American Law* (SJD Thesis, Harvard Law School, 1968), to his most recent work as co-editor of the leading practitioner work, Gore-Browne: see Boyle, AJ and Sykes, R, *Gore-Browne on Companies*, 44th edn loose-leaf (Bristol: Jordans, 1986).

Foss v Harbottle,[1] in the light of the Law Commission's recent proposals on share-holder remedies and the models developed in other common law jurisdictions.

The Law Commission's Consultation Paper on *Shareholder Remedies*[2] is a detailed and welcome response to the need to reform this area of company law. Other common law jurisdictions have recently refashioned or considered renovating shareholder remedies and this makes the Commission's foray into this realm especially timely.[3] Company law is a recent addition to the Commission's port-folio and its consultation document is the most important work that it has undertaken in this new field of interest. The Commission's 284 page Paper rep-resents the most exhaustive review of the field ever undertaken by a law reform agency in the United Kingdom. It is based upon extensive consultation, consid-eration of the law in other jurisdictions,[4] and a unique statistical survey of the practical operation of section 459 of the Companies Act 1985.[5] With admirable lucidity, it identifies usefully numerous defects in the law, makes imaginative efforts to address them and offers an explicit account of the principles which should guide reform.[6] It is also the first attempt to bring company law in line with Lord Woolf's recommendations on the reform of the civil justice system.[7]

The 'procedural thicket' surrounding the rule in *Foss v Harbottle*,[8] which gov-erns when shareholders can bring proceedings to enforce their or the com-pany's rights at common law, is a major axis within modern company law. Along with *Salomon v Salomon*,[9] it symbolises and constitutes the core of the classical conception of company law, helping to define its values, perimeters and self-identity, much like the elaborate rules governing estates and perpetuities in the classical conception of land law.[10] Being concerned with the enforcement of the rights of and in that most important of economic institutions, the incorporated business organisation, the Paper will, inevitably, engage with the balance of power as between shareholders, corporate management and society, and the aims and functions of legal regulation. For these reasons, and because of the mutual dependencies between the law and procedures governing shareholders' remedies and other aspects of company law, the reform of shareholders' reme-dies has a wider significance within and beyond the jurisprudence and practice of company law.

---

1 (1843) 2 Hare 461.
2 Paper No 142, (London: The Stationery Office, 1996). Hereinafter, 'the Paper'.
3 See, para 16.7–16.51; Appendix F, which summarises the 'oppression' or 'unfair prejudice' remedies and derivative actions in Australia, Canada, Ghana, New Zealand, Republic of South Africa and the United States of America; and Appendix G, which contains relevant extracts from legislation in Australia, Canada, Ghana, New Zealand, Republic of South Africa and the United States of America dealing with statutory rights to bring actions on behalf of a company.
4 Notably, Australia, Canada, Ghana, New Zealand and South Africa.
5 The statistics relating to the filing of s 459 petitions and the size of companies are contained in Appendix E. See, generally, Part 18: 'A New Additional Unfair Prejudice Remedy for Smaller Companies'.
6 Paragraph 14.11
7 The Rt Hon Lord Woolf, *Access to Justice: Final Report* (London: The Stationery Office, 1996), hereinafter 'the Woolf Report'. See, generally, Zuckerman, AAS and Cranston, R (eds), *Reform of Civil Procedure: Essays on 'Access to Justice'* (Oxford: Oxford University Press, 1996).
8 (1843) 2 Hare 461.
9 [1897] AC 22.
10 See, generally, the section entitled 'Reconceptualising company law', on p 232.

The purpose of this essay is to describe and assess critically the principal proposals canvassed by the Law Commission's Paper on Shareholder Remedies. It is also hoped that this discussion will illuminate the relationship between the Commission's proposals and current shifts in the character, values, languages and methods of company law. By treating the Paper in this way, I hope to advance a clearer understanding of the virtues, possibilities and potential difficulties that may arise from the Commission's proposals and also of the possible direction, paradoxes and dilemmas confronting company law reform at the end of the millennium.

> 'In an ideal world of making public policy, problems and objectives would be clearly defined, options rigorously canvassed and calculated choices made. In the real world this is a counsel of perfection; rationality must be pursued under severe constraints. Not only does one never start with a blank sheet but resources are limited (time being the most important); the problem as opposed to its symptoms may not be immediately identifiable; there are opposing interests which close off certain lines of inquiry and outcome; and values might be contested and a trade off necessary.'[1]

These words, by Ross Cranston, apply with singular aptness to the process of company law reform. In order to understand and evaluate the Law Commission's proposals it is necessary, therefore, to appreciate something of the larger context within which they were fashioned. The Commission's Paper is confined to legal matters and the larger context, in terms of how the proposals relate to current tendencies within company law, as well as its wider political and economic background, receive short shrift. This may be inevitable in works of this *genre*; but it is likely to impede an understanding of the nature, the changing forms, the possibilities and the limits of company law. In other words, it is liable to sustain what William Twining calls the 'lawyers' propensity to tunnel vision'.[2]

In order to do justice to the Commission's important and imaginative efforts, Parts One and Two of the essay set the Paper in its larger context. In part, this is to convey something which the Paper does not communicate well: namely, its place within the on-going changes in company law associated with de-regulation, re-regulation and the fragmentation of company law. My concern is less to endorse a particular normative view than to underscore the fact that certain movements are already under way in company law transnationally, and that these movements afford evidence of the development of a more fragmented, focused, flexible, contractual, equitable and relational company law. I will start, therefore, with a simplified outline of some of the assumptions and trends in contemporary corporate law that are also evident in the Law Commission's Paper. I will then describe the broad background to the Law Commission's Paper and to company law reform, then, subsequently, undertake an overview of and comment on the main recommendations canvassed by the Law Commission.

---

1 Cranston, R, 'The Rational Study of Law: Social Research and Access to Justice' in Zuckerman, AA and Cranston, R (eds), *Reform of Civil Procedure* (Oxford: Oxford University Press, 1996), p 31.
2 Twining, W, *Law in Context* (Oxford: Clarendon Press, 1997), p 57.

My argument is that company law has been changing rapidly since the 1980s, and that the Law Commission's Paper both reflects and advances several of the complex and contradictory tendencies at work in this field. Specifically, I hope to demonstrate the ways in which the Commission's proposals arose originally in the context of the debate concerning the reform of the law governing private companies, and of the influence of de-regulation on company law. By rejecting the creation of a new legal form for small businesses, the Commission was able to consider advancing the field of shareholder remedies through the modification of general company law, influenced by current concerns with value for money in public expenditure and access to justice (in particular, the need to reduce the time period and cost of litigation), empirical data on the major company law problems experienced by small businesses and overseas models of corporate law. The Commission's Paper is undoubtedly valuable and important in creating the space to re-think the legal and policy foundations of shareholder remedies. The radical restructuring of the economy, society and legal regulation since the 1960s means we cannot simply return to the model of classical company law to sustain law reform. We must, therefore, look to the future and construct a new synthesis embodying the best elements of the classical model that remain relevant, while discarding those which have become anachronistic. While the Commission's Paper both contributes to and is evidence of piecemeal changes within the field of shareholder remedies it largely fails to 'go back to basics' and evaluate, critique and re-construct the law governing shareholders' remedies in a root-and-branch fashion. This, however, was beyond the remit of the Commission both with respect to its narrow terms of reference and as a consequence of the fragmented and *ad hoc* character of the structure for company law reform in the UK. But it was accentuated by the dearth of empirical work on corporate business organisations, corporate law and markets and the conceptual confines of the legacy of classical company law, with its emphasis upon the peculiarities and independence of company law and of corporate obligations. The essential process of reconceptualising corporate law is likely to be advanced if a broader approach is applied to remedies and regulation, drawing upon economic and socio-legal studies of business, contracting and civil justice in order to better understand the culture and 'contractual environment' of the firm, and also by engaging with the problems of regulation, voluntariness, power, legitimate expectations and trust as they are being addressed, for example, in contemporary contract law, public law and 'equitable property'.[1]

PART ONE: A BRIEF OUTLINE OF RELEVANT PRINCIPLES AND TRENDS IN CONTEMPORARY COMPANY LAW

In this section I summarise and, hopefully, clarify several tendencies in contemporary company law that will be addressed in greater detail later in the essay. These tendencies are:

- A shift from a relatively unitary company law to one characterised by a plethora of different systems of regulation which have developed largely

---

1 On equitable property, see Gray, K, 'Equitable Property' (1994) *Current Legal Problems* 157.

independent of each other and yet are closely articulated both with each other and other power structures such as political economy. In fact, the existence of these different legalities or 'co-regulation'[1] is long-standing. However, it has tended to be repressed in company law scholarship as classical company law sought to accommodate them within a monolithic conception of company law (and corporate business enterprise) which, in turn, was premised upon a monolithic, state-centred conception of 'law' within liberal political thought. Since the 1960s, it has become increasingly difficult to contain this complex set of legal fields within monolithic conceptions of 'company law'. Because these different centres of company law are, to some extent, based upon different values and roles their co-existence may result in contradictory applications of the law and anomalies. From this perspective, company law has become a less well bounded and a less unified whole. Its centre has been displaced by a plurality of centres. Insofar as company law holds together at all it is not because it is unified, but because its differing elements can, in certain circumstances, be articulated together, albeit, always partially. Thus, it is constantly being 'de-centred' by forces outside itself, which opens up the possibility of new articulations and the forging of new centres of identity.[2]

- A resurgence in the belief in market forces and, therefore, contract as the most appropriate way of conceptualising modern business organisation. Paradoxically, this has been accompanied by increasing resort to more open-ended standards (such as fairness, reasonableness, reliance on reasonable expectations, participation, accountability, etc) to supplement the self-regulatory, facilitative and equitable frameworks within corporate law.

- The de-regulation and re-regulation of small companies, especially quasi-partnerships, giving incorporators greater freedom to manage their own affairs. Contract and precedents derived from partnership law are increasingly seen as important building blocks for facilitating this new voluntarism. This is further sustained by, and related to, the shift from mandatory to default and permissive forms of regulation. Mandatory laws that attenuate freedom of contract increasingly require rational justification.

- The re-examination of the traditional organising categories within company law influenced by the principles of market efficiency, cost-effectiveness, value for money, autonomy, access to justice, fairness, reliance and co-operation.

- Sharper distinctions between private and public companies as differentiation has become essential. Paradoxically, the recognition that most companies (private and public) create or reflect relationships — that is, that the contracts governing the internal relations within the company are frequently relational contracts — may result in a more complex and sophisticated differentiation where the boundaries between public and private companies are increasingly blurred.

1　On 'co-regulation', see the helpful elaboration in Ayres, I and Braithwaite, J, *Responsive Regulation* (Oxford: Oxford University Press, 1992) at p 102. See, also, Black, J, 'Constitutionalising Self-Regulation' (1996) 59 *MLR* 24, 27.

2　The fragmentation and restructuring of company law, of different legalities both closely inter-connected yet autonomous, is replicated in much of late modern law: see, generally, Santos, B de Sousa, *Toward a New Common Sense: Law, Science and Politics in the Paradigmatic Transition* (London: Routledge, 1995).

- The eschewal of the blanket application of regulation and the desire to carefully target intervention so that regulation is more efficient, effective and flexible.
- The increasing discretion of, and intervention by, the courts.
- The concern with increasing litigation and the encouragement of alternatives to litigation, such as alternative dispute resolution and arbitration.
- The concern to educate and, therefore, empower incorporators and shareholders with respect to the choices afforded by, and the responsibilities arising from, the law governing business associations. Related, thereto, is the principle that legal regulation should, where possible, be more flexible and user-friendly.[1]
- The preference for extra-legislative regulation such as by statutory instrument, changes in and through procedure, contract, etc.
- The tendency to treat the private company as the representative form of company within company law discourse and scholarship. The regulation of large public listed companies has been largely hived-off to the specialist world of the City and the new fields of securities regulation and financial services law.
- The development and enforcement of principles, standards and responsibilities concerned with sustaining and enforcing directors' duties and the reasonable expectations of shareholders even where this may undercut the majority rule of shareholders in general meeting and the prerogatives of corporate management.
- The rejection of a new form of business organisation for small companies with reform concentrating on modifying general company law (through shareholders' agreements, the development of standard-form tailored articles etc), so that it is more functional, pragmatic, flexible and focused to meet the needs of the particular type of company and the principal relationships concerned.
- Partnership as a model for the regulation and management of small companies, and the possible re-casting of partnership law, rather than company law, to better meet the needs of small business.
- The privatisation of company law through the development of extra-legal codes of practice.

PART TWO: BACKGROUND

Trends and tensions within contemporary company law — public companies

From the mid-nineteenth to the early twentieth century, English company law was usually characterised as relatively flexible, compact in size and *laissez-faire* in orientation. Since 1945, however, it has appeared ever more complex, obscure and elephantine. Confusion has been exacerbated by the manner in which

---

1   On the principle of flexibility and user-friendliness, see Farrar, JH, 'Fuzzy Law, the Modernization of Corporate Laws and the Privatization of Takeover Regulation' in Farrar, JH (ed), *Takeovers, Institutional Investors, and the Modernization of Corporate Laws* (Auckland: Oxford University Press, 1993), pp 2–3.

legislative reforms have been brought into force.[1] The culprits usually singled out as responsible for this state of affairs include the piecemeal and particularistic culture of the English legal system,[2] regulatory failure,[3] the low priority afforded to company law reform within the parliamentary process of law reform, poor parliamentary drafting, lack of consultation, and the fragmentary (i.e. step-by-step) yet over-inclusive transformation of company law that Britain is obliged to undertake under the EU's programme for the harmonisation of the laws of the Member States.[4] Just as Blackacre was, at least until recently, the

---

1 See, generally, Tunc, A, 'A French Looks at British Company Law' (1982) 45 *MLR* 1, 7–8; Sealy, LS, *Company Law and Commercial Reality* (London: Sweet & Maxwell, 1984) and 'More Haste, Less Speed' (1989) *The Company Lawyer* 210; Milman, D, '1967–1987: A Transformation in Company Law?' (1988) 17 *Anglo-American Law Review* 108; Farrar, JH, 'The United Kingdom Companies Act 1989' (1990) 17 *Canadian Business Law Journal* 150; Jacobs, E, 'Conceptual Contrasts — Comparative Approaches to Company Law Reform' (1990) 11 *The Company Lawyer* 215; The Company Law Committee, *The Reform of Company Law* (London: The Law Society, 1991). It has been claimed that North American corporate legislation is less detailed than that in the UK: see Branson, DM, 'Countertrends in Corporation Law: Model Business Corporation Act Revision, British Company Law Reform, and *Principles of Corporate Governance and Structure*' (1983) 68 *Minnesota Law Review* 53 at 73–88.

  The declining hegemony of the English law as a role model is not peculiar to company law. A similar state of affairs applies to other fields of law, such as contract law: see, for example, Beatson, J and Friedmann, D, 'Introduction: From "Classical" to Modern Contract Law' in Beatson, J and Friedmann, D (eds), *Good Faith and Fault in Contract Law* (Oxford: Clarendon Press, 1995), p 3.

2 See, for example, Atiyah, PS, *Pragmatism and Theory in English Law* (London: Stevens, 1987); and Sugarman, D, *In the Spirit of Weber: Law, Modernity and 'the Peculiarities of the English'* (Madison: Institute for Legal Studies, Wisconsin University, 1987).

3 See Teubner, G (ed), *Dilemmas of Law in the Welfare State* (Berlin: Walter de Gruyter, 1986) and Ogus, AI, *Regulation* (Oxford: Clarendon Press, 1994), pp 55–57. An important aspect of regulatory failure in corporate law has been the grounding of corporate regulation in increasing disclosure despite its high cost and doubtful utility: see, for example, Sealy, LS, *Company Law and Commercial Reality*.

4 On most of these 'causes', see Freedman, J, 'Reforming Company Law' in Patfield, F (ed), *Perspectives on Company Law, Vol 1* (The Hague: Kluwer Law International, 1995), p 197. Writing in 1990, David Milman observed that: '. . . [All] of the reforming Companies Acts since 1980 have been primarily motivated by a desire to fulfil our obligations to the European Community': Milman, D, 'Company Law in Transition' (1990) 24 *The Law Teacher* 3, 4. See, further, Buxbaum, RM and Hopt, KJ, *Legal Harmonization and the Business Enterprise* (Berlin: Walter de Gruyter, 1988); Sugarman, D and Teubner, G (eds), *Regulating Corporate Groups in Europe* (Nomos, 1990), pp 435–545; Wooldridge, F, *Company Law in the United Kingdom and the European Community* (London: Athlone Press, 1991); Hopt, KJ and Wymeersch, E (eds), *European Company and Financial Law* (Berlin: Walter de Gruyter, 1991); Prentice, D, *EEC Directives in Company Law and Financial Markets* (Oxford: Oxford University Press, 1991); Dine, J, *EC Company Law* (London: Chancery Lane Publishing, 1991); Cheffins, BR, 'European Community Company and Securities Law: A Canadian Perspective' (1991) 36 *McGill LJ* 1282; Thomas, R, *Company Law in Europe* (London: Butterworths, 1992); Andenas, M, 'The Future of EC Company Law Harmonisation' (1994) 15 *The Company Lawyer* 121; Xuereb, P, *Harmonisation of Company Law in the European Community* (Aldershot: Dartmouth, 1995).

  For a valuable examination of the parallel problems arising from the harmonisation of commercial law, see Goode, R in Cranston, R and Goode, R (eds), *Commercial and Consumer Law* (Oxford: Clarendon Press, 1993). Also relevant are the current debates surrounding the proposed 'Common European Code of Private Law', the alleged 'convergence' of the common law and civil law, and the extent to which they share a common legal culture: see Markesinis, B (ed), *The Gradual Convergence* (Oxford: Clarendon Press, 1994); Gessner, V, 'Global Legal Interaction and Legal Cultures' (1994) 7 *Ratio Juris* 132; Legrand, P, 'European Legal Systems Are Not Converging' *ICLQ* 45 (1996) 52; and Zimmermann, R, 'Savigny's Legacy: Legal History, Comparative Law and the Emergence of a European Legal Science' *LQR* 112 (1996) 576.

prototype English residential property, so the public limited company was treated as the paradigm of all companies for the purposes of company law, despite the fact that private companies are the typical form of business enterprise in the UK.[1] No wonder, then, that company law reform has tended to be piecemeal, incoherent, reactive and, at worst, ineffective.[2] As Gower *et al* put it:

> '[It cannot] . . . be said that our company legislation has not reacted to changing conditions . . . But if one looks at the major developments this century and at the problems that these have thrown up, it is difficult to avoid the conclusion that there has been a reluctance to recognize their implications for Company Law and that, when those implications have been recognised, the reaction has been to add to the existing framework without ever re-examining its foundations to ensure that they are still sufficiently sound to bear the weight of the expanding superstructure.'[3]

Moreover, the notion of a golden age of UK company law is largely mythic. The ideal of a unified company law characterised by rules of general application to all types of companies embracing the birth, life and death of the enterprise and capital market regulation was only possible by repressing, excluding and marginalising the plurality of overlapping legal rules and doctrines, subject-matter and values that were important to the understanding and operation of corporate law in practice.[4] In other words, the form and content of classical company law tended to be treated as individualised, unitary and acontextual.[5] Moreover, the inherent values that shaped the construction of company law during its classical period, from the mid-nineteenth century to the 1930s, was dominated by a belief in minimal regulation, freedom of contract and the

---

1 Sealy, LS, 'Small Company Legislation' (1993) *Law Society Gaz* Dec 8, 16.

2 See, for example, Sealy, LS, 'A Company Law for Tomorrow's World' *The Company Lawyer* 2 (1981) 195 and *Company Law and Commercial Reality* (London: Sweet & Maxwell, 1984); The Company Law Committee of the Law Society, *The Reform of Company Law* July 1991 no 255 (recommending the creation of a permanent, independent Company Law Commission to review company law, to monitor specific concerns and to undertake longer term planning and policy); Freedman, J, 'Reforming Company Law', in Patfield, F, (ed) *Perspectives on Company Law, Vol. 1* (The Hague: Kluwer Law International, 1995) 197; Patfield, F Macmillan, 'Challenges for Company Law' in Patfield, F (ed) *Perspectives on Company Law, Vol 1*, 1.

3 Gower, LCB, Prentice, DD and Pettet, BG, *Gower's Principles of Modern Company Law*, 5th edn (London: Sweet & Maxwell, 1992), p 70.

4 See, generally, Sugarman, D, 'Legal Theory, the Common Law Mind and the Making of the Textbook Tradition' in Twining, W (ed) *Legal Theory and Common Law* (Oxford: Basil Blackwell, 1986), p 26.

5 See, Sugarman, D, 'Corporate Groups in Europe: Governance, Industrial Organization, and Efficiency in a Post-Modern World' in Sugarman, D and Teubner, G (eds), *Regulating Corporate Groups in Europe* (Baden Baden: Nomos, 1990) 13, 19–22. Contrast, for example, company law's insistence upon the doctrine of the company as a *single* legal entity with the fact that all but small private businesses typically operate as pluralities, in the sense of group enterprises and networks. See, further, Hadden, T, *The Control of Corporate Groups* (London: Institute of Advanced Legal Studies, 1983); Bercusson, B, 'The Significance of the Legal Form of the Group Enterprise in the United Kingdom' in Sugarman, D and Teubner, G (eds), *Regulating Corporate Groups in Europe*, 267–284; Teubner, G, 'Enterprise Corporatism: New Industrial Policy and the "Essence" of the Legal Person' (1988) 36 *American Journal of Comparative Law* 130; and Blumberg, P, *The Multinational Challenge to Corporation Law: The Search for a New Corporate Personality* (New York: Oxford University Press, 1993).

beneficial role of market forces.[1] Subsequently, these have been clearly affected and to some extent displaced by other values that seek, among other things, to remedy the injustices of the free market.[2] In general, therefore, the unitary ideal of classical company law has not served modern company law well, and the fragmentation that has occurred is, for the most part, both necessary and beneficial.[3]

These problems have not been peculiar to the United Kingdom.[4] Nonetheless, since the 1970s, its corporate law has increasingly ceased to be a role model in the nations of the British Commonwealth which adopted the common law system and so-called 'mixed jurisdictions', such as South Africa.[5] In large measure

---

1 See, for example, Sugarman, D, 'A Socio-Historical Investigation of the Transformation of English Law c 1750–1914, with Special Reference to Company Law, Legal Education and Legal Scholarship' (Harvard Law School: SJD dissertation, 1985) Part Two; Atiyah, PS, *The Rise and Fall of Freedom of Contract* (Oxford: Clarendon Press, 1979), pp 562–570; Adams, J (ed), *Essays for Clive Schmitthoff* (Abingdon: Professional Books, 1983), p 29; Cornish, WR and Clark, G de N, *Law and Society in England 1750–1950* (London: Sweet & Maxwell, 1989), pp 246–266; Sugarman, D, 'Simple Images and Complex Realities: English Lawyers and their Relationship to Business and Politics' (1993) 11 *Law and History Review* 257, 272–277. Cf Lobban, M, 'Nineteenth Century Frauds in Company Formation: *Derry v Peek* in Context' (1996) 112 *LQR* 287.

2 See, Farrar, JH, *et al, Farrar's Company Law* 3rd edn (London: Butterworths, 1991) pp 22–23. See, generally, Friedmann, W, *Law and Social Change in Contemporary Britain* (London: Stevens & Sons, 1951), and the section entitled 'Reconceptualising company law', on p 234.

3 For a similar assessment with respect to contract law, see Nolan, D, 'The Classical Legacy and Modern English Contract Law' (1996) 59 *MLR* 603, 618.

4 In Australia, for example, corporation law has been notoriously complex. As Australia's Chief Justice Mason pointedly observed, 'Oscar Wilde, the supreme stylist, would have regarded our modern Corporations Law not only as uneatable but also as indigestible and incomprehensible': Mason, A, 'Corporate Law: The Challenge of Complexity' (1992) 2 *Australian Journal of Corporate Law* 1. The eventual response to this state of affairs was the creation of a corporation law simplification program which is now well under way: see, for example, The Corporations Law Simplification Program Task Force, *Plan of Action* (Barton: Attorney-General's Department, 1993); and The Corporations Law Simplification Program Task Force, *Plan of Action-Stage 2* (Barton: Attorney-General's Department, 1993). The complexity and growth of corporate law in Hong Kong, and its piecemeal reform, culminated in the current and comprehensive review of the Hong Kong Companies Ordinance, see Consultancy Report, *Review of the Hong Kong Companies Ordinance* (March, 1997) paras 11 and 104. I am grateful to Cally Jordan for providing me with details of the review of the Hong Kong Companies Ordinance.

5 See Sealy LS, *Company Law and Commercial Reality,* esp pp 62–75; and Gower, LCB, Prentice, DD and Pettet, BG, *Gower's Principles of Modern Company Law* 5th edn, p 70. Commonwealth countries look increasingly to each other and to the USA rather than to the UK. For example, the influential proposals for a new business corporation law for Canada were significantly influenced by the American Bar Association's, *Revised Model Business Corporation Act, 1984*: see Dickerson, RWV, Howard, JL and Getz, L, *Proposals for a New Business Corporations Law for Canada* (Ottawa: Information Canada, 1971) and the Canadian Business Corporations Act, RSC 1985, as amended. The recent reform of the New Zealand companies legislation also treated the UK model hitherto followed as too complex and obscure: see, generally, New Zealand Law Commission, *Company Law Reform and Restatement*, Report No 9 (Wellington: 1989) and McKenzie, PO, 'Corporate Law Reform: the New Zealand Experience' (1994) 4 *Australian Journal of Corporate Law* 129. Similarly, in Hong Kong, the appropriateness of following UK company law has been increasingly questioned: see Hong Kong, *Second Report of the Companies Law Revision Committee — Company Law* (April 1973); and Consultancy Report, *Review of the Hong Kong Companies Ordinance* (March,1997) paras 37, 38, 101–108, 141–148. Other Commonwealth countries that have increasingly rejected the UK role model include South Africa and Australia.

it has been superseded by the new exemplars of late modern company law: namely, the US Business Corporations Act 1984 (as revised), the Canada Business Corporations Act 1985 (as amended), the American Law Institute Principles of Corporate Governance (1994), and the New Zealand Companies Act 1993.

Recent changes in the organisation of work, production, governance and culture have rendered the ideal of a unitary company law even more problematic. Variously termed 'post-Fordism', 'post-modernism', the 'risk society', and 'the network society', these contradictory tendencies include the shift to more flexible, decentralised forms of labour processes and work organisation associated with greater work and production flexibility, the rise of the new 'information technologies' which, increasingly, supply much of the framework of society, of increasingly fragmented and specialised markets, the 'hollowing out' of the state,[1] the growth of a world market combined with the increasing scale of industrial, banking and commercial enterprises, the emergence of globalised economies whose substance consists of endlessly complex financial flows, and the gradual metamorphosis of industrial corporations from hierarchies of established offices to networks that sit uncomfortably with territorially based forms of organisation, such as the nation state.[2]

The new economy has created important opportunities for advanced business services, such as accountancy and the legal profession, to participate in and shape these processes as they are also being remade by them.[3] Since the 1960s, economic, political, technological and cultural forces have transformed the City of London.[4] There has been a dramatic increase in the 'number, size, speed of response, volatility and interaction of markets; [and] the increase of risk and the need for risk management . . .'[5] Markets and the range of financial

---

1   That is, the significant increase in the private provision of public services since the late 1970s: see, generally, Harden, I, *The Contracting State* (Buckingham: Open University Press, 1992); Forster, CD and Plowden, FJ, *The State Under Stress: Can the Hollow State be Good Government?* (Buckingham: Open University Press, 1996); Martin, S and Parker, D, *The Impact of Privatisation* (London: Routledge, 1997).

2   Lash, S and Urry, J, *The End of Organized Capitalism* (Cambridge: Polity, 1987) and *Economies of Sign & Space* (London: Sage, 1994); Giddens, A, *The Consequences of Modernity* (Stanford: Stanford University Press, 1990); Beck, U, *Risk Society* (London: Sage, 1992); Robinson, R, *Globalization* (London: Sage, 1992); Castells, M, *The Rise of the Network Society* (Oxford: Blackwell, 1996).

3   See, for example, Dezalay, Y, *Marchands de droit: La restructuration de l'ordre juridique international par les multinationales du droit* (Paris: Fayard, 1992); Flood, J and Skordaki, E, *Corporate Failure and the Work of Insolvency Practitioners: Professional Juridification and Big Corporate Insolvencies* (London: ACCA, 1992); Hanlon, G, *The Commercialisation of Accountancy* (London: Macmillan, 1994); Dezalay, Y and Sugarman, D (eds), *Professional Competition and Professional Power: Lawyers, Accountants and the Social Construction of Markets* (London: Routledge, 1995); Halliday, T and Carruthers, B, 'The Moral Regulation of Markets: Professions, Privitisation and the English Insolvency Act 1986' (1996) 21 *Accounting, Organisations and Society* 371; Dezalay, Y and Garth, B, *Dealing in Virtue: International Commercial Arbitration and the Construction of a Transnational Legal Order* (Chicago: University of Chicago Press, 1996).

4   On the development and significance of the City of London, see, generally, Ingham, G, *Capitalism Divided? The City and Industry in British Development* (London: Macmillan, 1984); Coakley, J and Harris, L, *The City of Capital* (Oxford: Blackwell, 1983).

5   Thrift, N, 'On the Social and Cultural Determinants of International Financial Centres' in Corbridge, S, Martin, R and Thrift, N (eds), *Money, Power and Space* (Oxford: Blackwell, 1994), pp 327, 345.

products have become greatly extended and diversified with investors having easier access to overseas markets.[1] The City's new, unorthodox, architectural creations are emblematic of its financial wealth, the reconfiguration of its power, traditions and self-identity, and the uncertainty that has enveloped it.[2] 'Big Bang',[3] the invasion of market forces, the intensification of competition, the rise of American-style mega-law firms which resemble their large, multi-national clients[4] and 'Yuppies' have called into question the homogeneity of the City,[5] the legal profession, the field of law,[6] including company law, and, therefore, the efficacy of the traditional mechanisms for regulating public corporations.[7]

A resurgence in the belief in the efficiency of markets has been coupled with an increasing emphasis on competition, 'enterprise culture',[8] individual responsibility, and de-regulation. Seen from this perspective, incorporation has become synonymous with entrepreneurship[9] and individual freedom, and traditional regulatory mechanisms are viewed as barriers and costs. These tendencies have been fuelled in part by the growing importance of global markets and global competition. The combination of banking and securities business within one group and the global structure of major investment/banking groups has accentuated long-standing potential conflicts of interest. Yet the pressure to de-regulate company law has been mediated by the breakdown of self-regulation, the

---

1 See, generally, the Symposium on the Internationalisation of the Securities Markets in (1986) 4 *Boston University International Law Journal* 1; and Oditah, F (ed), *The Future of the Global Securities Market* (Oxford: Clarendon Press, 1996).

2 See Whimster, S and Budd, L, 'Introduction', in Budd, L and Whimster S (eds), *Global Finance and Urban Living* (London: Routledge, 1992) p 20 and, generally, Sassen, S, *The Global City* (Princeton: Princeton University Press, 1991).

3 See, for example, Thomas, WA, *The Big Bang* (London: Macmillan, 1986); Gower, LCB, 'Big Bang and City Regulation' (1988) 51 *MLR* 1; Bradley, C, 'Competitive Deregulation of Financial Services Activity in Europe' (1991) 11 *OJLS* 545; Moran, M, *The Politics of the Financial Services Revolution* (London: Macmillan, 1991); Poser, NS, *International Securities Regulation* (Boston: Little, Brown, 1991); 'The Morning Ten Years After', *The Economist* (25 Oct 1996), pp 105–106.

4 Stanley, C, 'Enterprising Lawyers: Changes in the Market for Legal Services' *The Law Teacher* 25 (1991) 44; Flood, J, 'The Cultures of Globalization: Professional Restructuring for the International Market' in Dezalay, Y and Sugarman, D (eds), *Professional Competition and Professional Power*, 139.

5 Stanley, C, 'Cultural Contradictions in the Legitimation of Market Practice: Paradox in the Regulation of the City' in Budd, L and Whimster, S (eds), *Global Finance and Urban Living*, (London: Routledge, 1992), pp 142, 151, 156.

6 See, generally, Trubek, D, *et al*, *Global Restructuring and the Law: The Internationalization of Legal Fields and the Creation of Transnational Arenas* (Madison: Working Paper, Global Studies Research Program, 1993); Dezalay, Y, 'Introduction: Professional Competition and the Social Construction of Transnational Markets' in *Professional Competition and Professional Power*, Dezalay, Y and Sugarman, D (eds) 1; Arthurs, HW and Kreklewich, R, 'Law, Legal Institutions, and the Legal Profession in the New Economy' (1996) 34 *Osgoode Hall Law Journal* 1.

7 See, generally, Hancher, L and Moran, M (eds), *Capitalism, Culture and Economic Regulation* (Oxford: Clarendon Press, 1989).

8 See, generally, Keat, R and Abercrombie, N (eds), *Enterprise Culture* (London: Sage, 1991); Heelas, P and Morris, P (eds), *The Values of the Enterprise Culture* (London: Routledge, 1992).

9 Freedman, J, 'Small Business and the Corporate Form: Burden or Privilege?' (1994) 57 *MLR*, 556.

abuse of corporate status, the increase in fraud[1] and the need to create regulatory regimes adequate to police the new globalised markets. The preservation of investor confidence is imperative if London's pre-eminence in the highly competitive world of financial markets is to endure.[2] As increasing numbers of people invest, directly or indirectly, in public companies, and the impact of those companies on a wide range of interests beyond shareholders (eg, creditors, employees, the environment, etc) is acknowledged, the traditional grounds for intervention associated with market efficiency — such as the unequal distribution of information, the creation of a 'level playing field', the need to fill the inevitable 'gaps' that arise when parties contract, and the problem of negative externalities — have been augmented by the languages of 'fair dealing', 'corporate responsibility' and 'the stakeholder society'.[3] Thus, 'market' and 'intervention' paradigms of regulation continue to complement and compete with one another.

Anxiety concerning the lack of effective control of and sanctions against unscrupulous corporate management prompted Parliament to regulate unfairly prejudicial conduct in the company's affairs, to render incompetent directors personally liable for corporate debts on the grounds of wrongful trading,[4] and to extend the circumstances when the courts can disqualify individuals from directing or managing a company.[5] The control of corporate groups has attracted increasing attention.[6] And there are signs that in areas such as insider dealing, controls have been strengthened beyond the fiduciary relations of company law to the regulation of relationships in securities

---

1 A survey of the period 1984–1989 undertaken by accountants Ernst & Young indicates that fraud during this period risked sums totalling £4 billion, which is over 100 times the sums dealt with twenty years earlier: cited by Stanley, C, 'Cultural Contradictions in the Legitimation of Market Practice: Paradox in the Regulation of the City' in Budd, L and Whimster, S, *Global Finance and Urban Living* (London: Routledge, 1992), pp 142, 156. See, generally, Clark, M, *Regulating the City*, (Milton Keynes: Open University Press, 1986); and Levi, M, *Regulating Fraud* (London: Tavistock, 1987) and 'Fraudbusting in London: Developments in the Policing of White-Collar Crime' in Budd, L and Whimster, S (eds), *Global Finance and Urban Living* (London: Routledge, 1992), p 120.

2 See, generally, City Research Project, *The Competitive Position of London's Financial Services — Final Report* (London: Corporation of London, 1995).

3 See, generally, Lord Wedderburn, 'The Legal Development of Corporate Responsibility' in Hopt, KJ and Tuebner, G (eds), *Corporate Governance and Directors' Liabilities* (Berlin: Walter de Gruyter & Co, 1984), p 3; Prentice, DD, 'Directors, Creditors and Shareholders' in McKendrick, E (ed), *Commercial Aspects of Trusts and Fiduciary Obligations* (Oxford: Clarendon Press, 1992), p 73; and Parkinson, JE, *Corporate Power and Responsibility* (Oxford: Clarendon Press, 1995).
   On the justifications for state intervention, see Cheffins, BR, *Company Law: Theory, Structure and Operation* (Oxford: Oxford University Press, 1997), ch 3. While this important book appeared after this essay was completed, it is referred to in several footnotes.

4 On the regulation of unfairly prejudicial conduct, see the Companies Act 1985, s 459, which is further examined in this essay. With respect to liability for wrongful trading, see the Insolvency Act 1986, s 214. See, also, Milman, D, 'Personal Liability and Disqualification of Company Directors' (1992) 43 *NILQ* 1; Hicks, A, 'Acting on Wrongful Trading' (1993) 14 *The Company Lawyer* 16, 55; and McGee, A and Williams, C, *A Company Director's Liability for Wrongful Trading* (London: ACCA, 1995).

5 Under the Company Directors Disqualification Act 1986.

6 See Hopt, KJ (ed), *Groups of Companies in European Laws* (Berlin: Walter de Gruyter, 1973); Sugarman, D and Teubner, G (eds), *Regulating Corporate Groups in Europe* (Baden Baden: Nomos, 1990); and the contributions of Scott, J, Blumberg, PI, Hadden, T and Prentice, DD in McCahery, J *et al*, *Corporate Control and Accountability* (Oxford: Clarendon Press, 1993), chs 16, 17, 18 and 19 respectively.

markets.[1] The academic study of company law has fractured as its conceptual core has shrunk as more of the fields that hold company law together fragment in the wake of the political, economic and intellectual changes since the 1970s. Discrete fields such as securities regulation, financial services law, insolvency and personal property security interests have been established which are only tenuously connected to the conceptual framework of classical company law. Scholarly and media interest in corporate behaviour and white collar crime has increased, joined by interest groups, such as the Consumers' Association, and radio and television programmes, which report on corporate affairs. And the strains between the regulatory and the political concerns in policy making with respect to corporate regulation have accentuated, as in the fields of take-overs, mergers, financial services and corporate governance. In these ways, aspects of company law regulation have became more obviously politicised and, therefore, a matter of public interest.

Thus, in the wake of several public companies falling under the unfettered control of a fraudulent individual, the Cadbury Committee, established by the accountancy profession in 1992, recommended various counter-veiling mechanisms, through separate chairman and chief executives, at least three independent non-executive directors and the creation of formal remuneration and audit committees to ensure effective internal controls.[2] And after the furore concerning board room pay, the CBI established the Greenbury Committee, which led to more information on executive salaries being published and the creation of remuneration committees to report separately from the board.[3] In these ways, an additional layer of corporate governance was established: namely, formal, voluntary, codes of practice based on flexible principles rather than detailed legal obligations. However, these modest developments have been held by some to be an unreasonable burden on companies, and it is uncertain whether the momentum sustaining corporate governance reform will be sufficiently strong to prevent some retrenchment in this area. With respect to the rights of shareholders, it has been suggested that members should have a greater role in decisions concerning executive remuneration and be able to vote on directors' salaries at the annual general meeting. But it is the large, institutional shareholders who are seen as a major agent for improving corporate governance, although most institutional investors are reluctant to undertake serious intervention and many seldom vote.[4] Consideration is being given to

---

1   See Davis, PL, 'The European Community's Directive on Insider Dealing: From Company Law to Securities Markets Regulation?' (1991) 11 *OJLS* 92.

2   The *Report of the Committee on the Financial Aspects of Corporate Governance* (London: 1992), (the Cadbury Committee). See Finch, V, 'Board Performance and Cadbury on Corporate Governance' [1992] *JBL* 576 and Cheffins, BR, *Company Law*, pp 641–652.

3   *Directors' Remuneration: the Report of a Study Group Chaired by Sir Richard Greenbury* (London: 1995). On executive pay and shareholders, see Cheffins, BR, *Company Law*, pp 653–708.

4   See, generally, Stapledon, GP, *Institutional Shareholders and Corporate Governance* (Oxford: Clarendon Press, 1996), chs 3–5 and 11. Stapledon estimated that there were about 18 serious institutional interventions per year in the UK during 1990–1993, amounting to only seven-tenths of one per cent of quoted UK companies; that this was higher than the proceeding five years; and that this was not a low level compared with Australia and the United States (see pp 281–282). On the other hand, he also stresses that the amount of firm-level monitoring in the UK in the early 1990s was greater than was often assumed, and that more institutional intervention may occur 'behind the scenes than that which was reported in the press', p 154.

ways of encouraging them to act more responsibly, such as adopting the American practice of obliging pension funds to vote at the annual meetings of companies.[1] Given the resistance to additional regulation, however, it remains to be seen whether the new Government will seek to enhance the duties owed to shareholders and other 'stakeholders' in public companies.[2]

The boom in mergers and acquisitions (M & A) underlined the unfair and unequal treatment of shareholders, the incompleteness of disclosure of information, the asset-stripping activities of bidders and the social costs arising from take-overs.[3] In the late 1960s, the City of London created the City Panel on Take-overs and Mergers, a non-government, non-statutory body that regulates the conduct of bids involving companies listed on London's Stock Exchange, subject to appeal and judicial review by the courts.[4] Established, in part, to fend-off statutory intervention, the rhetoric of this privatised system stressed the virtues of flexibility, self-regulation and cost-effectiveness over a formal, legal regime. In practice, however, the system has taken on an increasingly hybrid character as it has become more complex, formalistic, managerialist, expensive

---

1 See, for example, The Labour Party, *Vision for Growth* (London: The Labour Party, 1997). A case can be made for voting to be compulsory for institutions as this would supplement their monitoring role: see Davies, PL, 'Institutional Investors in the United Kingdom' in Prentice, DD and Holland, PRJ (eds), *Contemporary Issues in Corporate Governance* (Oxford: Clarendon Press, 1993), p 92.

2 See, also, the joint DTI and the Treasury Paper of 1996 on 'Private Shareholders: Corporate Governance Rights'; and the Second Committee on the Financial Aspects of Corporate Governance, chaired by Sir Ronald Hampel, which is reviewing the role of executive, non-executive directors and shareholders in listed companies, and whose interim report is expected shortly.

   On corporate governance, see, generally, Hopt, KJ and Teubner, G (eds), *Corporate Governance and Directors' Liabilities* (Berlin: Walter de Gruyter & Co, 1984) 3; Gilson, RJ and Rose, MJ, 'Understanding the Japanese Keiretsu: Overlaps between Corporate Governance and Industrial Organization' (1993) 102 *Yale Law Journal* 871–906; Parkinson, JE, *Corporate Power and Responsibility* (Oxford: Clarendon Press, 1993); Prentice, DD and Holland, PRJ (eds), *Contemporary Issues in Corporate Governance*; Joseph McCahery *et al* (eds), *Corporate Control and Accountability*; Isaksson, M and Skog, R (eds), *Aspects of Corporate Governance* (Stockholm: Juristforlaget, 1994), Sheikh, S and Rees, W (eds), *Corporate Governance and Corporate Control* (London: Cavendish, 1995); Stapledon, GP, *Institutional Shareholders and Corporate Governance*; Stapledon, G and Lawrence, J, *Corporate Governance in the Top 100* (Melbourne: Centre for Corporate Law and Securities Regulation, 1996).

   See, also, the 'stakeholder society' debate: for a useful overview, see *The Special Issue on the Corporate Stakeholder Debate* (1993) XLII, No 3, *University of Toronto Law Journal*. See, also, Ireland, P, 'Corporate Governance, Stakeholding and the Company' (1996) 23 *Journal of Law and Society* 287.

3 See, for example, Johnston, M, *Takeover* (Harmondsworth: Penguin, 1986) and Fairburn, J and Kay, J (eds), *Mergers and Merger Policy* (Oxford: Oxford University Press, 1989). For a valuable American study, see Coffee, JC, Jr *et al* (eds), *Knights, Raiders and Targets* (New York: Columbia University Press, 1988). See, also, Brooks, J, *The Takeover Game* (New York: EP Dutton, 1987); Bruck, C, *The Predators' Ball* (New York: Simon & Schuster, 1988); and Burrough, B and Helyar, J, *Barbarians at the Gate: the Fall of RJR Nabisco* (New York: Harper & Row, 1990).

4 See, generally, Johnson, A, *The City Take-Over Code* (Oxford: Oxford University Press, 1980); Manser, WAP, *The UK Panel on Takeovers and Mergers,* Hume Occasional Paper No 21 (Edinburgh: David Hume Institute, 1990); and Lee, TP, 'Takeovers — The United Kingdom Experience' in Farrar, JH (ed), *Takeovers, Institutional Investors, and the Modernization of Corporate Laws*, p 192.

and juridified.[1] This tendency is strikingly evident in the new regime for controlling the financial markets in the United Kingdom, established by the Financial Services Act 1986, and associated with the establishment of the Securities and Investment Board (SIB) and the Self-Regulating Organisations (SROs).[2] Paradoxically, reforms made in the name of the free market have resulted in an increase in state power; or, more precisely, the de-regulation and commercialisation of the fields of financial services and the law (including the legal profession) produced greater market and state power reflected in and constituted by increasingly hybrid systems of regulation.[3] They have also led to public law process values being adopted, as exemplified in the principle that all shareholders of the same class should be treated equally in situations such as take-overs.[4]

Thus, the plurality of regulation and self-regulation that has long been associated with market activity[5] has been accentuated, as it has become progressively multi-layered and denser.[6] Responsibility for the policing of the financial markets is dispersed between the Stock Exchange, the SIB, the SROs, the Serious Fraud Office (SFO),[7] the DTI, the Crown Prosecution Service (CPS) and the

---

1 See, for example, Cane, P, 'Self-Regulation and Judicial Review' (1989) *Civil Justice Quarterly* 324 and Dezalay, Y, 'Technological Warfare: the Battle to Control the Mergers and Acquisition Market in Europe' in Dezalay, Y and Sugarman, D (eds), *Professional Competition and Professional Power*, p 77. This tendency may be further accentuated if recent European Union proposals concerning the harmonisation of the rules governing take-over bids are adopted. If adopted, the rules would make it likely that the Panel, or its successor, would function as a statutory body and that judicial review of its decisions would increase: see, further, the Department of Trade and Industry, *Proposal for a Thirteenth Directive On Company Law Concerning Takeover Bids* (London: DTI, April 1996).
   On juridification, see, generally, Teubner, G (ed), *Juridification of Social Spheres* (Berlin: Walter de Gruyter, 1987).
2 See Moran, M, *The Politics of the Financial Services Revolution* (London: Macmillan, 1991); Page, AC, and Ferguson, RB, *Investor Protection* (London: Weidenfeld & Nicolson, 1992); Large, A, *Financial Services Regulation* (London: Securities and Investment Board, 1993).
3 See, generally, Page, AC, 'Self-Regulation: The Constitutional Dimension' (1986) 49 *MLR* 141; Baldwin, R and McCrudden, C, *Regulation and Public Law* (London: Weidenfeld & Nicolson, 1987); Graham, C and Prosser, T (eds) *Waiving the Rules* (Milton Keynes: Open University Press, 1988); Stewart, P and Walsh, D, 'Changes in the Management of Public Services' (1992) 70 *Public Administration* 499; Power, M, *The Audit Explosion* (London: Demos, 1994); Black, J, 'Constitutionalising Self-Regulation' (1996) 59 *MLR* 24.
4 On the importance of the principle of equality of treatment in the regulation of take-over bids in the UK, see Prentice, DD, 'Take-Over Bids — The City Code on Take-Overs and Mergers' (1972) 18 *McGill LJ* 385, 402–407.
5 See, for example, Ferguson, RB, 'The Adjudication of Commercial Disputes and the Legal System in Modern England' (1980) 7 *British Journal of Law and Society* 141; Sugarman, D, 'Law, Economy and the State in England, 1750–1914: Some Major Issues' in Sugarman, D, *Legality, Ideology and the State* (London: Academic Press, 1983), p 213 at pp 215–218, 230–233; Hedley, S, 'The "Needs of Commercial Litigants" in Nineteenth and Twentieth Century Contract Law' (1997) 18 *Journal of Legal History* 85. And for a useful American example, see Lurie, J, *The Chicago Board of Trade 1859–1905: The Dynamics of Self-Regulation* (Urbana: University of Illinois Press, 1979).
6 See, generally, Picciotto, S, 'The Regulatory Criss-Cross: Interaction between Jurisdictions and the Construction of Global Regulatory Networks' in Bratton, WW *et al* (eds), *International Regulatory Competition and Coordination* (Oxford: Clarendon Press, 1996), p 89.
7 Established in 1987.

police.[1] Thus, even self-regulation is increasingly characterised by a multiplicity of regulation, raising important questions of regulatory co-ordination. Within the context of this complex set of legal fields, or 'interlegality',[2] hybrid systems of corporate law meld criminal law with contractual and equitable doctrines, supplemented with principles of a public law nature. Thus, the complex dialectic of regulation, de-regulation and re-regulation[3] — of private and public law — which has characterised the regulation of companies, both public and private. As concepts and practices have changed so there has been an increasing awareness of the manifold economic and social relations adopting the corporate form, the heterogeneous and hybrid forms of institutional structures adopted by business corporations[4] and the plurality of hybrid regulatory regimes that constitute and govern them. And these changing structures and regulatory frameworks operate in the context of increasing competition as between business corporations, among their legal and financial engineers, and as between the relevant regulatory watchdogs, national and transnational,[5] competition that is accentuated by globalisation.[6]

Trends and tensions within contemporary company law — private companies

While the de-regulation of large public companies is undoubtedly controversial, a consensus has emerged that some de-regulation of those small firms whose shares are not publicly traded may be desirable. The last major review of company law, the report of the Jenkins Committee in 1962, pointed to 'the

---

1   In practice, the rules are frequently flouted without censure. Both the Stock Exchange and the SIB have inadequate powers to punish offenders, and operate in a culture where public censure is rarely used even where important information is, in effect, withheld from the stock market. Most financial fraud offences, being criminal offences, require a higher burden of proof than civil offences. Not surprisingly, the DTI's conviction rate is low (though the SFO's is better — despite its high profile failures). Some commentators have, therefore, argued that more offences should give rise to civil as well as criminal liability as this might prove a more effective deterrent. For further discussion, see also Chapter 5.

    Since this was written the Government has announced the establishment of a 'super' securities commission to rationalise and improve the regulation of the financial markets and also the extension of civil liability in the field of securities regulation.

2   On the 'interlegality' of late modernity, see de Sousa Santos, B, *Toward A New Common Sense* (London: Routledge, 1995), pp 75–112.

3   See, generally, Majone, P (ed), *Deregulation or Re-regulation?* (London: Pinter Publishers, 1990). See, also, Prosser, T, 'Regulation, Markets and Legitimacy' in Oliver, D and Jowell, J (eds), *The Changing Constitution* (Oxford: Clarendon Press, 1994).

4   See, for example, Hadden, T, *The Control of Corporate Groups*; Scott, J, *Corporations, Classes and Capitalism* 2nd edn (London: Hutchinson, 1985), 'Corporate Control and Corporate Rule: Britain in an International Perspective' (1990) 41 *British Journal of Sociology* 351 and 'Networks of Corporate Power' (1991) *Annual Review of Sociology* 17; Teubner, G, 'The Many-Headed Hydra: Networks as Higher-Order Collective Actors' in McCahery, J *et al* (eds), *Corporate Control and Accountability* (Oxford: Clarendon Press, 1995), p 41.

5   For a useful case study, see Scott, C, 'Institutional Competition and Coordination in the Process of Telecommunications Liberalization' in Bratton, WW *et al* (eds), *International Regulatory Competition and Coordination* (Oxford: Clarendon Press, 1996), p 379.

6   See Dezalay, Y, 'Professional Competition and the Social Construction of Transnational Regulatory Expertise' in McCahery, J *et al* (eds), *Corporate Control and Accountability*, p 203.

multiplication of companies' and the abuse of the corporate privilege by small under-capitalised businesses.[1] It considered that there was a need to curb unnecessary incorporation. It recommended the abolition of the exempt private company so that all companies would be required to file accounts or have them audited. This recommendation was implemented by the Companies Act of 1967.[2] The Committee acknowledged the special difficulties of minority shareholders in private companies who are unable to dispose of their shares. In this context, it considered briefly whether a new form of business organisation, described as a corporate partnership, should be created, concluding that this was undesirable.

From the period coinciding with the publication of the Bolton Committee Report on Small Firms[3] in 1971, however, there was a gradual shift from the previous tendency to treat company law as unitary and the assumption that private companies required more regulation to bring them more closely in line with public companies. In its White Paper of 1973, 'Company Law Reform', the Government showed itself more sensitive to the particular problems of small companies. It considered that the classification of public and private companies should be amended to reflect more accurately the different requirements and responsibilities of the two corporate forms, that disclosure requirements should be determined by the size and status of the company and that public companies should be subject to a minimum paid-up capital requirement. It concluded that further research was required on the demand for a new corporate form for small businesses and the adequacy of the partnership and unlimited company before a new corporate form for small businesses could be adopted. No legislation resulted from the 1973 White Paper.

The Companies Act 1980, by establishing separate rules for private and public companies, aided their differentiation. It created a minimum capital requirement for public companies. Whereas all companies previously used the abbreviation 'Ltd' (unless otherwise exempted), public and private companies were now required to employ different designations.[4] And the contractual status of the relationship between shareholders and between shareholders and the company was set forth in the Companies Act 1980.[5] The Companies Act 1981 did not include a new form of incorporation for small companies, but it did create a more lenient regime for small and medium-sized companies as regards the filing of accounts. In the same year, the Department of Trade and Industry (DTI) published a consultative paper which included a scheme prepared by

---

1 Board of Trade, *Report of the Company Law Committee* (1962) Cmnd 1749. See, further, Law Commission, 'Reform of the Law Applicable to Private Companies: A Feasibility Study' in the DTI's *Company Law Review: the Law Applicable to Private Companies* (URN 94/529) (London: DTI, 1994) paras 1.2–1.8, on which I have drawn in preparing this paragraph.

2 Companies Act 1967, s 2 (abolishing the status of exempt private company).

3 *Report of the Committee of Inquiry on Small Firms: Small Firms* (1971) Cmnd 4811. For a useful survey which puts the Bolton Committee's findings in context, see Curran, P, *Bolton Fifteen Years On* (London: Small Business Research Trust, 1986). See, also, DTI, *Small Firms in Britain* (London: DTI, 1994).

4 See Sugarman, D, 'The Companies Act 1980: The Classification, Registration and Re-registration of Companies' (1980) 1 *The Company Lawyer* 135.

5 See s 14.

LCB Gower for a new form of incorporation for small firms.[1] The Law Society's response to the consultative document was, like most of the responses, equivocal. It concluded that many different forms of business organisations already existed, and that these should not be increased unless there was evidence of a clear demand for change. Its preference was to structure the requirements of the Companies Acts in areas such as disclosure by reference to size rather than the classification of the company.[2]

The Thatcher Government's desire to reduce government expenditure and the regulation of small companies was a major theme of its White Paper of 1985, *Lifting the Burden*.[3] This was followed by the Companies Act 1989, which undertook the further 'deregulation' of private companies. Of particular significance, was the adoption of an 'elective regime', which allows small private companies to contract out of some of the (hitherto) mandatory provisions of the Companies Acts.[4] In order to expedite deregulation, the Secretary of State was empowered to make regulations by statutory instrument enabling private companies to elect to dispense with compliance of the Act where this related primarily to the company's internal administration and procedure.[5] Within five years of the Act, 500,000 small companies had been exempted from the statutory audit and work on simplifying the accounting requirements of small companies was under way.[6]

The 1980s also saw the courts recognising the special needs of private companies through its development of the notion of the 'quasi partnership', a small private company that may be exempted from some of the formalities of com-

---

1 Cmnd 1871 (1981).
2 The Law Society, *Memorandum by the Society's Standing Committee on Company Law, A New Form of Incorporation for Small Firms* (1981) No 79. See, also, Sealy, LS, 'The New Form of Incorporation: A Personal View' (1981) 2 *The Company Lawyer* 128; Wooldridge, F, 'A New Form of Incorporation — Responding to the Gower Proposals' (1983) 3 *The Company Lawyer* 58; Milman D and Flanagan, T, *Modern Partnership Law* (London: Croom Helm, 1983), ch 10; Forum of Private Business, *A Report into Business Legal Structures* (London: 1991). See, generally, Freedman, J, 'Small Business and the Corporate Form' (1994) 57 *MLR* 555 and The Law Commission, 'Reform of the Law Applicable to Private Companies: A Feasibility Study' in the DTI's *Company Law Review: the Law Applicable to Private Companies* (URN 94/529) (London: DTI, 1994), paras 5.21–5.41, 6.1.
3 Cmnd 9571, July 1985.
4 See Part V headed 'Deregulation of Private Companies'. This was influenced by a report on the deregulation of private companies prepared by Professor LS Sealy for the Institute of Directors.
5 Companies Act 1989, s 117. Such regulations merely require the approval of both Houses by way of a resolution rather than the normal debate and scrutiny. Views differ on whether this incrementalism is desirable. On the one hand, it is questionable whether the increasing use of statutory instruments to by-pass parliamentary debate is the best way of achieving company law reform. Certainly, it encourages a 'trial and error' approach to company law reform. On the other hand, it does mean that corrections can be more easily made when an unintended or undesired consequence of a policy change comes to light.
6 In 1992, the DTI brought into force regulations implementing the Twelfth Company Law Directive, which permit the creation of single member private limited companies. The EU is currently undertaking a special programme on small and medium companies.

pany law but which may impose more stringent obligations on the directors and members akin to those applied in Partnership Law.[1]

Further impetus to relax and re-examine the rules of company law, as they applied to small companies, has come from the DTI. Since 1992, it has been undertaking an extensive re-appraisal of companies legislation during a lull in the EU's harmonisation programme,[2] '. . . largely driven by the philosophy of deregulation'.[3] A number of topics have been reviewed by working parties specially established for the purpose whose membership includes various expertise and interests. In 1993, the DTI created a Working Group on the law governing private companies to access whether 'it can be simplified and separately presented'.[4] The Working Group considered three options. The first was creating a new legal structure restricted to businesses owned and managed by five or fewer people (termed 'proprietary companies'). The second was disapplying all the sections of the Companies Act 1985 which are unnecessary for proprietary companies and simplifying others. The Group suggested that Table A should be substantially revised or replaced by a new table so that internal relations could be governed in a more flexible fashion. The final option was extending the elective regime applicable to private companies whereby statutory requirements may be relaxed or excluded by passing elective resolutions. It left open whether the regime should be extended to all small companies or only to proprietary companies.[5]

In April 1994, the Law Commission were invited to contribute to this work. The Commission was asked to carry out a feasibility study into the reform of the law applicable to private companies in the wider context of the needs of small business. In effect, its brief was to ascertain the best way to proceed. The Commission's study took account of the preparatory work of the Working Party, and its findings were published in November 1994.[6] But before we examine the Commission's findings, it would be helpful to first consider a significant research study that appeared while the Commission was undertaking its study, and which may have helped to shape its approach.

---

1 See *Re Duomatic Ltd* [1969] 2 Ch 365; *Ebrahimi v Westbourne Galleries Ltd* [1973] AC 360; *Cane v Jones* [1980] 1 WLR 1451. See, also, the development of the remedy for unfairly prejudicial conduct under the Companies Act 1985, s 459.

2 See, further, The Law Commission, 'Reform of the Law Applicable to Private Companies: A Feasibility Study', paras 1.11–1.16.

3 Freedman, J, 'Small Business and the Corporate Form' (1994) 57 *MLR* 555 n 6 citing DTI, *Deregulation — Cutting Red Tape* (London: DTI, 1994); *Deregulation Task Force's Proposals for Reform* (London: DTI, January 1994); Deregulation and Contracting Out Bill 1994; Padfield, F, 'The Reform of Company Law', *Palmer's In Company* (October 1993).

4 DTI Press Notice, 18 November 1992, cited in Freedman, 'Small Business and the Corporate Form' p 556; and on the Working Group, see Freedman, pp 556–557.

5 See, further, The Law Commission, 'Reform of the Law Applicable to Private Companies: A Feasibility Study', paras 5.3–5.5.

6 The Law Commission, 'Reform of the Law Applicable to Private Companies: A Feasibility Study', which was appended to DTI, *Company Law Review: the Law Applicable to Private Companies* (URN 94/529) (London: DTI, November 1994) being a 'Consultative Document Seeking Views on the Law Commission's Feasibility Study on Reform of Private Companies'.

Focusing, contract and new options within the existing structures of company law — Freedman's research and recommendations on small businesses

Those investigating this field were, seemingly, confronted by a paradox. There was little enthusiasm for the Gower proposals of 1981;[1] yet, criticism persisted that the legal forms available to business were unsuited to the needs of small firms.[2] This highlighted the dearth of systematic data on small firms and their attitudes towards the use of lawyers and legal forms. During 1990 and 1991, Judith Freedman, a member of the DTI's Working Group on the law governing private companies, undertook an empirical survey of small business owners and their accountants.[3] In July 1994, she published an important essay, drawing upon the findings of her research, in order to clarify the underlying issues that, in her view, were fundamental to the Commission's feasibility study.[4]

Her survey results indicated that the majority of small firm owners were not particularly interested in the question of legal form; that many small businesses were content with operating as an unincorporated form; that small firm owners often lacked an understanding of what was obtained by incorporation; and that they tended not to read legal documents, including their own memorandum and articles of association. Freedman's research also illuminated the long-acknowledged difficulties surrounding the formulation of a satisfactory definition of small companies.[5] In practice, private companies were extremely diverse in terms of their aims, structures and life cycles, and it was helpful to conceive of this heterogeneity as existing within a continuum. While some private companies do not wish to grow, others metamorphose into several different forms of company during their life cycle.[6] These findings highlighted a major obstacle to creating a new form of incorporation for small firms: namely, that it would be very difficult to determine which particular group (the one person firm, the husband and wife company, the family company, the private company which brings in outside finance, etc) to design a new legal form for, and it was not self-evident what configuration would be seen as improving the *status quo*. An examination of the law in other jurisdictions, especially the United States and New Zealand, also indicated that a special legal form was unnecessary. Thus, the way ahead was perceived as the development of new

---

1 Cmnd 1871 (1981).

2 See Freedman, J, 'Small Business and the Corporate Form', p 560.

3 This research was undertaken with Michael Godwin. See, Freedman, J and Godwin, M, 'Incorporating the Micro Business: Perceptions and Misconceptions' in Hughes and Storey (eds), *Finance and the Small Firm* (London: Routledge, 1994); Freedman, J and Godwin, M, *Legal Form, Tax and the Micro Business* (London: Institute of Advanced Legal Studies, 1991); Freedman, J and Godwin, M, 'Legal Form, Tax and the Micro Business' in Caley *et al* (eds), *Small Enterprise Development,* (London: Paul Chapman Publishing, 1992); Freedman, J and Godwin, M, 'The Statutory Audit and the Micro Company — An Empirical Investigation' [1993] *JBL* 105.

4 Freedman, J, 'Small Business and the Corporate Form', p 557.

5 A definition that was essential if Parliament were to be asked to create a new form of incorporation for small businesses.

6 Freedman, J, 'Small Business and the Corporate Form', pp 558–559.

options and standard form articles within the existing structure that fostered flexibility, giving choice to those engaged, but providing default provisions when the company's internal relations break down.[1] With respect to the need to protect third parties, such as creditors, Freedman distinguished between 'internal' provisions in the company's constitution that dealt with the internal relations within the company and which, therefore, could be left to shareholders to agree, without prejudicing third parties; and 'external' provisions of the company's constitution which did affect its relations with third parties and where leaving matters to the shareholders may not provide adequate protection.[2] She also argued that statutory standard form exit clauses, enabling shareholders to be bought out, would avoid the cost and uncertainty that arises from litigation, as is the case with the statutory remedy for challenging unfairly prejudicial conduct.[3]

Freedman cautioned against de-regulation becoming the sole basis for company law reform, arguing that regulatory provisions will be essential in any legal form offering limited liability. If people are dissuaded from incorporation that may not be bad: since '. . . in practice, discouraging firms from entering into an inappropriate regime may be the most deregulatory step possible'.[4] If incorporation involved choosing as between various standard form constitutional packages, such a scheme might usefully discourage incorporation in that business people would be forced, before they incorporate, to address their minds to the various relevant aspects of forming and running a limited company.[5]

The Law Commission's feasibility study on the reform of private companies of November 1994

The publication of the Law Commission's feasibility study on the reform of private companies was an important event for company law reform, being the Commission's first contribution to the field of company law and to the DTI's review of company law. Its objective was to assess the relative importance to small business of company law problems. It was agreed that the Commission would carry out its study over three to four months, which was acknowledged as too short a time to carry out a comprehensive survey.[6] The Commission canvassed the views of organisations representing small businesses, members of the DTI Working Group on private companies, individual company directors and professional advisors to small businesses. Its survey confirmed that small businesses do not regard company law problems as a high priority (save

---

1 Freedman, J, 'Small Business and the Corporate Form', pp 558–559.
2 Freedman, J, 'Small Business and the Corporate Form', p 557.
3 Under the Companies Act 1980, s 459. See Freedman, J, 'Small Business and the Corporate Form', p 582.
4 Freedman, J, 'Small Business and the Corporate Form', p 558.
5 Similarly, incorporation could be discouraged by greater education of small businesses as to the true fiscal effect of so doing since many small businesses are misconceived about the fiscal implications of incorporating their businesses: The Law Commission, 'Reform of the Law Applicable to Private Companies: A Feasibility Study', para 5.37.
6 Paragraphs 1.18, 1.21, 1.22.

in a few problematic areas)[1] and it noted the ambivalence to the idea of a new legal structure. It concluded that a new legal form for small business was not the right way to proceed, doubting that it would significantly assist small businesses. It noted and assessed briefly the other options considered by the DTI Working Group and Judith Freedman's recommendations for a flexible structure for small firms.[2] It recognised that incorporation tended to encourage small under-capitalised firms relative to unincorporated businesses and that company law reform had to be sensitive to this long-standing problem. It observed that any re-modelling of the internal relations between members on the lines of partnership precedents, thereby giving incorporators greater freedom to manage their affairs, was better undertaken by permissive regulation allowing incorporators to choose for themselves, rather than mandatory rules imposed on them from above, which 'would not meet the requirement of an incremental approach'.[3] As regards extending the elective regime, it doubted whether the relaxation of internal requirements would be of significant advantage to small businesses, since they do not find them a burden.[4]

While company law, generally, may not be a priority concern of small business, the Commission found that a number of their respondents were concerned with particular legal issues: namely, the requirements of audit and disclosure of companies' accounts, directors' duties and the means of resolving disputes between business owners. Its respondents evidenced '. . . great anxiety in relation to the lack of effective controls of, and sanction for, unscrupulous behaviour by directors'.[5] They also supported the clarification of directors' responsibilities and improvements in the resolution of internal disputes, such as arbitration, and the avoidance of unnecessary winding up proceedings.[6]

The Commission also received unsolicited correspondence from members of the judiciary, solicitors and barristers complaining that s 459 of the Companies Act 1985, which enables shareholders to apply to the court for relief where the company's affairs are being conducted in a manner which is unfairly prejudicial to the shareholders, leads to excessively long and expensive proceedings. It concluded that s 459 petitions are '. . . a particularly unsuitable mechanism for resolving disputes between members of small companies'.[7] It also noted that the lack of simple and cheap procedures for resolving internal disputes in private companies may deter investors such as pension funds from investing in them.[8]

---

1 See, below. It concluded that the major problems of small businesses in the UK are financial: lack of cash flow, inability to collect debts, and access to external finance: para 6.1.

2 See Freedman, J, 'Small Business and the Corporate Form'. It also considered the corporate structures in six overseas jurisdictions: paras 5.6–5.20.

3 Paragraph 5.39.

4 Paragraph 5.41.

5 Paragraph 5.42. The ineffectiveness of the legislation governing director disqualification, and the lack of resources in the government bodies responsible for enforcing this and allied areas of company law, may explain the concern expressed: see para 5.42.

6 Paragraphs 5.42–5.53.

7 Paragraph 5.45.

8 See para 5.46.

It suggested that minority shareholders might be given a statutory right to require the company to buy them out on the happening of certain events, such as changes in the company's constitution or embarking on substantial new transactions, without having to prove that the transaction complained of is unfair and unreasonable, as is the case under the New Zealand Companies Act 1993.[1] 'Additionally, or alternatively, other means of dispute resolution could be considered. These could be offered as an option for inclusion in the articles of the company.'[2]

The Commission also considered the reform of partnership law. Despite the inappropriate provisions that may be found in the constitutions of 'off-the-shelf' companies, the relative ease and cheapness with which they can be obtained is seen by incorporators as reducing the start-up costs of small companies. The Commission recognised that the absence of a standard form agreement for partnerships increases establishment costs for small businesses; and that such a standard form agreement could cover the effect of changes in the partnership and many other basic issues such as management of the business, partnership property, arbitration and dissolution.[3] More generally, the Commission concluded that 'reform of partnership law could assist as many, if not more, small businesses as would a reform of company law.[4] A reform of partnership law which addresses its main deficiencies, provides a statutory draft partnership agreement and possibly gives partnerships independent legal personality may well be of benefit to small business'.[5]

The 'contractual turn' and the form and style of regulation

Thus, the increasing sensitivity to the diverse range of businesses, the multi-layered character of regulation, and the need, therefore, for a more functional and focused approach to corporate law has been accompanied by a concern to advance shareholder choice and autonomy via the contractual terms governing the relationship between shareholders and between shareholders and the company. It has also been manifested in a shift away from mandatory forms of regulation. These tendencies are also evident in two discrete but overlapping movements, both of which derive from American corporate law debates and its engagement with law and economics scholarship. First, there has been a significant debate as to the best way to analyse and conceptualise companies. As a major shift from the administrative to the contractual allocation of resources

---

1 Paragraphs 5.46 and 5.47.
2 Paragraph 5.47. The consultative document also considered whether a separate Table A should be created for private companies, concluding that this should not be undertaken until after the DTI working groups on directors' duties and Part X of the Companies Act 1985 have completed their work: paras 5.48–5.49. It also examined certain uncertainties concerning shareholder agreements and concluded that these were not causing any practical difficulties to business: paras 5.51–5.59.
3 Paragraph 5.63. Freedman has opined that a statutory standard form partnership agreement could save unincorporated firms setting up costs much as incorporation does today: Freedman, J, 'Small Business and the Corporate Form' (1994) 57 *MLR* 584.
4 Paragraph 5.62.
5 Paragraph 6.5.

occurred, with the privatisation and 'contracting out' of public services,[6] so the contractual analysis of companies has, increasingly, supplanted the managerialist approach as the dominant method of conceptualising companies. Whereas the managerialist approach focuses on the imbalance of power and, therefore, the hierarchies within companies, the contractual approach treats the internal structures and external relations of the company as a series of contracts, the efficiency of which can be evaluated by market-based criteria. The desire to limit state intervention and advance market control, coupled with the evident utility of contractual approaches in addressing all types of companies and all corporate relations, has helped to underpin the influence of the contractual framework. It has encouraged company lawyers to see company law through the lens of contract, to re-examine and extend the contractual freedom within company law in the name of empowering the company's principal actors to organise matters as they see fit.[2] Moreover, it finds support in the doctrine that the articles of a company constitute a contract between the company and the members and the members *inter se*, which is now embodied in the Companies Act 1985.[3] Since majority rule cannot fill all the gaps in the parties' bargain, '. . . much of company law can be seen as offering rules which the parties would simply choose to spell out in full themselves were they compelled to address all future contingencies. And by offering such rules, transaction costs are thereby minimised'.[4]

Despite its merits, the contractual approach in company law has been subject to considerable qualification and criticism.[5] The articles of association are not like a classic, discrete contract for the sale of goods. The agreement between shareholders, especially in small companies, tends to be long-term and relational, requiring a different treatment to that afforded to discrete, 'one off contracts'.[6] 'Members of a company do not make a contract detailing what they and the

---

1 Since 1979, more than £60 billion of United Kingdom business has been transferred from the state to the private sector: see, generally, Harden, I, *The Contracting State* (Buckingham: Open University Press, 1992); Forster, CD, and Plowden, FJ, *The State Under Stress* (Buckingham: Open University Press, 1996); Martin, S and Parker, D, *The Impact of Privatisation* (London: Routledge, 1997).

2 See, generally, Easterbrook, F and Fischel, D, 'The Corporate Contract' (1989) 89 *Columbia Law Review* 1416 and their influential book, *The Economic Structure of Corporate Law* (Cambridge, Mass: Harvard University Press, 1991).
   It is ironic that the significant expansion of contract's role in society since the late 1970s occurred shortly after several commentators had predicted its declining role and, even, death: see, for example, Gilmore, G, *The Death of Contract* (Columbus: Ohio State University Press, 1974).

3 Section 14.

4 Riley, CA, 'Contracting Out of Company Law: Section 459 of the Companies Act 1985 and the Role of the Courts' (1992) 55 *MLR* 782.

5 See Brudney, V, 'Corporate Governance, Agency Costs and the Rhetoric of Contract' (1985) 85 *Columbia Law Review* 1403; Bebchuk, LA, 'The Debate on Contractual Freedom in Corporate Law' (1989) 89 *Columbia Law Review* 1395; Eisenberg, M, 'The Structure of Corporation Law' (1989) 89 *Columbia Law Review* 1461; Bratton, WW, Jr, 'The New Economic Theory of the Firm: Critical Perspectives from History' (1989) 41 *Stanford Law Review* 1471 and 'The "Nexus of Contract" Corporation: A Critical Appraisal' (1989) 74 *Cornell Law Review* 407; Parkinson, JE, *Corporate Power and Responsibility* (Oxford: Clarendon Press, 1993), pp 177–190; Teubner, G, 'Piercing the Contractual Veil? The Social Responsibility of Contractual Networks' in Wilhelmsson, T, (ed), *Perspectives of Critical Contract Law* (Aldershot: Dartmouth, 1993), p 211; the chapters by Bratton, WW, Jr, Teubner, G, Collins, H, in McCahery, J, *et al* (eds), *Corporate Control and Accountability*; and Cheffins, BR, *Company Law*, pp 31–46.

6 Riley, CA, 'Contracting Out of Company Law' (1992) 55 *MLR* 782, 785–786.

company are to do: they enter into a relationship in which they expect to bene-fit from whatever it is their company does do, as settled from time to time by themselves and the directors . . .'[1] Being part of the company's constitution, the articles operate as a constitutional framework within which the company func-tions. In consequence, the corporate contract is characterised by a process of active judicial review. Thus, the contractual approach ignores the hybrid char-acter of the company's constitution, with its discrete and relational contractual dimensions. '[Complete] contractual freedom is neither descriptively accurate nor normatively desirable'[2] since it may undermine co-operation and trust within the company, while denying those beyond the nexus of contracts (local residents, environmentalists, representatives of the public interest, etc.) any interest in the company's affairs.[3] An increasing reliance on contract, therefore, raises profound issues of control and accountability, much like the extension of self-regulation since the 1970s.[4]

Secondly, the application of functional, focused and contractual approaches to company law have been accompanied by a greater sensitivity to the variety of regulatory strategies, forms of regulation and the appropriate level that regula-tion might take. This has been associated with the desire to adopt the most eco-nomically efficient and socially desirable form of regulation in the particular circumstances.[5] A taxonomy of company law regulation would distinguish between mandatory provisions ('you shall not'), default provisions ('you are bound unless you have opted out'), and permissive provisions ('you may adopt a particular rule even though this may bypass or attenuate the usual rule'). In practice, such a taxonomy may not operate in a clear-cut fashion as one type of provision may shade into another. Nonetheless, a greater awareness of the range of company law rules, their costs and their benefits is likely to result in a more subtle and effective approach to regulation. The up-shot of this new body of work has been to problematise the steady growth of mandatory regulation. It has de-emphasised mandatory regulation (recognising that in some fields it has been creatively circumvented or ignored in practice) while, correspondingly, encouraging the greater use of default provisions (which fill contractual gaps much like a standard form contract — but require time and effort to do so) and permissive provisions (which have been at the cutting-edge of the de-regulation of small companies, but which may also involve significant transaction costs, and may affect third parties adversely).

---

1 Mayson, SW, *et al*, *Company Law* 13th edn (London: Blackstone, 1996), 147.
2 Riley, CA, 'Contracting Out of Company Law' (1992) *MLR* 782, 802.
3 See Collins, H, 'The Sanctimony of Contract' in Rawlings, R (ed), *Law, Society and Economy* (Oxford: Clarendon Press, 1997), p 78.
4 On self-regulation and the problem of accountability see, Page, AC, 'Self-Regulation: the Constitutional Dimension' (1986) 49 *MLR* 141. And on self-regulation by business, see Graham, G, 'Self-Regulation' in Richardson, G and Genn, H (eds), *Administrative Law and Government Action*. (Oxford: Clarendon Press, 1994); Ogus, A, 'Rethinking Self-Regulation' (1995) 15 *OJLS* 97; and Black, J, 'Constitutionalising Self-Regulation' (1996) 59 *MLR* 24.
5 See Farrar, JH, *et al*, *Farrar's Company Law*, p 99 and the American material cited there. See, also, Ribstein, LE, 'The Mandatory Nature of the ALI Code' (1993) 61 *George Washington Law Review* 984; Riley, CA, 'Contracting Out of Company Law' (1992) 55 *MLR* 782. See, now, the valuable discussion in Cheffins, BR, *Company Law*, ch 5.

These trends have emphasised the significant scope for self-regulation afforded by facilitative laws such as contract law and company law and the complex interaction between different forms of regulation emanating from 'above' and 'below'. Nonetheless, many important and difficult issues remain unresolved. These include the precise role of the courts, and the dangers posed by reducing the company and its constitution to just another network of contracts. The extent to which contract theory can be harnessed to broader organisational principles based upon co-operation, reliance and fairness remains one of the major challenges in this field.[1]

The Woolf Report and the reform of company law — enhancing company law's ability to deliver justice?

Cost effectiveness, concern about the high level of public expenditure on litigation and access to justice have become major issues in the re-shaping of the administration of civil justice. In 1994, Lord Woolf was appointed by the Lord Chancellor to review the civil justice system so as: to improve access to justice and reduce the cost of litigation; to reduce the complexity of the rules and modernise terminology; and to remove unnecessary distinctions between procedure and practice. In June 1995, Lord Woolf published his Interim Report entitled *Access to Justice*, and this was shortly followed by his Final Report of the same name.[2] The Woolf Report diagnosed bluntly the afflictions of the civil justice system in terms of its 'unrestrained adversarial culture' whereby the pace, extent and character of litigation are left almost completely to the parties and their lawyers. The Report's solution was case management: that is, the judicial take-over of the process of litigation, changing the ethos of civil litigation by shifting the responsibility for the management of civil litigation from litigants and their legal advisors to the courts.

It is hardly surprising that the Woolf Report, and allied changes and debates concerning public management and funding, now cast a long shadow over the reform of company law, as is evidenced in the Law Commission's review of shareholder remedies.

PART THREE: THE LAW COMMISSION'S CONSULTATION PAPER ON SHAREHOLDER REMEDIES

In February 1995, as part of the DTI's re-examination of several areas of company law, the Lord Chancellor and the President of the Board of Trade requested the Law Commission:

'. . . to carry out a review of shareholder remedies with particular reference to: the rule in *Foss v Harbottle* (1843) 2 Hare 461 and its exceptions; sections 459 to 461 of the Companies Act 1985; and the enforcement of the rights of shareholders under the articles of association; and to make recommendations.'[3]

---

1 See, generally, McCahery, J *et al* (eds), *Corporate Control and Accountability* (Oxford: Clarendon Press, 1993).
2 The Rt Hon Lord Woolf, *Access to Justice: Final Report* (London: HMSO, 1996).
3 Paragraph 1.2.

These were its terms of reference. Seventeen months later, the Commission published a Consultation Paper on shareholder remedies.[1] The Paper was circulated for comment and criticism only and does not represent the final views of the Commission.[2] Its recommendations are merely provisional, canvassing various options for reform. Indeed, the Commission invited suggestions as to any reform possibilities, irrespective of whether they were canvassed in the Paper.[3] A final report is expected during the Autumn of 1997.

An insight into the considerable effort involved can be gleaned from the following description of the Commission's work by the Law Commissioner with particular responsibility for company and commercial law reform, Ms Diana Faber:

'. . . I started by setting up an advisory committee that consisted of practising lawyers, academics and government officials. I also addressed meetings convened externally, for example at the CBI, in order to obtain views from businesses. Team working papers, based on detailed research and analysis of case law, legislation, academic articles and other sources of information, both domestic and international, were considered and commented upon by all these people . . .

Although the first drafts of our published documents are produced under the auspices of one of the five Commissioners, all of us read and comment on them in some detail. Some drafts undergo significant amendment as a result of this process.'[4]

The Consultation Paper discerned three 'main problems'.[5] First, the case law governing when shareholders can bring proceedings on behalf of the company (the rule in *Foss v Harbottle*[6] and its exceptions) is 'in certain respects . . . inflexible and outmoded'.[7] The rule can only be found in case law, much of which is complex, obscure and many years old and is in this respect virtually inaccessible, save to specialists in the field.[8] Under the aegis of this rule, an individual shareholder cannot usually litigate on the company's behalf. The principal authority with the right to initiate proceedings in the name of the company is

---

1 Paper No 142, (London: The Stationery Office, 1996). The Paper was completed for publication on 31 July 1996. The Paper was produced in consultation with the Scottish Law Commission, who agreed with its content and was responsible for the footnotes concerning Scotland: para 1.19 and p 7 n 37.

2 Comments were sought by 22 January 1997.

3 Paragraph 1.18.

4 Faber, D, 'The Work of The Law Commission' (1997) *Butterworths Journal of International Banking and Financial Law*, May, pp 199–200. Details of the persons and bodies whose assistance is acknowledged are contained in Appendix J. Ms Faber's team is currently assisting the Commission's Chairman, the Hon Mrs Justice Arden, (a company law specialist), in the report stage of the shareholder remedies project.

5 Paragraphs 1.4, 1.7.

6 (1843) 2 Hare 461. The leading modern case is *Prudential Assurance v Newman Industries (No 2)* [1982] Ch 204. There is a vast literature on the rule, but the classic starting point remains KW Wedderburn's seminal essay, 'Shareholders' Rights and the Rule in *Foss v Harbottle*' [1957] 16 *CLJ* 194 and [1958] 17 *CLJ* 93. See, also, for example, Gower, LCB, *The Principles of Company Law* 3rd edn (London: Stevens, 1969), pp 643–662; Farrar, JH *et al*, *Farrar's Company Law* 3rd edn (London: Butterworths, 1991), pp 443–453; Sealy, LS, Problems of Standing, Pleading and Proof in Corporate Litigation'; and Prentice, DD, 'Shareholder Actions: the Rule in *Foss v Harbottle*' (1988) 104 *LQR* 341.

7 Paragraph 14.1.

8 See paras 1.4, 1.6, 4.35 and 14.4.

the board of directors.[1] Thus, the role of individual shareholders in remedying wrongs to the company has been severely confined. Because the rule has been formulated and affirmed by the courts as one which limits derivative actions to set and exceptional circumstances, rather than one which governs the circumstances when shareholders can enforce actions vested in the company, its capacity for judicial development in the light of new circumstances is limited.[2] For example, an action to recover damages suffered by a company by reason of a director's breach of fiduciary duty cannot be brought by shareholders in the company unless the wrongdoers have control. Similarly, a minority cannot bring an action for damages suffered by the company by reason of the negligence of a director unless the negligence benefits the controlling shareholder. The enforcement of directors' duties is further undermined because shareholders in a company may ratify directorial wrongs. And minority shareholders have virtually no rights of access to vital 'inside' corporate information. In practice, litigation to enforce directors' duties is unlikely to arise unless there has been a change of control[3] or the company has gone into liquidation and the liquidator litigates on behalf of the company.

Since standing has to be determined as a preliminary issue by evidence demonstrating a *prima facie* case on the merits, two full court hearings may be required, thereby increasing the length and cost of a derivative action.[4] Moreover, it is difficult to distinguish between wrong done to the company (where the rule in *Foss v Harbottle* applies) and a wrong done to members personally (where the rule does not apply). Shareholders who initiate personal actions (ie actions to enforce their personal rights) will, if successful, directly benefit from the action, usually by way of damages. But shareholders who initiate derivative actions (ie actions to redress a wrong done to the company) will not, if successful, receive individual benefit from the action.[5] Shareholders may, therefore, be deterred significantly from bringing derivative suits, especially since the looser pays the winning party's costs and cannot benefit from the recently introduced limited contingency fee system (so-called 'conditional fees').[6] Thus, '. . . there is an overwhelming financial disincentive' on institutional (and ordinary) investors to take 'legal action against company directors or officers for breach of their fiduciary duties or duties of care and skill'.[7] For these reasons, the operation of the

---

1 The shareholders in general meeting cannot dictate how the board should exercise this power: see *Automatic Self-Cleansing Filter Syndicate v Cuninghame* [1906] 2 Ch 34 and *Breckland v London & Suffolk Properties* [1989] BCLC 100.

2 See para 4.35.
   Directors owe their duties to the company, not to individual shareholders: see *Percival v Wright* [1902] 2 Ch 421. When allied to the principle of majority rule, the shareholder's role is normally limited to participation in the decisions of the general meeting, such as whether to enforce breaches of directors' duties.

3 On shareholder litigation arising from changes in the control of public companies in take-over situations, see Bradley, C, 'Corporate Control: Markets and Rules' (1990) 53 *MLR* 170.

4 See, generally, paras 6.6–6.9. The extension of 'case management', with judges playing a more active role in managing court proceedings, might reduce this problem.

5 See, generally, Sealy, LS, 'Problems of Standing, Pleading and Proof in Corporate Litigation'.

6 See, generally, Prentice, DD, 'Some Aspects of the Corporate Governance Debate' in Prentice, DD and Holland, PRJ (eds), *Contemporary Issues in Corporate Governance*, pp 39–40.

7 Stapledon,GP, *Institutional Shareholders and Corporate Governance*, pp 131–132, and see, generally, pp 131–133.

rule in *Foss v Harbottle*[1] and its exceptions is unsatisfactory.[2] Thus, Canada and New Zealand introduced statutory derivative actions, so that *Foss v Harbottle* could be 'relegated to legal limbo without compunction'[3] and Australia and Hong Kong are currently contemplating its introduction in order 'to lay to rest the unruly ghost of *Foss v Harbottle* . . .'[4]

Secondly, it was often easier for minority shareholders to wind up the company on a just and equitable basis than to remedy wrongs done to the company and/or themselves. Following the recommendations of the Cohen Committee, Parliament created an alternative (and more flexible) remedy to winding up — under s 210 of the Companies Act 1948 — to assist minority shareholders, where the company's affairs were conducted in a manner oppressive to some part of the membership.[5] However, the courts circumscriptive interpretation of 'oppression' and drafting defects meant that few cases were successful.[6] In 1980, s 210 was replaced by a new free-standing remedy[7] that marked an important change in the treatment of shareholder remedies: the petition for the relief of unfairly prejudicial conduct, now embodied in ss 459–461 of the Com- panies Act 1985. This sought to address the drafting difficulties associated with s 210, thereby creating a more effective means of challenging controllers' conduct.[8] Section 459 provides shareholders with a remedy where the company's affairs are conducted in a manner 'unfairly prejudicial' to their interests.[9] The legislation does not

---

1 (1843) 2 Hare 461.
2 See, especially, Part 2 'A Shareholder's Personal Rights Arising from the Company's Constitution', Part 4 'A Shareholder's Right to Bring an Action on Behalf of the Company', and paras 14.1–14.3.
3 Dickerson, RWV, Howard, JL and Getz, L, *Proposals for a New Business Corporations Law for Canada* (Ottawa: Information Canada, 1971), p 482.
4 Consultancy Report, *Review of the Hong Kong Companies Ordinance* (March, 1997), p 152. Thus, several commentators have advocated the legislative reform of company law in the United Kingdom along the lines of that adopted in Canada: see, for example, Sealy, LS, '*Foss v Harbottle* — A Marathon Where Nobody Wins' (1981) 40 *CLJ* 29; Prentice, DD, 'Shareholder Actions: the Rule in *Foss v Harbottle*'; Lowry, J, 'A Plea for a Statutory Derivative Action' (1994) *Palmer's In Company*, 16 Nov, 1.
5 See para 7.3.
6 There were only two reported successful applications under s 210 during the 36 years of its existence.
7 In the sense that under the new remedy shareholders did not have to demonstrate grounds justifying a winding up order, as had been the case under the Companies Act 1948, s 210.
8 The historical background to the enactment of ss 459–461 is helpfully reviewed in paras 7.5–7.12.
9 The Companies Act 1985, s 459, as amended, provides that: 'A member of a company may apply to the court by petition for an order under this Part on the ground that the company's affairs are being or have been conducted in a manner which is unfairly prejudicial to the interests *of* its members generally or some part of the members (including at least himself) or that any actual or proposed act or omission of the company (including any act or omission on its behalf) is or would be so prejudicial' (italics supplied). For a useful analysis of s 459 and its case-law, see, for example, Prentice, DD, 'The Theory of the Firm: Minority Shareholder Oppression: Sections 459–461 of the Companies Act 1985' [1988] *OJLS* 55; Hannigan, B, 'Section 459 of the Companies Act 1985 — A Code of Conduct for the Quasi-Partnership?' [1988] *LMCLQ* 60; Riley, CA, 'Contracting Out of Company Law' (1992) 55 *MLR* 782; Boros, E, *Minority Shareholders' Remedies* (Oxford: Clarendon Press, 1995), ch 6 (which also deals with the Australian experience); Lowry, J, 'The Pursuit of Effective Minority Shareholder Protection: s 459 of the Companies Act 1985' (1996) 17 *The Company Lawyer* 67. The legislation of other jurisdictions is considered in Griggs, L and Lowry, JP, 'Minority Shareholder Remedies: A Comparative View' [1994] *JBL* 463.

specify the sort of conduct which might be so defined and provides the court with wide powers to grant a successful applicant any order it thinks appropriate.[1] This reform, when allied to a more activist judiciary,[2] has altered the prospect of shareholder actions. It has become the procedure most widely used by minority shareholders who experience breaches of directors' duties or other unsatisfactory conduct of the company's business. It provides remedies for types of conduct that cannot be remedied in any other way, especially in the context of private companies[3] and quasi-partnerships,[4] notably, the buying out of dissenting shareholders.

Indeed, s 459 has become a victim of its own success. Its general wording may encourage shareholders to put in issue anything that may be remotely

---

1 Companies Act 1985, s 461. The sheer breadth of this discretion explains its popularity, and contrasts starkly with the technical restrictions associated with *Foss v Harbottle* and its exceptions. Without prejudice to this general power, s 461(2) enumerates four merely illustrative orders which the court might make.

   Section 461(2)(c) was adopted following the recommendations of the Jenkins Committee (The Company Law Committee, chaired by Lord Jenkins, Cmnd 1749 (London: HMSO, 1962) to enable the court to authorise a minority shareholder to bring a derivative action without satisfying the rule in *Foss v Harbottle* (1843) 2 Hare 461. The Law Commission take the view that this provision is little used because it requires two full sets of proceedings: paras 7.11–7.12, 16.3. While the power has been rarely used, the courts have in fact rejected the notion that it necessarily requires two separate proceedings: see *Re a Company (No 005287 of 1985)* [1986] 1 WLR 281. For a recent broad interpretation of s 461(2), see *Lowe v Fahey* [1996] 1 BCLC 262, 268.

2 For example, whereas the courts confined 'oppression' to 'burdensome, harsh and wrongful' (*SCWS v Meyer* [1959] AC 324, 342 per Viscount Simmonds LC), they have expansively construed 'unfairly prejudicial' as to be distinguishable from 'unjust and inequitable': see *Diligenti v RWMD Operations Kelowna Ltd* (1976) 1 BCLR 36 per Fulton J. See, also, *Re a Company (No 008699)* [1985] BCLC 382 per Hoffman J. In some cases, membership interests have not been limited to their formal constitutional rights but have been extended to the protection of their legitimate expectations. It has been said that under s 459, the court's role is that '. . . of a medical practitioner presented with a patient who is alleged to be suffering from one or more ailments which can be treated by an appropriate remedy applied during the course of the continuing life of the company': *Re a Company (No 00314 of 1989), ex parte Estate Acquisition and Development Ltd* [1991] BCLC 154 per Mummery J.

   This development may be related to a more creative, interventionist role of the courts that can be discerned in some fields of company law, encouraged by the EU harmonisation programme: i.e., that legislation seeking to implement the EU's measures should not be interpreted in the traditionally conservative fashion epitomised by the literal rule of interpretation: see Milman, D, 'Company Law in Transition' (1990) 24 *The Law Teacher* 3, 5. And on the expansion of judicial intervention in the context of quasi-companies, see Hannigan, B, 'Section 459 of the Companies Act 1985 — A Code of Conduct for the Quasi-Partnership?' [1988] *LMCLQ* 60. The increased robustness of the courts may also be related to recent changes in the attitudes and values of the higher judiciary: see, generally, Rozenberg, J, *The Search for Justice* (London: Hodder and Stoughton, 1994), chs 1 and 2; Stevens, R, 'Judges, Politics, Politicians and the Confusing Role of the Judiciary' *The Human Face of Law* in Hawkins, K (ed) (Oxford: Clarendon Press, 1997), pp 245–289; Rozenberg, J, *Trial of Strength* (London: R Cohen, 1997).

3 Companies with a broad shareholder base are likely to manage their affairs through shareholder agreements, while shareholders in listed public companies are able to sell their stake in the company on the market. In private companies it is often the case that share transfer restrictions, problems relating to share valuation and the absence of buyers mean that aggrieved minorities cannot simply avoid acrimony and oppression by selling their investments.

4 Quasi-partnerships (ie small owner-managed companies) are a species of small private company. Often, most of the membership are involved in the management, and shareholder income is derived from salaries arising from managerial duties rather than from dividends. In this context, s 459 provides a vital remedy where minorities are excluded from management.

relevant. These proceedings often entail complex, factual, and/or historical investigations that can be unpredictable, expensive and potentially destructive of the company.[1] In *Re Elgindata*,[2] the costs of the 43-day trial totalled £320,000 and shares plunged in value from £40,000 to £24,000; and in *Re Macro (Ipswich Ltd)*,[3] the parties to this 27-day action claimed costs of £725,000. Small owner-managed companies are particularly at risk because the case-law on s 459 enables shareholders of those types of companies to resort to this remedy more easily than members of other types of companies; and because the consequent delays and lost management time are particularly detrimental to them.[4]

Proceedings under s 459 have blurred the classic distinction between corporate wrongs remedied by derivative actions[5] and personal wrongs remedied by personal actions. This is because it is used to redress allegations which previously might have been subject to a derivative action or a personal action to enforce the companies constitution under s 14 of the Companies Act 1985.[6] Yet many shareholders may not have access to the advice of an expert in company law when undertaking a petition under s 459. And those advisors who are not experts in company law, such as Citizens' Advice Bureaux and smaller firms of solicitors, may not have the specialist resources[7] and expertise to be able to predict whether or not a court is likely to find that there has been unfairly prejudicial conduct.[8] For these reasons, the Paper evaluates critically the operation of ss 459–461 in terms of its 'efficiency'[9] and cost-effectiveness.

Thirdly, the Paper examines the legal problems that may arise when shareholders seek to enforce: their personal rights under the company's constitution; their statutory rights (ie those rights that the Companies Act 1985 confers on members); and their rights in shareholder agreements. The principal difficulties discerned concern the enforcement of rights that a shareholder has in a capacity other than that of a member, such as a director or solicitor; the identification of personal rights conferred by the articles; and the fact that s 14 of the

---

1 See Part C 'Unfair Prejudice Remedy' and paras 14.5–14.6.

2 [1991] BCLC 959.

3 [1994] 2 BCLC 354.

4 See para 14.5.

5 On derivative actions, see Boyle, AJ, 'The Derivative Action in Company Law' (1969) 13 *JBL* 120 and Hollington R, *Minority Shareholders' Rights* 2nd edn (London: Sweet & Maxwell, 1994), paras 2–013–2–016.

6 See para 7.2.

7 The Paper contends that 'Such people may have an additional difficulty in that some cases under the section are only reported in specialist series of reports': para 20.5.

8 Paragraph 14.6 and p 141 n 9. The Paper draws a distinction between company law experts, who 'are not troubled by the generality of the wording' (p 141 n 9) because the case-law provides sufficient guidance as to the likely outcome of a case; and non experts, such as CABs and smaller firms of solicitors, who may not have the specialist reports and even books needed to understand the law and predict outcomes: para 14.6 and p 141 n 9. This dichotomy is not wholly persuasive. One might go further than the Commission and concede that even company law specialists may not agree on whether or not a court will find that certain conduct was unfairly prejudicial. On the other hand, the Paper seems to assume that s 459 actions are more unpredictable than other specialist areas of company law, an assumption for which there is no evidence.

9 Paragraph 1.7.

Companies Act 1985 does not state that the company is bound by the articles as if it had executed them under seal.[1]

In order to address these difficulties, the Paper canvasses four strategies: the partial abrogation of *Foss v Harbottle*[2] and the creation of a new derivative action;[3] a new action giving shareholders in small companies the right to have their shares purchased where they have been wrongly excluded from management;[4] the streamlining and more effective 'case management' of shareholders' actions;[5] and the introduction of three new model regulations into Table A to assist shareholders to help themselves and minimise litigation.[6] With respect to the problems relating to the enforcement of the articles of association, the Commission concluded that they are either outside its terms of reference or are not causing hardship in practice.[7]

The Commission's proposals and allied recommendations will now be considered, followed by a general assessment of its helpful study.

New derivative action

The Paper proposes the partial abolition of the rule in *Foss v Harbottle*[8] and the creation of a new derivative action.[9] The new derivative action would enable a member to enforce any cause of action vested in the company against any person arising from any breach or threatened breach of duty by any director of any of his or her duties to the company (including claims against third parties as a result of such breaches).[10] If there is no breach of duty by a director, a shareholder could not bring the action and the company would be left to bring proceedings itself.[11] The proposal would partially abrogate the rule in *Foss v Harbottle*[12] as the old requirements of 'fraud' and 'wrongdoer control' would no longer apply in this context. 'Our aim', it says, 'is to create a more flexible and modern criterion for leave to bring a derivative action than fraud on the minority'.[13]

By rendering to a shareholder *locus standi* to bring a derivative action as co-extensive with the breach of directors' duties, rather than majority rule, the proposal would extend the ability of shareholders to police corporate wrongs. In effect, the proposal would widen the shareholder's interest beyond the right

1 See, generally, paras 2.1–2.39, 14.7–14.9, 19.1–19.2.
2 (1843) 2 Hare 461.
3 Part 16: 'A New Derivative Action'.
4 Part 18: 'A New Additional Unfair Prejudice Remedy for Smaller Companies'.
5 Part 17: 'Case Management by the Courts of Shareholder Proceedings'.
6 Part 19: 'Articles of Association'.
7 Paragraphs 14.7–14.9.
8 (1843) 2 Hare 461.
9 Paragraph 21.1 and see, generally, Part 16: 'A New Derivative Action'.
10 Paragraph 15.2.
11 This is the situation in South Africa (where shareholders can also bring a derivative action under the common law); but contrasts with the situation in Canada, New Zealand and under the draft Australian legislation, where there is no statutory circumscription of the derivative action.
12 (1843) 2 Hare 461.
13 Paragraph 16.1.

to participate in the general meeting's decision on whether to take action for the breach of duty to a new corporate interest in compliance with such duties. This is important given the uncertainty surrounding whether a shareholder can bring a personal action against directors for breach of duties.[1] Insofar as this proposal is likely to render the duties of directors more meaningful in that (costs aside) they can be more effectively enforced, then the proposal could represent an important advance in the accountability of corporate directors. In order to avoid any abuse of the new action, strict judicial control at all stages applies,[2] largely inspired by the Woolf Report.[3] Where possible, the new procedure would be governed by rules of court, rather than statutory provisions, that could be easily amended in the light of changing circumstances.[4]

The action would also be available for breach of directors' duties of care and skill. This welcome proposal addresses a major defect in the current law. Where companies have a cause of action against directors for negligence the company may, nonetheless, be disinclined to bring the action itself. Shareholders seeking to enforce the directors' duties of care and skill on behalf of the company have had a Herculean task. Presently, a derivative action based upon negligence may only be brought if it can be shown that the majority have profited by the negligence;[5] and a petition under s 459 cannot be used to police negligence as such, but only serious mismanagement.[6] By encouraging the development of a shareholder's interest in competent, as well as honest management of the company's affairs, this proposal may result in the more effective policing of managerial incompetence.[7]

---

1 At common law, the general principle is that directors owe their duties to the company and not to shareholders individually: see *Burland v Earle* [1902] AC 83, 93. Thus, shareholders can only challenge a breach of such duties if they can either establish that there is a fraud on a minority or that there is a breach of the shareholder's personal rights. Stanley Beck has argued that any breach of directors' fiduciary duties should give rise to a personal action ('The Shareholders' Derivative Action' (1974) 52 *Canadian Bar Review* 159, 171–172). But the extension of personal rights to include breach of directors' duties was apparently rejected in *Prudential Assurance v Newman (No 2)* [1982] 2 WLR 31 (CA). Cf *Re a Company (No 005136 of 1986)* (1986) 2 BCC 99, 528 where Hoffman J held that a breach of shareholders' contractual rights under the articles will occur where directors use their powers for an improper purpose. Moreover, s 459 may be used to remedy corporate wrongs including breach of directors' duties, notably in private companies and small public companies (see *Re a Company (No 005136 of 1986)* (1986) 2 BCC 99) as well as secure personal remedies directly against third parties (see *Lowe v Fahey* [1996] 1 BCLC 262, 267–268). Thus, the Commission's proposal should be seen in this context of the gradual, halting and problematical extension by the courts of the minority shareholders' ability to remedy breaches of directors' duties.
2 Paragraph 15.2.
3 The Rt Hon Lord Woolf, *Access to Justice: Final Report* (London: HMSO, 1996).
4 Paragraph 15.3.
5 See *Pavlides v Jensen* [1956] Ch 565. Although it was recently approved (see *Multinational v Multinational* [1983] Ch 258 per Dillon LJ at 382 F and 389 D–E) it was distinguished in *Daniels v Daniels* [1978] Ch 406 by Templeman J and *Prudential Assurance v Newman Industries (No 2)* [1981] Ch 257, 313 D–E by Vinelott J on the basis that the directors did not enjoy any personal benefit from their negligence.
6 Paragraph 16.9.
7 On the reluctance of the judiciary to extend the low duties of care and skill that have usually applied to directors, see, generally, Finch, V, 'Company Directors: Who Cares About Skill and Care' (1992) 55 *MLR* 179.

The new action would also be available for breach of duty by officers and employees other than directors where there has been 'a fraud on a minority'.[1] The jurisprudence of Foss v Harbottle[2] would continue to apply in this context and petitioners would, therefore, have to establish wrongdoer control and that the breach of duty was unratifiable. The reason for the Commission strictly confining such actions is a variant on the traditional 'fear of floodgates opening' argument: namely, that extending the new procedure to embrace breaches of duty by others apart from directors might result in excessive shareholder interference in company management.[3] The Commission also claim that in most situations of this sort there would also be a breach of duty by the directors and, therefore, a right of action under the new procedure.[4] In view of the acknowledged difficulties surrounding the old law, and the lack of evidence to support the Commission's fears, it is disappointing that it chose to preserve the common law derivative action in this context. Nor is this recommendation consistent with a law reform process concerned to secure greater simplicity, certainty and justice. A more rational solution would be for all breaches of duty and allied claims to be actionable under a single, statutory derivative action, thereby supplanting entirely the common law, as is the case in other common law jurisdictions.

The Commission sensibly concluded, that the new statutory action should abrogate the common law action in those areas where the statutory action is available as it would lead to confusion to allow both common law and statutory actions.[5] Thus, an action under the new statutory procedure would only be capable of being so brought, and not also under the exceptions to Foss v Harbottle.[6]

The court's discretion to grant leave to bring the new derivative action would operate within a procedural framework, enlightened by the principles developed by those common law jurisdictions that have a statutory derivative action and by Lord Woolf's Report on Access to Justice.[7] In order to allow a company sufficient time to determine what to do about the action, shareholders would be required to serve a notice on the company calling on it to institute proceedings

---

1 Paragraph 16.10.
2 (1843) 2 Hare 461.
3 Paragraph 16.10.
4 Paragraph 16.11.
5 However, consultees are asked whether actions within the 'special majority' exception to Foss v Harbottle should be governed by specific rules of court requiring the court's leave for the continuation of the action; and if so, which of the matters set out in para 16.20 (or other matters) should apply to such actions: see para 16.14. On the face of it, it is difficult to see why further reliance on court discretion, with its attendant uncertainties, is required in this context.
6 (1843) 2 Hare 461. Paragraphs 16.12–16.13, following the approach adopted in Canada and New Zealand and recently proposed in Australia: see ibid.
   In order to secure greater simplification, consistency and certainty, perhaps consideration should be given to the repeal of s 461(2)(c), which was enacted to enable the court to authorise a minority shareholder to bring a derivative action without satisfying the rule in Foss v Harbottle but which has been rarely used given the attractions of the unfair prejudice remedy and may not be needed if the Commission's recommendations for a new derivative action are implemented. 'A more orderly development of the law would result from one point of access to a derivative action and would allow for a body of experience and precedent to be built up to guide shareholders': Beck, S, 'The Shareholders' Derivative Action' which was adopted by the Law Commission's Paper at para 16.13.
7 The Rt Hon Lord Woolf, Access to Justice: Final Report (London: HMSO, 1996).

within one month, specifying the grounds of the proposed derivative action, and stating that, if the company fails to do so, the shareholder would commence a derivative action.[1] This requirement would be waived, however, if the shareholder could show that urgent relief was required or if the court dispensed with the requirement. If the company commenced an action, but failed to prosecute it diligently, it would be open to a shareholder to apply to the court for leave to take over the action.[2] The court would, normally, consider leave at the close of the pleadings, but could do so earlier. It is acknowledged that the leave stage may be complex and lengthy and that it would necessitate case management of the kind advocated by the Woolf Report.[3] In these circumstances, the application for leave would normally be heard by a judge rather than a Master.[4]

Under the current law, a shareholder seeking to bring a derivative action has to prove fraud and control on a *prima facie* basis. In part, to avoid the risk of a mini-trial or a detailed investigation of the merits at the leave stage, which would be time consuming and expensive, the Commission rejected creating a threshold test on the merits of the case, a sensible decision as such a test would be difficult to apply in practice.[5] 'Parties should not', says the Paper, 'go into the legal merits in detail on the application for leave unless it is clear that there is a high degree of probability of success or failure.'[6]

The court, when considering whether or not to grant leave, 'should take into account all the relevant circumstances without limit'.[7] Without prejudice to this very broad discretion, it is proposed that the court should consider the following matters: whether the applicant is acting in good faith;[8] whether the

---

1 This recommendation would seem to be sound, although it is unlikely that petitioners will be able to formulate the basis of their actions in detail without access to the company's records.

2 Paragraphs 16.5–16.17. In the circumstances, the court would have to consider the criteria for leave as set out in paras 16.20 and 16.27–16.44. If it granted leave, the court would have the same powers in relation to the proceedings as in any other derivative action: para 16.17.

3 Paragraph 16.18. See, also, The Rt Hon Lord Woolf, *Access to Justice: Final Report* (London: HMSO, 1996), ch 5.

4 Paragraph 16.18. See, also, The Rt Hon Lord Woolf, *Access to Justice: Final Report* (London: HMSO 1996) ch 1, para 4 on the active management of litigation as being part of the judge's function, and that in more complex cases the function of the procedural judge would normally be performed by Circuit judges and High Court judges, rather than Masters and district judges. Unless the court otherwise directs, all the parties to the action would be parties to the application for leave and would be entitled to receive evidence filed on it: see para 16.19. It is not clear that the latter requirement will do anything to address the considerable difficulties experienced by minority shareholders in obtaining information on the management of the company in order to bring a successful action: see, generally, Haddon, T, *Company Law and Capitalism* 2nd edn (London: Weidenfeld and Nicolson, 1977), pp 280–282.

5 Paragraphs 16.22–16.25. The case would necessarily be one which the court decides or has decided has a realistic prospect of success. Following the example of the Woolf Report, the court would have new powers to dispose of weak cases and hopeless issues: see paras 16.22, 17.4 and 17.16.

6 Paragraph 16.22.

7 Paragraph 16.25. See, also, para 16.20.

8 See paragraphs 16.27–16.31. While the applicant's good faith would be relevant, it would not be a prerequisite to the grant of leave, a view which seems to be sound as it would discourage mini-trials on the issue (see para 16.31). The Paper asks whether 'good faith should be defined for these purposes': para 16.31. It is difficult to see how the advantages of defining 'good faith' are not outweighed by the disadvantages of including an appropriate definition.

proceedings are in the interests of the company;[1] that the wrong has been or may be ratified by the company in general meeting;[2] the views of an independent organ that for commercial reasons the action should or should not be pursued;[3] and the availability of alternative remedies.[4] The principal reasons for articulating these factors is to prevent the company from being exposed to trivial or groundless lawsuits or being held to ransom by irate shareholders.

Following the position in Canada, New Zealand and South Africa, the court would not be bound to refuse leave where ratification has occurred.[5] By refusing to identify the will of the corporation with the will of the majority in this way the principle of majority rule would be weakened since the courts are no longer bound by (nor can simply retreat behind) the views of the majority. Instead, it is the judges, not the majority, that could now deny the company of its right of action.[6]

The Commission were not persuaded that creating a special power to appoint an independent expert to investigate and advise the court on the action (as exists under the Australian draft statutory action) would be advantageous.[7]

With respect to remedies, the Paper considered whether it should be open to the court to make an order granting a personal benefit to the shareholder bringing the derivative action, such as an order that the defendant wrongdoers buy the applicant's shares.[8] It concluded that such a power was unnecessary

---

1 See paras 16.32–16.34. So as not to encourage mini-trials on the issue, the court would not be bound to refuse leave if the proceedings were not in the interests of the company: para 16.33. However, the court should have regard to the views of the directors and in general not substitute its (ie the court's) judgment on what is in the company's interests (para 16.34). Query, whether, in the light of the broad discretion conferred upon the courts, it is realistic to expect that the court could prevent the substitution of their judgement for that of the management in this context?

2 See paras 16.35–16.37. On the issue of ratification, see Lowry, J, 'Reconstructing Shareholder Actions: A Response to the Law Commission's Consultation Paper *Shareholder Remedies*' (1977) *The Company Lawyer* 18, 247.

3 See para 16.38. The Paper does not specify what is meant by 'independent organ', but we can probably assume that it means an organ of the company (eg the shareholders, the directors). Any legislation on the point would have to clarify what constituted an 'independent organ'. The views of the independent organ would not necessarily be conclusive on the issue of leave (para 16.38).

4 See paras 16.39–16.40. The availability of an alternative remedy would not necessarily be conclusive on the leave issue: para 16.40.

5 See paras 16.35–16.37.

6 See, generally, Welling, BL, *Corporate Law in Canada*, 2nd edn (Toronto: Butterworths, 1991), pp 541–552; and the Consultancy Report, *Review of the Hong Kong Companies Ordinance* (March, 1997), pp 151–152.

7 Paragraphs 16.46–16.47. The Law Commission's cursory treatment of this subject may be explained by its controversial nature. It might be seen as undercutting the principle that in general the court should not substitute its judgement for that of the board in commercial matters: see para 14.11. Moreover, the legal profession strongly opposed Lord Woolf's initial proposals on single experts, and his Final Report does not envisage a large role for them: The Rt Hon Lord Woolf, *Access to Justice: Final Report* (London: HMSO, 1996), ch 13, paras 16–24.

8 Paragraphs 16.48–16.50, which explain that under the relevant laws in Canada, New Zealand and Ghana, compensation may be paid to members rather than the company.

since the case-law on s 459 enables a shareholder to obtain a personal remedy for a wrong done to the company.

The Commission left open the question of whether provision should be made for multiple derivative actions, that is, whether a shareholder in a parent company may bring a derivative action on behalf of a subsidiary or associated company within the group.[1] Although it is not clear from the Paper, this remedy might prevent a company from evading its responsibilities to shareholders by operating its business *via* subsidiary companies and, therefore, has much to commend it.

It could be argued that a statutory derivative action is unnecessary because the common law action has been somewhat overshadowed by s 459 petitions. And that the simplest and most efficient way to proceed is to clarify and slightly broaden s 459 and to introduce North American style 'appraisal rights', that is, a statutory buy-out remedy providing shareholders with the opportunity to compel the company to buy their shares, possibly limited to certain specified occurrences.[2] The Commission considered this question briefly, in the context, exclusively, of channelling all proceedings into s 459 actions. It rejected this option on three counts. First, from '. . . the point of view of limiting costs and making economical use of court time, it may be better if the issues are confined to the wrong to the company if this is the substantial complaint, and the issues would be so confined at trial if the proceedings were a derivative action.'[3] Secondly, a cause of action vested in the company is not affected by the grant of personal relief under s 459. 'The advantage of a derivative action is that it offers the possibility that, in appropriate circumstances, the company's cause of action may be enforced without a liquidation.'[4] Thirdly, '. . . creditors are likely to be better off and treated equally if wrongs to the company are remedied by relief for the company, rather than its shareholders personally under section 459'.[5]

On balance, a statutory derivative action is desirable. In addition to the reasons indicated by the Commission, it is a proven way of removing or attenuating the diverse obstacles for shareholders associated with the rule in *Foss v Harbottle*. Additionally, it is claimed that a statutory derivative action has a prophylactic effect which is salutary.[6]

In sum, the new derivative action is attractive insofar as it '. . . eliminates the noisome case-law spawned by the 1843 case of *Foss v Harbottle*',[7] at least with respect to breaches of duty by directors; and that it results in the more effective

---

1 Paragraph 16.51 and p 215 at para 29.
2 See, for example, Cheffins, B and Dine, J, 'Shareholder Remedies: Lessons from Canada' (1992) 13 *The Company Lawyer* 89, 95.
3 Paragraph 16.4.
4 Paragraph 16.4.
5 Paragraph 16.4. The Commission concluded that an applicant should have the right to choose whether to bring a derivative action or proceedings under s 459, or cumulative claims under both. It also opined that the courts have adequate powers to order issues to be tried separately and, in the case of duplication of remedies, to require election between them: see para 16.6 and *Slough Estates Ltd v Slough Borough Council* [1968] Ch 299. See, generally, paras 16.4–16.6.
6 Consultancy Report, *Review of the Hong Kong Companies Ordinance* (March, 1997), pp 149 and 152.
7 Consultancy Report, *Review of the Hong Kong Companies Ordinance* (March, 1997), p 150.

enforcement of directors' duties, encouraging shareholders to use the action where it is possible to substantiate breaches of duty, rather than the more expansive proceedings involved in establishing unfairly prejudicial conduct under s 459.

From a comparative perspective, the Commission's proposal is, essentially, modest and evolutionary. Whereas the Commission's proposal significantly limits the availability of the derivative action to breaches of directors' duties, in Canada, New Zealand and under the draft Australian legislation, there is no statutory circumscription of the availability of the derivative action. Under the Canadian Business Corporations Act (CBCA), for example, shareholders may bring an action on behalf of the company, but only with the permission of the court.[1] The CBCA specifies three conditions that must be satisfied before the court will grant permission to sue so as to ensure that the company is not subject to unmeritorious litigation.[2] On the other hand, the unfairly prejudicial remedy is the remedy of first choice, and is likely to remain so, since it makes it easier for shareholders to get into court, and it offers an exceptional range of remedies. In practice, therefore, there may be no need for the derivative action to do much more than facilitate the enforcement of the duties of corporate management.

Case management and greater judicial discretion

In order to streamline litigation and induce early settlement, the Commission recommends that a system of case management, prompted by the Woolf Report,[3] should operate in respect of all shareholder proceedings. As the Paper explains:

> 'A decision could be taken at the case management conference, for example, to direct, in an appropriate case, the trial of the issue whether the relationship between the members of a company falls within the type contemplated in the case of *Ebrahimi*.[4] Following the hearing and determination of this issue would be a further review at which the court and the parties could decide, in the light of that determination, which of the claims the applicant should pursue. If the court held that there was no *Ebrahami*[5] type relationship, the court would not hear issues based on an alleged legitimate expectation, so time and costs would be saved.'[6]

In all shareholder proceedings, judges would be given the power, exercisable at any stage after the service of the defence, to dismiss any claim or part of a claim or any defence which had no realistic prospect of success.[7] In order to encourage the parties to consider other means than litigation for resolving disputes or issues between them it is proposed that the rules governing shareholder proceedings should include an express reference to the power to adjourn at any

---

1 Canadian Business Corporations Act 1974–75–76, s 239(1). Reproduced in the Paper at p 266.
2 Canadian Business Corporations Act 1974–75–76, s 239(2). Reproduced in the Paper at p 266.
3 The Rt Hon Lord Woolf, *Access to Justice: Final Report* (London: HMSO, 1996).
4 *Ebrahimi v Westbourne Galleries Ltd* [1973] AC 360.
5 *Ebrahimi v Westbourne Galleries Ltd* [1973] AC 360.
6 Paragraph 17.11.
7 Paragraph 17.16.

stage to enable parties to make alternative arrangements for disposing of the case or any issue in it.[1]

The Paper considers that substantial savings in time and costs might occur if the courts adopted a proactive approach to the exercise of their power to determine the nature of the evidence to be put before it. On each occasion when the case is reviewed, the court would consider making directions as to how facts should be proved. A more radical proposal is that judges could exclude evidence where they are satisfied that it would not have a bearing on the issues that needed to be decided, thereby saving time and costs.[2] Rule 5.1 (I) of the Draft Civil Proceedings Rules that accompany the Woolf Report proposes that the court '. . . may exclude an issue from determination if it can do substantive justice between the parties on the other issues and determining it would therefore serve no worthwhile purpose.'[3] The Commission believes that the new Rule should apply to all shareholder proceedings.[4]

The Paper proposes that the rules of court governing the new derivative action should provide that the company may convene a meeting of shareholders to consider a resolution as to whether the proceedings should be continued.[5] Applicants would be unable to enter into any compromise or abandon the proceedings without the leave of court.[6]

Given that minority shareholders have scant rights of access to the 'inside' corporate information necessary to underpin a shareholders' action, it is disappointing that the effort to streamline litigation has not addressed the thorny issue of disclosure and the asymmetry of information between management and shareholders, or between large and small shareholders, with respect to the enforcement of shareholders' rights.

A limited 'appraisal' or 'buy-out' remedy for small companies

In an innovative study of the court files of the 156 section-459 petitions to the High Court in 1994 and 1995, the Commission found that 96 per cent related to private companies, just under 85 per cent of which had five or fewer shareholders, and that the vast majority alleged exclusion from management. In almost 70 per cent of cases the remedy sought was the purchase of the petitioners' shares and in nearly 21 per cent it was the sale of the respondents' shares.[7] The most common ground on which petitioners under s 459 seek a non-

---

1 Paragraph 17.7. This power already exists: see para 17.7 n 32.
2 Paragraph 17.19. This would represent a major change as currently the court cannot exclude evidence that is legally relevant and admissible.
3 The Rt Hon Lord Woolf MR, *Access to Justice: Draft Civil Proceedings Rules* (London: HMSO, 1996), pp 18–19.
4 Paragraph 17.19.
5 Paragraph 17.7. Comments are sought on whether the court should have additional powers to determine whether any shareholder should or should not be permitted to vote at such a meeting: para 17.7. If the court did not have this power there is a real danger that those voting would not be sufficiently independent.
6 Paragraph 17.10. This proposal may have been influenced by r 23.1 of the Federal Rules of Civil Procedure (USA) governing derivative actions, which adopts a similar approach.
   The court's power to add or substitute applicants would remain unchanged: para 17.9.
7 The statistics relating to the filing of s 459 petitions and the size of companies are contained in Appendix E. The full results are contained in Appendix E, Table 1.

discounted valuation of their shareholding is that the relationship between the members falls within the quasi-partnership type contemplated in *Ebrahimi v Westbourne Galleries Ltd*.[1] Reflecting these findings, the Commission is canvassing views on whether an additional remedy for shareholders of smaller companies is needed which permits shareholders in private companies which have no less than two and not more than five shareholders, between whom there is a relationship such as that set out in *Ebrahimi*, to obtain a purchase order for their shares at a fair value without discount for the fact the applicant's shares represent a minority shareholding, if the applicant can prove exclusion from management and that before his or her exclusion from management there was an agreement or understanding between all the shareholders that he or she should participate in the conduct of business.[2] As we have seen, the generality of the wording of s 459 tends to encourage shareholders to make many allegations of fact, some trivial and some serious, in order to bolster their claims. The remedy for smaller companies would not require evidence that the affairs of the company are being or have been conducted in a manner which is unfair and unreasonable. This should necessitate the proving of fewer issues of fact. Thus, litigation should be shorter and cheaper than that associated with s 459 cases.

The Paper recognises that this proposal is open to several objections. The limitation of this remedy to companies of five shareholders or fewer is artificial and arbitrary.[3] Inevitably, it would be easy to evade any conditions based upon the number of shareholders.[4] For example, a majority might issue more shares to prevent a minority from utilising the action.[5] On the other hand, the limitation attempts to ensure that the relief is effectively targeted, that the new action and, therefore, litigation is confined, and that there is no serious reduction in the protection of third parties.

Another possible objection to the proposal is that it might generate additional litigation, albeit, more focused than much of the current litigation under

---

1 [1973] AC 360. That is, that in addition to the company being small or private the circumstances include one or more of the following elements: (a) an association formed or continued on the basis of a personal relationship involving mutual confidence; (b) an agreement or understanding that all or some of the shareholders shall participate in the conduct of the business; (c) restrictions upon the transfer of the members' shares in that company so that if confidence is lost, or one member is removed from management, the member cannot simply take her or his stake and go elsewhere. See, further, paras 8.5–8.12.

2 Paras 18.4–18.5. Cf 'It is surely the case that a prerequisite for further reforms which are aimed at a sub-group of small or private companies based on size is a thorough census of the registered company stock so that thresholds can be formulated based on real needs and not anecdotal evidence': Freedman, J, 'Small Business and the Corporate Form' (1994) 57 *Modern Law Review* 555, 573.

3 The Commission's proposal may have been influenced by the New Zealand Companies Act 1993, which gives shareholders the right to require the company to purchase their shares in certain circumstances and does not require proof of unfair and unreasonable conduct: see The Law Commission, 'Reform of the Law Applicable to Private Companies: A Feasibility Study', which was appended to DTI, *Company Law Review: the Law Applicable to Private Companies* (URN 94/529) (London: DTI, November 1994) being a 'Consultative Document Seeking Views on the Law Commission's Feasibility Study on Reform of Private Companies' paras 5.46–5.47. In contrast to the Commission's proposal, this provision is not limited by the number of shareholders.

4 Paragraph 18.7.

5 Although this would be for an improper purpose and, therefore, open to challenge. See, further, para 18.7 and p 182 n 8.

s 459.[1] The Commission considered that an applicant should not have to choose between the two remedies. There is a risk of a multiplicity of litigation, rather than a reduction of the issues, since shareholders might seek relief under both the existing law and the new remedy. The Commission's response to these criticisms — namely, case management and the active use of the court's discretion to determine the order in which issues are tried — is not wholly reassuring.[2]

This proposal is a circumscribed version of the 'appraisal' or 'buy-out' remedy that exists in other common law jurisdictions. This remedy was developed originally in the United States to enable shareholders unhappy with fundamental but legitimate changes in the company's activities to be bought out without the necessity of judicial intervention.[3] Its *raison d'être* is that it avoids litigation. It is, therefore, a relatively cheap and certain remedy. In Canada and New Zealand, it is conceived as a supplement to, rather than a replacement of, other remedies which the shareholder might utilise, such as the unfairly prejudicial remedy.[4] The Commission's proposal, in contrast to analogous provisions in the United States, Canada and New Zealand, is limited to small companies on the basis of exclusion from management and involves a court ordered purchase of the shareholder's stake in the company.[5] Given the Commission's desire to create cheaper alternative dispute mechanisms, it might have been worthwhile to investigate the extent to which the broader-based buy-out remedies that exist in Canada and New Zealand might be appropriate in the UK.

The Paper's heavy reliance upon the exercise of discretion by the court is also evident in its decision that the valuation of the shares does not require a specified procedure, such as by reference to an independent accountant, but that this could be left to the court since it can make such an order in an appropriate case.[6] In recent years, the courts have, increasingly, indicated their concern at the possible conflicts of interest that may arise where the valuers are the company's own auditor or even an independent accountant. It may be that it is the unacceptability of exposing the petitioner to these dangers which encouraged the Commission to opt for a court valuation.[7]

In short, the proposal would increase access to justice by guaranteeing a purchase without discount, which s 459 does not. It is also more focused than s 459 and therefore is less likely to generate costly and lengthy litigation. But it

---

1 Paragraph 18.7.

2 Paragraph 18.11.

3 Recourse to the courts would occur, however, where there was disagreement concerning the valuation of the shareholder's interest. See, generally, the American Bar Association, Committee on Corporate Laws, Model Business Corporations Act, 1984, s 13.

4 See, for example, MacIntosh, JG, 'The Shareholders' Appraisal Right in Canada' (1988) 13 *Canadian-United States Law Journal* 299.

5 Contrast this with Freedman's advocacy of a fully fledged, statutory 'buy-out' remedy which it is claimed would avoid the cost and uncertainty that arises from litigation, as in the case of section 459 petitions: see Freedman, J, 'Small Business and the Corporate Form', p 582.

6 Paragraph 18.8. The Paper rejects the extension of a statutory remedy in no-fault situations: see para 18.10.

7 See, further, Prentice, DD, 'Minority Shareholder Oppression: Valuation of Shares' (1986) *LQR* 179; Hannigan, B 'Purchase Orders Under s 459' (1987) *Business Law Review* 21; Riley, CA, 'Contracting Out of Company Law' (1992) 55 *MLR* 782, 798–802.

is very limited in scope and arbitrary with respect to those who might benefit from it. And it would not avoid the necessity of judicial intervention, as is the case in other common law jurisdictions.

Model articles

The Paper canvasses three 'self-help' remedies that would be embodied in new model articles to be added to Table A:[1] a shareholder exit article for smaller private companies,[2] an arbitration and alternative dispute resolution regulation,[3] and share valuation machinery where shareholders are being bought out by the remaining shareholders and no agreement can be reached on value.[4] The aim is to encourage shareholders to provide in advance for what will happen if there is a dispute, thereby avoiding litigation.[5] It seems that they are premised upon a desire to further reduce the number of claims brought under section 459, as well as improving the position of minority shareholders in quasi-partnerships.

The shareholder exit article for smaller private companies would be restricted to those companies that have fewer than ten members and are not public companies.[6] It would arise where an ordinary resolution had been passed attaching the rights of exit to particular shares.[7] Provision is made for the valuation of the shares in the event of a failure to agree a price.[8] The shareholder exit article is limited to private companies with fewer than ten members. This restriction seems arbitrary and easy to avoid. The Law Society's Company Law Committee were of the opinion that exit rights should be available to all shareholders, irrespective of the type and size of the company.[9] They also observed that the protection that this proposal would afford an aggrieved minority is limited:

> 'In the first place, the draft requires the holders of a majority of the shares to pass a resolution attaching the relevant rights to specified shares. It is difficult to imagine that a majority would be prepared to attach rights (which might be against their

---

1 Thus, requiring secondary legislation only. See, generally, Part 19: 'Articles of Association' and Appendix H, 'Proposed New Regulations to be Inserted in Table A'.
2 Paragraphs 19.3–19.11 and Appendix H, draft regulation 119.
3 Paragraphs 19.12–19.15 and Appendix H, draft regulation 120.
4 Paragraphs 19.16–19.17 and Appendix H, draft regulation 121.
5 For a valuable account of 'default' rules and contractual consent in company law, see Cheffins, BR, *Company Law* (Oxford: Clarendon Press, 1997), ch 6.
6 Paragraph 19.3.
7 Paragraph 19.4.
8 The outgoing member can request the President of the Institute of Chartered Accountants in England and Wales to appoint an independent accountant to determine the fair value of the relevant shares: para 19.7 and Appendix H, draft regulation 119(5). On the disadvantages of a valuation other than that undertaken by a court, see Riley, CA, 'Contracting Out of Company Law' (1992) 55 *MLR* 782, 798–800.
9 See, further, *The Law Society's Company Law Committee Memorandum on Shareholder Remedies: Law Commission Consultation Paper 142* (London: The Law Society, January 1997) 7. Freedman argues that given the vast majority of existing private companies are likely to have fewer than ten members, any relaxation of internal provisions designed to assist companies with small numbers of shareholders should be available to all private companies: Freedman, J, 'Small Business and the Corporate Form', p 583. As with the similar limits imposed on the additional unfair prejudice remedy for smaller companies, consultations would have been enhanced if the Paper had contained a more sustained justification of the restrictions proposed based on the number of members.

own interests) to shares held by a minority. However, the article appears to allow the majority to attach these rights to their own shares — presumably then enabling them to compel a dissatisfied minority to buy them out if he complains.'[1]

One of the findings of the Law Commission's survey of 1994 on small businesses and company law was that small businesses were concerned about the difficulties of resolving internal disputes.[2] There was evidence that such disputes can and do result in the winding up of companies which are otherwise financially viable. The Forum of Private Business recommended that machinery for resolving internal disputes, such as a compulsory reference to arbitration, should be included in any new form for small businesses.[3] During the last decade, various tentative steps have been taken within the civil justice system to encourage party negotiations and settlement under the label of 'alternative dispute resolution' ('ADR').[4] Lord Woolf's proposals on the reform of the civil justice system in England and Wales envisage an enhanced role for ADR through the court's ability to take into account whether parties have unreasonably rejected the possibility of ADR or have behaved unreasonably in the course of ADR.[5] Pilot mediation and ADR schemes are currently underway, and the Lord Chancellor's Department has published a plain English guide on ADR, designed to make the general public more aware of methods of resolving disputes which do not involve litigation.[6] Indeed, ADR has become an international movement whose implications for corporate law have yet to receive detailed attention. In Canada's leading commercial jurisdiction of Ontario, for example, alternative dispute resolution has flourished, and mandatory mediation has recently been introduced as a precondition to non-family law civil litigation. Thus, the Commission's, albeit brief, consideration of ADR is a welcome first step in the effort to consider the implications of ADR for corporate law. The object of the arbitration and alternative dispute resolution regulation, as proposed by the Commission, is to encourage incorporators to avoid litigation. If a dispute is referred to arbitration, a sole arbitrator would be chosen by the parties or, in default, by the President of the Institute of Chartered Accountants in England and Wales.[7] When the issue of a reference to arbitration arose, the parties would have to consider whether the dispute was appropriate for alternative dispute resolution (ADR). If

---

1 *The Law Society's Company Law Committee Memorandum on Shareholder Remedies: Law Commission Consultation Paper 142*, 2.

2 The Law Commission, 'Reform of the Law Applicable to Private Companies: A Feasibility Study', which was appended to DTI, *Company Law Review: the Law Applicable to Private Companies* (URN 94/529) (London: DTI, November 1994) being a 'Consultative Document Seeking Views on the Law Commission's Feasibility Study on Reform of Private Companies' para 5.43.

3 The Forum of Private Business, *A Report into Business Legal Structures* (London: 1991).

4 See, for example, Burn, S, 'Alternative Dispute Resolution in the UK' in Smith R (ed), *Shaping the Future: New Directions in Legal Services* (London: Legal Action Group, 1995), p 237. Practitioner works include Beavan, A, *Alternative Dispute Resolution* (London: Sweet & Maxwell, 1992) and Brown, H and Marriott, A, *ADR Principles and Practice* (London: Sweet & Maxwell, 1993).

5 The Rt Hon Lord Woolf, *Access to Justice: Final Report*, para 18. For a critical evaluation of the Woolf Report's approach to ADR, see Roberts, S, 'Litigation and Settlement' in Zuckermann, AAS, and Cranston, R (eds) *Reform of Civil Procedure* (Oxford: Oxford University Press, 1996), p 447.

6 The Rt Hon Lord Woolf, *Access to Justice: Final Report,* para 18.

7 Appendix H, draft regulation 120(2). Insofar as disputes turn upon the legal interpretation of the articles, query, whether it would be more appropriate to appoint a lawyer as arbitrator?

the parties agreed to resolve their dispute through ADR, the arbitration procedure would be suspended.[1]

Currently, there is no remedy to which shareholders can resort (in the absence of unfairly prejudicial conduct) where they are all agreed that one or more should sell their shares to the rest, but no agreement can be reached on value. The Commission have, therefore, designed a regulation which provides an agreed valuation procedure. The regulation states that no discount is to be made for the fact that the shares form part of a minority shareholding. However, incorporators would be free to make some other provision for the basis of valuation.[2]

Within the new landscape of civil litigation envisaged by the Woolf Report, the civil justice system will be responsive to the needs of litigants and this includes: enhanced provision of advice and assistance to litigants through court-based or duty advice and assistance schemes; that the courts will provide more information to litigants through leaflets, videos, telephone helplines and information technology; court staff will provide information and help to litigants on how to progress their case; and there will be ongoing monitoring and research of litigants' needs.[3] No doubt with this new landscape in mind, the Commission is seeking consultee's views as to the best methods of alerting advisers and incorporators to the proposed self-help articles. The Law Society's Company Law Committee has suggested that a booklet could be produced and made available, free of charge, by Companies House, to all those enquiring about incorporating a new company. It advocated that commercial vendors should also be encouraged to make the same or a similar leaflet available.[4]

Remedies for breach of contract in the articles of association

It is probably not possible, under s 14 of the Companies Act 1985, to enforce rights which a member has in some other capacity (so-called 'outsider rights'), for example, as a director or solicitor of the company. The Commission took the view that this particular issue was beyond its terms of reference and that, in any case, 'outsiders' would normally have a separate contract between the company and themselves which they could enforce.[5]

A further difficulty concerns the identification of those rights in the contract in the articles of association which are the personal rights of shareholders. Where there are breaches of the articles which are ratifiable, the shareholder does not have a personal right in the articles. Where an article confers a personal ('insider') right, a breach of that article is unratifiable. The Commission's

---

1 Appendix H, draft regulation 120(1). The Woolf Report and commentators alike have recognised that the claims made for ADR may be exaggerated, and the Woolf Report acknowledged the need for monitoring, careful evaluation and support.
2 Paragraphs 19.16–19.17 and Appendix H, draft regulation 121.
3 The Rt Hon Lord Woolf, *Access to Justice: Final Report*, para 9.
4 *The Law Society's Company Law Committee Memorandum on Shareholder Remedies: Law Commission Consultation Paper 142*, p 8.
5 Paragraph 14.7. In Canada and New Zealand, shareholders may apply to court for a compliance and restraining order against the company to ensure that the company and its directors comply with the corporate constitution, thereby, helping shareholders to enforce their personal rights: see, for example, the Canadian Business Corporations Act 1985, s 247.

widespread consultations indicated that this was not causing problems today; and that a comprehensive definition of what constitutes a personal membership right under s 14 of the Companies Act 1985 is unrealistic since the matter depends upon the specific articles and the circumstances of the alleged breach.[1]

Reform of proceedings under sections 459–461[2]

The Paper considers several possible reforms to the 'unfairly prejudice' remedy. It takes the view that it would not be appropriate to find parliamentary time for the simplification of s 459 alone. However, if s 459 is amended in other respects, the opportunity should be taken to make it clear that it is specific conduct, rather than the affairs of the company overall, that has to be shown to be unfairly prejudicial.[3] It is hoped that this change would focus attention on specific conduct, demonstrating that it is not every aspect of the company's affairs in the relevant period that is in issue. This, in turn, might reduce the number of tactical allegations made without limiting the conduct on which a party could rely.[4]

The statistical analysis of s 459 indicated that just under ten per cent of cases involve allegations of conduct over a period of five years or more. Reported cases, however, include allegations spanning as much as 40 years, adding to the length and cost of cases. Thus, the Paper favours a limitation period on s 459 claims, canvassing views on its length.[5] Now it is commonly alleged that the majority shareholder has failed to provide information about how the company is run. In these circumstances, a claimant may only discover the basis for a claim or be able to adduce evidence of on-going unfair conduct after a substantial period of time. In these circumstances, a limitation period of the kind being canvassed might work unfairly. In any case, petitions concerning events spanning a lengthy period of time are confined, in practice, because only present shareholders can avail themselves of the s 459 remedy.[6]

---

1 Paragraphs 20.2–20.4.
2 A useful survey of the procedural aspects of ss 459–461, particularly in the light of the access to justice debate, is contained in Part 11: 'Procedural Matters'.
  The Paper also canvasses views on whether the shareholder's current rights of discovery in court proceedings are adequate. Inspired by the Woolf Committee recommendations, it seeks views on whether a right of pre-action discovery similar to that available in relation to personal injuries claims (including a right against non-parties) should be available in relation to derivative actions, s 459 actions and claims under any new unfair prejudice remedy: paras 20.40–20.43.
3 Paragraphs 20.15–20.16.
4 Paragraph 20.16.
5 Paragraphs 20.9–20.11. It further recommends that where the conduct impugned constitutes the invasion of a legal right or some duty, the length of the limitation period should not be less than that (if any) which applies to that wrong: para 20.11. It also recommends that the limitation period should run from the date when the applicant ought reasonably to have known the relevant facts: para 20.12; that the courts should not have discretion to permit proceedings brought outside the limitation to continue (para 20.13); and that there should not be a limit on the age of the allegations upon which parties can rely in s 459 proceedings (para 20.14).
6 See, also, *The Law Society's Company Law Committee Memorandum on Shareholder Remedies: Law Commission Consultation Paper 142*, pp 8–9 at point 57.
  Given the claims made for active case management elsewhere in the Paper, is this a situation where active case management by the courts might help to ensure that sufficiently focused cases did not resort to lengthy historical exegesis unless this was really necessary?

The remedy under s 122(1)(g) of the Insolvency Act 1986 of winding up on just and equitable grounds is frequently pleaded in the alternative to s 459 since winding up is not available as a remedy under ss 459–461.[1] Seeking a winding up, in the alternative, may be to invoke the proverbial sledgehammer to crack open a nut. It can profoundly undermine the smooth running of the company's business where this is unreasonable in the circumstances. The Paper invites views on whether s 461 should be amended so as to enable the court to make a winding-up order (unless there is some other adequate remedy); and if so, whether an applicant should require the court's leave to apply for winding-up proceedings under s 459 so as to deter unnecessary applications.[2] In order to discourage the abuse of petitions for winding up, it would be useful if any such proposal were framed so that it was clear that winding up was only a remedy of last resort.[3]

Other amendments to s 459 were considered and rejected.[4] The Paper contends that '. . . it is preferable to have the very general wording of the section as it now stands, with scope for an evolving interpretation by the courts' rather than define the phrase 'unfairly prejudice'.[5]

The Commission considered that there was no justification for permitting former members to bring derivative actions.[6] But it left it open whether a former member should have standing to petition under s 459. Although it has been held that former shareholders do not have standing to petition under s 459,[7] it has been forcefully argued that they should be able to bring such claims.[8] The Paper was agnostic on this point, and it asked consultees whether they consider that the lack of availability of the s 459 remedy to former members causes problems.[9] As indicated above, it could be argued that this qualification is valuable in

---

1   The general impact of the Insolvency Act 1986 on shareholder remedies is examined in Part 13 of the Paper.

2   Paragraphs 20.24–20.28. On the background to this matter, see the useful discussion in paras 8.1–8.2, 8.18–8.24. The Paper left open this matter because it is not clear that bringing winding up within s 461 would curb the inappropriate use of winding-up petitions nor reduce the allegations in issue. The Commission places its faith in active case management as the best way of policing the improper use of a winding up order: see para 20.27.

3   See, also, *The Law Society's Company Law Committee Memorandum on Shareholder Remedies: Law Commission Consultation Paper 142,* p 9 at point 63.

4   Paragraphs 20.17–20.23.

5   Paragraph 20.23.

6   Paragraphs 20.32–20.33.

7   *Re a Company (No 00330 of 1991)* [1991] *BCLC* 597. Former members of the company may be joined as a party to actions under section 459 where relief is sought against them: see, for example, *Re a Company* [1986] BCLC 68.

8   Prentice, DD, 'The Theory of the Firm: Minority Shareholder Oppression', p 64. In Canada, the class of complainant is broadly defined and includes members, former members, directors, former directors or officers of a corporation or any of its affiliates and any other person who, in the discretion of the court, is a proper person to make an application: Canadian Business Corporations Act 1985 as amended, s 238. The recent review of the Hong Kong Companies Ordinance, if implemented, would also extend its unfairly prejudicial remedy to include members and former owners, directors and former directors or executive officer and the financial secretary: Consultancy Report, *Review of the Hong Kong Companies Ordinance* (March, 1997), p 152.

9   Paragraphs 20.34–20.38.

that it limits petitions concerning matters that took place in the long and distant past.[1]

Finally, the Paper requests views on whether authoritative, non-statutory guidance on the application of s 459 might be helpful; and if so, how it might best be provided and disseminated?[2] Such guidance might take the form of a leaflet produced by or on behalf of the DTI. The Paper acknowledges that it might be difficult to secure the resources needed to produce such material, and that there would have to be a commitment to up-date it to ensure that it was not misleading.[3]

PART FOUR: RE-THINKING SHAREHOLDER REMEDIES — RESEARCH, RECONCEPTUALISATION AND REFLEXIVITY

Despite the undoubted value of the Commission's proposals, they largely fail systematically to re-examine and reconceptualise corporate law as it affects shareholder remedies in the light of the changes to corporate law and the economy outlined in Part Two of this essay. However, this preference for incremental reform and, therefore, a failure to return to first principles, was inevitable given the Commission's narrow terms of reference and the fragmented structure for company law reform in the UK. It was accentuated by the dearth of empirical work on corporate business organisations, corporate law and markets and the conceptual confines of the legacy of classical company law, with its emphasis upon the peculiarities and independence of company law and of corporate obligations. The essential process of reconceptualising corporate law is unlikely to be advanced until a broader approach is applied to remedies and regulation, drawing upon economic and socio-legal studies of business, contracting and civil justice in order to understand better the culture and 'contractual environment' of the firm, and also by engaging with the problems of regulation, voluntariness, power, legitimate expectations and trust as they are being addressed beyond the classical perimeters of corporate law. These issues are considered briefly below.

The Law Commission and the process of company law reform

The Paper on shareholder remedies highlights the problems and the possibilities arising from the Commission's role in the process of company law reform. The Commission's brief was relatively narrow and technical. Moreover, it was difficult to justify the expenditure of scarce public funds on the investigation of topics such as directors' duties which are already being considered by the DTI and its working groups. Thus, the Commission's Paper is not as wide-ranging and coherent as might have been hoped. In fairness to the Commission, however, the problem stems in part from its complex and delicate relationship with

---

1 Cf *The Law Society's Company Law Committee Memorandum on Shareholder Remedies: Law Commission Consultation Paper 142*, pp 8–9 at point 57.

2 Paragraphs 20.6–20.8. See, also, paras 14.6 and 20.5.

3 See para 20.8. One might add that special skills would be required to produce material that was lucid, succinct and accurate and which also addressed the technicalities that may be vital for a real understanding of the law.

that body responsible, traditionally, for company law reform, the Department of Trade and Industry (DTI); its ambiguous and unaccountable position in the law making process; its understandable desire that its time-consuming initiatives should bear fruit; its corresponding fear of controversy; and an omnipresent pressure to confine its work to incremental, technical measures, a pressure which the Commission has usually resisted.[1] All these forces can, perhaps, be discerned in the form and substance of the Commission's Paper.

Thus, the review was 'conducted under the present law' in view of the DTI's promised, but delayed, work on directors' duties.[2] Also excluded from consideration are the content of directors' duties, issues as to the accountability of directors, the personal rights of shareholders to enforce the articles, the rights of shareholders as 'outsiders' (such as directors, employees and creditors), the division of power between members and directors, the content of shareholders' rights and the problems arising from nominee shareholdings and the electronic share settlement system, CREST.[3] Likewise, common law remedies in contract, tort and restitution and the areas covered by the DTI consultative document, *Shareholder Communications at the Annual General Meeting*,[4] are outside the project.[5] Moreover, 'The project', says the report, 'is concerned only with the machinery by which the duties owed in law can be enforced'[6] thereby reproducing the artificial separation of 'procedure' from 'rights' and 'substance' from 'form'.

Clearly, all law reform projects have to be bounded if they are be tenable. Nonetheless, the perimeters drawn here may be unduly confined. Changes to the machinery by which duties are owed will invariably impact upon those duties and the balance of power between competing interests. As Lord Wedderburn observed, *Foss v Harbottle* '. . . is not just an obscure Rule . . . ; its tentacles creep into every part of company law'.[7] Thus, the reform of remedies in isolation from the effect of the changes being proposed on other related areas of concern is unlikely to produce satisfactory law reform and may actually accentuate the complexity and incoherence of the law. The problem here is that two different bodies, the DTI and the Law Commission, have divided up company law reform between themselves and some at least of the topics under investigation are closely inter-connected. As a result, it is difficult to progress on one front without reference to the outcome of other work undertaken by another body.

What is the relationship between the Commission's Paper and the nineteen consultation documents on aspects of company law reform published by the DTI since April 1995? In effect, the thrust of the Commission's proposals is to enhance the lot of minority shareholders; whereas currently the DTI is seeking to reduce disclosure of information in the context of small companies. As one commentator has observed pointedly:

---

1 See, generally, Cretney, SM, 'The Law Commission: True Dawns and False Dawns' (1996) 59 *MLR* 631.
2 P 1 n 1.
3 Paragraphs 1.5, 1.9, 1.10.
4 April, 1996.
5 P 7 n 36.
6 Paragraph 1.5.
7 Lord Wedderburn, 'Derivative Actions and *Foss v Harbottle*' (1981) 44 *MLR* 202, 210.

'Would the designer of a rational system of company law reform appoint a company law commissioner and then negotiate with her about which part of company law she would like to look at, at the same time pursuing a larger programme of potentially fundamental reform outside the Commission?'[1]

The same commentator has argued persuasively that company law reform would be enhanced if the specialist teams working on company law at the DTI and the Law Commission were combined and based at the DTI, possibly with a Company Law Commissioner co-ordinating efforts and liasing with other parts of government and interest groups.[2] Until changes of this kind are implemented, company law reform will, almost invariably, appear more fragmented and overly-confined than is both necessary and desirable.

The problem of values

The duties owed to shareholders, and the rights and remedies of shareholders, raise not merely technical questions but also, inevitably, involve taking positions on the values and purposes of company law. The Commission's Paper offers a brief and tentative account of the principles which should guide the law on shareholder remedies.[3] These principles are: that the company is normally the proper plaintiff; that individual shareholders should not be able to undertake proceedings on behalf of the company which the majority of shareholders can regulate by ordinary resolution; that the court should have regard to the decisions of the directors on commercial matters made in good faith; that a member is taken to have agreed to the terms in the company's constitution; that shareholders should not involve the company in unnecessary litigation; and that all shareholder remedies should be made as efficient and cost effective as can be achieved in the circumstances.

This welcome statement of principles is marred, however, by its abstraction and superficiality. The relationship between these principles and between these principles and the specific proposals of the Commission is neither clear nor explicit. The fact that these principles may conflict or contradict one another in practice, and how this might be resolved, is not addressed. Why these principles have been chosen rather than others is simply ignored. The result is a set of principles which largely preserves free from legal regulation certain core areas of managerial prerogative. This is neither justified by recent developments in the field of shareholders' remedies nor reflected in the substance of the Commission's recommendations. For example, the Commission acknowledges elsewhere in the Paper that 'As a matter of policy we are trying to facilitate shareholders' remedies'[4] and this is borne out in its proposals.

---

1 Freedman, J, 'Reforming Company Law' in Patfield, F (ed) *Perspectives on Company Law, Vol 1* (The Hague: Kluwer Law International, 1995), p 211; and on the relationship between the DTI and the Law Commission, see pp 211–213. Thus, the current structure of company law reform prevented the Commission from performing its role, as stipulated in the Law Commission Act 1965, including the systematic renovation of the law, the simplification and modernisation of the law, and the elimination of anomalies.

2 Freedman, J, 'Reforming Company Law', pp 211–213, 221. On the need for a single authority responsible for company law reform, see, also, The Law Society's Company Law Committee, *The Reform of Company Law*. Cf Gower, LCB, 'Reforming Company Law' (1980) 14 *The Law Teacher* 111.

3 Paragraph 14.11.

4 Paragraph 16.49.

The values articulated in the Woolf Report included the delivery of just results, treating litigants fairly, offering appropriate procedures at a reasonable cost and remedies that were adequately resourced and, therefore, effective. Lord Woolf said that his overriding concern was '. . . to ensure that we have a civil justice system which will meet the needs of the public in the twenty-first century'.[1] While the Paper is not unsympathetic to these concerns, it nonetheless falls short of imaginatively examining their implications for company law.[2] Central here is a failure to articulate the normative case for interfering in and controlling inter-shareholder contracts and the decisions of directors and corporate controllers. In this light, the new principles of efficiency and cost effectiveness are valuable but hardly do justice to the bases of current legislative and judicial intervention, and our understanding of the character of successful business enterprises over the long term.[3]

The reconfiguration of the derivative action/personal action dualism?

For some time now, the boundaries separating actions shareholders can bring on behalf of the company (derivative actions) and personal actions which shareholders can bring in their own right have been in a state of flux, and may be intertwined in practice. But the blurring of this classic procedural dualism has been significantly aided and abetted by the development of the courts' jurisdiction under s 459 of the Companies Act 1985 which has, in effect, recognised the hybrid character of wrongs in this area. Common allegations made in petitions under s 459 include a misappropriation or diversion of corporate assets, excessive remuneration and non-payment or payment of inadequate dividends. Several s 459 cases have determined that a shareholder may have a personal interest in directors complying with the duties that they owe to the company. Moreover, the rarely used s 461(2)(c) of the Companies Act 1985 allows a petitioner who succeeds in proving unfairly prejudicial conduct under s 459 to then bring a derivative action in the name of the company.

Although the matter is not directly addressed in the Paper, there is a strong indication that the Commission does not regard the derivative-personal action dualism as sacrosanct. As the Paper acknowledges, 'To maintain a distinction in available relief based solely on the cause of action pleaded may perpetuate the current problems facing litigants in deciding whether to bring a personal or derivative action'.[4] Indeed, the implication of the Paper is that this is neither desirable nor feasible in practice. Such an effort would thwart its policy goal of facilitating shareholder remedies. Yet the Paper does seek to reinstate the classic division between derivative and personal actions by

---

1 The Rt Hon Lord Woolf, *Access to Justice: Final Report*, para 23.
2 Cf Unger, R, 'Legal Analysis as Institutional Imagination' in Rawlings, R (ed), *Law, Society and Economy* (Oxford: Clarendon Press, 1997), ch 8.
3 See, for example, Kay, J, *Foundations of Corporate Success* (Oxford: Oxford University Press, 1993).
4 Paragraph 16.49.

proposing a new derivative action which the Commission hopes will prove more attractive to shareholders than hitherto. In short, the Paper seems to downgrade rather than de-construct the traditional dichotomy between derivative and personal actions.

Originally, derivative actions, with their foundations in majority rule and the business judgement rule, were perceived to be at the core of litigation concerning the affairs of the company. Personal actions were thereby limited and marginalised. Arguably, the dichotomy rendered the law more certain by carefully confining the range of personal actions and, therefore, the amount of shareholder litigation. The significant development of personal actions under s 459 has brought about a re-orientation in the balance between derivative and personal actions whereby the latter has, in practice, come to predominate, and shareholder litigation has been liberalised. The attempt to give greater weight to the special needs of private companies has been crucial in this process. The Law Commission's Paper, being concerned primarily with improving shareholders' remedies in private companies, provides further impetus for this development. The Paper's proposals are likely to lead to further convergence between the two actions as case management is similarly applied to derivative and personal actions and the foundations underpinning the new derivative action and personal actions become more-or-less coterminous. As a result, the earlier role of the dualism in checking litigation has been further diminished.

The Woolf Report and company law — some problems and possibilities

Clearly, the reform of civil justice will have a major impact on the operation of shareholder remedies. For too long, matters pertaining to civil procedure and the administration of civil justice have been separated artificially from the teaching and scholarship of company law. The Commission's reflections on the possible implications of implementing the Woolf Report on shareholder remedies is, therefore, important in its own right. Here we will consider briefly some of the problems, paradoxes and possibilities arising from the Paper's discussion of Lord Woolf's proposed reforms of civil litigation.

The Paper's proposals concerning the implementation of the Woolf Report are relatively brief and uncritical. As a result, several important questions are not addressed. First, the special needs of shareholder litigants (as distinct from other litigants), and the significance of the vast spectrum of companies and shareholders that might be involved, are not considered. In other words, the Commission's treatment of the Woolf Report is rather less focused than other topics considered in the Paper.

Secondly, the Paper fails to address the concern surrounding 'case management'. It has been argued that by increasing the discretion exercised by the courts, case management may accentuate uncertainty and expense and, therefore, curtail access to justice. Research conducted in the United States indicates that case management increases the cost of litigation because it generates more work for lawyers.[1] It is also argued that case management will produce undesirable results. 'The American experience is that the court-management system often results in the judge at the pre-trial conference leaning on the parties in the hope of pushing them ('in their own best interests') toward settlement. The judge's concern to judge the case is subverted by his new concern to achieve a settlement'.[2] It has also been contended that judicial control and simplified procedures will not remove the incentives that lawyers have for complicating and protracting litigation, thereby, subverting the new arrangements.[3]

On the one hand, the Commission seeks to provide alternative remedies to s 459 in order to reduce lengthy and costly litigation, in part, because s 459 gives the courts very wide discretionary authority. On the other hand, the thrust of several of its major proposals (the new derivative action, the new unfair prejudice remedy for small companies, the vesting of share valuation in judges in the special remedy for small companies, case management, etc) is to rely heavily on, and further extend, the exercise of discretion by the court. This may encourage uncertainty and costs as shareholders bring more rather than less evidence in the hope of persuading the court to exercise its discretion in their favour. Similarly, expanding judicial discretion and the avenues available for shareholders to bring actions may draw judges into the realm of commercial decisionmaking. Exemplary as Woolf is, it is no panacea. It poses many dilemmas, not least in the context of company law. Thus the tension in Woolf, which is replicated in the Paper, between the desire to improve access to justice and the recognition that more litigation may not necessarily be in the best interests of business and society.[4]

Thirdly, there is concern that the philosophy of greater court control may, in practice, elevate efficiency above the other goals of a civil justice system, such as fair justice. There is also unease that it may (albeit, unwittingly) express a managerialist dynamic associated with the increasing power of the central state and governance by 'experts'.[5] Seen from this perspective, case management involves increased trust in professional expertise and, above all, the courts: is this warranted?

Lastly, the engagement with the Woolf Report provides a positive opportunity to confront directly the much neglected issues of fairness, justice and ethics in company law. The principles and concerns of the Woolf Report provide an

---

1   See, for example, Resnick, J, 'Managerial Judges' (1982) 96 *Harvard Law Review* 374; Zander, M, 'Why Lord Woolf's Proposed Reforms of Civil Litigation Should Be Rejected' in Zuckerman, AAS and Cranston, R (eds), *Reform of Civil Procedure* (Oxford: Oxford University Press, 1996), pp 79–96. For a valuable overview of some of the empirical research available to Lord Woolf, see Cranston, R, "The Rational Study of Law": Social Research and Access to Justice' in Zuckerman, AAS and Cranston, R (eds), *Reform of Civil Procedure* (Oxford: Oxford University Press, 1996), pp 31–60.

2   Zander, M, 'Why Lord Woolf's Proposed Reforms of Civil Litigation Should Be Rejected', p 87.

3   Zuckerman, AAS, 'Lord Woolf's Access to Justice: Plus ça change . . .' (1996) 59 *MLR* 773.

4   Case management is unlikely to operate effectively unless it is properly tested and refined in practice, and is sustained by adequate resourcing, judicial training and careful monitoring.

5   See, generally, Sommerlad, H, 'Managerialism and the Legal Profession: a New Professional Paradigm' (1995) 2 *International Journal of the Legal Profession* 159; Wall, DS, 'Legal Aid, Social Policy and the Architecture of Criminal Justice: the Supplier Induced Inflation Thesis and Legal Aid Policy' (1996) 23 *Journal of Law and Society* 549.

ideal occasion for re-assessing company law's relationship with morality and its ability to deliver justice.

Litigation costs and access to justice

Despite the 'access to justice' debate, and its important implications for share-holders' remedies, the Paper has relatively little to say about the question of costs and how these should be borne as between the company and shareholders.[1] In common law derivative actions, a shareholder will not be entitled to legal aid, but the plaintiff may include in an application under RSC, Ord 15, r 12A(13) para-graph (2) an indemnity out of the assets of the company in respect of costs incurred or to be incurred in the action and the court may grant such indemnity upon such terms as may, in the circumstances, be appropriate.[2] The court has no jurisdiction under s 459, unlike common law derivative actions, to grant the peti-tioner an advance order requiring the company to indemnify the petitioner as to costs. However, in contrast to shareholders bringing a common law derivative action, petitioners under s 459 are eligible for legal aid.[3] Would the costs of the new statutory derivative action and the new additional remedy for smaller com-panies be normally borne by the company? And would legal aid be available to petitioners under either remedy? The Paper does not address these questions. It is clear, however, that the 'loser pays all' rule of costs and the fact that sharehold-ers will, normally, have little to gain from a successful derivative action[4] would continue to prevail. In this context, the Commission's view that the possibility of a costs indemnity order would be a 'significant incentive' to use the new derivative action, instead of s 459 proceedings, is somewhat optimistic.[5]

Clearly, the use of one particular remedy, as against another, will be shaped, crucially, by the issues of costs and legal aid. It is difficult to see how shareholders will be able to remedy breaches of duty if there is not adequate provision for costs. Despite the introduction of case management, wealthier and more powerful parties will continue to enjoy a tactical advantage over their opponents, for example, by additional expenditure and access to specialised legal services. This is particularly the case where 'repeat players', who benefit from the leverage derived from their frequent use of civil litigation (such as corporate management) are pitted against those who have only occasional recourse to the settlement process and the courts

---

1　The discussion of costs and legal aid takes place in paras 6.10–6.15, 11.26–11.28, 17.8, 17.13–17.15.
2　This order came into force on 1 September 1994. Prior thereto, the Court of Appeal had held that a shareholder who brings the action may be entitled to be indemnified by the company at the end of the trial for any costs he or she has incurred, provided the shareholder acted reasonably in bringing the action, even if it fails: *Wallersteiner v Moir* (No 2) [1975] QB 373: see, also, Prentice, DD, '*Wallersteiner v Moir:* A Decade Later' [1987] *The Conveyancer* 167.
3　Paragraph 11.26 and n 72. On indemnification from the company under s 459, see, also, Prentice, DD, 'The Theory of the Firm', pp 65–67; and E Boros, *Minority Shareholders' Remedies* (Oxford: Clarendon Press, 1995), pp 164–165.
4　See Boyle, AJ and Sykes, R, *Gore-Browne on Companies*, 44th edn loose-leaf (Bristol: Jordans, 1986), para 28.9.
5　Paragraph 18.1. Cf with respect to derivative actions, the Canadian Business Corporations Act, s 242(4) provides that a court '. . . may at any time order the corporation or its subsidiary to pay to the complainant interim costs, including disbursements, but the complainant may be held accountable for such interim costs on final disposition of the application or action'.

('one-shooters').[1] Access to justice depends upon both the existence of legal rights and remedies and the ability to enforce them. It '... requires that litigants be able to make full use of the law and legal institutions; and that the outcome of disputes and claims should be determined by the merits of the arguments of the parties and not by inequalities of wealth, power or experience ... A civil justice system which seeks to promote equal access to just outcomes requires procedures which maximise opportunities for entry into the system and offers procedures that minimise the effects of resource inequalities on outcomes'.[2] It would be pertinent, therefore, for the Commission to re-consider its proposals in the light of the need for effective access to just results, and to investigate, specifically, the extension of conditional fees to cover derivative suits and other litigation where shareholders endeavour to protect and enforce their rights.[3]

Company law reform and 'the information black hole'[4]

Whilst the Law Commission's guiding principles for resolving the problems identified[5] are likely to receive broad approval, more searching questions about the nature of company law and the role of shareholder remedies need to be addressed. What are company law and shareholder remedies for? who are they for? and whose interests and values do they protect? There has been a tendency to ignore these questions and, equally important, there is a dearth of factual data that might inform such debate.[6] Given the absence of an accurate picture of how company law operates in practice, the Commission's resort to empirical research is especially welcome. Nonetheless, this research was limited in nature and scope. It did not, for example, investigate the views and experience of consumers of legal services in the context of shareholder litigation and alternative dispute resolution. Nor did it explore the factors that propel or deter shareholders from using the law, and the criteria that they use to assess the utility and

---

1 This nomenclature derives from the seminal work of Galanter, M, 'Why the Haves Come Out Ahead: Speculations on the Limits of Legal Change' (1974) 9 *Law and Society Review* 347 and 'Reading the Landscape of Disputes' (1983) 31 *UCLA Law Review* 40. With respect to England, see, for example, Genn, H, *Hard Bargaining* (Oxford: Clarendon Press, 1987), Wheeler, S, *Reservation of Title Clauses* (Oxford: Oxford University Press, 1991); and Ingleby, R, *Solicitors and Divorce* (Oxford: Clarendon Press, 1992).

2 Genn, H, 'Access to Just Settlements: the Case of Medical Negligence' in Zuckerman, AAS and Cranston, R (eds), *Reform of Civil Procedure* (Oxford: Oxford University Press, 1996), p 394.

3 The question of conditional fees receives scant attention: see para 6.15. The Vice-Chancellor, Sir Richard Scott, has recently called for wider use of contingency fee arrangements and the use of tax incentives to encourage litigation insurance (1997) *The Times*, 17 May.

4 The term is coined by Hazel Genn: see Genn, H, 'Access to Just Settlements: the Case of Medical Negligence' (above), p 393.

5 Paragraphs 14.10–14.13.

6 With respect to company law, see, generally, Freedman, J, 'Small Business and the Corporate Form', pp 572–573. See, generally, Genn, H, 'Access to Just Settlements', pp 395–96; Purcell, T and McAllister, G, 'Filling the Void in Civil Litigation Disputes — A Role for Empirical Research' in Smith, R (ed), *Shaping the Future* (London: Legal Action Group, 1995); Cranston, R, 'The Rational Study of Law: Social Research and Access to Justice'; Cranston, R, '"A Wayward, Vagrant Spirit": Law in Context Finds it Rich and Kindly Earth' in Wilson, G (ed), *Frontiers of Legal Scholarship* (Chichester: John Wiley, 1995), p 1; Partington, M, 'Implementing the Socio-Legal: Developments in Socio-Legal Scholarship and the Curriculum' in Wilson, G (ed), *Frontiers of Legal Scholarship*, p 92.

fairness of legal procedures.[1] The nature of corporate law litigants (who uses the courts? are they largely very rich?); the extent to which alternative dispute resolution works; and the nature, quality and efficiency of legal advice and assistance before proceedings are issued are just some of the many important questions that have not been addressed systematically. Similarly, we need to know how corporate relations are constituted and the function and the role of the law and lawyers therein. Without sound empirical research to sustain them, law reform programmes may fail to accomplish their goals.

Research which uses economic theory to provide insights into corporate law is also essential. For example, how does corporate law affect choice of remedies; do different legal remedies affect choice differently; can we assess the cost of one legal stratagem or remedy relative to another; can we undertake a cost-benefit analysis of alternative remedies and systems of regulation (self-regulation, judicial, legislative, etc)? It is also important that the regulation of companies takes the role of advanced professional services such as the legal and accountancy professions seriously. The influence of the lawyers' financial interest in making litigation more complex and lengthy, and in mediating and avoiding the law, has been a long-standing complaint of the English legal system.[2] Even in the seemingly mundane world of the creditors' meeting in insolvent liquidations, '. . . insolvency practitioners, as an emerging professional group, use the meeting space to establish within their own group power and territory and that creditors whose interests the meeting is being held are, in effect, marginalized and relegated to the role of audience'.[3] These problems have been compounded by the new economy which has enabled these professional 'hired guns' to construct new markets for their services, at the same time as shape the new forms of organisation and regulation, transnational and national, private and public, and the boundaries delineating the private and the public. Business enterprises, legal knowledge and the regulatory environment are all affected by this process.[4] In short, there is a huge

---

1 See Genn, H, 'Access to Just Settlements: the Case of Medical Negligence', pp 393, 395–396 and 407. For suggestive empirical research that could be adapted to address these issues, see: Tyler, T, 'What is Procedural Justice? Criteria Used by Citizens to Assess the Fairness of Legal Procedures' *Law & Society Review* 22 (1988) 104; O'Barr, WM and Conley, JM, 'Lay Expectations of the Civil Justice System' *Law & Society Review* 22 (1988) 137; Lind, E Allan *et al*, *The Perception of Justice: Tort Litigants' Views of Trial, Court Annexed Arbitration and Judicial Settlement Conferences* (Rand Institute for Civil Justice, 1989). See, generally, Genn, H, 'Understanding Civil Justice' (Unpublished Inaugural Lecture, University College, London, 12 December 1996).

2 On the influence of lawyers' financial interests, see Zuckerman, AAS, 'Reform in the Shadow of Lawyers' Interests' in Zuckerman, AAS and Cranston, R (eds), *Reform of Civil Procedure*, p 61. On lawyers and avoidance, see McBarnet, D, 'Legal Creativity: Law, Capital and Legal Avoidance' in Cain, M and Harrington, CB, *Lawyers in a Postmodern World* (Milton Keynes: Open University Press, 1994), p 73.

3 Wheeler, S, 'Empty Rhetoric and Empty Promises: the Creditors' Meeting' (1994) 21 *Journal of Law and Society* 350, 351.

4 See, for example, Dezalay, Y, *Marchands de droit: La restructuration de l'ordre juridique international par les multinationales du droit;* (Paris: Fayard, 1992); Flood, J and Skordaki, E, *Corporate Failure and the Work of Insolvency Practitioners* (London: ACCA, 1992); Hanlon, G, *The Commercialisation of Accountancy*, (London: Macmillan, 1994); Dezalay, Y and Sugarman, D (eds), *Professional Competition and Professional Power* (London: Routledge, 1995); Halliday, T and Carruthers, B, 'The Moral Regulation of Markets: Professions, Privatisation and the English Insolvency Act 1986' (1996) 21 *Accounting, Organisations and Society* 371; Dezalay, Y and Garth, B, *Dealing in Virtue* (Chicago: University of Chicago Press, 1996).

void in our knowledge of the civil justice system, of which corporate law is but one component, which can only be addressed by systematic empirical research.

It is to the Commission's credit that, since its first sortie into company law, it has recognised the lack of factual data in this field and has undertaken modest surveys and statistical studies as well as drawn upon the available empirical research. But the void that needs to be filled is a big one, and a clearly defined, systematic and goal-orientated empirical research programme is a prerequisite for an effective and efficient programme of corporate law reform.

Reconceptualising company law

The discipline of company law did not emerge fully formed but was constructed largely by judges and lawyers, and only belatedly taken up by legal academics.[1] In substance, classical company law was a patch-work quilt of doctrines appropriated from fields such as agency, partnership, contract, torts, and public law, held together by a common conceptual core that asserted that company law was an autonomous legal discipline. Company lawyers created a distinctive field by conceptualising the company as an *institution* or thing, as opposed to a regulatory technology.[2] By the end of the classical period of modern legal education and scholarship (ie *circa* 1914), private and public law, jurisprudence and legal history, were dominated by similar criteria of relevance, which served simultaneously to separate them from one another, while recasting them in an analogous fashion. Seen from this perspective, law was a subject of great technical complexity which nonetheless was unified and coherent because it was grounded in a handful of general principles. This classical conception of legal scholarship was sustained by a battery of distinctions: common law/statute law, law/politics, law/state, law/morality, legal/empirical, law/business, form/ substance, means/ends, private law/public law, law/history, law/theory that made it more tenable to regard law as 'pure' and 'scientific'.[3] The field of

---

1 This section largely summarises my long-standing and forthcoming research on the creation and development of company law, and also on the history of legal education. This work will contain a more detailed and nuanced account of the developments and take-for-granted assumptions outlined here. See, generally, Horwitz MJ, *The Transformation of American Law, 1780–1860* (Cambridge, Mass: Harvard University Press, 1977) and *The Transformation of American Law 1870–1960: The Crisis of Legal Orthodoxy* (New York: Oxford University Press, 1992); Atiyah PS, *The Rise and Fall of Freedom of Contract*; Ireland, P, 'The Triumph of the Company Legal Form, 1856–1914' in Adams, J (ed), *Essays for Clive Schmitthoff* (Abingdon: Professional Books, 1983), pp 29–58; Cornish, WR and de Clark, GN, *Law and Society in England, 1750–1950*, pp 246–266; Freyer, T, *Regulating Big Business* (Cambridge: Cambridge University Press, 1992); Robb, G, *White Collar Crime in Modern England* (Cambridge: Cambridge University Press, 1992); Slinn, J, 'Solicitors and Business Regulation: Attitudes to Company Law in the Nineteenth Century' in Swann, EJ (ed), *The Development of the Law of Financial Services* (London: Cavendish, 1993), p 143; Andrews, N, 'Comment on Corporate Law and Historical Methodology' (1996) 3 *Canberra Law Review* 15. Cf Simpson, AWB, 'The Horwitz Thesis and the History of Contracts' (1979) 46 *University of Chicago Law Review* 533; Barton, JL, 'The Enforcement of Hard Bargains' (1987) 103 *LQR* 188; Lobban M, 'Nineteenth Century Frauds in Company Formation' (1996) 112 *LQR* 287.

2 This was true of other fields of law too: see, generally, MacCormick, N, 'Law as Institutional Fact' (1974) 90 *LQR* 102.

3 See, generally, Sugarman, D, 'Legal Theory, the Common Law Mind and the Making of the Textbook Tradition' and 'The Legal Boundaries of Liberty: Dicey, Liberalism and Legal Science' (1983) *MLR* 102.

classical company law was constituted on this terrain, and its conceptual core was, essentially, similar to much of the private and public law of the classical period.

Thus, judicial supervision over the internal affairs of the company was reduced to a bare minimum through the development, for example, of: majority rule;[1] the separate personality of the company;[2] the doctrine that it was not normally open to individual shareholders to bring an action on behalf of the company against, for example, the directors;[3] the limited nature of the 'contract' in the articles of association;[4] the doctrine that corporate management was vested in the board of directors;[5] the principle that the courts should be hesitant about interfering in the affairs of companies, and should not second guess management;[6] and the rule that directors owe their duties to the company and not to the shareholders.[7] While equity was increasingly marginalised, procedure was often elevated over substance. Questions of reasonableness and fairness were for the parties to decide, and not for the courts. In sum, company law was re-classified from a 'privilege' to a 'right', from a creature of public law to a creature of private law.[8]

As in other legal fields, certainty, predictability and stability were achieved by keeping parties to their bargains. Only if third parties were affected might the courts and Parliament intervene. As a result, the legal machinery that existed to police the abuse of power by and within the company was circumscribed significantly. Increasingly, contract became the dominant conceptual framework within company law. And reflecting classical contract law's obsession with freedom of contract and the autonomy of the parties, judicial supervision was largely eschewed.[9] Thus, classical company law developed a conception of the relationship between shareholders *inter se*, and between shareholders and the board of directors, which emphasised the individually subordinate position of the shareholder within the firm (relative to the separate persona of 'the company' and the board of directors), thereby, preserving largely free from legal regulation certain core areas of the managerial prerogative. The relationships of power and dependence that arose within and as between companies received short shrift. In these ways, the newly emerging limited liability company was, increasingly, freed from the regulatory public law assumptions that dominated the law of corporations.

---

1 *Mozley v Alston* (1847) 1 Ph 790.
2 *Salomon v A Salomon & Co Ltd* [1897] AC 22.
3 *Foss v Harbottle* (1843) 2 Hare 461.
4 For example, *Hickman v Kent or Romney Marsh Breeders' Association* [1915] 1 Ch 881.
5 *Automatic Self-Cleansing Filter Syndicate v Cuninghame* [1906] 2 Ch 34 and *Breckland v London & Suffolk Properties* [1989] BCLC 100.
6 *Howard Smith Ltd v Ampol Petroleum Ltd* [1974] AC 821, 832 *per* Lord Wilberforce.
7 *Percival v Wright* [1902] 2 Ch 421.
8 See, generally, Hurst, JW, *The Legitimacy of the Business Corporation in the United States 1780–1970* (Madison: University of Wisconsin Press, 1970); and Sugarman, D, 'A Socio-Historical Investigation of the Transformation of English Law', etc, Part Two.
9 See, for example, *Foss v Harbottle* (1843) 2 Hare 461 and *Salomon v A Salomon & Co Ltd* [1897] AC 22. See, generally, Sugarman, D, 'A Socio-Historical Investigation of the Transformation of English Law', etc, Part Two.

This model of company law both reflected and sustained certain notions of the nature of the market, the firm and the state. Like other fields of classical law, it tended to draw a stark divide between coercion and the market, the state and the market, and coercion and contract. At its simplest, the market and the firm were characterised as singular, individualised, neutral, individualistic, competitive, atomistic, autonomous, private (ie non-governmental) and non-coercive; while the state or the public sphere was characterised as coercive, political, dangerous and unstable. Crucial, here, was the centrality of the separation of 'public law' from 'private law'; and the notion that unrestrained competition was synonymous with the public good.[1]

Clearly, such wave-of-the-wand treatment of the general trends in classical company law must, necessarily, recognise the deviations, variations and simplifications that arise from such an exercise. It is undoubtedly the case that in company law, like other fields of law, the textbook writers tended to undervalue the role played by equity in practice. Although directors were re-classified from 'trustees' to 'agents', and their duties of care and skill were severed from their fiduciary duties, and thereby diluted, they nonetheless continued to be bound by the strict liability doctrines of fiduciary relations, albeit, that the doctrine of *Foss v Harbottle* created numerous obstacles to their enforcement.[2]

In the modern period, corporate law sought increasingly to control business corporations. In particular, since 1945, modern corporate law was transformed by the growth of statutory and self-regulatory supervision. Many of the assumptions and stark dualisms of classical company law began to disintegrate, although they continue to be influential. This became possible as the public and the private, and private law and public law, became increasingly indistinguishable. This involved recognising the coercive and regulatory character of contract and private law generally. Seen from this perspective, the voluntaristic model of company law, characterised by freedom of contract and self-regulation, not only facilitated individual autonomy but also facilitated and legitimated the exercise of power over others. Thus, state intervention and voluntarism were not polar opposites. Indeed, state action and, therefore, law were essential to the creation of individual autonomy and a regime characterised by voluntarism.

Similarly, the notion of companies as discrete, contractual entities has, increasingly, been challenged by the idea of companies as 'legal persons' with their own legitimate purposes operating within a *shared* framework of action.[3] This conceives of markets and the environment of the company as, in part, shaped by norms which seek to direct economic activity in ways that thwart or attenuate the destructive effects on unbridled competition, recognising the singularity of the firm and the imperatives of intra and inter-organisational co-operation, trust and mutual dependence as the foundations of corporate success.[4] This move-

---

1 See, generally, Atiyah, PS, *The Rise and Fall of Freedom of Contract* (Oxford: Clarendon Press, 1979).
2 Sugarman D, 'A Socio-Historical Investigation of the Transformation of English Law, c 1750–1914', etc, Part Two.
3 Cf Hirst, P, *Representative Democracy and its Limits* (Cambridge: Polity, 1990), pp 75–78.
4 Kay, J, *Foundations of Corporate Success* (Oxford: Oxford University Press, 1993); Deaking, S, Lane, C and Wilkinson, F, 'Trust or Law?' (1994) *Journal of Law and Society* 329; Macaulay, S, 'Non-Contractual Relations in Business' (1963) 28 *American Sociological Review* 55; 'Symposium: Law, Private Governance and Continuing Relationships' in (1985) *Wisconsin Law Review* No 3.

ment is further evident in contemporary society where loss of trust is a major feature experienced within and between private and public organisations.[1]

Notwithstanding these changes, the judicial supervision of business corporations continued, for the most part, to be circumscribed.[2] Since the 1960s, as formalism in private and public law began to give way to an increasing concern with procedural and substantive fairness, so gradually the courts in company law cases also changed. This, in turn, is beginning to be allied to a greater sensitivity to the diverse forms of business corporations and, therefore, to the different types of shareholders. The control of the abuse of discretion and the protection of legitimate expectations has occurred using the conceptual building blocks of equity and public law. However, despite the malleability and adaptability of the conceptual core of company law, its in-built tensions and contradictions, as well as its complexity, have intensified. In these ways the fragmentary, hybrid character of late modern corporate law has become further fragmented and hybridised. Thus, the schizophrenic character of contemporary company law.

So the problem for company lawyers is to how to create a new synthesis, possibly drawing upon the best of the classical model, the modern model (regulatory, state-centred) and the late modern model (hybrid, fragmented, de-centred, contractual, equitable) of corporate law, whilst also fashioning a more appropriate conceptual framework for the twenty-first century. This might recognise the similarities of issues and concepts that arise as between company law and other fields of law; but it would also acknowledge the special nature of corporate power and governance and, therefore, the distinctive types of legal discourse that may be necessary to help to maintain an environment within which business corporations and society may prosper.

CONCLUSION

I hope that I have demonstrated how the Commission's proposals arose originally in the context of the debate concerning the reform of the law governing private companies, and of the influence of deregulation on company law. This explains its principal focus on private companies and the creation of more cost-effective remedies for their shareholders. By rejecting the creation of a new legal form for small businesses, the Commission was able to consider advancing the field of shareholder remedies through the modification of general company law, influenced by current concerns with value for money in public expenditure and access to justice (in particular, the need to reduce the time period and cost of litigation), empirical data on the major company law problems experienced by small businesses and overseas models of corporate law. Its important proposals should be seen as part of an essentially on-going, incremental and longer-term process that both reflects and sustains larger and significant changes currently underway in corporate law. And like all good discussion papers, it has clarified problems, issues and possible solutions, while raising as many questions as it answers.

---

1 Beck, U, *Risk Society*.
2 See, for example, the interpretation of the Companies Act 1948, s 210.

Specifically, the proposed attenuation of *Foss v Harbottle*[1] and the creation of a derivative action triggered by breach of directors' duties represents a cutting back of majority rule and the principle that the courts are reluctant to intervene in the affairs of the company, and an increased reliance on judicial discretion, notions of substantive justice and a general concern with the enforcement of directors' duties already manifested in the development of s 459. In other words, it indicates that in company law, as in other fields of contemporary law, greater weight is being attached to fairness and the protection of reasonable expectations. From this perspective, the decline of *Foss v Harbottle* and the rise of unfairly prejudicial remedy, allied to the proposed derivative action, is akin to, and possibly of a similar magnitude of importance as, the decline of consideration in contract law, and its replacement by the rules of equitable estoppel and economic duress.[2]

We should not loose sight of the striking symbolic significance involved in 'laying to rest' the jurisprudence of *Foss v Harbottle*. For the case has increasingly symbolised the bizarre, pre-modern, irrational (in the Weberian sense)[3] world of classical company law. The hyper-technicality that surrounds the doctrine's artificial distinction between corporate and personal wrongs and remedies, with its elevation of form (procedure) over substance, and the uncertainties surrounding when breaches of articles amount to corporate wrongs as opposed to 'internal irregularities', and what are ratifiable and unratifiable wrongs, does have a Dickensian character. Seen from this perspective, the doctrine of *Foss v Harbottle*, like the Chancery suit in *Bleak House*[4] and the Circumlocution Office in *Little Doritt*,[5] is a maze, a labyrinth or a prison. No wonder, then, that other common law jurisdictions have taken special pleasure in putting '. . . a well deserved nail in the coffin of that 1843 nuisance, *Foss v Harbottle*'.[6]

Yet one person's irrationality may be another's rationality. The doctrine of *Foss v Harbottle* is both irrational (in the Weberian sense); and, insofar as it sought to limit litigation, it is also functionally and rationally successful. In these days, when the cost of litigation on the public purse as well as the parties has become omnipresent, the old doctrine may retain some modest virtues, which perhaps explains why the Commission resisted the temptation to finally send it packing. Indeed, given the Commission's significant reliance on judicial discretion, such a reluctance may be understandable. Yet this highlights a tension that the Paper does not really address: namely, the desire to reduce public and private expenditure arising from litigation and the increasing reliance on judicial discretion. If the courts, as well as the lawyers, are part of the problem, then it may seem

---

1 (1843) 2 Hare 461.

2 For contrasting assessments, see Beatson, J, 'Innovation in Contract Law' in Birks, P (ed), *The Frontiers of Liability* (Oxford: Oxford University Press, 1994), vol 2 and Chen-Wishart, M, 'Consideration, Practical Benefit and the Emperor's New Clothes' in Beatson, J and Friedmann, D (eds), *Good Faith and Fault in Contract Law*, p 123.

3 That is, indicative of a pre-modern conceptual mode which lacks at least an element of modern notions of organisational rationale. See, generally, Sugarman, D, *In the Spirit of Weber: Law, Modernity and 'the Peculiarities of the English'* (Madison: Institute for Legal Studies, Wisconsin University, 1987), which I have drawn upon in this and the next paragraph.

4 Dickens, C, *Bleak House* (1852–1853) (Oxford: Oxford University Press, 1996 edition).

5 Dickens, C, *Little Dorrit* (1855–1857) (Oxford: Oxford University Press, 1996 edition).

6 Consultancy Report, *Review of the Hong Kong Companies Ordinance* (March, 1997), para 132.

odd to cast the courts as the solution. The problem is not peculiar to company law. It is manifested in the contemporary tendency to treat a substantial part of private and public law as springing from '*ex lege* rules'.[1]

In fact, the Commission, sensibly, seeks to develop a spectrum of remedies and allied stratagems that are more-or-less dependent upon judicial review, along with those, such as the model articles, which are not. While some remedies, such as the new derivative action may improve the decision-making process by enabling members to exercise greater 'voice' in governance decisions,[2] others (such as the new remedy for small companies and the model articles) provide relatively easy, low cost 'exit' mechanisms from the company where this might otherwise not be the case.[3] In effect, the Paper may herald a move towards an integrated or co-ordinated approach to shareholders' remedies, recognising that a plurality of shareholder remedies is necessary. As the American Law Institute put it: '. . . [No] single technique of accountability (including market and legal remedies) is likely to be optimal under all circumstances. Each has its characteristic and well-known limitations, and, as a result, shareholders are best served by an overlapping system of protections'.[4]

The development of an 'overlapping system of protections' raises the question of how to ensure that the overall balance between 'exit' and 'voice' is appropriate. Will current preoccupations with less litigation and, therefore, with the facilitation of 'exit' unduly weaken or discourage 'voice'; or will this be counterbalanced by the unfair prejudice remedy and the new derivative action? In part, this requires us to clarify the conceptual and policy basis grounding shareholder remedies. For example, do the remedy for unfairly prejudicial conduct and the new derivative action function to provide relief to those who have suffered harm as a result of the unconscionable behaviour or excessive dependence of the kind associated with fiduciary relations, as in equity; or do they function to improve the decision-making process of bodies where the public interest has a stake, as in public law? Or, do they seek to perform both equitable and public law functions?

As the Paper recognised, the law on shareholder remedies recognises two types of companies, namely the quasi-partnership and other sorts of companies.[5] This distinction is reflected in the development of the unfair prejudice remedy, as well as the remedy of winding up on just and equitable grounds. In essence, higher obligations and standards, and therefore more extensive judicial review, may apply to the shareholders of quasi-partnerships, as opposed to other types

---

1 With respect to this tendency in contract law using these terms, see Beatson, J and Friedmann, D, 'From "Classical" to Modern Contract Law' in Beatson, J and Friedmann, D (eds), *Good Faith and Fault in Contract Law*, pp 3, 16. As regards company law, see Prentice, DD, 'The Theory of the Firm' and Riley, CA, 'Contracting Out of Company Law' (both stressing the inevitable role of the courts in filling the gaps in a company's articles and shareholders' agreements).

2 This will, of course, depend on how the Commission finally deal with the question of 'costs'.

3 This is simply an application of Hirschman's well-known generalisation that members of an organisation have to choose between 'exit' and 'voice': see Hirschman, AO, *Exit, Voice, and Loyalty* (1970).

4 ALI *Principles of Corporate Governance* (St Paul, Minn: ALI Publishers, 1994) vol 2, 291 cited in Consultancy Report, *Review of the Hong Kong Companies Ordinance* (March, 1997), para 131.

5 Paragraph 8.10 n 31.

of company. And it is this equitable jurisdiction that has sustained much of the development of the unfairly prejudicial remedy.[1] However, the unfairly prejudice remedy is also available to shareholders in public companies. In *Re Blue Arrow plc*, Vinelott J considered whether the petitioner, a shareholder in a public listed company, could have legitimate expectations founded on an undisclosed agreement. Striking out the petitioner's claim, he said: '. . . it must be borne in mind that this is a public company, a listed company, and a large one . . . Outside investors were entitled to assume that the whole of the constitution was contained in the articles . . . There is in these circumstances no room for any legitimate expectation founded on some agreement or arrangement made between the directors and kept up their sleeves and not disclosed to those placing the shares with the public through the Unlisted Securities Market'.[2] Should the same approach apply to the shareholders of those companies that are not quasi-partnerships but are also not large, listed public companies? The logic of 'focusing' (ie tailoring intervention and remedies to the nature and structure of the firm), coupled with the recognition that the familiar dichotomy between public and private companies obscures the existence of a large continuum embodying a variety of firms, would seem to encourage the development of a less arbitrary and a more nuanced approach to shareholder remedies. Both conceptually, and in terms of the objectives of legal regulation, is the quasi-partnership/other company dualism the best way to organise and develop shareholder remedies in the 1990s? In part, this is to recognise that the relational character associated with quasi-partnerships may also extend to larger firms in certain circumstances. Further reforms extending focusing beyond quasi-partnerships to a larger sub-group of companies based on the size and nature of the firm would require careful and sustained research, as well as the protection of third parties.

The Paper's greater responsiveness to the needs of shareholders in terms of advice, information and assistance is undoubtedly an advance. But it also raises difficult questions. As we saw, empirical research indicates that most business people do not want to read legislation or even a page of a booklet and that, on cost and other grounds, it is probably undesirable to leave members to draft their own agreement as to how the company should be run. It was in this context that the Commission has begun to explore the development of standard form articles, and more generally the reform of partnership law as a way of assisting small businesses. This welcome initiative could make an especially important contribution to the reform of company law. Indeed, it would perhaps be fairer to judge the Commission's Paper on shareholder remedies in the light of its forthcoming proposals on the reform of partnership law.

I have emphasised that the Commission's role in company law is one which is necessarily incremental in approach. It is important to recognise that '. . . in achieving comprehensive change incrementalism has the advantage that corrections can be more easily made as any undesirable consequences of a change in policy become manifest. In any event, incrementalism is all that is possible in some instances because of resource constraints, a clash of interests and a lack of

---

1 The distinction between quasi-partnership/other companies plays an analogous role to the distinction between 'consumer' and other contracts in contemporary contract law.
2 [1987] BCLC 585, 590. See, generally, the Law Commission Paper at para 9.53.

consensus on values'.[1] Yet among its many virtues, the Commission's Paper also encourages us to take stock, to reconsider many of the assumptions of classical and modern company law and the systems of regulation of which they are a part, especially in the light of the major changes taking place in regulation and governance during the last decade of the century.

In raising these questions, we establish an agenda or prospectus for the reappraisal of the objectives and techniques of corporate law. In order to proceed, however, it would be advisable to seek:

> '... much greater clarity in answer to such questions as, what are we trying to achieve through legal regulation, and how do we hope to achieve a successful intervention for this purpose by using the law? In their turn, these questions lead to further inquiries about how we may best construct and support a market with the flexibility to release the energy of economic innovation, and at the same time prevent this market from devouring or compromising institutions sustaining social solidarity.'[2]

Addressing these questions will call for doctrinal and technical expertise, institutional imagination, inter-disciplinary collaboration, sustained debate and reflexive methodologies.[3] Such, then, may be the vocation of the company lawyer of the twenty-first century.[4]

---

1 Cranston, R, 'The Rational Study of Law': Social Research and Access to Justice' in Zuckerman, AA and Cranston, R (eds), *Reform of Civil Procedure* (Oxford: Oxford University Press, 1996), pp 31, 58.

2 Collins, H, 'The Sanctimony of Contract', p 89.

3 By reflexive, I mean methodologies that systematically reflect upon the assumptions, categories and values of knowledge: see, generally, Bourdieu, P, *An Invitation to Reflexive Sociology* (Cambridge: Polity, 1992). The importance of such reflexivity for company law is nicely brought out in the following observation on contemporary company law: 'One thing for sure is that in spite of all legislative change we cannot escape the fundamental conceptual questions which need to be addressed ... The problem is that we constantly start in the middle when what we need to do is to go back to first principles. If there is one weakness of legal education in British Commonwealth jurisdictions it is an unwillingness ... to transcend the black letter law and to think conceptually about the subject and the underlying policies, and for this we pay the price of high cost and intellectual incoherence': Farrar, JH, 'Fuzzy Law, the Modernization of Corporate Laws and the Privatization of Takeover Regulation', p 11.

4 Cf Eisenberg, M, 'The Structure of Corporation Law'(1989) 89 *Columbia Law Review* 1461; Bratton, WW, 'The New Economic Theory of the Firm' (1989) *Stanford Law Review* 1471; Bradley, C and Freedman, J, 'Changing Company Law' (1990) 53 *MLR* 397; Selznick, P, *Law, Society and Individual Justice* (New York: Russell Sage Foundation, 1969); Graham, C, 'Regulating the Company' in Hancher, L and Moran, M (eds), *Capitalism, Culture and Economic Regulation* (Oxford: Clarendon Press, 1989); Ramsay, I, 'Corporate Law in the Age of Statutes' (1992) 14 *Sydney Law Review* 474; Wheeler, S, 'The Business Enterprise' in Wheeler, S (ed), *A Reader on the Law of the Business Enterprise* (Oxford: Oxford Univeristy Press, 1994), p 1; Mitchell, LE (ed), *Progressive Corporate Law* (Boulder: Westview Press, 1995); Patfield, F Macmillan, 'Challenges for Company Law' in *Perspectives of Company Law* Vol 1 (The Hague: Kluwer Law International, 1995); Cheffins, BR, *Company Law* (Oxford: Oxford University Press, 1997).

Chapter 12

SHARE BUY-BACKS

Ben Pettet[1]

INTRODUCTION

The statutory provisions permitting public companies to purchase their own shares[2] seem to have become popular at long last. Listed plcs have been setting up share buy-backs in a variety of circumstances. In 1995–1996, £1.4 billion worth of share buy-backs were conducted in the UK market.[3]

When the reforms were being debated, there did not seem to have been much enthusiasm for overturning the prohibition on public companies purchasing their own shares,[4] although there seemed no shortage of good reasons for permitting private companies to do so.[5] Yet it is now clear that Parliament was, in fact, providing a facility that businessmen were eventually going to find useful.[6] The purpose of this essay is to take a fresh look at the purchase of shares in the context of the recent popularity of share buy-backs.

---

1 Senior Lecturer in Laws, University College London.
2 Contained in ss 162–170 and 178–182 of the Companies Act 1985. Further provisions in ss 171–177 enable private companies to utilise capital in payment for their shares in certain circumstances.
3 *Financial Times* 25 March 1996. The USA has seen similar developments. According to Lehman Brothers, share buy-backs in 1996 amounted to 14 billion dollars; *Financial Times* 22 March 1997. For an account of developments in Australia, see Cotton (1995) 16 *Company Lawyer* 287.
4 'For these reasons there is a case for consideration, at least, of an extension of the power of a private company to re-purchase its own shares . . . The case for an extension in relation to public companies is of a different character.' *The Purchase by a Company of its Own Shares. A Consultative Document* (HMSO Cmnd 7944, 1980) paras 15–16. The document was written by Professor Gower.
5 *Ibid*, paras 11, 15.
6 The idea was certainly in the minds of some people at the time; see para 10 of the Consultation Document: 'Others have suggested that larger companies with surplus liquid assets might more usefully employ them in informal reductions of capital by buying up their shares rather than by looking round for outlets for further diversification.'
Another use of the public company provisions that is now going to become popular is their essential structural role in the existence of Open Ended Investment Companies (OEICS). This possible use was also clearly foreseen by the 1980 Consultation Document. *Ibid*, paras 11(h) and 16. According to a recent press report, 'The Association of Unit Trusts and Investment Funds predicts that Oeics will come to dominate the unit trust industry within a few years' — 'There will not be many unit trusts left by mid-1999 — a large proportion of trusts will have been converted to Oeics.' *Financial Times* 28 April 1997.

THE COMMON LAW BACKGROUND

In 1887, the House of Lords took the decision to prohibit companies from buying their own shares.[1] The case which gave rise to this opportunity was *Trevor v Whitworth*.[2] The insolvent company was in liquidation and was faced with a claim from the executor of a deceased shareholder for the balance of the purchase price of shares which the shareholder had sold to the company.[3] The articles of association provided that:

> '[A]ny share may be purchased by the company from any person willing to sell it, and at such price, not exceeding the marketable value thereof, as the board think reasonable.'[4]

The decision proceeded largely on the technical basis that the purchases were *ultra vires* the company as being neither 'in respect of or as incidental to any of the objects specified in the memorandum'.[5] But the speeches were heavy on rationale and it is clear that their Lordships felt that the practice was thoroughly undesirable and unlawful for reasons other than being beyond the powers of the company as defined in the memorandum. Indeed, Lord Macnaghten went so far as to say that even 'if the power to purchase its own shares were found in the memorandum of association . . . it would necessarily be void'.[6] The main thrust of the rationale against allowing share purchase was expressed in the form that a proponent of the practice was on 'the horns of a dilemma',[7] (and a dilemma which was made 'perfect'[8]), namely that if the shares purchased by the company were going to be resold then this was 'trafficking' in shares and if they were not then it was a reduction of capital which was unlawful because it fell outside the statutory provisions regulating reductions.[9] The need for careful regulation of reductions in accordance with the maintenance of capital principle was stressed:

> 'The creditors of the company which is being wound up . . . find coming into competition with them persons, who, in respect only of their having been, and having ceased to be shareholders in the company, claim that the company shall pay to them a part of that capital . . . The capital may, no doubt, be diminished by expen-

---

1 For an interesting account of the earlier case law and the developments going on in the USA at about the same time see Trichardt, Organ and Cilliers *The Purchase by a Company of its Own Shares: The English Rule vs The American Rule* (Bloemfontein: Centre for Business Law UOFS, 1989), pp 4–7.

2 (1887) 12 AC 409.

3 There was an issue as to whether the shares were being purchased by a director on his own account but it was held that the purchase was in fact made by him on behalf of the company. *Ibid* at 413.

4 Article 179. By art 181, it was provided that 'Shares so purchased may at the discretion of the board be sold or disposed of by them or be absolutely extinguished, as they deem most advantageous to the company'.

5 *Ibid* at 416, *per* Lord Herschell.

6 *Ibid* at 436.

7 *Ibid* at 425, Lord Watson citing James LJ in *Hope v International Society* (1876) 4 Ch D 335.

8 *Ibid per* Lord Herschell at 419, citing Brett, JA in *Hope*.

9 Then contained in the Companies Act 1867, ss 9–13, now ss 135–138 of the Companies Act 1985. 'When Parliament sanctions the doing of a thing under certain conditions and with certain restrictions, it must be taken that the thing is prohibited unless the prescribed conditions and restrictions are observed.' *Ibid* at 437–438, *per* Lord Macnaghten.

diture upon and reasonably incidental to all the objects specified. A part of it may be lost in carrying on the business operations authorised. Of this all persons trusting the company are aware and take the risk. But I think they have a right to rely, and were intended by the legislature to have a right to rely, on the capital remaining undiminished by any expenditure outside these limits, or by the return of any part of it to the shareholders.'[1]

On the facts, it seemed fairly clear that a systematic breach of the maintenance principle was being perpetrated despite the argument that the purchases were being carried out to facilitate the retention of family control; and even if the purchases were for this purpose it was:

'A practice which became more and more confirmed as the company's affairs became more and more embarrassed . . . The figures are instructive. In December 1880 the company owed its bankers, who were secured creditors, £20,202. Up to that date, from its commencement in 1865, it had spent £16,202 in the purchase of its own shares. By December 1883 the debt to the bankers had increased to £30,490 and the sum spent in the purchase of its shares amounted to £32,935. By means of these purchases that large sum, more than one-fifth of the nominal capital of the company, had been withdrawn from the fund to which . . . the creditors have a right to look. In 1884 the company went into liquidation, and the creditors are unpaid.'[2]

Although the courts developed a few marginal exceptions,[3] *Trevor v Whitworth* remained the main source of authority until the legislature intervened in the early 1980s.

ANALYSIS OF THE LEGISLATION

The first legislation was contained in the Companies Act 1980 which codified the basic common law rule.[4] While this legislation was passing through Parliament, moves were afoot to consider the possibility of extending the exceptions to the legislation, to the extent permitted by the EC Second Directive.[5] The DTI issued a Consultative Document[6] and, in due course, the Companies Act 1981 brought in the wider exceptions.

All the relevant legislation[7] is now contained in ss 143–149, and 159–181 of the

---

1 *Ibid* at 414–415, *per* Lord Herschell.
2 *Ibid* at 434, *per* Lord Macnaghten.
3 See *Kirby v Wilkins* [1929] 2 Ch 444; *Re Castiglione's Will Trusts* [1958] 549.
4 Section 35(1) provided '. . . [N]o company limited by shares or limited by guarantee and having a share capital shall acquire its own shares (whether by purchase or subscription or otherwise)'. Some attempt was made to codify also the common law exceptions: 'A company limited by shares may acquire any of its own fully paid shares otherwise than for valuable consideration and any company may acquire its own shares in a reduction of capital duly made': s 35(2). See also ss 35(4) and 36–37.
5 Directive 77/91/EEC mainly arts 19–22, 24 and also 39 (redeemable shares).
6 See n 4 on p 243 above.
7 It is not proposed to deal, in this essay, with the provisions regulating the provision by a company of financial assistance for the acquisition of its shares *by another*; ss 151–158 of the Companies Act 1985. While these are sometimes seen as an 'extension' of the rule in *Trevor v Whitworth*, it is submitted that the better view is that they are really an unrelated area, dealing with abuses that do not, technically, involve a reduction (or a potential reduction) in the capital yardstick of the company. For an analysis of these provisions, the reader is referred to my articles in (1988) 3 *Journal of International Banking Law* 96 and (1995) 9 *Journal of International Banking Law* 1.

Companies Act 1985. The basic prohibition is contained in s 143, which provides:

> 'Subject to the following provisions, a company limited by shares or limited by guarantee and having a share capital shall not acquire its own shares, whether by purchase, subscription or otherwise.'[1]

The exceptions are set out in a list in s 143(3), so that the prohibition is expressed not to apply to:

> '(a) the redemption or purchase of shares in accordance with [sections 159–181];
> (b) the acquisition of shares in a reduction of capital duly made;
> (c) the purchase of shares in pursuance of an order of court under section 5 (alteration of objects), section 54 (litigated objection to resolution for company to be re-registered as private) or Part XVII (relief to members unfairly prejudiced); or
> (d) the forfeiture of shares, or the acceptance of shares surrendered in lieu, in pursuance of the articles, for failure to pay any sum payable in respect of the shares.'

This is mainly[2] a gathering-together list of exceptions which already exist or are already dotted about in other parts of the Act. The main exceptions are, obviously, the general ones referred to in paragraph (a).

Section 162(1) contains the main permission:

> 'Subject to the following provisions of this Chapter, a company limited by shares or limited by guarantee and having a share capital may, if authorised to do so by its articles,[3] purchase its own shares (including any redeemable shares).'

Shares purchased are treated as cancelled.[4] The type of permission required depends on whether the share purchase is an 'off-market'[5] purchase or a

---

1 The sanctions are contained in s 143(2), which provides for a fine for the company and fines or imprisonment for the officers in default. The purported acquisition is void. It has been held that s 143 was not contravened when a company acquired another company which held shares in it: see *Acatos & Hutcheson plc v Watson* [1995] 1 BCLC 218 and Nolan 'The Veil Intact' (1995) 16 *Company Lawyer* 180. Other recent litigation on s 143 is *Vision Express Ltd v Wilson* [1995] 1 BCLC 419, although it is difficult to derive any general principle from the case.

2 Section 143(3) also makes it clear that a company may acquire any of its own fully paid shares 'otherwise than for valuable consideration' such as by way of gift. In ss 144–149, there are complex provisions dealing with companies having beneficial interests in their own shares and designed to prevent circumvention of the prohibition in s 143.

3 The necessary authority is, normally, supplied by art 35 of Table A.

4 Section 162(2) and s 160(4).

5 The Act provides a definition in s 163(1): 'A purchase by a company of its own shares is *off-market* if the shares either — (a) are purchased otherwise than on a recognised investment exchange; or (b) are purchased on a recognised investment exchange but are not subject to a marketing arrangement on that investment exchange.' There follows, in s 163(2), a further definition by which a company's shares are subject to a marketing arrangement on a recognised investment exchange 'if either — (a) they are listed under Part IV of the Financial Services Act 1986; or (b) the company has been afforded facilities for dealings in those shares to take place on that exchange without prior permission for individual transactions from the authority governing that investment exchange and without limit as to the time during which those facilities are to be available'. Overseas investment exchanges are not RIEs for these purposes: s 163(4).

'market'[1] purchase. With off-market purchases, the company may only make the purchase if the contract is approved in advance.[2] Obviously, this would not be possible in the case of a market purchase and so the legislation here requires merely prior authorisation in general meeting.[3] In view of the frequency with which share buy-backs are conducted by listed plcs, these days, it is not surprising to find that seeking permission from the shareholders at a company's annual general meeting has become a routine practice[4] even if there is no immediate intention to use it. An example of the proposed ordinary resolution taken from the 1995 Annual Report[5] of Hanson plc, (in the early stages of its demergers) runs as follows:

> 'That the company be and is hereby generally and unconditionally authorised to make market purchases (within the meaning of s 163(3) of the Companies Act 1985) of up to an aggregate of 518.6 million ordinary shares of 25p each at a price per share (exclusive of advance corporation tax and expenses) of not less than 25p and not more than 105 per cent of the average of the middle market quotations for such an ordinary share, as derived from the Stock Exchange Daily Official List, for the ten dealing days immediately preceding the day of purchase; such authority to expire at the conclusion of the annual general meeting to be held in 1997, save that the company may purchase shares at any later date where such purchase is pursuant to any contract made by the company before the expiry of this authority.'

The note to this item shows the continuity and the context:

> 'The company was authorised at the last annual general meeting to purchase up to 517.3 million of its ordinary shares. This authority has not been used and expires at the conclusion of this annual general meeting. The resolution renews and extends the authority to allow the company to purchase up to 518.6 million of its ordinary shares (representing approximately 10% of the issued ordinary share capital) for a further year.

> The directors have no present intention of using this authority and, in reaching any decision to purchase ordinary shares, will take into account the company's cash resources, capital requirements and the effect of any purchase on earnings per share.'

The provisions make various other specifications applying to share purchases, so that the shares must be fully paid up,[6] there may be no purchase if, as a result

---

1 Defined in s 163(3) as '. . . a purchase made on a recognised investment exchange, other than a purchase which is an off-market purchase by virtue of [s 163(1)(b)]'. The main examples, in practice, of market purchases are those made of shares listed on the London Stock Exchange or the Alternative Investment Market (AIM).

2 The terms of the proposed contract must be authorised by special resolution before the contract is entered into: s 164. Not surprisingly, the owner of the shares is, effectively, barred from voting on the resolution: s 164(5), and there are various other conditions and extensions: ss 164, 165.

3 Section 166 (1). Various details are laid down in s 166, for example by s 166(2) 'that authority (a) may be general for that purpose, or limited to the purchase of shares of any particular class or description; and (b) may be unconditional or subject to conditions.' By s 166(3), 'the authority must (a) specify the maximum number of shares authorised to be acquired; (b) determine both the maximum and the minimum prices which may be paid for the shares; and (c) specify a date on which it is to expire'.

4 Described recently by Mr Andrew Teare, Chief Executive of Rank plc, as a matter of 'good housekeeping'. *Financial Times* 11 April 1997.

5 At pp 28–29.

6 Sections 162(2) and 159(3).

of the purchase, there would no longer be any member of the company holding shares other than redeemable shares[1] and there is a requirement for disclosure by delivery of particulars to the Registrar of Companies.[2]

It is in the provisions concerning the payment for the shares that Parliament meets some of the challenges posed by the rationale of *Trevor v Whitworth*. One of the main objections was that it would operate as an unlawful reduction of capital:

> 'The shareholders receive back the moneys subscribed, and there passes into their pockets what before existed in the form of cash in the coffers of the company, or of buildings, machinery, or stock available to meet the demands of the creditors.'[3]

This problem is avoided by requiring that the shares may only be purchased out of distributable profits of the company or out of the proceeds of a fresh issue of shares made for the purpose. The drafting by which this is achieved is convoluted, for the statute, by s 162(2), imports these rules from the provisions governing the redemption of redeemable shares (s 160) where the underlying principles concerning maintenance of capital are identical. On the other hand, also applicable here, but standing alone and not imported, are the provisions of s 170, which require the establishment of a capital redemption reserve to the extent that the payment for the purchase[4] of the shares is out of distributable profits. The capital redemption reserve, effectively, makes those profits undistributable and so preserves the capital yardstick. It is important to realise the significance of these rules, for unless it can comply with them, a public company wishing to buy back its shares will have to resort to a formal reduction of capital under the comparatively cumbersome and restrictive statutory mechanisms provided in ss 135–138.[5]

With private companies, with which this essay is not concerned primarily, it is possible to reduce the capital yardstick in some circumstances. Where various conditions, set out in ss 171–177, are satisfied the Act permits the use of capital to the extent of what it calls 'the permissible capital payment'.[6] The *Trevor v Whitworth* objection is met, to a large extent, by the existence of numerous safeguards, such as the need for directors' declarations as to solvency, and enhanced protection for creditors.

The other main objection emanating from *Trevor v Whitworth* was that a purchase of its own shares would enable the company to traffick in its own shares, meaning buy and sell for profit. This is, effectively, prevented by the provision that the shares purchased are treated as cancelled.[7] There are also two additional safeguards. If the company were to buy its own shares in an effort to force up or support the market price, the directors and the company itself could face liability for market manipulation under s 47(2) of the Financial Services Act

---

1 Section 162(3).
2 Section 169. Other matters are dealt with in s 167 (assignment) and s 178 (effect of failure to purchase).
3 *Ibid* at 416, *per* Lord Herschell.
4 Or redeemable shares redeemed under ss 159–160.
5 See, eg *Re Chatterley Whitfield Collieries* [1948] 2 All ER 593.
6 *Ibid*, s 171(3).
7 See n 4 on p 246 above.

1986; although, given the prevalence of the practice, the case would, presumably, have to be an extreme one.[1] The directors might, conceivably, also face liability for Insider Dealing, in some circumstances.[2] It is not immediately obvious how the Act might apply, because the shares purchased are treated as cancelled and so a profit on resale is not a possibility; similarly, avoidance of a loss is not possible since the company will not be holding any shares on which to avoid a loss. However, the following example might illustrate the possibility. Suppose a listed company had an issued share capital of 200m £1 shares with assets of £200m and a market price of £1 per share. The directors own 50m shares between them. Confidentially, the directors receive some good news about the company's prospects which shows it to be worth twice as much as previously thought. Before the news is made public, they cause the company to buy-back 100m of its shares at the market price of £1. After the buy-back, the position is that the assets now stand at £300m (the new value of £400m minus the buy-back cost of £100m) and there are now only 100m shares in issue, now worth £3 each. Half of these are owned by the directors and they have, in a broad sense at least, made a nice profit.[3]

Arguably, the directors ('individuals') have procured[4] the dealing by another 'person'[5] and fall within s 52(1).[6]

THE COMMERCIAL RATIONALE OF BUY-BACKS

Many different commercial reasons lie behind the decision of a company to set up a buy-back. It is worth considering some of the more specific reasons which have arisen in recent years.

Trading price of shares undervalues company's assets

In a situation where the traded price of the shares of the company is thought by the directors to be undervaluing its assets then, assuming that the directors' view of the situation is correct, a buy-back will provide a method of increasing the value of the remaining shares and so wipe out the discount in the traded price.[7]

A recent example is that of Mercury European Privatisation Investment Trust (Mepit) which:

> '. . . plans to buy back more of its shares before July in an attempt to narrow its discount to net assets . . . Although Mepit bought 53m of its shares, equivalent to 9

---

1 Section 47(2) provides: 'Any person who does any act or engages in any course of conduct which creates a false or misleading impression as to the market in or the price or value of any investments is guilty of an offence if he does so for the purpose of creating that impression and of thereby inducing another person to acquire, dispose of, subscribe for or underwrite those investments or to refrain from doing so or to exercise, or refrain from exercising, any rights conferred by those investments'.

2 Under the Criminal Justice Act 1993.

3 Profit is not defined by the legislation other than by s 53(6).

4 Section 55(1)(b).

5 The company.

6 Another possibility is liabilty for encouraging under s 52(2)(a).

7 A reason advanced by Nowlan & Abrahams in 'Share Buy-Backs' (1994) 278 *Tax Journal* 10.

per cent of the share capital, towards the end of last year, the £618m trust is currently running at a 17 per cent discount to net assets. The move narrowed the discount by about 5 per cent, but only temporarily . . . Mepit is, in some ways a victim of its own initial marketing success. The razzamatazz of its early 1994 launch attracted thousands of private investors, many of whom had never put money in an investment trust. Some subsequently changed their minds and the steady drift of private investors out of the trust continues to hold the discount stubbornly high. Mercury says a share buy-back, combined with increased marketing, will narrow the discount – but it said the same thing this time last year, to no concrete effect . . .'[1]

Cash surplus to requirements

Companies which have cash which is surplus to their current needs will sometimes find that this dilutes their average earnings per share. This is because they get a higher return on their trading and acquisition activities than they can by investing the money. If this is the situation, a share buy-back will enhance the future earnings per share of the remaining shares.[2]

An example arose in 1995:

'Boots, the retailing and healthcare group, said it had "no inhibitions" about handing back more of its £600m-plus cash pile to shareholders if it could not find "sensible" acquisitions . . . Boots has already returned £508m to shareholders through a buy-back last November . . . "If we can't see any sensible use for the cash in the medium term we have no inhibitions about returning that cash to shareholders in the most effective way".'[3]

Enhancement of earnings per share

Earnings per share might also be enhanced by a buy-back in a whole variety of other situations, such as where the cancelled share capital was to be replaced by a cheaper source of funding. As an example, Boots again, in the following year:

'Boots halved its cash pile yesterday, buying back about 5 per cent of its equity for £300m . . . Its offer to buy 51.36m shares at up to 580p was quickly oversubscribed by institutional shareholders and closed in just over an hour . . . The purchase should enhance Boots' earnings per share by several percentage points and therefore bolster the share price, analysts said . . . Boots said the buy-back would help it make better use of its balance sheet: it would save on dividend payments and debt was cheaper to service than equity.'[4]

Fending off unwanted takeover bids

Buy-backs can be found having a role in capital restructuring designed to fend off unwanted takeover bids. For example:

---

1 *Financial Times* 22 May 1997.
2 A reason suggested by Edge in 'Do We Have an Imputation System or Not?' (1996) 375 *Tax Journal* 2. A reason also advanced by Nowlan & Abrahams *loc cit* n 7 on p 249 above.
3 *Financial Times* 2 June 1995.
4 *Financial Times* 28 June 1995.

'Littlewoods, the family-owned retail and football pools group, is offering to buy out any family shareholders who wish to sell their holding in a share buy-back worth up to £250m, in a move seen as a defensive measure against a potential £1.2bn takeover bid.'[1]

Returning surplus cash to shareholders

Returning surplus cash to the shareholders can also avoid uncertainty over the directors' business intentions.[2]

Against rival bidder in takeover

The suggestion of a buy-back has even been used as a weapon against a rival bidder in a takeover bid, as part of an attempted deconstruction of the rival's financial management policies:

'Gehe, the German group engaged in a £650m bid battle for Lloyds Chemists, suggested yesterday that UniChem, the rival bidder, would be better off buying back its own shares . . . In a circular to shareholders in both Lloyds and Unichem, Gehe said that UniChem could enhance its earnings by 13% this year by buying back 20% of its shares.'[3]

THE TAX SAGA

The Inland Revenue have been taking an interest in buy-backs for a long time and recent months have seen developments in the tax treatment of buy-backs. One matter which they were finding particularly irksome was having to pay a tax credit to tax-exempt institutions, such as pension funds.

The broad principles of the background to this phenomenon were put succinctly by the Revenue themselves in a recent Press Release:[4]

'As a general principle, where a company makes a purchase of its own shares any excess paid over the amount of repayment of capital for the shares is a distribution of profits. As a result, the company has to account for advance corporation tax and a tax credit is made available, by the Exchequer, to the recipient of that distribution. The tax credit is sufficient to cover any liability to lower or basic rate tax. Higher rate taxpayers have additional tax to pay, and those who are not liable to, or are exempt from, tax can obtain payment of the tax credit.'

Reliance on the provisions allowing them to cancel a tax advantage in ss 703–709 of the Taxes Act 1988 seemed to have been foreclosed by unhelpful case-law. In *Sheppard v IRC (No 2)*,[5] it had been held that, where an exempt body received income of a kind within its tax exemption, this could not be regarded as a tax advantage. The Revenue were in the process of challenging this, in *USS v IRC*,[6] when they decided to resort to legislation. Possibly, this was

---

1 *Financial Times* 24 November 1995.
2 Nowlan & Abrahams, *loc cit*.
3 *Financial Times* 4 January 1997.
4 Press Release of 5 December 1996.
5 [1993] STC 240.
6 The case is analysed by Wainman in 'Tax Advantage' (1996) 380 *Tax Journal* 6.

prompted by the Reuters £600 million scheme to issue special dividend shares[1] and the Revenue's Press Release was nicely timed, one day ahead of the Reuters meeting, to obtain shareholder approval.[2] Perhaps this was felt to be sufficient notice for them, on the basis that they would be likely to get the news more quickly than anybody else.

The Press Release of 8 October 1996 set out the problems and the proposed remedy. The rationale was contained in the statement of the then Chancellor of the Exchequer, Kenneth Clarke:

> 'We have recently seen companies buying their own shares or paying special dividends in such a way that the proceeds end up[3] almost entirely in the hands of those entitled to payment of a tax credit. This has costs for the Exchequer, and if action is not taken soon that cost would escalate. I therefore propose to bring forward legislation in the next Finance Bill to remove payable credits in some circumstances. The new rules will take effect from today. The Inland Revenue will continue to monitor the situation and we will not hesitate to take any necessary further action should further evidence of abuse appear.'

The Revenue then set out the details of the proposed changes in the following terms:

> '1. The Chancellor's proposal is to amend the treatment of particular transactions so that, although they will remain, as now, distributions of the company, there will be no payable tax credit. The income tax liability of taxpayers who receive such distributions will be unaffected by the change. Shareholders who previously would have been able to claim payments of tax credits on the distributions will no longer be able to do so.
>
> 2. The new treatment will apply to the following distributions made on or after 8th October 1996:
>   (a) a redemption, repayment or purchase by a company of its own shares;
>   (b) a distribution where there are arrangements by virtue of which the amount and timing of the distribution are associated with a transaction, or transactions, in shares or securities, including special dividends linked to share consolidations, and special dividends following a takeover where those dividends are effectively part of the bid.
>
> 3. Where such distributions are made, they will be treated in the same way as foreign income dividends (FIDs). Accordingly, companies which make such distributions must account for advance corporation tax (ACT). Any vouchers issued in respect of the distribution must show the distribution as a FID, on which notional lower rate income tax (which is not repayable) has been borne but on which there is no tax credit. UK companies which receive such distributions will be able to use them to frank FIDs or similar distributions . . .
>
> 4. The Government will also be introducing a clarificatory change to the provisions contained in section 703 *et seq*, Taxes Act 1988. These provisions prevent share-

---

1   Special dividends give rise to similar problems to share buy-backs, in this context.

2   '"The move was brought forward because we know of several deals in the pipeline between now and the Budget" said a government official.' *Financial Times* 9 October 1996.

3   With special dividends, the shares acquire a premium value to tax-exempt shareholders with the result that ordinary shareholders sell out before collecting their special dividends, so that the exempt shareholders collect the greater part of the dividends and then get the tax credits. A similar result is produced on a buy-back if the sale is targeted on tax exempt institutions.

holders from obtaining a tax advantage from various artificial transactions in securities. The change will make it clear that a tax advantage can include obtaining a payable tax credit.'

The results of the proposed changes were summarised:[1]

'. . . [T]he position of taxpayers will remain largely unaffected. They will receive distributions which are treated as having borne lower rate income tax. That income tax will not, however, be repayable, and there will be no payable tax credit for those who are not liable to, or are exempt from tax . . .

The treatment of special dividends which are not linked to share consolidations, takeovers or other transactions in shares or securities will remain unchanged, as will the purchase by a company of its own shares from dealers . . .

The change will produce an estimated yield for the Exchequer of £80 million in 1996/97, £200 million in 1997/98 and £400 million for 1998/99.'[2]

In due course, the Finance Act 1997 contained the amendments in ss 69–73 and Sch 7.

CONCLUSIONS

Share buy-backs have become an essential component of the finance director's armoury in his battle to manage the company's capital flexibly and efficiently. They have aroused controversy and still do, even after the tax changes: 'Beguiling buy-backs',[3] 'Some buyback myths',[4] 'No heresy in share buy-backs',[5] 'Magic of a buy-back'.[6]

Directors stand accused of wasting shareholders' money, for those who remain in the company have to bear the unnecessary cost of buying out others at premium prices. Against this, it is said that the directors are making a very low risk, earnings enhancing investment, on behalf of those shareholders who remain in the company. Obviously, much will depend on the economics of each particular situation. Sooner or later, we will see some interesting battles in annual general meetings, when directors seek the 'routine' s 166 authority.[7]

---

1 These are the main points. This is not an exhaustive summary.
2 Further details were announced in the subsequent Press Release of 26 November 1996 and draft legislation was contained in the Press Release of 5 December 1996.
3 The Lex Column *Financial Times* 12 December 1996.
4 Jackson *Financial Times* 22 March 1997.
5 *Financial Times* 27 February 1997.
6 *Financial Times* 21 December 1996.
7 Litigation, even, might not be unthinkable; see, eg, *Rutherford, Petitioner* [1994] BCC 876.

Chapter 13

HOW REGULATION FINDS ITS WAY THROUGH THE CORPORATE VEIL

Joanna Gray[1]

INTRODUCTION

Professor Boyle's retirement takes place in the centenary year of the report of the decision in *Salomon v A Salomon Co Ltd*[2] which makes one marvel at just how much the business and legal environment has changed for companies over that 100 year period. It would be surprising nowadays to find a boot manufacturer that did *not* employ the corporate form and any such company would be subject to a plethora of detailed statutory and regulatory obligations. These obligations arise not just under company law but under many of the different areas of regulatory law which impinge directly on business activity. A Salomon & Co Ltd had, in the 1890s, no need of a technical compliance directorate to keep the company on the right side of health and safety, environmental, product standard, packaging and marketing legislation and regulation and thus avoid the swingeing penal and quasi-penal sanctions that often attach to contraventions of such regulatory strictures. In fact, Aron Salomon would most probably hang up his cobbler's last and cast around for another type of living, less hidebound by law, to pass on to his family.[3] This essay attempts to show how an increasingly important onslaught on the impenetrability of the corporate veil comes from statutory regulatory provisions, reflecting the growing role of regulation in business life.

There are many interesting legal and policy issues that arise around the related issues of corporate personality and corporate responsibility. One easily over-looked technique which regulatory laws often employ is an extension of the sanction of criminal liability so that it reaches beyond and behind the corporate veil to impose liability for regulatory contravention on a company's directors and officers as well as the company itself. In terms of regulatory efficacy, this type of what are hereinafter referred to as 'officer liability' provisions is, potentially, a useful weapon for enforcers of regulation and framers of regulatory provisions as it gives them a way of getting round the doctrine of corporate personality and pinning responsibility for the company's actions on those human actors behind the veil of incorporation who are responsible for the company's regulatory contravention in the first place. Thus these provisions represent a quite deliberate setting aside by the legislature, for policy reasons,

---

1 Senior Research Fellow in Company Law, Institute of Advanced Legal Studies, University of London.
2 [1897] AC 22.
3 Suggestions that spring readily to mind include counselling, running a dating agency or religious sect, and horse whispering.

of the principle that flows logically from the doctrine of separate corporate personality, that the company and only the company bears responsibility for its acts and omissions.

The first part of this essay examines some of these provisions and considers the Court of Appeal decision in *Attorney-General's Reference (No 1 of 1995)*[1] and its implications for company directors in a business world of increasing regulatory complexity. This decision sheds some light on judicial interpretation of these 'officer liability' statutory provisions.

The second part of the essay then assesses the Court of Appeal's reasoning in the light of recent appellate case-law on the responsibility of companies under criminal and regulatory statutes for acts and omissions of their officers and employees.

At first sight, these officer liability provisions may seem unrelated to the issue of corporate responsibility. The question for the law when considering corporate responsibility is: 'In deciding whether a company has done or failed to do something for the purposes of determining its liability under a criminal, or regulatory provision then, of all the actors who constitute the company *'de facto'*, whose acts are attributable to the company so that they can be said to be the acts of the company *'de jure'* and thus determine the company's responsibility?'.

As the cases post *Tesco Supermarkets v Nattrass*[2] show, there is no simple answer to this question but the increasing sophistication with which the courts have begun to tackle it could, it is argued here, be usefully imported into the interpretation of the 'officer liability' provisions considered in the first part of this article. It is an immutable fact that, as regulation of all aspects of companies' conduct increases, the issues of (i) when is a company liable under a criminal or regulatory provision for the misdemeanours of its employees?; and (ii) when are its officers liable under such provisions for the company's misdemeanours? will continue to occupy the courts and the linkage between these two questions may become clearer.

PART ONE: 'OFFICER LIABILITY' PROVISIONS

In the complex regulatory age in which companies now do business, with a myriad of specific statutory criminal and regulatory offences in existence, directors can find that such an offence can, if committed by the company, be visited upon their heads as well. The obvious rationale for this is that it gives the primary corporate offence extra 'bite' and deterrent effect by looking through the corporate veil and fixing those officers who were responsible for the corporate offending with criminal liability as well.

Examples of 'officer liability' provisions

Some examples of statutory provisions which put company directors at risk in this way include the following:

---

1 *Attorney-General's Reference (No 1 of 1995)* [1996] 1 WLR 970.
2 *Tesco Supermarkets Ltd v Nattrass* [1971] 2 WLR 1166.

Companies Act 1985, s 733 — Offences by Bodies Corporate:

'**(1)** The following applies to offences under any of sections 21, [failure to comply with Part VI disclosure of interests in shares provisions], 216(3) [non-compliance with s 212 notice], 394A(1), [non-compliance with duty to make statement on ceasing to hold office as auditor] and 447 to 451 [non-compliance with and obstruction of company investigations]

(2) Where a body corporate is guilty of such an offence and it is proved that the offence was occurred with **the consent or connivance or was attributable to any neglect on the part of any director, manager, secretary or similar officer** of the body or any person who was purporting to act in any such capacity, he as well as the body corporate is guilty of an offence and is liable to be proceeded against and punished accordingly . . .'

In like vein, s 432 of the Insolvency Act 1986 'Offences by Bodies Corporate' fixes a company's officers with liability for certain Insolvency Act offences:

'**(2)** Where a body corporate is guilty of an offence to which this section applies and the offence is proved to have been committed with **the consent or connivance of, or to be attributable to any neglect on the part of, any director (sic)** . . . he, as well as the body corporate is guilty of the offence and liable to be proceeded against and punished accordingly.'

More sector specific regulatory statutes adopt the same approach. For example, Financial Services Act 1986, s 202:

'**(1)** Where an offence under this Act committed by a body corporate is proved to have been committed **with the consent or connivance of, or to be attributable to any neglect on the part of . . . and director** . . . he, as well as the body corporate, is liable to be proceeded against and punished accordingly.'

and s 96(1) of the Banking Act 1987 does exactly the same thing with corporate offences committed under that Act.[1]

These types of provision can be seen as legitimate responses to the doctrine of separate corporate personality which, in their absence, would render many regulatory offences unable to reach and touch those individuals to whom the offending is '*de facto*', if not '*de jure*', attributable. It is interesting to note that all of the provisions mentioned apply not just to directors and officers but also to members where the affairs of the company are managed by the members.[2] These provisions are not intended to impose strict liability on the individuals concerned. Their liability is expressed to be fault based in that it requires proof of their consent, connivance or causal neglect.

However, what if a company director is ignorant of the fact that an offence has been committed by his company? He is running the company, in good faith, but in such a way as means the company has unwittingly strayed into business territory that is subject to specific statutory regulation (the very existence of which the director is unaware) and has thereby offended. Is that primary

---

1 A trawl through health and safety and environmental regulatory legislation would provide many more examples, eg Employers' Liability (Compulsory Insurance) Act 1969, s 5.
2 Section 733(3) of the Companies Act 1985, Insolvency Act 1985, s 432(3), Financial Services Act 1986, s 202(2).

corporate offence to be visited on the directors through the operation of a statutory provision for secondary 'officer liability' even if the director argues he did not 'consent' to its commission by the company because he was unaware of even the fact of its commission?

In other words, what meaning does the precept 'ignorance of the law is no excuse' have in an era where it is, some businessmen would argue, all too easy to do business in such a way that offends against some specific statutory edict or other. Should not the fact that the company is itself strictly liable for the offence be a sufficient deterrent without imposing an additional criminal liability on the ignorant officer for his 'consent or connivance' in an offence which he was unaware was even being committed?

The question of what *mens rea* is required to prove 'consent' in the context of these 'officer liability' provisions received attention from the Court of Appeal in *Attorney-General's Reference (No 1 of 1995)*.[1] This appeal concerned the liability of directors of an unlicensed deposit-taking business.

Section 3(1) of the Banking Act 1987 stipulates that:

> '. . . no person shall . . . accept a deposit in the course of carrying on a business which for the purposes of this Act is a deposit-taking business unless that person is an institution for the time being authorised by the Bank [of England] under . . . this Act.'

Section 96(1) stipulates further:

> 'Where an offence under this Act committed by a body corporate is proved to have been committed with the consent or connivance of, or to be attributable to any neglect on the part of any director, manager, secretary or other similar officer of the body corporate, or any person who was purporting to act in any such capacity he, as well as the body corporate is guilty of an offence . . .'

The respondents to this appeal, one of whom was a director and the other a deemed director of an investment and insurance brokerage company, had been charged with consenting to the offence of the carrying on by the company of an unlicensed deposit-taking business in contravention of s 3(1) of the Banking Act 1987. The respondents were completely ignorant of the need for the company to have a licence and the trial judge therefore withdrew the s 3 charges from the jury on the grounds that the respondents could not have the requisite consent:

> '. . . the sole ground upon which I find there is no case to answer is that which was centred on the word 'consent' in section 96(1) of the Banking Act 1987 under which counts 1 and 2 are drawn. It does seem to me that a section 3 offence is indeed a strict liability offence, but that it is made otherwise where it concerns directors or persons purporting to act as directors; that is each of these defendants. In that regard I hold that a particular awareness must be proved, and . . . evidence adduced of a particular awareness of the director . . . including a lack of awareness of authorisation. That lack of awareness of authorisation . . . requires a specific application of the conscious mind to that point . . .'[2]

---

1 *Op cit* at n 1 on p 256.
2 Comments of trial judge extracted in CA judgment at p 978 E–F.

The trial judge thought that the use of the word 'consent' in s 96 of the Banking Act 1987 meant that Parliament required this specific *mens rea* on the part of the director charged, whereas the corporate offence was one of strict liability.

The Attorney-General referred two points of law to the Court of Appeal:

(a) Whether on a charge against a company director of consenting to the acceptance of a deposit contrary to ss 3 and 96 of the Banking Act 1987, ignorance of the law as to the requirement of the authorisation of the Bank of England is a defence; and
(b) What *mens rea* constitutes 'consent'.

To these questions the Court of Appeal answered 'no' to the first and, in respect of the second, held that proof that a defendant knew the material facts which constituted the offence by the body corporate and agreed to its conduct of its business on the basis of those facts gave that defendant sufficient *mens rea* to constitute consent.

The judgment of the Court of Appeal drives home to executive company directors the importance of continually subjecting the way in which they are conducting all the various aspects of their business to critical legal and regulatory audit:

> 'A director who knows that acts which can only be performed by the company if it is licensed by the Bank, are being performed when in fact no licence exists and who consents to that performance is guilty of the offence charged. The fact that he does not know it is an offence to perform them without a licence, i.e. ignorance of the law, is no defence . . . [the] suggestion that the director must have actively addressed his mind to the question of licences is wholly unreal. If the two directors, who were wholly responsible for the company's business activity, were ignorant of the need for a licence it can readily be inferred that they knew they did not have one. The concept of a director who is ignorant of the law requiring a licence, focusing his mind on the question of whether he has or has not obtained one is academic. Had anyone approached the defendant directors and asked: "Have you a licence or authorisation from the Bank of England?" the ready answer would have been "No", probably supplemented by "I did not know I needed one." There would have been no need for a search, an inquiry or a focusing of the mind. Since the question had not occurred to them they would know that the company did not have one.'[1]

What hope for the blissfully ignorant art director?

The Court were at pains to point out that the effect of their ruling on this point was not to create an absolute offence out of s 96(1) in respect of directors:

> 'There could, for example, in a company with a number of directors responsible for different limbs of the company's business, be a director who believed the licence had been obtained and was not therefore consenting to the offences committed by the company.'[2]

---

1 *Per* the Lord Chief Justice at pp 980 H–981 A.
2 *Ibid*, p 981 B.

Thus, the Court of Appeal's analysis leaves room for a degree of exculpation in the case of a large functionally differentiated board of directors for, let us say, the creative art director who believed the necessary licence had been obtained by one of the more technical directorates; he could not be said to be consenting to the commission of the offence. However, what if such a director was just as ignorant of the need for a licence as the managing director and the rest of the board were? This, in fact, would be more likely to be the case in reality since such a director would be more likely to leave all matters of legal compliance to his colleagues. The terms of the Court of Appeal judgment seem to suggest that in this situation (which is, after all, more understandable and even desirable in that it would make for more efficient functioning of the board) then he would not be excused as he could not be said to have 'believed the licence had been obtained . . .' as he too was as ignorant of the law as the rest of the board and was, therefore, just as consenting to the commission of the corporate offence within the meaning of s 96(1) as they were.

The Civil division of the Court of Appeal considered the effect of this type of 'liability of officer' provision in *Richardson v Pitt-Stanley & Others*.[1] Section 5 of the Employers Liability (Compulsory Insurance) Act 1969 imposed criminal liability on any officer of a company who consented or connived, etc. in a company's failure to insure against liability to employees for personal injury. This case concerned an unsuccessful attempt to argue that s 5 also, impliedly, imposed a civil liability on the company's officers who were in contravention of it so that an injured workman could recover damages from such officers. The attempt failed, but the dissenting judgment of Sir John Megaw, who would have allowed for the existence of such a civil remedy, reaffirms that, whereas the corporate statutory liability was absolute, that of the officers under s 5 was not and 'relevant fault' must be proved:

> '. . . in order that the liability should exist, for the purpose of civil proceedings under . . . section 5, it is necessary for the employee to establish that the director in question consented to or connived at the failure to insure, or facilitated that failure by any neglect: in other words, there has to be shown a relevant fault on the part of the individual, other than the mere fact that he has general responsibilities as a director.'[2]

The only 'relevant fault' which the Court of Criminal Appeal has required in *A-G's Reference (No 1 of 1995)* is that the defendant officer be proved to know the material facts which constitute the offence by the body corporate and to have agreed to its conduct of its business on the basis of those facts. This could quite easily cover less immediately involved directors who have only the most general of responsibilities for the area of business in which the corporate offence falls. That might be thought unfair and potentially inefficient in that this interpretation renders all directors potentially criminally liable for matters which are, in practice, far removed from their areas of knowledge, expertise and responsibility. Although the Court of Appeal may not consider its decision here to mean that it is imposing strict liability on such directors those same directors could well be forgiven for thinking that it does, since that is what it would feel like for them.

---

1 [1995] 2 WLR 26.
2 *Ibid*, p 37.

This decision should serve to remind all company directors and officers, no matter what the demarcation of their area of responsibility for the company's business, of the importance of keeping a watching brief on legislative developments that do or could pertain to their company's overall business. Not an easy task for the busy and stretched executive who may, quite justifiably, feel that operating within a functionally differentiated board as he does, he should be able and entitled to rely on those of his fellow directors whose task it is to 'know the law' and secure compliance with it, to do so. Of course, to suggest that the Court of Appeal's decision should have been otherwise and perhaps recognised the reality of the way many boards allocate responsibility amongst their members is to run the risk of fragmenting the legal content of a company director's duties. Moving away from a unitary view of what constitutes a company director's responsibilities, at least for the purposes of applying these officer liability provisions, at first sight may seem to carry with it the danger of a return to the lax amateurism of the days of *The Marquis of Bute's Case*.[1] Another concern might be that if the courts were to take a more subjective view of the *mens rea* needed for these regulatory offences then a board of directors might try to structure itself so that no one single individual on it could ever be said to know sufficient of both the content of applicable regulatory law *and* the operations of the company to assume personal liability for consenting to or conniving in regulatory contraventions. However, it is suggested that the courts should see the chief executive and other senior executive officers as being in such a position, despite what they may claim to the contrary. Such an approach chimes with the view that the regulators themselves are beginning to take (in the financial regulatory sector at least) of 'who should be seen to be responsible for what' when it comes to enforcement of regulatory standards.[2] To put it crudely, the buck has to stop somewhere with a real person, not just a corporate person, for sanctions for regulatory contraventions to have any sting in their tail. But the law ought to try as far as possible to 'sting' the right person, ie someone who actually knew or whose job it was to know about the non-compliance and who can do something about it in the future. To sting the 'wrong' person does not further the regulatory law's goals and will only create a disincentive for certain types of individual and function to be represented at board level which could have deleterious wider and long-term consequences.

Accessory liability provisions vs lifting the corporate veil the old fashioned way

Another very recent decision of relevance and interest in any centenary celebration of *Salomon* is the decision of Carnwath J earlier this year in *Securities*

---

1 [1892] 2 Ch 100. The Marquis of Bute, having inherited the office of President of the Cardiff Savings Bank from his father when he was but six months old, and having attended just one board meeting in 38 years, was held not to be liable for lending irregularities within the bank's operation.

2 A Consultation Document from the Securities and Futures Authority (September 1996) *Proposals to amend Guidance and the Rules in Relation to the Responsibilities of Senior Executive Officers* created a stir of interest in that it sought, post-Barings, to make senior management responsible for compliance failures within their firm whether or not they were directly responsible. The Securities and Investments Board has published Draft Guidance on the Responsibilities of Senior Management (July 1997).

and Investments Board v Scandex Capital Management A/S and Jeremy Bartholomew-White.[1] The decision covered many points on the system of authorisation and enforcement introduced by the Financial Services Act 1986 but what was especially interesting was the SIB's attempts to pierce the corporate veil of the first defendant company in order to fix the second defendant with personal liability for the many and various regulatory contraventions by the first defendant. The first defendant, Scandex Capital Management, ('Scandex'), was a Danish company, now in liquidation, of which the second defendant, Mr Bartholomew-White, was managing director and in which he held one third of the share capital. Scandex had conducted foreign exchange trading for and on behalf of UK investors and had sent mailshots directed at investors into the UK, had made unsolicited calls offering forex trading services and had also made misleading statements about, *inter alia*, the level of commission Scandex was charging its clients. Significant losses were incurred by UK investors as a result of their dealings with Scandex. Scandex had been operating in Denmark on the basis of interim authorisation from Finans (the Danish investment business regulatory authority) under transitional provisions of Danish law implementing the Investment Services Directive ('ISD'), pending Finans' determination of its application for full authorisation to do investment business. This, it was claimed on behalf of the defendants, entitled Scandex to do investment business in the UK under the Euro-passporting provisions of the ISD which are given effect by s 31 of the Financial Services Act 1986. That argument was rejected by the Court, with the effect that the company's investment business was, therefore, unauthorised and in contravention of the Financial Services Act 1986. There were other contraventions of specific regulatory provisions of the Financial Services Act 1986 as well, but the basic one of interest to us was the unauthorised doing of regulated investment business.

The SIB took enforcement proceedings against Mr Bartholomew-White, as well as Scandex, on the basis that he was personally responsible for Scandex' unauthorised investment business because the business of Scandex should be treated as his business by a process of 'lifting the corporate veil' and seeing through it in order for the court to say that it was he, not just the company, who had done unlicensed investment business. Relying on the few and far between case law examples where the courts have characterised companies as mere covers or shams,[2] the SIB argued that Scandex was nothing more than a strategic cloak for Mr Bartholomew-White's illegal forex dealing activities. However, in language which shows what a sea change has occurred over the past 100 years in judicial thinking since the lower courts expressed such suspicion and hostility to companies in *Salomon*, Mr Justice Carnwath ruled that the conditions for lifting the veil of incorporation were not satisfied for the purposes of giving the SIB summary judgment on this point and, indeed, were unlikely to be satisfied at any trial of this issue:

> 'The cases in which the veil has been lifted are generally ones where the company is being used as a means of shifting responsibility from the person (company or indi-

---

1 Unreported: judgment date 26 March 1997.
2 *Gilford Motor Co v Horne* [1933] Ch 935; *Jones v Lipman* [1962] 1 WLR 832; *Re H* [1996] 2 All ER 391.

vidual) who would otherwise be liable or might reasonably be expected to be liable. That element is not present in this case. There was no reason to expect Mr Bartholomew-White to undertake investment business in his own name, and nothing unusual in him doing so through a company. He was fully entitled to organise his affairs in that way. Thus even if it were shown that he was the sole and effective mind of Scandex, I doubt whether that would be sufficient to establish the grounds for lifting the veil. It may well be established that Scandex was set up as a vehicle for avoiding the restrictions on investment business in the UK, but on the facts the restrictions being avoided were those applicable to Euro Currency [Mr Bartholomew-White's previous forex trading company which had been based in London] rather than to Mr Bartholomew-White as an individual. Furthermore it cannot be said that Scandex was clearly "a one man company". Mr Bartholomew-White was a one-third shareholder and only one of the directors. The evidence of the SIB appears to me consistent with the case of a major shareholder who also acts as managing director — a situation which is very common and has never been thought to justify lifting the veil.'

So much for the SIB's attempt to lift the corporate veil in order to make Mr Bartholomew-White liable primarily for contraventions of the FSA 1986, but the SIB had markedly more success with that part of their enforcement action which was based on provisions in the Financial Services Act 1986 which enable action to be taken against those 'knowingly concerned' in various contraventions thereof, including the most basic contravention of all – doing regulated investment business without authorisation.[1] Unfortunately, in the light of the discussion above of the Court of Appeal's decision in *Attorney-General's Reference(No 1 of 1995),* Mr Justice Carnwath did not settle the question of law as to the appropriate standard of knowledge required to establish that a person is 'knowingly concerned' in another's contravention of the Financial Services Act. He did not need to address this question as there was no difficulty in finding that Mr Bartholomew-White was knowingly concerned in Scandex' contraventions that took place after he had been put on notice of them by correspondence he received from the SIB, so on the facts of this case, the provision clearly applied.

Hence, the SIB managed to establish that Mr Bartholomew-White was 'knowingly concerned' in Scandex' contraventions of investor protection legislation, and thus he was made subject to restitutionary orders to be used to compensate investors, although they were unable to establish that he was actually party to the offending transactions and deeds himself, on the basis that company law could not set aside Scandex' corporate veil.

This decision is a neat recent illustration of just how useful these types of accessory/secondary liability provisions are at getting regulation to bite when the rather tight strictures of case-law prevents the lifting of the corporate veil to allow the particular regulatory law through to reach the 'real' perpetrators. If enforcers reach a dead end with an appeal to courts to lift the veil, as is more than likely in most cases, they can often achieve the same result by using these statutory 'officer liability' provisions.

---

1 The court has power to make restitutionary orders against persons 'knowingly concerned' in another's regulatory contraventions under ss 6(2) and 61(1) of the FSA 1986. See Court of Appeal decision in *SIB v Pantell SA* [1993] Ch 256.

PART TWO: RECENT TRENDS IN CORPORATE REGULATORY AND CRIMINAL RESPONSIBILITY

Turning now to the separate but (it is argued) related question 'when is a company liable under a criminal or regulatory provision for the acts of its employees?' This question has spawned some of the most interesting recent appellate decisions[1] and theoretical literature concerned with company law.[2] It is the uneasy co-existence of the doctrine of separate corporate personality and the need to establish *mens rea*/fault on the part of a company in so many criminal and quasi-criminal offences that gives rise to difficulty for the law.

However, as recent appellate case-law has shown, there is nothing immutable about the doctrine in this context and the Law Lords have, recently, subjected it to some sophisticated analysis in decisions dealing with transmission of a company's employees' *mens rea* 'upwards' to fix the company itself with responsibility under regulatory and statutory provisions:[3] the acts of the employee becoming those of the company, liability moving in the opposite direction to that in which it travels under the 'officer liability' provisions considered above — where the liability of the company becomes that of the individual officer, rather than vice versa.

When considering the question of corporate criminal/regulatory responsibility, Lord Hoffmann's reasoning in *Meridian Global Funds Management Asia Ltd v Securities Commission* seems entirely appropriate for the variegated statutory and regulatory age in which companies now do business:

> '. . . given that [the rule in question] was intended to apply to a company, how was it intended to apply? Whose act, (or knowledge or state of mind) was *for this purpose* intended to count as the act etc. of the company? One finds the answer to this question by applying the usual canons of interpretation, taking into account the language of the rule (if it is a statute) and its content and policy.'[4]

This moves us away from an overly simplistic reliance on the 'directing mind and will' approach to the liability of a company for the acts of its employees in *Tesco Supermarkets Ltd v Nattrass*.[5] Organisation theory and practice have certainly moved away from this simple vertical command and control model of how a company functions. In an age of flatter corporate hierarchies, 'empowered' front line employees and devolved decision making, Lord Hoffmann's decision has considerable resonance in the real commercial world.

---

1 *El Ajou v Dollar Holdings plc* [1994] 1 BCLC 464, CA; *Seaboard Offshore Ltd v Secretary of State for Transport* [1994] 2 All ER 99, HL; *Meridian Global Funds Management Asia Ltd v Securities Commission* [1995] 3 WLR 413, PC; *In re Supply of Ready Mixed Concrete (No 2)* [1995] 1 AC 456, HL.

2 See in particular Fisse B and Braithwaite J, *Corporations, Crime and Accountability* (Cambridge University Press, 1993); Wells C, *Corporations and Criminal Responsibility* (Oxford University Press, 1994).

3 See in particular the analysis of Lord Hoffmann in *Meridian Global Funds Management Asia Ltd v Securities Commission* [1995] 2 AC 500; *In re Supply of Ready Mixed Concrete (No 2)* [1995] 1 AC 456.

4 *Per* Lord Hoffmann at p 419 F in *Meridian* (*op cit*). For the facts and an excellent analysis of the *Meridian* decision and the issues raised therein see 'A fresh insight into the corporate criminal mind' Robert-Tissot, Simon, *The Company Lawyer* (1996) Vol 17 No 4 p 99.

5 [1972] AC 153.

A company's actions speak louder than its words

The decision of the House of Lords in *In re Supply of Ready Mixed Concrete (No 2)* is further evidence of this shift away from a formula for determining corporate responsibility based on a simple model of corporate organisation of vertically structured hierarchy with an élite cadre exercising 'Command and Control' and being the only people in the company capable of imbuing it with criminal responsibility. This appeal arose out of breaches of certain injunctions that had been obtained by the Director General of Fair Trading prohibiting further contravention of Restrictive Trade Practices legislation by four companies which were suppliers of ready mixed concrete.

After the original injunctions had been obtained all four companies had adopted compliance systems designed to ensure that there would be no further breaches of the legislation and prohibited their employees from entering into illegal price fixing and market sharing agreements. However, despite the existence of these clear prohibitions, certain employees of the companies continued to meet in local pubs and carve up the Oxfordshire ready mixed concrete market between them, ostensibly on behalf of the companies that employed them. In enforcement and contempt proceedings in the Restrictive Practices Court, three of the companies admitted contempt and pleaded their internal compliance arrangements, which were designed to prevent such illegal arrangements and practices, as mitigation only. The fourth company, however, denied contempt, relying on its compliance prohibitions as a defence and disowning the actions of its non-compliant employee who, without the company's knowledge or authority, purported to make it party to the illegal arrangements. This argument did not impress the Restrictive Practices Court but succeeded in the Court of Appeal and, as a consequence, two of the other companies which had at first admitted their contempt sought and obtained leave to appeal the original orders of the Restrictive Practices Court. These appeals were also successful and it was against that decision of the Court of Appeal that the Director General of Fair Trading appealed successfully to the Lords.

The comments of Lord Templeman are especially significant in the context of the present discussion of what the limits of corporate responsibility for the acts of its employees should be:

> 'The decisions of the Court of Appeal [in these two appeals] infringe two principles. The first principle is that a company is an entity separate from its members but, not being a physical person is only capable of acting by its agents. The second principle is that a company, in its capacity as supplier of goods, like any other person in the capacity of taxpayer, landlord or in any other capacity, falls to be judged by its actions and not by its language. An employee who acts for the company within the scope of his employment is the company. Directors may give instructions, top management may exhort, middle management may question and workers may listen attentively. But if a worker makes a defective product or a lower manager accepts or rejects an order, he is the company.'[1]

Companies are not protected from legal responsibility for the acts of their employees by the existence of quality control and preventative compliance

---

1 *Per* Lord Templeman at p 465 D–E.

systems designed to ensure that all employees act in such a way that legislation and regulation are never infringed. No matter how seemingly watertight and superior those controls are — if someone within the company subverts them and takes the company outside the law the company cannot escape ultimate responsibility by pleading that it tried its best and its preventative systems ought to have worked. The simple fact is they did not, and the task of the law here is to punish effective non-compliance no matter from where it was generated within the company.

Lord Nolan makes this clear:

> 'The [Restrictive Practices] Act is not concerned with what the employer says but with what the employee does in entering into business transactions in the course of his employment. The plain purpose of section 35(3) is to deter the implementation of agreements or arrangements by which the public interest is harmed, and the subsection can only achieve that purpose if it is applied to the actions of the individuals within the business organisation who make or give effect to the relevant agreement or arrangement on its behalf.

> This necessarily leads to the conclusion that if such an agreement is found to have been made without the knowledge of the employer, any steps which the employer has taken to prevent it from being made will rank only as mitigation. Liability can only be escaped by completely effective preventive measures.'[1]

'By your deeds ye shall be judged' is the clear message to companies from both this decision and that of the Privy Council in *Meridian Global Funds Management Asia Ltd v Securities Commission*, with a much wider category of natural persons within the company now being seen to constitute the legal person of the company for the purposes of the company's responsibility under statutory and regulatory offences and controls. Although Lord Templeman's view of corporate organisation, as evinced by his words extracted above, is open to the criticism that it remains wedded to an overly simplistic vertical hierarchy based on 'Command and Control' theories of business functions, at least the result of his decision is to recognise that the real '*de facto*' ability of a company to evade or break external legal controls resides as often as not at the interface between the company and the public (in the case of consumer protection legislation), or the environment (in the case of environmental protection legislation), or the factory floor (in the case of health and safety legislation). These places are exactly where the law is designed to protect and regulate the company's business and are often a very long way, in terms of the corporate culture and power structure, from the head office, where supposedly preventative compliance systems are promulgated.

It therefore seems entirely appropriate that the law on corporate responsibility has been moved along in this way from the position in *Tesco Supermarkets Ltd v Nattrass*. The fictitious separate corporate person must now take responsibility for its employees' acts where its own systems of controlling those employees have failed. This may, indeed, seem harsh and the law should, of course, always be alive to the risks of designing its liability rules in such a way as to provide a gross disincentive to businesses to continue operating. Lord Nolan acknowledges this, but tosses the remedy into the lap of the legislature:

---

1 *Per* Lord Nolan at p 475 B–C.

'How great a burden of the devising of such [completely effective] preventive measures will cast upon individual employers will depend upon the size and nature of the particular organisation. There are, of course, many areas of business life, not only in the consumer protection field, where it has become necessary for employers to devise strict compliance procedures. If the burden is in fact intolerable then the remedy must be for Parliament to introduce a statutory defence for those who can show that they have taken all reasonable preventive measures.'[1]

In the current climate of visible failures of compliance systems — particularly in the emotive and politically damaging area of retail financial services[2] — it would be very surprising indeed if Parliament were to even consider introducing such an exculpatory defence for companies whose control systems fail.

The company as victim

The artifice of separate corporate personality is also laid bare when one considers the company as 'victim' rather than 'perpetrator'. One is forced to ask questions like 'did the company know X or was it deceived as to X?' in the context of deception and fraud offences for deception operates on the state of mind of its victim and of course ascertaining what and where is the mind of a company, as opposed to a natural person, is no easy task. Ascertaining where the corporate criminal mind is and what is going on inside that mind for the purposes of the company's responsibility under criminal and regulatory offences has created the exciting case-law we have just considered. The decision of the Court of Appeal in *R v Rozeik*[3] raises some of the same questions but in the direct converse situation — it concerns the company as victim rather than the company as perpetrator: Of all the various actors, who go to make up a company, whose knowledge should be attributed to the company for the purposes of its being said to be ignorant of or *sciens* to a deception? It is a truism to say that the same question of legal principle posed in different litigation contexts often yields different answers, and the decision in *R v Rozeik* bears that out.

The factual background to the appeal in *R v Rozeik* was commonplace enough. The defendant had been convicted of obtaining by deception cheques from finance companies, contrary to s 15 of the Theft Act 1968. It was alleged that the defendant had made dishonest applications for funds to finance companies using false information and false invoices relating to equipment hire-purchase agreements. However, the prosecution accepted that the branch managers of the finance companies may not have been deceived, indeed they were probably aware that the defendant's representations were false. There was, however, no evidence put forward by the prosecution to show that the branch managers were acting in any way dishonestly or could be said to be a party to the defendant's fraud. At the defendant's trial, the judge had directed the jury to ignore the effect of the state of mind of these branch managers when deciding the question of whether or not the companies were deceived, for the judge told the

---

1 *Per* Lord Nolan at p 475 D–E.
2 Witness the mis-selling of personal pensions; Jardine Flemings's failure to control their Hong Kong fund manager, Mr Colin Armstrong, and his breaches of regulation at the expense of several Flemings unit trust funds; Morgan Grenfell's recent failure of controls vis-à-vis unit trust management.
3 [1996] 1 *WLR* 159.

jury to assume simply that the branch managers knew that the information supplied was false. He went further and directed that, quite apart from the branch managers, if *any* other employee or employees within the companies were deceived by the false invoices into doing something which resulted in cheques being obtained by the defendant then that was sufficient to find him guilty of 'obtaining by deception' from the companies.

The defendant appealed against his conviction under s 15 of the Theft Act 1968, basing his appeal on two grounds. The first ground was that the judge had misdirected the jury on the point of which persons within a company constituted the company's state of mind for the purposes of its being deceived. The judge was wrong to decide that persons within a company other than those responsible for making decisions to authorise the respective transactions were persons who could be deceived and whose deception could be attributed to the company, for the purposes of s 15 of the Theft Act 1968. The second ground of appeal was that the trial judge had also been wrong to direct the jury to ignore the relevance of the fact that the branch managers most likely knew of the defendant's deception. In making that direction in those terms, the judge was, effectively, inviting the jury to assume the managers had acted dishonestly and were a party to the defendant's fraud. This, the defendant argued in his appeal, was a matter for the prosecution to prove (something it had not sought to do), not something that the jury should be invited to assume. So, since the branch managers' likely knowledge should not have been ignored by the jury, the defendant argued that it should be imputed to the companies which, therefore, could not be said to have been deceived for the purposes of s 15 of the Theft Act 1968.

The Court of Appeal allowed the defendant's appeal, Lord Justice Leggatt giving the judgment of the court. Counsel for the defendant summarised his contention on attribution of knowledge for the purposes of a company being deceived thus:

> '. . . where one employee is deceived by a representation but either the true position or the falsity of the representation is known to another employee in a position of equality or superiority to the employee deceived the company cannot be said to have been deceived . . . The offence is committed against the company, and not the individual employee, so if the company is fixed with knowledge of the true position it is not deceived.'[1]

This question, obviously, needed to be examined in the light of *In re Supply of Ready Mixed Concrete (No 2)*; and *Meridian Global Funds Management Asia Ltd v Securities Commission*, since they both concerned the attribution of acts and knowledge of its employees to a company in order to fix it with liability as a perpetrator; and the Court of Appeal was now seised of the exact converse situation. So, the Court of Appeal asked: 'whose state of mind represented the state of mind of the company for the purpose of ascertaining whether it had been deceived into entering into the hire-purchase agreements?' The answer was, evidently, the relevant branch managers *whose job it was* to process and approve these loan transactions. Nor could their knowledge that the invoices were false be attributed to the company, for if it could, then the company could not possibly have been said to have been deceived and the appeal must succeed.

---

1 *Per* Leggatt LJ at p 162 A–B.

The Court of Appeal ruled that the trial judge was wrong to direct the jury to ignore the branch managers' knowledge and it agreed with the defendant's argument that such a direction should only have been made if the prosecution had proved that the managers were acting dishonestly and were privy to the fraud. Lord Justice Leggatt explained the reason for the doctrine that the dishonest knowledge of a company's officers cannot be attributed to the company:

> 'The reason why the company is not visited with the manager's knowledge is that the same individual cannot both be party to the deception and represent the company for the purpose of its being deceived. Unless therefore it was proved that the managers were party to the fraud, with the result that their knowledge can be disregarded, their knowledge must be imputed to the companies, and the fact that other employees were deceived could not avail the companies.'[1]

The Court of Appeal also made some interesting comments on the defendant's contention that the trial judge had been wrong to direct that the deception of 'any' employee within the company would suffice to constitute the deception of the company. The court focused on the meaning of the word 'obtained' in s 15 of the Theft Act 1968. Who exactly was the cheque obtained from? The Court of Appeal said it was not correct to say that the cheque had been 'obtained', in this sense, from a typist or an employee who had a mere clerical role in the process, but rather cheques could be obtained in the s 15 sense only from those who 'had a responsibility to ensure that the cheques were not signed unless satisfied that the money should be paid',[2] in other words, the signatories of the cheques. 'Who signed the cheques?' thus becomes a crucial question in a case like this one where the branch managers were most probably party to the fraud. If it was an accomplice manager alone who signed then there could not be said to be any obtaining by deception, but if an 'innocent' signatory also had to sign the cheque then it was possible to say that the cheque was obtained by deception. So, where the cheques which were the subject of the indictment had been signed by the branch managers alone, the defendant's conviction was most certainly bad and even where the cheques were signed by other 'innocent' employees or co-signed by a manager with another 'innocent' employee, the fact that the trial judge's direction to the jury had been overly wide — in that he said it was enough if '*any employee*' was deceived (and had therefore failed to focus the jury on the state of mind of the signatory) — this meant that the convictions in relation to those other co-signed cheques were unreliable too. Hence, all of the defendant's convictions under s 15 were quashed.

Should the law develop a different rule of attribution of knowledge to cover the 'company as victim' situation to that which now prevails in the 'company as perpetrator' situation? Lord Justice Leggatt explored this interesting and important question in this appeal:

> 'Whether or not a company is fixed with the knowledge acquired by an employee or officer will depend on the circumstances. It is necessary first to identify whether the individual in question has the requisite status and authority in relation to the act or omission in point: *El Ajou v Dollar Holdings plc* [1994] 2 All ER 685. It follows from this that information given to a particular employee, however senior, may not

---

1 *Per* Leggatt LJ at p 164 F–G.
2 At p 165 H.

be attributed to the company if that employee is not empowered to act in relation to that particular transaction. An employee who acts for the company within the scope of his employment will usually bind the company since he *is* the company for the purposes of the transaction in question: see per Lord Templeman in *In re Supply of Ready Mixed Concrete* [1995] 1 AC 456. The company may be liable to third parties or be guilty of criminal offences even though that employee was acting dishonestly or against the interests of the company or contrary to orders. But different considerations apply where the company is the victim, and the employee's activities have caused or assisted the company to suffer loss . . . In cases in which the company is the victim the person or persons who stand for its state of mind may differ from those who do so in cases in which a company is charged with the commission of a criminal offence. The latter are less likely to represent what Viscount Haldane LC in *Lennard's Carrying Co Ltd v Asiatic Petroleum Co Ltd* [1915] AC 705 called "the directing mind and will" of the company.'[1]

The range of employees and officers of a company who are able, in law, to make a victim of the company is therefore more restricted than those who are able by their acts, statements or omissions to constitute it a perpetrator. This appears to be a conclusion we can safely draw from the juxtaposition of this appeal with the recent decisions in *Meridian Global Funds Management Asia Ltd* and *In re supply of Ready Mixed Concrete*. But what is especially interesting about what the Court of Appeal did in *Rozeik* was that it looked into the company's internal organisation and asked what were the functions and responsibilities of its various officers and employees and it then took those into account in designing an attribution of knowledge rule which would make sense of the particular offence of deceiving a company. Although the court framed a narrower attribution rule than the House of Lords did in *In re Supply of Ready Mixed Concrete* and than Lord Hoffmann did in *Meridian,* the really important thing to note was that the courts, in all three of these cases, were unafraid to examine the internal workings of the company and ask who did what within the company? and what was the purpose of the legal rule in question? Having ascertained answers to those questions, then and only then did they go on to frame an attribution rule that gave the law in question efficacy and real meaning.

CONCLUSION

How are these two separate strands, considered in Parts One and Two, related to each other? What has corporate criminal and regulatory responsibility (and its flipside of corporate victimhood) got to do with the problem of interpretation of officer liability provisions? In dealing with the former question, the courts have demonstrated recently a greater sensitivity and surer feel for the realities of the way statutory regulatory controls actually impact upon the corporate organisation. They have formulated legal principles of responsibility in such a fashion as to give legal controls maximum efficacy and have given management the strongest possible incentive to make compliance systems substantively effective rather than simply literally correct. This 'effects centred' approach could be imported usefully by courts faced with the

---

1 Pp 164 B–C, 165 D.

problems of deciding whether an ignorant company director has the requisite *mens rea* for secondary responsibility for the illegal acts of the company under an officer liability provision. A re-examination of the comments of Lord Hoffmann in *Meridian Global Funds Management Asia Ltd v Securities Commission,* extracted above, reveals that he sees as integral to the process of ascertaining whose act/knowledge/state of mind is to be attributed to the company for the purposes of determining its responsibility under XYZ law the need also to ask the questions — what is XYZ law there to do? what policy objective is it designed to achieve? what effect is it supposed to have on the way in which companies do business? Therefore, if we flip this reasoning over and apply it to the questions tested in *A-G's Reference (No 1 of 1995),* it may point the way to a fairer basis for deciding what degree of fault or *mens rea* will suffice to render an officer liable for the offence of his company. The content of and policy behind the statutory corporate offence that is being visited upon an officer could first be examined. Then the extent of the knowledge or ignorance of the state of the company's affairs which constitute the offence that is possessed by the officer charged would be assessed. If, given the content and policy of the particular corporate offence, it is reasonable and efficient for the officer charged to leave all questions of legal compliance in the relevant area of the company's business to another officer or officers then he should not be said to be consenting to the offence simply by virtue of the fact that he knew the company's business was being conducted in a particular way. Surely, it is about time company law began to recognise the realities of doing business in an ever-changing regulatory age and that the way in which it attributes liability to officers should recognise the way in which those officers attribute tasks and responsibilities amongst themselves.

Chapter 14

CONTRACTING WITH INDIVIDUAL DIRECTORS

Brenda Hannigan[1]

INTRODUCTION

Many company law reform initiatives have taken place in the past decade with the topics covered ranging from accounting formats and audit exemptions for small companies to the implementation of CREST and public offer regulations, to single member private companies, elective regimes and de-regulation.[2] Much attention has been paid to corporate governance, with the publication of the Cadbury and Greenbury Reports,[3] while the Law Commission has published reports and consultation papers on involuntary (including corporate) manslaughter and shareholder remedies.[4] The driving force behind all this activity has been a rapidly changing business world, yet despite this it is necessary to go back to 1989 for the last major reforming statute, in the form of the Companies Act of that year, which addressed such diverse areas as accounts and auditors, investigation powers, *ultra vires* and the authority of the board. Many of the reforming measures, over the years, have been designed to de-regulate smaller companies and to improve standards in larger ones. Overall, the aim has been to provide a modern legal framework for the one million businesses which operate as registered companies. Business requires that the law should be clear and accessible; it should be readily understood; it should be certain in its application and, in particular, it should offer security to those third parties who deal with registered companies in millions of transactions each year. It is with this last issue that this essay is concerned, namely the security of third parties when contracting with a company, most specifically when they contract with an individual director who purports to bind the company.

This issue of the security of third parties contracting with a company was addressed, in part, by the Companies Act 1989 in the reforms (now contained in the Companies Act 1985, ss 35 and 35A) relating to the *ultra vires* doctrine and the authority of the board.

Section 35 ensures that a third party is immune from any challenge to a transaction based on any limitations on the company's capacity. In practice, this reform is

---

1 Reader in Corporate Law, University of Southampton.
2 For details of reforms over the past decade see the DTI's annual report each year to Parliament, the most recent being *Companies in 1996–97* (HMSO).
3 *Report of the Committee on the Financial Aspects of Corporate Governance (1992)* (the Cadbury Committee); *Directors' Remuneration*, Report of a Study Group chaired by Sir Richard Greenbury (1995); see also the Preliminary Report of the Committee on Corporate Governance (the Hampel Committee).
4 Law Commission *Legislating the Criminal Code: Involuntary Manslaughter* Law Com No 237 (1996); Law Commission *Shareholder Remedies* Consultation Paper No 142 (1996); Law Com No 246 (1997).

largely irrelevant as the width of most company's objects clauses means that it is extremely unusual now for a transaction to be *ultra vires* in the first place. Furthermore, the Companies Act 1989 has also made it easier for companies to alter their objects clauses[1] and companies can adopt an object which simply states that the company is to carry on business as a general commercial company.[2]

As a corollary to the *ultra vires* issue, s 35A dealt with the important issue of the authority of the board. It provided that, in favour of a person dealing with a company in good faith, the power of the board of directors to bind the company, or authorise others to do so, was deemed to be free of any limitation under the company's constitution.[3] The statutory provisions then ensure that it is very difficult for a person to be in bad faith.[4] In practice, this reform too is less significant than might initially appear. The drafting of modern management articles in the common form of article 70 of Table A means that all powers of management are vested in the board with very limited powers retained by the company in general meeting and so it is unlikely that a third party will be hindered, in any event, by any lack of authority in the board.

What the reforms did not address was the position of the third party who deals with an individual director whom the company subsequently asserts had no authority to enter into the disputed transaction. The solution to that problem lies not in the statute but in agency and in finding that the individual did have actual or apparent authority to contract on behalf of the company.

ACTUAL AUTHORITY

A company director may have express or implied actual authority. Express actual authority arises from an explicit conferring of authority on a director. This might be done with respect to a particular transaction and may be evidenced by formal board resolutions. As we shall see below, an individual director may find it advantageous to seek to have express authority conferred upon him explicitly in this way, as this may resolve subsequent internal disputes as to where authority lies with respect to a particular matter.

Implied actual authority arises from the position which the individual holds, but no implied authority will spring from the position of director as such, for an individual director has no authority to act outside of the collective board.[5] However, if an individual director is appointed to a position such as that of managing director then implied authority will authorise him to do all such things as fall within the usual scope of that office.

---

1 See CA 1985, s 4 substituted by CA 1989, s 110.
2 See CA 1985, s 3A inserted by CA 1989, s 110.
3 CA 1985, s 35A(1) inserted by CA 1989, s 108.
4 A person is presumed to have acted in good faith unless the contrary is proved: CA 1985, s 35A(2)(c); a person is not to be regarded as acting in bad faith by reason *only* of his knowing that an act is beyond the powers of the directors under the company's constitution: s 35A(2)(b); and a party to a transaction with a company is not bound to enquire as to whether it is permitted by the company's memorandum or as to any limitation on the powers of the board to bind the company or authorise others to do so: s 35B.
5 *Re Haycraft Gold Reduction and Mining Co* [1900] 2 Ch 230.

The leading authority is *Hely-Hutchinson v Brayhead Ltd*,[1] where the company chairman also acted as its de facto managing director and entered into contracts on the company's behalf on his own initiative. He subsequently reported them to the board which acquiesced in this practice. Litigation ensued when the board refused to honour an undertaking which the director had given on behalf of the company to a third party to indemnify the third party against certain losses and to guarantee the repayment of certain funds.

The Court of Appeal found that the director lacked express actual authority. Also, there was no implied actual authority on the basis of his post as chairman of the company as that office, of itself, did not carry the authority to enter into contracts without the sanction of the board. However, as the de facto managing director, he did have implied actual authority authorising him to do all such things as fell within the usual scope of that office. This would be implied from the circumstance that the board, by their conduct over many months, had acquiesced in his acting as managing director and committing the company to contracts without the necessity of sanction from the board.[2] The business of the company involved taking over other companies and operations of that kind were undertaken by this de facto managing director. Indemnities and guarantees of the type in issue were an integral element of such transactions. It was, therefore, within the usual scope of the office in that company for the managing director to commit the company to a third party in this way.[3]

The usual scope of the office of managing director

On the facts, it was clear in that case that the transaction did fall within the usual scope of the office. In general, however, how do we identify the usual scope of the position of managing director? It would extend, presumably, to all the usual range of business matters appropriate to a person in that position, but this does not advance the debate. If we were to consider particular matters, such as the power to hire and fire employees; to transfer shares; to borrow money; to make acquisitions and disposals; to give guarantees and indemnities; and to initiate litigation, and then to ask whether those powers are clearly within the usual scope of the office of managing director, the answer may not be clear-cut. It has been said that the office extends only to the commercial business of the company and so share transfers, for example, would not be within the usual scope.[4] On the other hand, acquisitions and disposals are clearly commercial matters, but would they always fall within the usual scope of the office or would it depend on the scale of the acquisition or disposal and the practice in the particular company?

Harold Holdsworth & Co v Caddies[5] would support the view that there is no usual scope to the office and it is a matter for each company to decide. The position will vary from company to company, depending on the size of the business, with the functions to be performed depending on the way in which a particular

---

1 [1968] 1 QB 549, [1967] 3 All ER 98, CA.
2 [1968] 1 QB 549 at 584, [1967] 3 All ER 98 at 103, CA.
3 [1968] 1 QB 549 at 587–588, [1967] 3 All ER 98 at 104–105.
4 See *George Whitechurch Ltd v Cavanagh* [1902] AC 117.
5 [1955] 1 All ER 725, [1955] 1 WLR 352.

business is organised.[1] This difficulty in identifying the usual scope of the office may mean that, factually, it will be easier to assert and establish the existence of apparent authority (discussed below) rather than to establish that there is implied actual authority. The tendency to resort to apparent authority, in such circumstances, also means that the courts have had limited opportunities to identify the usual scope of the office.

A case which might suggest that the usual scope of the office is actually rather limited is *Mitchell & Hobbs (UK) Ltd v Mill*.[2] The company, in this case, was a small private company with two directors, R (the managing director) and P. The shareholders were R (66%), P (17%) and M (17%). M was also the company secretary. R fell out with P and M and initiated an action on behalf of the company against M for the return of £3,900 which M had withdrawn from the company's bank account. M stated that he had withdrawn the money to protect it from being dissipated by R in breach of his duties to the company. M applied to have the action struck out.

The company's articles were in the form of Table A, article 70 which vests all powers to manage the business in the board subject to any directions by special resolution of the company in general meeting. The articles also contained Table A, article 72 which allows the directors to delegate to any managing director such of their powers as they consider desirable to be exercised by him.

The court found that no directions had been given to the board by the general meeting under article 70 and, therefore, the management of the company was vested in the board. *Breckland Group Holdings Ltd v London & Suffolk Properties Ltd*[3] has confirmed that the initiation of litigation in the company's name is a matter of business and as such falls within the ambit of the board's powers under article 70.[4] It followed that R had no authority to initiate litigation under article 70.

It was also argued that a managing director, *ex virtute officii*, had the power to institute proceedings. The court agreed that:

> '... as reg 72 makes clear, in a particular case the managing director may have powers over and above those enjoyed by his co-directors because they may have delegated those powers to him and, if they have done, so be it.'[5]

However, on the facts there was no delegation of power to the managing director and, therefore, article 72 did not assist R.

Initially, this might seem a rather curious outcome. A managing director is found to have no powers over and above those of his co-directors unless powers are expressly delegated to him under article 72. This would seem to run counter to commercial reality and the practice which has developed over the years of regarding a managing director as having authority to manage the business which is almost co-extensive with that of the board.

1 See *Bishopsgate Investment Management Ltd v Maxwell (No 2)* [1994] 1 All ER 261 at 264, [1993] BCLC 1282 at 1285.
2 [1996] 2 BCLC 102.
3 [1989] BCLC 100.
4 This case ended speculation on this issue based on *Marshall's Valve Gear Co Ltd v Manning Wardle & Co Ltd* [1909] 1 Ch 267.
5 [1996] 2 BCLC 102 at 108.

The important distinction which must be drawn, however, is between internal divisions of power (ie between the general meeting and the board and between the board and individual directors) and external issues such as the authority of a managing director to contract with third parties. The power to initiate litigation is a management power which, under the articles, is vested in the board. This means that the board, collectively, must undertake the action on behalf of the company.[1] As Deputy Judge Anthony Machin QC noted, the possibility of each of a board of 24 directors, if such was the case, being able to initiate litigation would give rise to such a plurality of litigation that article 70 could not be interpreted in that way.[2]

There is, therefore, no power in an individual director, whether the managing director or any other director, to initiate litigation in the company name. Hence the importance, noted above, of granting the director express actual authority if it is desired to give him any specific internal authority. Of course, it may be unrealistic to expect such formality in small companies of the type involved in *Mitchell & Hobbs (UK) Ltd v Mill*[3] but, in the absence of such express authority, the power to act on behalf of the company remains vested in the collective board.

This is not to say, however, that the decision in *Mitchell & Hobbs (UK) Ltd v Mill*[3] has unduly diminished the status of a managing director, for whatever the internal constraints, a managing director will, externally, possess very wide implied actual or apparent authority to act on behalf of the company and a third party will be affected by those constraints only where he knows or is put on inquiry as to any limitations (discussed below).

APPARENT AUTHORITY

The *locus classicus* on apparent authority, as far as company directors are concerned, is the judgment of Diplock LJ in *Freeman and Lockyer v Buckhurst Park Properties (Mangal) Ltd*,[4] where he identified the following key elements which must be present before a company can be bound by the acts of an agent who has no actual authority.

It must be shown:

'(a) that a representation that the agent had authority to enter on behalf of the company into a contract of the kind sought to be enforced was made to the contractor;

(b) that such representation was made by a person or persons who had "actual" authority to manage the business of the company either generally or in respect of those matters to which the contract relates;

---

1 Exceptionally, a shareholder may undertake an action derivatively on behalf of the company where the wrongdoers control the company and the action can be brought within the fraud on the minority exception to the rule in *Foss v Harbottle* (1843) 2 Hare 461. As to the rule in *Foss v Harbottle* and its exceptions, see *Palmer's Company Law* (25th edn, 1992) para 8.806 *et seq.*

2 *Mitchell & Hobbs (UK) Ltd v Mill* [1996] 2 BCLC 102 at 108.

3 1996] 2 BCLC 102.

4 [1964] 2 QB 480, [1964] 1 All ER 630, CA. See Milman & Evans 'Corporate Officers and the Outsider Protection Regime' (1985) 6 *Company Lawyer* 68.

(c) that he (the contractor) was induced by such representation to enter into the contract, that is, that he in fact relied upon it; and

(d) that under its memorandum or articles of association the company was not deprived of the capacity either to enter into a contract of the kind sought to be enforced or to delegate authority to enter into a contract of that kind to the agent.'[1]

To some extent, the statutory reforms, noted above, have diminished the significance of the fourth requirement identified by Diplock LJ, above. Limitations on the company's capacity are no longer relevant in respect of an act done by the company following the enactment of CA 1985, s 35 abolishing the *ultra vires* doctrine as far as third parties are concerned, while limitations on the board's power to delegate are no longer relevant, following CA 1985, s 35A. Notwithstanding the statutory reforms, apparent authority cannot be relied upon, however, where the third party is aware of some limitation which prevents the individual's authority arising, or is put on inquiry as to the extent of the individual's authority.[2] Furthermore, the doctrine of constructive notice has not been abolished (despite the inclusion of a provision to that effect in the Companies Act 1989[3]) and so third parties are affected with knowledge of the company's constitution which may restrict (although it is unlikely) the apparent authority of an individual director.[4] Equally, the 1989 reforms did not affect the indoor management rule in *Royal British Bank v Turquand*[5] and this may assist a third party by allowing them (where there has been a holding out of a director by someone with authority) to assume that there has been compliance with all matters of 'indoor management'.

The authority of an agent

Apparent (or ostensible) authority is then the authority of an agent as it appears to others[6] and it can operate both to enlarge actual authority[6] and to create authority where no actual authority exists.[7] For apparent authority to arise, the

---

1 [1964] 2 QB 480 at 505, [1964] 1 All ER 630 at 646. See Brown 'The Agent's Apparent Authority: Paradigm or Paradox' (1995) *JBL* 360 who criticises this approach as inappropriate to today's dynamic corporate commerce.

2 *A L Underwood Ltd v Bank of Liverpool* [1924] 1 KB 775, CA; *B Liggett (Liverpool) Ltd v Barclays Bank Ltd* [1928] 1 KB 48; *Morris v Kanssen* [1946] AC 459, [1946] 1 All ER 586, HL; *Rolled Steel Products (Holdings) Ltd v British Steel Corpn* [1986] Ch 246, [1985] 3 All ER 52. CA 1985, s 35B which frees a third party from any obligation to enquire, does not assist the third party in this instance, since it only applies with respect to limitations on the powers of the board of directors to bind the company or authorise others to do so.

3 CA 1989, s 142 (inserting s 711A in CA 1985) has not been brought into force.

4 *Ernest v Nicholls* (1857) 6 HL Cas 401. Constructive notice can only operate negatively to cut down an authority which might otherwise appear to exist; it cannot be used to support an authority of which the third party was unaware: *Rama Corpn Ltd v Proved Tin and General Investments Ltd* [1952] 2 QB 147, [1952] 1 All ER 554; *Houghton & Co v Nothard, Lowe & Wills* [1927] 1 KB 246.

5 (1856) E & B 327; although it is unnecessary now, in the light of the statutory reforms noted above, for a third party to rely on it in many cases. See also *Mahony v East Holyford Mining Co* (1875) LR 7 HL 869.

6 See *Hely-Hutchinson v Brayhead Ltd* [1968] 1 QB 549 at 583, [1967] 3 All ER 98 at 102, *per* Lord Denning.

7 See *First Energy (UK) Ltd v Hungarian International Bank Ltd* [1993] BCLC 1409.

agent must have been held out by someone with actual authority to carry out the transaction. An agent cannot hold himself out as having authority, for our law does not recognise the self-authorising agent.[1] The acts of the principal must constitute a representation that the agent had a particular authority and must be reasonably so understood by the third party[2] who relied on the representation in entering into the contract.[3] In determining whether the principal had represented his agent as having authority to enter into the particular transaction, the court will consider the totality of the principal's conduct.[4]

The commonest form of holding out is permitting the agent to act in the conduct of the principal's business[5] and, in many cases, the holding out consists solely of the fact that the company has invested the agent with a particular office, eg 'managing director' or 'secretary'.[6]

> 'In the commonly encountered case, the ostensible authority is general in character, arising when the principal has placed the agent in a position which in the outside world is generally regarded as carrying authority to enter into transactions of the kind in question. Ostensible general authority may also arise where the agent has had a course of dealing with a particular contractor and the principal has acquiesced in the course of dealing and honoured transactions arising out of it.'[7]

In *Freeman and Lockyer v Buckhurst Park Properties (Mangal) Ltd*,[8] the director in question managed the company's property and acted on its behalf and, in that role, employed the plaintiff architects to draw up plans for the development of land held by the company. The development ultimately collapsed and the plaintiffs sued the company for their fees. The company denied that the director had any authority to employ the architects.

The court found that, while he had never been appointed managing director (and therefore had no actual authority, express or implied), his actions were within his apparent authority and the board had been aware of his conduct and had acquiesced in it.[9]

1 *Freeman and Lockyer v Buckhurst Park Properties (Mangal) Ltd* [1964] 2 QB 480, [1964] 1 All ER 630, CA; *British Bank of the Middle East v Sun Life Assurance Co of Canada (UK) Ltd* [1983] BCLC 78, [1983] 2 Lloyd's Rep 9, HL; *Armagas Ltd v Mundogas SA* [1986] AC 717, [1986] 2 All ER 385, HL.
2 *Egyptian International Foreign Trade Co v Soplex Wholesale Supplies Ltd, The Raffaella* [1985] BCLC 404 at 411, [1985] 2 Lloyd's Rep 36 at 41, CA, *per* Browne-Wilkinson V-C.
3 *Rama Corpn Ltd v Proved Tin and General Investments Ltd* [1952] 2 QB 147, [1952] 1 All ER 554; *Freeman and Lockyer v Buckhurst Park Properties (Mangal) Ltd* [1964] 2 QB 480, [1964] 1 All ER 630.
4 *Egyptian International Foreign Trade Co v Soplex Wholesale Supplies Ltd, The Raffaella* [1985] BCLC 404 at 411–412, [1985] 2 Lloyd's Rep 36 at 41, CA.
5 *Freeman and Lockyer v Buckhurst Park Properties (Mangal) Ltd* [1964] 2 QB 480 at 505, [1964] 1 All ER 630 at 645, *per* Diplock LJ.
6 *Egyptian International Foreign Trade Co v Soplex Wholesale Supplies Ltd, The Raffaella* [1985] BCLC 404 at 411, [1985] 2 Lloyd's Rep 36 at 41, CA, *per* Browne-Wilkinson V-C. In *Panorama Developments (Guildford) Ltd v Fidelis Furnishing Fabrics Ltd* [1971] 2 QB 711, [1971] 3 All ER 16, the company secretary, as the chief administrative officer of the company, was found to have apparent authority to enter into contracts connected with the administrative side of the company's affairs.
7 *Armagas Ltd v Mundogas SA (The Ocean Frost)* [1986] AC 717 at 777, [1986] 2 All ER 385 at 389, *per* Lord Keith.
8 [1964] 2 QB 480, [1964] 1 All ER 630, CA.
9 [1964] 2 QB 480 at 509–510, [1964] 1 All ER 630 at 648.

Distinction between categories of authority

As is clear from comparing the decisions in *Hely-Hutchinson v Brayhead Ltd*[1] (implied actual authority) and *Freeman and Lockyer v Buckhurst Park Properties (Mangal) Ltd*[2] (apparent authority), it is difficult to distinguish between these categories of authority.[3] As Diplock LJ explained in *Freeman and Lockyer*, actual authority is a legal relationship between principal and agent created by a consensual agreement to which they alone are parties, while apparent authority is a legal relationship between the principal and contractor created by the representation made by the principal to the contractor; and to that relationship the agent is a stranger.[4] The distinction, essentially, is between authority arising from the relationship between the principal and agent (as in *Hely-Hutchinson*) and authority arising from the relationship as the principal allows it to appear to third parties.[5] In the company context, there may be considerable overlap between the two categories with both, possibly, arising from the position held by the individual director.

Dealing with individual or de facto directors

The combined effect of the decisions in *Hely-Hutchinson v Brayhead Ltd*[6] and *Freeman and Lockyer v Buckhurst Park Properties (Mangal) Ltd*[7] is to ensure that a managing director has extensive authority as far as third parties are concerned either through implied actual authority or apparent authority. However, a third party may wish or need to rely on an individual director who is not the managing director: the bank may deal with the finance director; the garage with the transport director; the computer supplier with the marketing director; indeed, a third party may deal with someone who turns out to be a de facto director, ie someone not validly appointed as a director at all but someone held out as a director by the company.[8]

The issue is whether third parties are able to assert that authority has arisen in each of these cases. There is no implied actual authority arising from a position held, for the director holds no position in these cases unless the courts undertake to identify the usual scope of the office of the transport director, or the finance director, or the personnel director in the same way as they have done with respect to the position of managing director. They may well be willing to do so, recognising that changing business practices have created executive

---

1 [1968] 1 QB 549, [1967] 3 All ER 98.

2 [1964] 2 QB 480, [1964] 1 All ER 630, CA.

3 Indeed, Diplock LJ in *Freeman and Lockyer* thought the trial judge might have concluded that there was actual authority there also, see [1964] 2 QB 480 at 501, [1964] 1 All ER 630 at 643, CA.

4 [1964] 2 QB 480 at 502–503, [1964] 1 All ER 630 at 644.

5 See, generally, *Bowstead & Reynolds on Agency* (16th edn, 1996) paras 3-001–3-005.

6 [1968] 1 QB 549, [1967] 3 All ER 98.

7 [1964] 2 QB 480, [1964] 1 All ER 630, CA.

8 As to de facto directors, see *Re Hydrodam (Corby) Ltd* [1994] 2 BCLC 180, [1994] BCC 161; *Re Moorgate Metals Ltd* [1995] 1 BCLC 503.

positions with distinctive and well-defined roles.[1] It is much more likely, however, that the third party will have to rely on apparent authority arising from a holding out by the company. Evidence would have to be produced to meet the Diplock criteria set out above and, in the case of the de facto director, it would be necessary to produce evidence, first, that he is a de facto director and, secondly, that as a director he had apparent authority to enter into contracts of the type in question.

Undoubtedly this can be done, but should third parties dealing in ordinary commercial transactions be put to the burden of establishing such an agency relationship? Professor Prentice, in his report on *Reform of the Ultra Vires Rule*,[2] which preceded the 1989 reforms, considered this issue and proposed that the acts of an individual director should be made binding on the company. He noted:

'Such a reform might be objected to as conferring too much power on a director and as striking the wrong balance between protecting a third party on the one hand and protecting a company against unauthorised acts of its organs or agents on the other. However, the modern reality is that companies often act through an individual director and therefore to make the acts of an individual director binding on the company would merely bring the law into line with prevailing commercial practice . . . If a company was made liable for the acts of an individual director, it would have to be careful whom it appointed to the board but this enhanced sense of caution is to be welcomed.'[3]

Yet, despite this recommendation and a concern to enhance the security of third parties dealing with companies, the reforms contained in the Companies Act 1989 failed to deal with this issue. Third parties must, therefore, continue to rely on agency to confer on them the security which the Companies Act fails to provide. In fact, the suggestion that the legislation should confer authority on individual directors may seem a modest reform in the light of the potential scope of agency which may confer authority not just on individual directors but on managers below board level. Furthermore, a failure to address the practical realities by statute may force the judiciary to strain the boundaries of agency to reflect those realities.

One of the most interesting cases, in this regard, is *First Energy (UK) Ltd v Hungarian International Bank Ltd*[4] where the Court of Appeal found that a senior manager of a bank specialising in commercial lending had no actual or apparent authority to make an offer of credit facilities to a customer; nor did he have

---

1 This has already happened to the position of company secretary, with the Court of Appeal in *Panorama Developments (Guildford) Ltd v Fidelis Furnishing Fabrics Ltd* [1971] 2 QB 711, [1971] 3 All ER 16 finding that the company secretary did have apparent authority to enter into contracts connected with the administrative side of the company's affairs. In his modern role, a company secretary has ceased to be a mere administrative officer and has become an important executive of the company. Cf *George Whitechurch Ltd v Cavanagh* [1902] AC 117.

2 Professor Prentice's report was published as a DTI Consultative Document, see DTI, *Reform of the Ultra Vires Rule*, a Consultative Document (1986).

3 See Professor Prentice's report, *supra* para 29, p 29.

4 [1993] BCLC 1409, [1993] 2 LL Rep 194; noted Reynolds (1994) 110 *LQR* 21. See also Brown 'The Agent's Apparent Authority: Paradigm or Paradox' (1995) *JBL* 360.

any actual authority to communicate any offer of credit facilities from the bank's head office to the customer. However, the court found that his position gave him apparent authority to communicate to the customer an offer of credit facilities from the head office. Therefore, the bank was in breach of contract when it refused credit facilities after the customer had accepted an offer so communicated. By putting him in that position, the bank clothed him with authority to communicate head office approval of credit facilities,[1] there being no requirement that the authority to communicate decisions should be commensurate with the authority to enter into a transaction of the kind in question on behalf of the principal.[2]

It might be argued that this decision goes too far,[3] but it needs to be remembered that, in *First Energy*, the bank conferred apparent authority on its branch manager to communicate its decisions by the position to which it had appointed him. In this way, it can be distinguished, perhaps, from the decision in *Armagas Ltd v Mundogas SA (The Ocean Frost)*[4] where the House of Lords rejected the idea of the self-authorising agent. In *The Ocean Frost*, the agent's position (vice-president (transportation) and chartering manager) was known not to carry authority to enter into the particular transaction (a three-year charterparty) and, therefore, there was nothing on which to found authority other than the agent's own representation that he had sought and obtained authority. Such a representation has always been insufficient to bind the principal.[5] Nevertheless, the decision in *First Energy*, even if it can be distinguished from *The Ocean Frost*, does enable apparent authority to be based on a representation which is nothing more than the appointment of a person to a particular position and, in that respect, it is pushing at the boundaries of the concept of apparent authority as arising from a representation by a principal to the third party.[6] In so doing, this judgment opens up the broader debate, beyond the scope of this essay, as to the appropriate conceptual basis for agency, whether grounded on a consensual relationship or imposed by law to protect third parties; and the appropriate weight to be given to the internal and external dimensions of the agency relationship.[7]

At another level, the judgment may be particularly significant in the context of agents who are appointed to the position of company directors. Applying the approach in *First Energy*, it would seem that, on this basis, third parties may be able to rely on a director having apparent authority to communicate decisions

---

1 [1993] BCLC 1409 at 1422, [1993] 2 Lloyd's Rep 194 at 204. Cf *British Bank of the Middle East v Sun Life Assurance Co of Canada (UK) Ltd* [1983] BCLC 78, [1983] 2 Lloyd's Rep 9, HL: a branch manager of an insurance company had no authority, by virtue of his title, to bind the company to a third party.

2 [1993] BCLC 1409 at 1426, [1993] 2 LL Rep 194 at 206.

3 See *Bowstead & Reynolds on Agency* (16th edn, 1996) para 8-023: '. . . any easy admission of the agent's statement of his own authority as creating apparent authority involves a departure from the basic principle of apparent authority for which no general justifying principle seems ready to hand'. See also Reynolds (1994) 110 *LQR* 21.

4 [1986] AC 717, [1986] 2 All ER 385, HL.

5 Furthermore, as the Court of Appeal noted in *First Energy*, the transaction at issue in *The Ocean Frost* had a number of unusual features: see [1993] BCLC 1409 at 1419, [1993] 2 Lloyd's Rep 194 at 202.

6 See Brown (1995) *JBL* 360; Reynolds (1994) 110 *LQR* 21.

7 See *Bowstead & Reynolds on Agency* (16th edn, 1996) para 1-023; Brown, *supra*.

made by the board. As Evans LJ noted in *First Energy*, the practical position is that a board of directors or other senior management cannot always communicate directly with third parties and there must be someone authorised to communicate on their behalf. He went on:

'It is not the practice, so far as I am aware, in normal commercial transactions for written proof, e.g. of board decisions, to be demanded by contracting parties and even where this may occur, e.g. in large-scale financing transactions, the third party must always rely ultimately on some individual who has been held out as having or who appears to have the necessary authority to communicate with him . . . Moreover there is clearly no requirement that the authority to communicate decisions should be commensurate with the authority to enter into a transaction of the kind in question on behalf of the principal.'[1]

A third party who cannot establish any actual or apparent authority vested in a director to bind the company to a particular transaction will be able to argue that the director, like the senior manager in *First Energy*, did have authority to communicate decisions of the board and so, perhaps, to hold the company to the transaction.

Whatever its merits and demerits, the approach to the precise agency issues central to *First Energy* was driven by wholehearted judicial support for an approach to these issues which recognises the need for realism and certainty in commercial affairs.

Steyn LJ noted:

'A theme that runs through our law of contract is that the reasonable expectations of honest men must be protected. It is not a rule or a principle of law. It is the objective which has been and still is the principal moulding force of our law of contract.'[2]

On the facts in *First Energy*, to have denied the authority of the bank manager to communicate the offer of credit facilities would have been, Steyn LJ said, to fly in the face of the way in which, in practice, negotiations are conducted between trading banks and trading customers who seek commercial loans.[3] Nourse LJ and Evans LJ, in their judgments, also stressed the need to recognise the commercial realities.[4] It was in recognition of those same commercial realities that Professor Prentice would have extended protection to third parties dealing with individual directors.

This judicial recognition of commercial reality is also evident in the different context of the decisions in *El Ajou v Dollar Land Holdings plc*[5] and *Meridian Global Funds Management Asia Ltd v Securities Commission*.[6]

In *El Ajou v Dollar Land Holdings plc*,[7] the court accepted that a company's directing mind and will may be found in different persons for different activities of

---

1 [1993] BCLC 1409 at 1425–1426, [1993] 2 Lloyd's Rep 194 at 206.

2 [1993] BCLC 1409 at 1410, [1993] 2 Lloyd's Rep 194 at 196.

3 [1993] BCLC 1409 at 1423, [1993] 2 Lloyd's Rep 194 at 204.

4 See [1993] BCLC 1409 at 1425, *per* Evans LJ, at 1427, *per* Nourse LJ.

5 [1994] 2 All ER 685, [1994] 1 BCLC 464, CA.

6 [1995] 2 AC 500, [1995] 3 All ER 918, PC.

7 [1994] 2 All ER 685, [1994] 1 BCLC 464, CA.

the company. Here, the fraudulent intent of a non-executive chairman of the company was imputed to the company and he was, therefore, the directing mind and will of the company with respect to a particular transaction; in that case, the receipt of funds which were the proceeds of fraud. In consequence, his knowledge was the company's knowledge. This is a very practical response to the difficulties involved in attributing knowledge to a corporate entity. It recognises that, in many instances, a company will not act through the collective board but through an individual director and sometimes (as with the knowing receipt of the proceeds of fraud) that individual director should be treated as the company. Likewise, in *Meridian Global Funds Management Asia Ltd v Securities Commission*[1] where, on a true construction of the relevant statute and in view of the policy of the legislation, it was appropriate to attribute the knowledge of a senior employee (the chief investment officer) of an investment management company to the company. Accordingly, the company knew that it was a substantial shareholder in another company when that was known to the employee; and the company was, therefore, in breach of a requirement for shareholders who knew they were substantial shareholders to disclose that fact.

Where the board does not embody the company

These decisions recognise that policy objectives in differing areas may require that we step away from the idea of the board as embodying the company and seek alternative groups or individuals whom we can treat as the company, or whose knowledge we can attribute to the company for the purpose of liability. It is highly desirable that companies should not retain ill-gotten gains by hiding behind abstruse arguments as to the directing mind and will of the company, as opposed to focusing on who in the company knew of the wrongdoing. It is highly desirable, in the context of the regulation of investment companies and the enforcement of technical provisions such as those relating to the disclosure of interests in shares, that the knowledge of employees should be attributed to the company for those purposes. The activities likely to amount to breaches of the law in such situations will rarely, if ever, be conducted by the board, as opposed to executive directors or managers further down the chain of command. A failure to attribute their knowledge to the company and, in consequence, holding the company liable would, as Lord Hoffmann noted, put a premium on the board paying as little attention as possible to what its managers were doing.[2]

These decisions stress that we do not need to see the board and only the board as the company. They also place an onus on the board to monitor the conduct of individual directors and employees to avoid civil and criminal liabilities which may otherwise arise. Likewise, in the context of everyday commercial transactions, there is no reason to limit authority to contract to the board. The commercial reality is that individual directors enter into contracts on behalf of their companies with third parties and that should be recognised by the law without the necessity of resorting to detailed and complex agency rules to hold the company to such transactions.

---

1 [1995] 2 AC 500, [1995] 3 All ER 918, PC. See Sealy (1995) *CLJ* 507.
2 *Meridian Global Funds Management Asia Ltd v Securities Commission* [1995] 2 AC 500 at 511, [1995] 3 All ER 918 at 927.

Shifting the onus to the company

Of course, there is a question of balance as between reflecting commercial reality and convenience, on the one hand, and exposing shareholders and creditors to untold contractual liabilities through the activities of unscrupulous directors, on the other. That fair balance is struck by shifting the onus to the company. At the moment, the company is only bound if the third party can establish the necessary agency relationship, whereas the position should be that the company is bound unless the third party knows or is put on inquiry as to some limit on the agent's authority. If there are concerns as to the potential liabilities of companies if individual directors are given unrestricted authority to contract on behalf of the company, then the onus is on the company to monitor the conduct of individual directors and to remove any director whom the company feels cannot be trusted with such extensive authority.

The Department of Trade and Industry may wish to revisit the reforms, with respect to a company's capacity and the powers of the board, in the Companies Act 1989. Specific issues remain to be clarified about those provisions, such as the need for two special resolutions in CA 1985, s 35; the relationship between the provisions and the rule in *Turquand's Case*; and the abolition of the doctrine of constructive notice in view of the failure to implement the provision to that effect in the Companies Act 1989. Any review of this area must give serious consideration, on this occasion, to Professor Prentice's recommendation that a company should be bound by the acts of individual directors. Commercial certainty would be best served by a statutory statement to that effect.

Chapter 15

MODELS OF COMPANIES AND THE REGULATION OF GROUPS

Janet Dine[1]

INTRODUCTION

Tony Boyle has always been a source of inspiration and new ideas. I hope that this essay will provide us with topics for many future discussions.

THEORIES AND MODELS OF COMPANIES

The models of companies which have been adopted in various jurisdictions are shaped by the theories concerning the place of companies within society. Different theories concerning the origin and purpose of corporations shape the model of company adopted and thus shape the relationship which companies have with all the participants in their economic activity and with their regulators. A key element in determining the model and, therefore, the relationship with participants and regulators is the way in which the 'corporate veil' is viewed. The strength and purpose of the corporate veil is derived directly from the theories which shape the model adopted in any jurisdiction. The status of the corporate veil contains the essence of the model of company adopted and also contains important lessons for those seeking to regulate companies. This essay seeks to examine the way in which disparate theories give rise to different models of companies, and examines the implications of this for regulators and seeks to apply the analysis to the regulation of groups.

The role of corporate personality

The concept of separate corporate personality plays an important role in the corporate governance debate. To a greater or lesser extent, companies are considered as entities separate from those who form and invest in them. The strength and importance of the 'corporate veil' is a direct reflection of each society's theory concerning the role and derivation of companies.

An illustration of the way in which a separate entity may come into existence can be given by drawing a parallel with international law and the development of the EC. The network of treaties which bind States gives rise to treaty obligations and rights, but it is only when the 'new community legal order' was invented[2]

---

1 Professor of Law, Essex University. Senior Visiting Fellow at the Institute of Advanced Legal Studies. My thanks to my colleagues Steve Anderman, Sheldon Leader and Gerry McCormack for assistance in writing this piece.
2 Case 26/62 *NV Algemene Transport-en Expiditie Onderneming van Gend en Loos v Nederlandse Administratie der Belastingen* [1963] ECR 1.

that the Community truly became a separate legal personality. There is a similarity between this process and the contracts entered into by shareholders in forming a company. On formation of the company, a separate legal order is formed which has rights and duties independent from the rights and duties of the shareholders.

Theories of company law

Space does not permit an extensive discussion of theories and models of companies and regulatory structures. The following sets out a brief outline of stylised theories and models in order to show the importance of the links between them.

Theories of company existence are all important in the understanding of the appropriate corporate governance model. They affect the strength of the corporate veil and the degree of State interference that is deemed appropriate in the conduct of company affairs, as well as the range of interests that compose the 'interests of the company'. Three theories that are important are the contractual, the concessionary and the communitaire theories. In the contractual theory,[1] two or more parties come together to make a pact to carry on commercial activity and it is from this pact that the company is born. This tends to limit the 'interests of the company' to the interests of those contractors. It also emphasises the free enterprise rights of the contractors and limits the social responsibility of the company, as well as strengthening the corporate veil, because any denial of the right to use the free enterprise tool which is available tends to interfere with this concept of the company.

The concession theory has two branches. The existence and operation of the company may be seen as a concession by the State in granting the ability to trade using the corporate tool, particularly where it operates with limited liability. The theory does not give a clear signal as to the 'interests of the company', although it may remove some of the more extreme emphasis on the interests of the founders and thus be responsible for a more equitable mix of interests. This theory will also encourage the State to interfere with the corporate veil as the company is, essentially, a State creation. This is particularly so where a public interest is perceived to be at stake.

More interesting, perhaps, is the 'bottom-up' concessionary theory,[2] which sees the company as an extension of the contracting partners' original compact, but seeks to show that in coming together and using the corporate tool, the contractors have created an instrument which has a real identity separate from and quite distinct from the original contracting partners. The company, if you like, 'floats free' from its founders and becomes a separate person with its own interests. This theory enables us to be open to a constituency model because the interests of the company are no longer anchored in the interests of the original contracting partners. If we take the analogy of a balloon lifting from the ground, we can now see that, in the balloon's basket, are no longer just the

---

1 Different from the nexus of contracts theory. See Parkinson, *Corporate Power and Responsibility* (Clarendon, 1995).

2 My theory, but inspired by lectures given by Professor Sheldon, Leader of Essex University.

owners; employees and creditors will join them as part of the commercial concern. The difficulty with this theory and model is that it provides constituencies but gives us few clues on how to balance the competing interests and arrive at the interests of the company as a whole. It is not impossible that a fight will break out in the basket of the balloon and someone will be thrown overboard! This theory, however, will give the company a strong corporate veil, based as it is on the contractual free enterprise approach. It will, therefore, discourage government interference, at least in the details of corporate management.

The third theory to consider is the commutaire theory, in which the company is not a concession by the State but is an instrument of the State itself. This model was familiar in the former Communist countries. It has two consequences: the company has no strong commercial identity as it has become a political tool with diffused goals. Although the diffused goals will give it considerable social responsibility it will remove its commercial focus. Further, the corporate veil will be more or less non-existent as the State is merely using the corporate tool to further its ends.

The efficacy of the company as a commercial tool may well depend on it gaining a separate existence and a strong corporate veil. The diffusion of goals is widely regarded as inefficient.[1] On the other hand, a very narrow focus of its goals on the interests of a small sector of those involved in a commercial enterprise gives a distorted picture of the reality of the commercial endeavour — which involves the investment of the capital of the owners, the lives and endeavours of the workforce and the risks taken by the creditors. The most useful foundational theory may well be the concession theory, and, in particular, the 'bottom-up' concession theory. What is required are refinements to this foundation which give us models of companies and governance which will enable the company to reach decisions without conflict between the relevant inside parties. How can decisions be reached which will enable the balloon to navigate the skies of commerce without a danger of anyone being jettisoned from the balloon basket? It is this refinement which leads to the development of the enterprise and associative models of companies and their governance.

Models of companies

The contractual model
Based on the contractual theory, this model regards a company as primarily if not solely the property of and co-extensive with the owners. At the formation stage, the owners alone are involved. The UK courts have tended to carry this theory into the period when the company is fully operational. This has the major consequence that the wishes of the shareholders are seen as the overriding consideration for management, who are obliged to act 'in the best interests of the company'. Numerous cases equate the interests of the shareholders with the interests of the company.[2] This has the effect of excluding other interests from consideration in the way in which the company is run, in particular leav-

---

1　Howard, 'Corporate Law in the 80s — an overview' (1985) Law Society of Canada Lectures. See also, American Law Institute's Principles of Corporate Governance (tentative Draft No 2) 13 April 1984. For a contrasting view, see James Boyd White (1985) *Yale LJ* 416.

2　Sealy, *Cases and Materials in Company Law* 6th edn (Butterworths, 1996), pp 178–182. An extreme example is perhaps *Parke v Daily News Ltd* [1962] Ch 927 (but now see CA 1985, s 719).

ing creditors and employees as 'outsiders'. This model is reflected in the structure of UK companies, where employee directors are rare and shareholders elect the whole of the management team. Although this model would seem, at first sight, to be a simple one, it has built-in complications. For example, shareholders are not an amorphous body. Different shareholders will have different interests at any one time. The interest of an aged shareholder intent on enjoying the good life may differ radically from the young shareholder just starting out in life. Thus attempts by the UK courts to pin down the true meaning of the 'interests of the company', even in applying this simple theory, have been fraught with difficulty and division.[1]

Separation of ownership and control

The famous research of Burle and Means showed that the ownership and control of companies was, increasingly, in different hands. The identification of the shareholders with the company no longer represented reality. This could have led to a re-identification of the company as the creature of its professional managers but, instead, the tendency has been to regard the company more and more as an entity in its own right and to struggle to identify what are the interests of the company as distinct from its shareholders. Critical theorists have argued, from a Marxist perspective, that the separation of ownership and control necessarily leads to a depersonalisation of the relationship between capital and labour,[2] but this need not be the case provided that an inclusive model of this separate legal entity is chosen, rather than a divisive one. What are the alternatives?

The constituency model

So that the decision-making of directors involves interests other than those of shareholders, some have suggested a move to a constituency or stakeholder model of company law.[3] As we have seen, there is a strong basis for this type of model in the 'bottom-up' concessionary theory. There are two variants of this model. The different theoretical underpinning has important implications for determining which parties should have a corporate governance role. The first variant of the model sees the company as run in the interests of shareholders, it being in the interests of shareholders to take account of other interest groups, because to ignore them would damage shareholder interests. This approach is exemplified by legislation which details the interests which must be considered by directors in determining their actions, while enforcement is left in the hands of shareholders.[4] The importance of the routing of the constituency interests through the interests of the shareholders is that the logical group to enforce

---

1 *Allen v Gold Reefs of West Africa* [1900] 1 Ch 656, *Dafen Tinplate v Llanelly Steel Co* [1920] 2 Ch 124, *Greenhalgh v Arderne Cinemas Ltd* [1951] Ch 286.
2 See, for example, Ireland, Paddy, Grigg-Spaul, Ian and Kelly, Dave, 'The Conceptual Foundations of Modern Company Law' 14 *Journal of Law and Society* No 1, p 50.
3 See RSA inquiry, *Tomorow's Company*: '[Directors] must, as fiduciaries have regard to the interest of shareholders, but that obligation is not related to the holders of shares at one particular time — it is related to the general body of shareholders from time to time . . .'; TUC, 'Your Stake at Work' 1996; Political Economy Research Centre, 'Stakeholder Capitalism: Blind Alley or Best Hope' (Sheffield University, 1996); Deakin and Hughes, *Enterprise and Community, New Directions in Corporate Governance* (Blackwell, 1997).
4 See, for example, CA 1985, s 309, discussed further below.

those interests are the shareholders themselves. In the second variant of the model, it is accepted that interests of other groups must be taken into account because such an approach benefits the company directly. In this variant, the company is seen as encompassing interests other than those of shareholders. 'Interests of the company' are then seen as including at least the interests of employees and creditors, as well as shareholders. The distinction between the two variants is that, in the second, it is more clearly the company which has the corporate governance role and it is less clear that shareholders should have an exclusive role in acting on behalf of the company to ensure that it is run in its best interests. It could be argued that the company should be able to depend on other interested groups to ensure its proper management. Both variants of this model are able to absorb the tendency of the courts to give different weight to the degree of interest of the constituencies, which will vary at different times in the history of the company, reflecting not least the financial health of the company. Thus, it is likely that creditors will be considered to be more important than shareholders when the company is insolvent. It is a model hard to control, because groups of interested parties are considered relevant because they comprise a described group and not because of any analysis of how closely they are, in fact, involved with the interests of the company.

The enterprise model

While still rooted in the constituency theory, an enterprise model differs from a constituency model in that the directors not only have to take into account the interests of others than shareholders, but also, those interests are regarded as part of the company, having a corporate governance role of their own inside the decision-making process. The contrast can be drawn between the obligation of directors to take account of the interests of employees under the Companies Act 1985, s 309 (which has no enforcement mechanism open to employees, only to shareholders) and the election of employees to the boards of companies. A further example would be the ability of a person named in the articles of association to nominate members of the supervisory board.[1] This article would probably be used by banks to involve themselves in corporate decision making. This model is the classic model developed in Germany and Holland and reflected originally by the draft EC Fifth Directive and European Company Statute.

The associative model

At Essex University, a team[2] is developing an associative model of a company. It is postulated that all who have dealings with a company have, potentially, two rights.[3] They will usually form a contractual relationship with the company, but if their association with the company becomes very close (as in many contracts of employment or contracts for loans), a different relationship, an associative relationship[4] will arise and this will give the holder of such a right a corporate governance role. The holder of such a right will be able to argue that

---

1 For example, Article 4A of the EC Draft Fifth Directive on Company Law. See Dine and Hughes, *EC Company Law* (Bristol: Jordans), looseleaf chapter 8.
2 Steve Anderman, Janet Dine, James Gobert, Sheldon Leader, Bob Watt.
3 This idea was first propounded by Sheldon Leader in respect of shareholders, see Patfield (ed), *Essays in Company Law* (Kluwer, 1995).
4 This idea was first propounded by Bob Watt in respect of employment contracts.

the company is not being run in its own best interests because associative rights are being disregarded. The great value of this model is that corporate governance roles are available to particular persons or groups, when they can show that their interests should be considered as part of the company's interests rather than because they belong to a particular group. Thus, the interested parties have the advantage of the enterprise model, in that they become insiders, but their interests are less likely to be institutionalised or frozen at a particular point of time, because the associative interests in a company will be constantly changing. Thus, the corporate governance right will only be available to a person who can prove that *at that moment in the history of the company* their interests should be an important element for management to take into account when determining the interests of the company. This right is different from, but might complement, a right of representation in the corporate governance structure, and may be particularly valuable where, for example, employee representatives on a supervisory board wish to argue that their interests have been totally ignored. So far as UK company law is concerned, it would represent a small shift from the mixed contract/constituency model that exists. The courts have required interests of creditors to be taken into account in certain situations[1] and the Companies Act 1985, s 309 requires managers to take account of the interests of employees while other cases equate the interests of shareholders with the interests of the company. Those holding associative rights would not be as powerful as if they had representation on the decision-making body of the company, although it would always be open to a company to adopt the enterprise model as well, ensuring a really tight model of 'insider' governance.[2] The challenge to management decisions would be by derivative action, reflecting similar features to a shareholder derivative action. Thus, such an action could only be brought to defend the interests of the company and the eventual 'winner' of any successful action would be the company itself. The action would only succeed where the court was able to determine that the interests of the company had been contravened. Where associative rights had been totally disregarded, the action would succeed, but where associative rights had been considered and other interests had prevailed, a successful action would be rare indeed.

That the associative model represents only a small shift from the current model is shown by the fact that an employee shareholder would already be in the position postulated, but it may provide a different source of enforcers who, by definition, have a long-term connection with the company and, unlike the second variant of the constituency model, are not defined solely by their membership of a particular group.

One great advantage of this model is that it is immensely flexible and can serve a variety of purposes. Mayer[3] made the point that insider or outsider governance structures would serve different purposes. The associative model could be structured by those controlling it, so that if 'outside' governance was

---

1 *Lonhro v Shell Petroleum* [1980] QB 358, affirmed [1980] 1 WLR 627 (HL).
2 Mayer, Colin in 'Enterprise and Governance' (IOD, 1995), p 10, draws a distinction between 'insider' governance by a small number of interests who have long-term involvement in the company and 'outsider' governance, where the power to control management is widely dispersed.
3 *Op cit*, p11.

the aim, short-term loans and employment as well as diversity of shareholding could be used to prevent a tight structure of corporate governance. If, on the other hand, a really tight corporate governance was required, the company might move towards an associative plus enterprise structure, reflecting the philosophy embodied in the early Commercial Code of The Czech and Slovak Republics, where the definition of an enterprise gives us some clues as to the underlying policy and theory of company law in these countries. Section 5 of the Commercial Code (subsequently amended) defined an enterprise as 'the aggregate of all its tangible and intangible assets and the skills applied by its staff to its business activity'. This, clearly, signals an inclusive enterprise approach to companies.

THE REGULATION OF DIFFERENT MODELS

Models of companies and regulatory structures

We have seen that where society has created companies with strong corporate veils, strong internal regulation is required. Many jurisdictions adopt a system where, theoretically, the general meeting of the body of shareholders has considerable power to make decisions which affect the management of the company by using the vote attached to their shares. This theoretical power of control is, in practice, severely limited. If the majority of the shares in a company are held by those controlling that company (and they often are) those controllers can perpetrate all kinds of wrongdoing, to the detriment of the minority, and then vote that the company should not take legal action to gain compensation.

The reality of 'shareholder control', models of control and regulation

The danger of adopting a model of company which relies on shareholder control is that, in many jurisdictions, it has been less than useful in controlling management. The whole purpose of providing a company with separate personality is to enable a separation of ownership and control. This enables the directors to use their energies for the benefit of the company, and not act as agents of the ownership pressure group. However, the separation has become extreme in many cases so that shareholders are no longer an effective governance mechanism. This has occurred for many well known reasons.[1] In large companies, small investors are apathetic, caring only for the return on investment. Institutional investors see their primary duty to their investors as best served by leaving a company where management difficulties are experienced, rather than becoming involved. Further, the supply of information is in the hands of management, as may be a significant quantity of 'active' shares and proxies. To rely on shareholders as a governance mechanism is, therefore, to allow directors almost complete discretion, subject to the unpredictable whims of the market, as to corporate control. For that reason, among others, some jurisdictions have adopted a governance mechanism which relies on a two-tier management

---

1 For a full analysis see Parkinson, *Corporate Power and Responsibility* (Clarendon, 1995).

structure, allowing a supervisory board a greater or lesser degree of control over the executive directors.

A further consideration is relevant in considering what controls there are over companies. This is the different models of regulation which States can adopt on any particular issue. Here it is proposed to offer for consideration an outline of three models of regulation which can be applied to companies. Of course, most systems of regulation 'mix and match' various aspects of regulation but, in order to understand systems of control, it is useful to consider which system has been favoured when a regulatory structure is under consideration.

The first model is the adoption of penal or quasi-penal rules in order to prevent a particular aspect of behaviour. This author has argued elsewhere[1] that, used in isolation, this is an ineffective way of attempting to regulate commercial behaviour. Because of the very serious results to the company of a successful prosecution of either the company or one of its senior managers, a criminal investigation is likely to be seen as a threat to be resisted. This leaves the regulator outside the company trying to pierce the corporate veil in order to gain sufficient information on which to base a prosecution. In these circumstances, the corporate veil will resist penetration and the bubble will remain intact. It is for this reason that prosecutors have violated the right not to self-incriminate in order to strengthen their hand.[2] Such behaviour, however, raises questions of violation of fundamental rights. If prosecutions cannot be effective without doing so, does this not indicate that there is something amiss with the method of regulation? However, it must be borne in mind that the existence of criminal sanctions may deter some from behaving in the prohibited way. A small number of successful prosecutions may, therefore, not be a true reflection of the success of a measure.

A second model of regulation is one where the regulator has a dual purpose. Some aspect of the regulator's existence benefits the company which is regulated. The regulator both confers benefits and acts as policeman. An example is a stock exchange. Anyone reading the rules of a stock exchange might be forgiven for thinking that the sole purpose of the body is to regulate the sale of shares. However, its primary purpose is to *facilitate* those sales. For that purpose, it may demand information from a company and it will be freely given because the result will be the benefit of a stock exchange listing. It will, therefore, be at an advantage when policing issues are at stake. Because of the cosier relationship, the corporate veil is less opaque. The downside is, of course, that the regulator may confuse the two disparate functions and be effective at neither.

The third model of regulation seeks to put in place a system of internal controls which prevent aberrant behaviour. This will include all the methods of internal corporate governance. In this system, the corporate veil does not obstruct because this is regulation from the inside. An example would be the systems of control in banks and insurance companies which identify transactions which are likely to be money laundering transactions.[3] It may well be noted that one very significant factor in the Leeson saga was the failure of internal controls.

---

1 Dine, *Criminal Law in the Company Context* (Dartmouth, 1995).
2 McCormack, Gerard, 'Investigations and the Right to Silence' (1993) *JBL* 425; Dine, *op cit*, chapter 9.
3 In the UK, the Money Laundering Regulations 1993, SI 1993/1933.

Most systems will rely on a mixture of these models to ensure control over private companies and their managers. A full picture cannot be built up without studying all the pressures applied by legislation. This essay is limited to some of the controls put in place by structural company law.

Fitting theories and models together

How do the theories and models fit with the models of regulatory structures? We have seen that the 'outside' criminal or quasi-penal approach is particularly ineffective where there is a strong corporate veil. It should work well, therefore, with a commutaire-based system but less so within companies based on theories other than the commutaire. We have seen that a strong corporate veil gives impetus and focus to commercial activity, but it also poses difficulties with penal models of regulation. The importance of either the dual regulatory approach, with 'user-friendly' regulators, or a strong internal system in corporate structure, based on other theories, becomes evident. The user-friendly regulator system is particularly appropriate to areas of industrial endeavour where there is small variation between the aims and commercial field of the regulated. Appropriate rules can be easily formulated. Where the great mass and diversity of the ordinary commercial endeavour is concerned, appropriate rules are necessarily more difficult to formulate. The emphasis must, therefore, be squarely on a strong internal control mechanism and the development of appropriate models of corporate governance within companies based on theories other than the commutaire must strive towards this end.

MODELS AND GROUPS

Models and the management of groups

When the management of groups is considered, a strong corporate veil, as generated by models based on theories other than the commutaire, tend to obscure the 'group' interest and isolates companies as separate units. This creates an unreal situation which various jurisdictions have attempted to combat in different ways. Perhaps the most extreme example of separate units is the UK. We have seen that the contractual model is, in part, a product of a free enterprise approach with a strong corporate veil with which the State will be loath to tamper. Historically, at least, this is the UK model and much of the jurisprudence concerning groups has been developed on this basis. We thus see a very strict approach to the separateness of companies within groups and the consequent 'blinkered' approach to advice to corporate managers.[1] The corporate veil is regarded as so strong and sacrosanct that managers must focus only on the company they are serving at the moment of decision making, regardless of the global well-being of the group of which that company is a part.

1　See the cases examined in the next section.

In UK case-law there is no formal or informal recognition of group interests

Do companies with a significant cross-shareholding have a special relationship? In the UK, while for many tax and accounting purposes groups of companies are treated as one unit,[1] the courts are reluctant to admit the reality of interrelated companies acting in any other way than as a number of separate entities tied together by their relationship as significant shareholders in each other.

The approach of the UK courts is epitomised by Templeman LJ in *Re Southard & Co Ltd*:[2]

> 'English company law possesses some curious features, which may generate curious results. A parent company may spawn a number of subsidiary companies, all controlled directly or indirectly by the shareholders of the parent company. If one of the subsidiary companies, to change the metaphor, turns out to be the runt of the litter and declines into insolvency to the dismay of its creditors, the parent company and the other subsidiary companies may prosper to the joy of the shareholders without any liability for the debts of the insolvent subsidiary.'

The approach is confirmed by the cavalier treatment by the courts of 'letters of comfort'. Thus, in *Re Augustus Barnett & Son Ltd*,[3] the company was a wholly owned subsidiary of a Spanish company. The subsidiary traded at a loss for some time, but the parent company repeatedly issued statements that it would continue to support the subsidiary. Some of the statements were made in letters written to the subsidiary's auditors and published in the subsidiary's annual accounts for three successive years. Later, the parent company allowed the subsidiary to go into liquidation and failed to provide any financial support to pay off the debts of the subsidiary. In deciding that this did not constitute fraudulent trading on the part of the parent company, Hoffman J accepted that the assurances of the parent were without legal effect.[4]

This attitude reached a high (or low) point in the decision in *Adams v Cape Industries*,[5] where the Court of Appeal endorsed the use of subsidiaries which had been created specifically to reduce the potential liability of the parent company for claims by employees founded on asbestosis contracted in the course of their employment. This was held to constitute a legitimate use of the corporate form. The court also refused to accept that the relevant companies formed a 'single economic unit' for jurisdictional purposes. The plaintiffs had submitted[6] that the group should be treated on the basis of a single commercial entity because justice so demanded. In giving the judgment of the court, Slade LJ expressed sympathy. He said:

---

1 See, for example, Companies Act 1985, s 258.
2 [1979] 3 All ER 556.
3 [1986] BCLC 170.
4 They were not fraudulent because Hoffman J accepted that they were true when made. The subsequent change of mind did not make them fraudulent retrospectively.
5 [1990] BCLC 479.
6 On the basis (*inter alia*) of *The Roberta* (1937) 58 Ll LR 159, *Harold Holdsworth v Caddies* [1955] 1 All ER 725, *DHN Food Distributors v London Borough of Tower Hamlets* [1976] 3 All ER 462 and *Commercial Solvents Corp v EC Commission* (Cases Nos 6–7/74 [1974] ECR 223.

'To the layman at least the distinction between the case where a company itself trades in a foreign country through a subsidiary, whose activities it has full power to control, may seem a slender one.'[1]

But he argued that in the absence of an agency relationship between companies they should continue to be treated as separate legal entities:

'If a company chooses to arrange the affairs of its group in such a way that the business carried on in a particular foreign country is the business of the subsidiary and not its own, it is, in our judgment, entitled to do so. Neither in this class of case nor in any other class of case is it open to this court to disregard the principle of *Salomon v Salomon* [1897] AC 22 merely because it considers it just so to do.'[2]

Community law, German law and concepts of 'undertaking' or 'enterprise'

Community law and German law have tended to adopt a wider enterprise view of company structures. In the wide participation in management there are even glimpses of a commutaire approach, with the company existing to serve wide social purposes as well as its own commercial interests. This leads to a much weaker corporate veil and the greater willingness of the courts and legislature to interfere in the management of the company and define the parameters of the entity with which it is dealing. This can be seen both in Community competition law and in the German approach to groups.

In *Centrafarm*,[3] the European Court of Justice said:

'Article 85, however, is not concerned with agreements or concerted practices between undertakings belonging to the same concern and having the status of parent and subsidiary, if the undertakings form an economic unit within which the subsidiary has no real freedom to determine its course of action on the market, and if the agreements or practices are concerned merely with the internal allocation of tasks as between undertakings.'

German law and the EC proposed Ninth Directive

In Germany, there is a law of groups which has been placed on a statutory footing. The Konzernrecht[4] is applicable only to stock corporations,[5] although a vigorous body of developing law applies it to other companies.

Under this law, a distinction is made between contractual and *de facto* groups of companies. In contractual groups, the creditors of the subsidiary are protected by a legal obligation of the parent towards the subsidiary to make good losses at the end of the year. Shareholders, other than the parent company, have a right to periodic compensation payments and must be offered the opportunity of selling their shares to the parent at a reasonable price. They have a right to an

1 [1990] BCLC 479 at p 512.
2 *Ibid* at p 513.
3 Case 15/74 *Centrafarm BV and Adriaan de Peijper v Sterling Drug Inc* [1974] ECR 1147.
4 Konzernrecht: para 291 *et seq* of the Atiengesetz or Stock Corporation Act of 1965.
5 In Germany, in 1988, there were 2,373 stock corporations as against about 400,000 GmbH (Deutsche Bundesbank, Jahresbericht 1989, 52, quoted by Hopt in Schmitthoff and Wooldridge (eds), *Groups of Companies* (London: Sweet & Maxwell, 1991).

annual dividend, which is calculated according to the value of their shares at the time of the formation of the contractual group and the likelihood of such dividends without the formation of the group. The board of the subsidiary has to give a report on all transactions, measures and omissions during the past year which result from its membership of the group.[1] The conclusion of the contract between members of the group is encouraged by the ability of the parent company to induce the subsidiary to act against its own interests, thus legitimising the concept of the interests of the group as a whole. However, the concept has been little used. Hopt[2] observes that most groups have chosen 'cohabitation without marriage certificates'.

Despite problems experienced in the operation of the German law, the draft proposal for an EC Ninth Company Law Directive took a similar route. The proposal would have affected groups of companies and public limited companies controlled by any other undertaking (whether or not that undertaking was itself a company). The proposal was that there should be a harmonised structure for the 'unified management' of groups of such companies and undertakings. The proposal was that rules would be laid down for the conduct of groups which were not managed on a 'unified' basis. Unless an undertaking which exercised a dominant interest over a public limited company formalised its relationship and provided for some prescribed form of 'unified management', it would be liable for any losses suffered by a dependant company, provided the losses could be traced to the exercise of the influence or to action which was contrary to the dependant company's interest.

United States approaches

In the US, it is recognised that dominant shareholders have fiduciary duties towards both the company and other shareholders. Thus, dominant shareholders are distinguished from other shareholders. The latter, as in the UK, are permitted to vote their shares according to their own selfish interests. In *Southern Pacific Co v Bogert* 250 US 483 (1919), the Supreme Court stated:

> 'The rule of corporation law and of equity invoked is well settled and has been often applied. The majority has the right to control; but when it does so, it occupies a fiduciary relation toward the minority, as much so as the corporation itself or its officers or directors.'[3]

The principle is widely, if not unanimously, accepted by the states. However, the implications of the doctrine vary widely. Two states have adopted, by legislation, a general principle which authorises contracts between parent and subsidiary companies subject to certain conditions of fairness and procedural requirements for adoption or ratification. In other states, a voluminous body of case law is evidence of the different and uncertain effects of the doctrine. Part V

---

1 Paragraph 312 of the Stock Corporation Act, mirrored by Article 7 of the proposed EC Ninth Directive.
2 Schmitthoff and Wooldridge (eds), *Groups of Companies* (Sweet & Maxwell, 1991).
3 There are echoes here of the UK case *Allen v Gold Reefs of West Africa* [1900] 1 Ch 656, where Lindley MR stated that the power of a majority is subject to 'those general principles of law and equity which are applicable to all powers conferred on majorities and enabling them to bind minorities'.

of the American Law Institute's *Principles of Corporate Governance: Analysis and Recommendations* deals with the duties of dominating shareholders. Ability to control over 25% of the voting equity would give rise to a presumption of control. It is a strange feature of the definition of control that it focuses solely on control of shareholders' votes. In Tentative Draft No 5[1] control is defined as:

> 'the power directly or indirectly, either alone or pursuant to an arrangement or understanding with one or more other persons, to exercise a controlling influence over the management or policies of a business organisation through the ownership of equity interests, through one or more intermediary persons, by contract or otherwise.'

Transactions between a dominating shareholder and the corporation are valid if:

(i) the transaction is fair to the corporation when entered into; or
(ii) the transaction is authorised or ratified by disinterested shareholders, following disclosure concerning the conflict of interest and the transaction, and does not constitute a waste of corporate assets at the time of the shareholder transaction.

If the transaction is ratified according to (ii), the burden of proving unfairness is on the challenging party. Otherwise, it is for the dominant shareholder to prove the fairness of the transaction. A transaction is 'fair' if it falls 'within a range of reasonableness'.

Conflicting duties of loyalty owed by directors who sit on boards of parents and subsidiaries are also judged on a 'fairness' scale:[2]

> 'In the absence of total abstention of an independent negotiating structure, common directors must determine what is best for both parent and subsidiary.'

The interrelationship between companies thus focuses principally on the companies as significant shareholders. The difficulty in formulating rules to control the power given to dominant companies in a constituency based system with a strong corporate veil is evident from the differential application of the rules which varies widely from State to State and the considerable volume of case-law. However, the valuable notion of taking into account the interests of members of a group without simply regarding them as a commercial whole is clearly established.

Why not a notion of 'the best interests of the group'?

So far as the concept of the benefit of the group as a whole is concerned, there are a number of reasons for not developing and/or relying on such a concept. First, it would only work with any degree of success where the group was arranged as an hierarchy, so that there is an identifiable 'holding' company which is used to make strategic policy for the whole group. Many groups are not structured in this way. Otherwise, numerous boards will be purporting to make decisions 'in the interests of the group' with no clear grasp of long-term policy. Further, the composition of the group will change from time to time as controls over companies shift, as will the degree of involvement of any of the constituent

---

1 Section 1.05
2 Commentary, p 60 following *Weinberger v UOP Inc* 457 A 2d 701, discussed by Tunc, Andre, in Schmitthoff and Wooldridge (eds), 'The Fiduciary Duties of a Dominant Shareholder' *op cit*.

companies. The identification of the 'benefit of the group' does not solve either of these problems, although it is sometimes thought to do so at least for some purposes.[1] The identification of companies with cross-shareholdings as a single entity tends to disguise the importance of the degree of involvement of each individual company with its associated companies.

Secondly, it destroys the separate identities of the companies within the group. It is to be assumed that the group is operated as a batch of separate companies for particular reasons. Since there is no limit to the size of a company, the reasons for forming separate entities lies elsewhere and may be for legitimate business reasons, such as creating a division with managerial autonomy. In these circumstances, to destroy the barriers between entities may remove real business convenience. It is much better to adopt the view that each management should take into account the interests of *all* constituencies which have formed an associative relationship with the company, including those other companies with which it is linked. The focus is still on the interests of the particular company for which the director works and the entities remain separate but linked in the way originally intended.

Characteristics of a desirable system

Identifiable characteristics of a desirable system include: an ability of managements to act in the best interests of the company on whose board they sit, *recognising the effect of the relationship between their company and other companies*, ie bringing their world vision into realistic focus.

Thus, the dominating company should take account of its subsidiary *as a company* rather than the focus being exclusively on the relationship between a company and a significant shareholder, as tends to be the case in the US. Unless a strict contractual approach is taken, a company is separate from its shareholders so that shareholder rights in a company will not equate to the rights of those shareholders as members of a subsidiary company.

We are looking for a system which retains the notion of the individuality of separate companies within a group, which ameliorates the worst features of viewing them completely separately and which focuses on the rights of the company as a company shareholder, not just a significant shareholder, while avoiding the rigidity of the German approach.

A modest step forward?

Companies with significant cross-shareholdings relate to each other as companies as well as significant shareholders. If it were accepted that, as shareholders, an associative relationship could develop giving corporate governance rights, as is suggested above, then it should also be the case that such rights could develop to enable a company to protect its interests *as a company* and not just as a shareholder. Once it is accepted that a company's interests are not solely those of its shareholders, there will be occasions on which those two interests diverge. This

---

1 Hadden in McCahery, Picciotto and Scott (eds), *Corporate Control and Accountability* (Clarendon, 1993). Hadden, 'Liabilities in Corporate Groups: A Framework for Effective Regulation' *I Gruppi Di Societa* (1996) Vol 12.

approach would require directors to consider the interests of the individual company, but take account of its place within its group where the relationship between companies is sufficiently close. It steers a middle line between the rigidity of the German system, the isolationist UK system and the commercial unit approach of the EC. It lays emphasis on the interests of the company, in contrast to the emphasis in the US, and it raises many issues as to how it would work, which I hope may be the subject of future debate.

Chapter 16

COMPANY LAW REFORM IN THE UK AND EUROPEAN HARMONISATION

Mads Andenas[1]

THE SURREAL

My first encounter with academic company law, as a newly appointed law lecturer, was at an SPTL seminar in the rather grand Old Library in All Souls,
Oxford in 1991. It was on 'Examining the Company Law Syllabus'. I made copi-
ous notes and the event made such an impression that I have since kept them
filed in my bookshelf between two volumes of *Butterworth's Company Law Cases*.[2]

Professor Len Sealy from Cambridge presented the arguments for teaching
company law through the cases. He suggested to purge 'some cases which by
general consensus are outworn', but admitted that the 'temptation is to go on
teaching them all until the outlines of future development begin to take shape'.
And he pointed out, with elegance and irony: 'There are many reasons why we
may be tempted not to discard our lecture notes on ultra vires and to continue to
regale our audiences with all the learning we have accumulated over the years'.
He feared that 'the pressure to keep the cases in the syllabus is very much
demand-driven', in spite of the new legislation making many of them obsolete.
Caroline Bradley from the London School of Economics introduced a critical
and economic approach. She argued for 'beginning with Coase'; not failing to
remind that Ronald Coase had developed much of his important contribution
to the understanding of why we have companies before he left the LSE for
Chicago University.

In the ensuing discussion, Alastair Alcock from Buckingham spoke in favour of
a more practical approach. His years in a financial institution had made it clear
to him that one could not understand, even less teach, company law without
having been involved in a public issue. Company law teachers had to be familiar
with the workings of the City and to impart this to their students. Ian Grigg-
Spall from Kent forcefully challenged this perspective, merely by standing up
with his beard and donnish clothes as Alastair Alcock, in his city suit, had sat
down. Students should instead be offered a Marxist method, without which
they would understand very little: 'you have to begin with Marx, to teach them
Das Kapital'.

The seminar was a rather surreal experience. It showed a breadth and diversity
of perspective which must count as an asset in an academic community. What it

---

1 Senior Lecturer in Law, King's College, London.
2 The quotations from my notes may not be correct and my recollections are subjective. Some of
   the papers from the seminar are published in Birks (ed), *Examining the Law Syllabus* (Oxford
   University Press, 1993).

lacked was a discussion of the major issues of policy and reform, at the time (or any time). How does one involve students in discussions about corporate governance; what should be the role of shareholders and management; of directors' and auditors' liability; of shareholder action, and of employee participation. The role of European Community law was not touched upon. Questions were not raised about the impact of company law harmonisation on any of the policy issues, or how (or whether) to teach students to use Community legislation, or the emerging case-law of the European Court.

There was breadth and diversity of perspective but the most pressing issues were left out. Walking down Broad Street on the way to the railway station, I had this feeling of getting out of a time warp. On reflection, the event had more of a timeless quality. It could just as well have taken place some 20 years earlier. The worry is that it could also take place some 20 years later as well.

THE SECOND ENCOUNTER

My next encounter with academic company law was putting together a special edition of *Company Lawyer* on 'Europe and the Single Market'. Tony Boyle contributed with an article on directors' duties, minority shareholder rights and employee participation.[1] He set out the rather unsatisfactory state of the case-law on directors' liability and shareholders' remedies. He then discussed the provisions of the draft Fifth Company Law Directive[2] and the extent to which they provide a satisfactory avenue of reform. Finally he turned to the provisions about employee participation and board structure. His approach was open: will the draft Directive offer any solutions to the problems of English company law? It was also very realistic. The Conservative Government at the time was not going to support either extended liability for directors, shareholder remedies or employee participation. He pointed out that further harmonisation and reform depended on a change of government.

I had by then learnt to recognise two types of company lawyers. One type was not particularly interested in what went on in other jurisdictions (the English variety being more internationally oriented than continental or US colleagues in that some would pay attention to developments in other common law jurisdictions). The other type was interested enough, giving papers and writing articles propagating features of their own (inherently superior) legal system and at the same time making it clear that it would not be possible to transplant elements of other systems to their own.

The company lawyers I had got to know by then recognised European Community company law as another jurisdiction but with only incidental and unfortunate impact on their own jurisdiction. The study of EC company law had as its objective to point out its weaknesses compared with the domestic system or to argue for the introduction of elements of their own system into EC law. They worried that EC harmonisation would lead to 'petrification' of

---

1 'Draft Fifth Directive: Implications for Directors' Duties, Board Structure and Employee Participation' (1991) 13 *Company Lawyer* 6.
2 1983 OJ No C 240, 1991 OJ No C 321.

national company laws because Directives would be more difficult to amend that national legislation. It is difficult, by the way, to find many instances of successful company law reform projects on a national level that justify the concern that less will happen if Directives are adopted.

Tony Boyle's is a third position. Under his editorship and authorship, *Gore Brown on Companies* and *Boyle and Birds' Company Law* have analysed and explained the provisions of EC company law and how it is part of English company law to practitioners and students. It is done better and in greater depth than in any of the preceding company law texts.[1]

But his most original contribution lies in the way in which he has made use of the harmonisation process in his discussion of company law reform and in his willingness to consider, and adopt, elements of other European systems.

In his *Company Lawyer* article,[2] Tony Boyle looked at the approaches that a Labour government might take to company law harmonisation. The main gain would be that the UK would no longer block the process because of dogmatic opposition to employee representation and general anti-European bile. The prospects turned out to be much longer than they appeared in 1991, and it is only with Labour's election victory in 1997 that the reappraisal of UK policy can take place.

THE HARMONISATION AHEAD

The new Labour Government coincides with a series of Commission initiatives in the area of company law harmonisation. They cover most of the outstanding measures in the Commission's original programme. Their adoption will complete a harmonised company law structure in the Community. The nine major company law Directives adopted have already achieved a certain degree of harmonisation in important areas. The case-law of the European Court has laid down strict requirements to the transposition in the Member States. There may be objections that the more recent Directives and proposals have attempted to embrace the different solutions of the laws of the Member States, perhaps to the extent that it defeats the very purpose of harmonisation. The UK shares the responsibility for this with other Member States for being unwilling to enter into agreements entailing changes in domestic law.

In February 1997, the Commission issued a Consultation Paper on Company Law raising the question of the fundamental direction of future harmonisation. In his covering letter, Director General John Mogg says that the paper 'is aimed at making company law better suited to the realities of the single market'. The main questions are: Is further harmonisation of company law necessary to complete the internal market? What part should the EU play in the regulation of corporate governance? Or in the effort to simplify and deregulate?

---

1 Chapter 1 of the 3rd edition (Bristol: Jordans, 1995) of *Boyle & Birds' Company Law* is a good example of this.
2 'Draft Fifth Directive: Implications for Directors' Duties, Board Structure and Employee Participation' (1991) 13 *Company Lawyer* 6, 9.

The Commission Consultation Paper is an initiative to promote constructive talks on the pending proposals for new Directives. They have all been stalled in the Council, in no small measure due to UK opposition. The Commission states that: 'the lack of any discussions or mutual contact brings with it the risk that a common view of the usefulness of existing or future Community legislation in this field might become blurred or even disappear altogether'.

The fundamental question is what is the purpose of Community harmonisation of company law. The UK line has been that there must be a positive justification for each harmonisation measure and the Conservative Corporate Affairs Ministers usually have had problems in finding such justification.

A starting point is that an internal market depends on the right of establishment. Differences in company legislation will increase transaction costs and limit the right of establishment. Free movement of companies may even depend on a common company law jurisdiction based on EC regulations and not on harmonised, national company law. Free movement of capital and free provision of services depend on doing away with restrictions on share ownership and on the exercise of voting rights. Reporting requirements must be harmonised, far beyond what is the case today, before an English analyst can make much out of German or Greek annual accounts.

It is the UK with its financial services industry that should have the most to gain from company law harmonisation. There is some support for claiming that the model of English company law is generally accepted as the most suited to the development of modern financial markets. The important Directives concerning financial reporting, corporate governance and take overs make use of the English model, either as an alternative to other continental models or even to their exclusion. The victory of the true and fair view in the Fourth Directive[1] over the German or French corresponding concepts and the victory of the Take Over Code in the draft Thirteenth Directive[2] are the best illustrations.

The UK position, up till now, seems to have been aimed at obstructing the harmonisation process. The first step is protracted negotiations with other Member States which have not been willing to enter into any agreement which entails changes in domestic law. When all demands are finally met, the UK may still object with the argument that the Directive is useless, having become too general and leaving too much to the discretion of the Member States. This is still a possible outcome of the discussions about the draft Thirteenth Directive on Take Overs.

The most important measure blocked by the UK is the Fifth Directive on the Structure of Public Limited Companies. Corporate governance is at the core of company law and harmonisation has to include that. The many differences between the Member States seem to have been accommodated and it is the UK veto against any form of workers' participation that has proved to be the stumbling block. The Commission's approach is presented in a Communication from 1995 on worker information and consultation. It seems to build on a gradual approach where different measures on notification of, and participation by, employees will go a long way towards establishing the position that the UK has not wanted to recognise in the company law Directives.

1 1978 OJ No L 222/11.
2 1990 OJ No C 240, 1996 OJ No C 161.

The Commission recently published a broad study under the title *The simplification of the operating regulations for public companies in the European Union*. It is produced by Ernst & Young and deals mainly with the corporate governance issues of the draft Fifth Directive. It supports the draft Directive and makes a number of other recommendations. In addition to its analysis of existing proposals and adopted Directives, it also contains a technical report on the law of corporate governance in the Member States. The study is a clear demonstration of the utility of comparative research and how important this is as a background for future company law harmonisation. A new trend is also reflected in several of the most recent OECD country reports. They include studies of corporate governance and corporate finance of EU Member States. There is an emerging economic scholarship which has to be taken into account.

The European Company Statute[1] has been held back by the UK for the same reasons as the draft Fifth Directive. In May 1997, a group headed by Viscount Etienne Davignon suggested solutions to the worker participation issue. In June 1997, the Council gave broad support to the group and considered that a graduated approach was a possible way forward.[2]

The European Bankruptcy Convention seems close to some form of final adoption, perhaps as a convention between all the Member States excluding the UK, unless New Labour changes all of that. Analysis of the text of the Convention is important at this stage, but the recent process has shown how many questions are far from resolved by adopting the Convention. The need for substantive harmonisation of the relevant law is highlighted.

In 1995, the Commission launched a broad study of the different ways in which the accounting profession is organised in different Member States. In 1996, it presented a Green Paper[3] on the role, the position and the liability of the statutory auditor. The focus of the Green Paper is on the free provision of auditing services in the Internal Market. It does also propose action at Community level to implement international auditing standards. It does not propose any specific action in order to strengthen the enforcement of the requirements of Community law.

A MISGUIDED DISCUSSION

An example of a rather misguided discussion on a Community harmonisation measure is the one on the revised proposal by the European Commission for a Thirteenth Company Law Directive on Take Overs.

In 1996, I was asked by the House of Lords' Select Committee on the European Communities to submit a memorandum on the matter.[4] The Committee came out against the Commission's proposal, finding little benefit in it and that it might pose dangers for the future of the City Take Over Code and Take Over Panel.[5] I shared that view when I first looked into the matter

---

1 1991 OJ No C 138.

2 1997 OJ No C 227/1.

3 COM(96) 338 final.

4 *Takeover Bids* Thirteenth Report of the Select Committee on the European Communities, Session 1995–96 (HL Paper 100), p 97.

5 *Ibid*, pp 41–42.

some years ago.[1] I was later convinced that this was wrong having spent some more time on study and reflection.[2] The Centre of European Law at King's College organised a seminar on the revised Take Over Directive in 1996 and the discussion showed convincingly, in my mind, that the case against adopting the Directive is indeed a weak one. However, the House of Lords' Select Committee and the press comments went the other way, and the critics have won the day in the UK debate.

The Department of Trade and Industry consultation paper of April 1996 provided a solid basis for any discussion of the proposed Directive on take-over bids,[3] in particular on any possible negative impact on the present system of take-over regulation in the UK. The submission from the Financial Law Panel, also of April 1997, dealt with the possible risk that the proposed Directive may pose to the present UK system. That submission answers most of the questions posed in the DTI paper, and the conclusion was that the proposed Directive will not threaten the UK system. I believed that the authority of the Financial Law Panel, its general mission to deal with legal risks affecting the UK financial market, its general competence and the additional specialist expertise drawn upon in drafting its submission, would put an end to the discussion of the questions it has answered so clearly. It did not.

In the DTI's consultation paper, views were invited on whether the adoption of the Directive would:

(i)   further cross-border take overs; and
(ii)   have any negative impact on the City Code and the Take Over Panel.

Would the proposed Directive further cross-border take overs?

Professor Len Sealy points out that the proposed Directive first and foremost attempts to harmonise safeguards for the protection of shareholders and others. Little attention is given to the issue of making it possible for take overs to take place.[4] He also points out differences in corporate cultures in the Member States, and he finds it unreasonable to expect the Community to effect a transformation in respect of take overs.[5]

Professor Ross Cranston regards it as: 'not an unreasonable hypothesis that the take over directive, when effective, will not radically change the environment of EC countries regarding hostile take overs, at least not for the time being, since the institutional and cultural barriers will remain'.[6]

---

1   See 'The Proposed Thirteenth Directive on Take Overs: Unravelling the United Kingdom's Self-Regulatory Success' in Andenas, Mads and Kenyon, Slade (eds), *EC Financial Market Regulation and Company Law* (London: Sweet & Maxwell, 1993), 135 at p 149.

2   See Andenas 'Future of the Take Over Directive' (1993) 14 *Company Lawyer* 113.

3   1996 OJ No C 162/5.

4   Sealy, 'The Draft Thirteenth EC Directive on Take Overs' in Andenas, Mads and Kenyon, Slade (eds), *EC Financial Market Regulation and Company Law* (London: Sweet & Maxwell, 1993), p 135, at p 144.

5   *Ibid*, p 146.

6   Cranston, 'The Rise and Rise of the Hostile Takeover' in Hopt and Wymeersch (eds), *European Takeovers* (Kluwer Law International, 1992), p 77, at p 92.

There have been several recent developments in the area of take-over regulation in the Member States. In most Member States, the promotion of a market for corporate control[1] is accepted as an important structural economic reform issue or supply side reform. The OECD now includes in its country reports an analysis of corporate governance and the role of financial markets in that context.[2] More efficient equities markets are considered important as an instrument to achieve a responsive management and cheaper funding for medium-sized and larger companies.

There is a development in all the other Member States to reassess the importance of the equity markets in the economy. It must be remembered that few Member States have had a market for equities with a volume large enough to have potential effects on the real economy. Member States look to the UK model when they adopt a regulatory system of their own. This will have a strong effect on the corporate cultures in a medium-term perspective.

The proposed Thirteenth Directive must be seen in the broader context of the corporate governance provisions of the other company law Directives. In the proposed Fifth Directive, the European Commission has included strict limitations on the power of Member States to allow exceptions from the principle of one share, one vote.[3] Two techniques have been developed in the company law of Member States. One is to divide shares into classes carrying different voting rights. The other is to restrict the number of voting rights on shares belonging to the same shareholder, either as a limitation on ownership or the exercise of voting rights. The first technique is severely circumscribed and the second is prohibited in the most recent Commission proposal.[4] (The background to the most recent proposal is an initiative by the UK Government to reduce barriers to take overs in the Community.) If adopted, these provisions will contribute to changes in corporate practices in many Member States facilitating a market of corporate control, both domestically in each Member State and at a Community level.

The programme of company law harmonisation has achieved the adoption of Directives on many important issues. The disagreement on the corporate governance provisions of the proposed Fifth Directive, mainly the UK's veto against employee representation, has held up further progress. Of course, also, the proposed Thirteenth Directive deals with aspects of corporate governance.[5]

The proposed Directive is based on Article 54 of the EC Treaty on measures to abolish restrictions on the freedom of establishment. In Article 58 EC, companies are accorded the same right of establishment as natural persons under Article 52 EC. The proposed Directive is the thirteenth company law Directive proposed by the Commission in a programme of company law harmonisation

---

1 For a theoretical discussion of general concepts in the light of US regulation, see Esterbrook and Fischel 'Corporate Control Transactions' 91 *Yale LJ* 698 (1982). See otherwise the article by Professor Cranston, (*op cit*) and Caroline Bradley 'Corporate Control: Markets and Rules' (1990) *MLR* 170.
2 See, in particular, *Germany* OECD Economic Surveys 1994–95 (Paris, 1995).
3 The Commission proposal for a fifth company law Directive of 1983 and 1988.
4 Amendments to the Commission proposal for a fifth company law Directive of May and December 1990.
5 See Andenas 'The future of EC company law harmonisation' (1994) 15 *Company Lawyer* 121.

to give effect to the right of establishment. Harmonised company law is presumed to reduce the obstacles on cross-border establishment. At the same time, Member States may wish to establish certain common minimum standards to prevent companies from going to the less restrictive jurisdiction (the so-called 'Delaware effect').

Take-over regulation is part of the internal market measures listed in the Commission's 1985 White Paper. It can affect the freedom to provide services (Article 59 EC) and the free movement of capital (Article 67 EC). A European market for corporate control may be an important contribution to the development of an internal financial market.

The proposed Directive has already had an impact in several Member States. They have introduced take-over regimes based upon the provisions of the proposal which has had, in effect, the function of a Commission recommendation. The introduction of a mandatory bid and other elements of the City Code has been accompanied by a gradual elimination of certain take-over defences. Most of the latter process has taken place within the domestic systems of stock exchange regulation.

Professor Sealy and Professor Cranston are right in that the adoption of the Directive will not alter cultural or institutional obstacles to the creation of a market for corporate control. They do not, however, say that it cannot contribute to a development in this direction.

Seen in the context of other developments, there is every reason to expect that the adoption of the Directive will strengthen the creation of a market for corporate control and cross-border mergers. It will promote the internal market process of creating an internal financial market, with not only a market in services and investment but also one with even more direct consequences for the integration of European industry.

UK banks, brokers and law firms will provide a large proportion of the services involved when this market grows. They already do so, and a clear basis in the City code formalised in a Directive, can only strengthen their position.

The 1989 and 1996 proposals

The Directive is, in its revised form, very brief and general. There are clear objections to the use of a framework Directive in this area.

Already, the 1989 proposal could be criticised for its lack of detail. It set out relatively detailed requirements and minimum standards for the conduct of take overs of listed public companies, following the City Code closely. However, being a typical minimum standards Directive, the 1989 proposal left considerable discretion to Member States. It has been criticised for leaving important elements in a regulatory vacuum.[1] The substantive minority shareholder protection was a mandatory bid obligation. This obligation was not satisfactorily developed, leaving the regulation of the price of the offer to Member States'

---

1 'The Proposed Thirteenth Directive on Take Overs: Unravelling the United Kingdom's Self-Regulatory Success' in Andenas and Kenyon Slade *EC Financial Market Regulation and Company Law* (Kluwer Law International, 1993), p 149.

discretion. There was no Directive provision akin to the '2% in 12 months' provision of rule 9 of the City Code regulating the consolidation of control. This could allow the bidder to execute a market sweep at the lowest available price immediately after the mandatory bid terminates. There was no 'cooling off' provision similar to rule 35 of the City Code restricting subsequent offers or purchases of target company shares by the same bidder. This could allow the bidder to hold the target in a continuous state of siege. Another important provision excluded from the 1989 proposal is in the City Code's Substantial Acquisition Rules, seeking to reduce shareholder inequality by decelerating attempts to secure share accumulations of between 15% and 30%. Furthermore, the 1989 proposal imposed no analogous method of regulation of the acquisition of stakes below the threshold set in Article 4 (33% as compared to the City Code's 30%). Finally, the Substantial Acquisition Rules also introduce certain tender offer procedures without any counterpart in the 1989 proposal.[1]

When the negotiations over the 1989 proposal were suspended in 1991, it was due to strong opposition from several Member States. The climate for take overs had also changed. The 1989 proposal followed a period of high merger and take-over activity. The recession brought on a period of relative inactivity that reduced the incentive to press on with the proposal. When the European Commission revitalised it at the Edinburgh Council in 1992, it was included on the list of Directives to be revised according to the principle of subsidiarity, adopted in the EC Treaty earlier in that year. This did not follow from considerations relating specifically to the Directive, but was a more arbitrary inclusion on a list of Directives that were not considered important enough to harm core Community policies. The answers to the Commission's 1993 questionnaire to the Member States followed the established dividing lines, but allowed the Commission to conclude that: 'a majority indicated their preference for a directive which established general principles to govern take overs, but which did not attempt detailed harmonisation, as in the text originally proposed'.

The objections to the revised 1996 proposal as a framework Directive apply equally strongly to many other internal market measures where the principle of subsidiarity is given effect. This is not a strong UK argument against the proposal in the light of its general approach to the principle of subsidiarity.

The mandatory bid is no longer obligatory in the 1996 proposal as Member States can ensure the necessary protection by equivalent means. This will let the German government conclude that their company laws provide protection rendering the mandatory bid unnecessary. It must be remembered that the mandatory bid adds to the costs of a take over. If a Member State will create a take-over regime, reducing the take-over defences, but without the additional transaction cost of a mandatory bid requirement, this should be acceptable as long as the protection offered is equivalent.

---

1   See Andenas 'Future of the Take Over Directive' (1993) 14 *Company Lawyer* 113 and 'The Proposed Thirteenth Directive on Take Overs: Unravelling the United Kingdom's Self-Regulatory Success' in Andenas and Kenyon Slade *EC Financial Market Regulation and Company Law* (Kluwer Law International, 1993), p 149.

The Directive and the Take Over Panel

The UK position, well stated in the DTI paper, remains that a take-over Directive must not interfere with the present non-statutory take-over regulation. It is argued that a Directive will interfere since, at present, the City Code and the Take Over Panel do not have a statutory base. The Panel has, formally speaking, no legal sanctions at its disposal, but the SIB's Conduct of Business Rules impose an obligation on authorised persons to observe the Code so that it may now be indirectly enforced through the mechanisms established by the Financial Services Act 1986. The Panel is also a designated authority for the purpose of disclosure of information under section 180 of the Act, making an exception from the restrictions which otherwise apply.

The 1996 proposal allows Member States to designate a self-regulatory body as supervisory authority under its Article 4. This act of designation under an adopted Directive may not require legislation in the UK. It is clear that if the designation is made through a statutory instrument, the proposal does not make it necessary to give the body statutory powers so long as its present non-statutory powers are considered sufficient.

There is little reason to fear that a statutory base for the Code and Panel will lead to more intense judicial review or additional remedies. The Court of Appeal in *Datafin*[1] focused not on the source of authority but on the activities of the Panel. Third party reliance was among the reasons for the Court's refusal to quash the Panel's decision. Lord Donaldson MR explained the use of the limited remedy of a declaration with prospective effect with 'the special nature of the Panel, its functions, the market in which it is operating, the time scales which are inherent in that market'.[2] A statutory base would not change what His Lordship describes as this 'workable and valuable partnership between the courts and the Panel in the public interest'. It may be of interest to note the attitude of the courts to self-regulatory organisations with delegated statutory authority under the Financial Services Act 1986. This is summed up by Sir Thomas Bingham MR in a recent case in these words: 'these bodies are amenable to judicial review but are, in anything other than very clear circumstances, to be left to get on with it'.[3]

Nor will courts, necessarily, be put in a different position because take-over regulation is based upon a Directive. This will depend on the rights accorded by the Directive. The 1989 proposal stated that the Directive should not affect the law of Member States concerning the liability of competent authorities (Article 6.6). The 1996 proposal is amended to clarify that it does not have any impact on the Take Over Panel in this respect: it 'does not affect the power which courts may have in a member state to decline to hear legal proceedings and to decide whether or not such proceedings affect the outcome of the bid provided that an injured party enjoys adequate remedies' (Article 4.5). It will be sufficient with 'an appeals procedure operated by the supervisory authority' and the present appeals procedure operated by the Panel qualifies here.

---

1 *R v Panel on Takeovers and Mergers, ex parte Datafin plc* [1987] QB 815.
2 [1987] QB 815, 842.
3 *R v Securities and Futures Authority, ex parte Panton*, unreported, 20 June 1994, CA.

It is clear to me that the last alternative of Article 5.5 about 'the right to take proceedings before the courts to claim compensation' does not create any additional rights. It will leave the rights of compensation under UK law as they stand today. It is contrived to attempt to build a further liability, either for the supervisory authority or private parties, on this provision. If this is considered a problem in any way, it must be possible to remedy it by an amendment in the next stage of negotiations under the Council.

The adoption of a Directive does not have to lead to further delay as a consequence of references to the European Court. The Court of Appeal has been very restrictive in allowing Article 177 references to the European Court where it could lead to delay with detrimental effects. In *Else*,[1] the Court of Appeal overturned a High Court order for a reference in a case concerning a Stock Exchange decision under one of the listing Directives. The case had many similarities with prospective cases relating to an adopted take-over Directive, and it clearly demonstrates that there would have to be very good reasons indeed for a reference in cases such as this and where the effects of delay would be considerable.[2]

Subsidiarity

The subsidiarity issue is here whether the aims of take-over regulation are best achieved by regulation at Community level. The answer is probably still positive. The very disagreement between Member States shows that leaving this area to national legislation would not result in a take-over regime that would promote cross-border take overs or a Community market for corporate control.

CONCLUSIONS

It is difficult to find any support for the fear of a take-over Directive leading to more litigation and undermining the City Code and the Take Over Panel. The English case-law is clear, and no new Community law rights are created which could change the present position in English law. The proposal is closely based on the model of the City Code and would extend the principles of English take-over regulation to the other EU Member States.[3] It will contribute to a lowering of the barriers to take overs in Europe, and it will benefit UK business.

The main problem with the 1996 proposal is that it is too general and leaves too much to the discretion of Member States. With the disagreement between Member States on so many issues in the take-over area, a more detailed Directive would be preferable. However, the 1996 proposal will be a first step, and as one of many measures with an impact on take-over bids, including the

---

1 *R v Stock Exchange ex parte Else* [1993] 1 All ER 420.
2 This is developed, extra-judicially, in Bingham 'The National Judge's View' in Andenas *Article 177 References to the European Court* (London: Butterworths, 1994), p 43.
3 The take-over Directive has come to symbolise the very essence of the prevailing English capital markets model. Michel Albert talks about 'la substitution de la bourse à la banque' as a feature of 'le néocapitalisme anglo-saxon . . . défendue à la Commission de Bruxelles par le vice-président Sir Leon Brittan', see *Capitalisme contre capitalisme* (Paris: 1991), p 18. M Albert advocates the institutional, more consensus-oriented model of capitalism that he claims to find in France, Italy and Germany.

other company law Directives, the stock exchange Directives and the invest-ment services Directive, it can provide the foundation for an effective EU take-over regulation.

However, I do not think Tony Boyle is too worried about the set back for the take-over Directive. His concern is not primarily to export features of the English company law regime such as the take-over rules. He has pointed out that there are alternative mechanisms of corporate control in, for instance, German company law. I believe he would rather put the Fifth Directive top of the list of legislative priorities, making use of some of those mechanisms in English company law.

I am sure he would be right. But the discussion about the Thirteenth Directive is no less misguided for that reason.

INDEX

References are to page numbers; n indicates that the reference is to a footnote.